Frederick Bentham

The Art of
Stage Lighting

Second Edition, Revised and Expanded

THEATRE ARTS BOOKS

First edition 1968

Second edition, revised and expanded,
published in 1976 by
Theatre Arts Books
333 Sixth Avenue
New York, New York
10014

© Frederick Bentham, 1968, 1976

ISBN: 0-87830-009-0

Text set in 11/12 pt Monotype Baskerville, printed by photolithography,
and bound in Great Britain at The Pitman Press, Bath

Preface to Second Edition

I HAVE seen the Sydney Opera House, been all over it in fact, but more important I have attended public performances there. When the first edition of this book was written one wondered if that building was ever going to open and at what cost. Much the same queries have dogged our own National Theatre complex. Although I have seen productions in the Lyttelton, the Olivier is not open as yet; but I have been over the building several times and have examined much of the special equipment—in particular the spotlights made by CCT Theatre Lighting and the control systems by Rank Strand Electric. Which brings me to the fact that I am no longer an active member of that firm. After forty-two years there—responsible nearly the whole time for research and development and for the writing and the teaching about it—Rank and I agreed to part.

I am not the man for the large organization and the only wrench was parting with *Tabs*. After all, up to the end of 1973 I had written something for that journal ever since it began in 1937 and had been editor from September 1957. Thanks to the Association of British Theatre Technicians, of which I am a founder member and the present chairman, I have been able to continue my idea of *Tabs* with their journal *Sightline* while *Tabs* itself has added "Stage Lighting International" to its title. This is significant and has a significance for the present book as well. To me stage lighting cannot be separated from the design of the building in which it finds itself any more than it can from the design of the scenery it illuminates.

No light means that none of these things exists visually at all for the audience. We cannot have a theatre without light, for a theatre is by definition a place for viewing. If this holds for the director it also holds for the scene designer, and still more for the architect. Light is the most intractable medium he has to handle in creating his building. It alone insists that it can travel only in straight lines. Sound, air, actors, and audience can be made to turn corners, to squeeze through gaps, and in the case of the first-named, can even be reinforced when attenuated. Not so light. It travels direct from source to object, in this case the actor, and thence it is reflected as straight lines to the eyes of the audience.

Paradoxically, the whole reason for theatre, the actor's craft—the acting—is the only subject that can be completely left out of a book on stage lighting.

It does not matter to stage lighting whether the acting is rotten or superb; all it demands is that the actor shall warm to the glare of the footlights, or their latter day substitutes, and seek the limelight. For the rest, theatre planning, architectural and scene design, stage layout, production, electrical technology, physics in the shape of optics and colour, manufacturing processes and economics, all are of vital concern. Never was a material so much depended on, and yet so dependent itself, as light. It is responsible for the origin of the whole of what we see in the theatre and yet it cannot convey any message whatever by itself; it is invisible until it strikes something and is reflected into our eyes. In this process it can be more readily impeded and obstructed than any other material in the theatre. Thus it is that all of us who practise stage lighting have constantly to concern ourselves with matters that appear to be outside our subject. Even on the simplest level, when a supplier is asked by an architect to put forward a stage lighting scheme he has to begin a probe which some find inquisitive and even impertinent. What kind of scenery, if any? What shape and colour is the auditorium and how is it lit? How many does it seat? What is the ceiling over the audience going to be like? And the roof over the stage? Also the back wall?

A recent intensive tour of theatre in Australia going from one city or town to another in a matter of days and seeing several "theatres" each day served to present a reminder of the diversity of building and of the activity therein. Incidentally let no man think that the only stimulating new theatre there is the notorious opera house! Although Australia is so enormous and so empty the similarities of their theatre problems to ours are remarkable. Is this because most of the population originally came from here? The stage lighting equipment certainly did. In North America the scene is quite different. Although some people tend to think of an Anglo-American school of lighting on the one hand and the German school on the other, I do not see how this notion can be sustained. It is true that the Germans have not succumbed, as we have, to the multi-lantern complexity but at the control we and they believe in a full set of dimmers and this is fundamental.

Imagine it, to buy my latest in computer memory systems (DDM) and then to go and muck it up by having only 90 dimmers patched to 460 circuits—to quote an actual and recent example in the United States. Not only this but the large number of firms supplying equipment makes it difficult to compare the philosophy behind one product and another. We are beginning to see this in Britain now that there is no longer the undisputed leadership of one firm. The chapter on lighting control was much harder to write now that it could no longer be an expression of what I had done or intended to get done. It is not so much the technological development since my last edition, great though it is, which makes the subject complicated but rather that it has opened the door for everyone. A new stage control may originate with any firm or consultant. The new control devices and systems which proliferate each, it may be assumed, aim to simplify but carry the complication of unfamiliarity. At the light-producing end—the lanterns—this particular problem certainly does not exist. There is little real change to report. Thus the image of stage lighting can be thought of as a player in a tuxedo caressing the keys of his control while a bloke in a boiler suit at the end of a long ladder fights to focus a nearly red hot spotlight! The purpose of this new edition is to put over in a readable manner the essential and increasingly technical background which provides both the disciplines and the opportunities to express oneself in the art of stage lighting.

Fortunately the basic principles of lighting and colour and the way one goes about applying them to the stage change but little. Elsewhere there is much that is new or heavily revised. A brand new Chapter 1 sets the scene at a time when we may have reached our peak in building and equipping the establishment theatre. Chapter 2 now takes into account places as diverse as the Olivier and the Young Vic, while in Chapter 3 the history of stage lighting is brought to but a decade away. Obsolescence and new development have greatly extended that amalgam of today and yesterday which the equipment in current use in our theatres inevitably represents; in consequence Chapter 13 is much enlarged.

The new long Chapter 8 on lighting control brings together most of the examples current in order to describe, contrast and discuss the philosophies behind memory systems. If these are not to herald an age of the moron punching the crossfader as the only control he feels at home with, then we must adopt tighter ergonomic disciplines for their design. If we are calling up cue numbers, for example, why cannot we all do it the same way? I sometimes think that all the niggling differences are there to hide which firm is copying what. Surely the computer keyboard is a good basis for numbers but neither the Post Office or the various manufacturers have made up their minds. If the piano or typewriter had been invented at the present time, one thing is certain: they would never have got their standard keyboards!

Acknowledgements

I should like to thank my wife for her direct help as German translator and interpreter. These are roles in which she has made herself well-known on the expeditions, conferences and meetings we have attended together for many years now. I have thereby been able to exchange less stilted views with German-speaking theatre people than might otherwise have been the case. In getting the large amount of new material on paper I have relied heavily on Barbara Berrington for the typing and as a reader to keep some control on what is, I gather, my rather individual use of English grammar! The services of "B" Bear have been—as always—unique; they cover almost everything in the book from first draft to final indexing.

Photographs—where not otherwise acknowledged—are courtesy of Rank Strand Electric. They either show equipment currently marketed or come from the *Tabs*/Strand Electric photographic archive which not surprisingly is the source best known to and, I sometimes think, only really comprehensible in its full richness, by me. Photographs otherwise are hard to come by—particularly of productions lit to show the true contrast range—and to ask for the cast as well is to call for the impossible. Similarly, such architectural photographs as exist almost invariably show empty theatres; be it black box or baroque, that is no way to see a theatre.

Thanks are also due to the following for help in providing illustrations: Fig. 6, Christ's Hospital, photo by the Architectural Press; Fig. 8, The National Theatre, photo by *The Times*; Fig. 11, *Stage Lighting* by Theodore Fuchs, New York, 1929; Fig. 13, *Illustrated London News*, 1928; Figs. 14 and 15, Cie Clemançon, Paris; Fig. 17, The General Electricity Company, U.S.A.; Fig. 48, Ludwig Pani of Vienna; Figs. 89, 92 and 94, Thorn Lighting Ltd., Theatre Lighting Division; Fig. 90, Century Lighting, New York; Figs. 103, 136*b*, 147 and 148, lighting designed by Richard Pilbrow; Figs. 104 and 105, original layout and photo by William Lorraine; Fig. 111, CCT Theatre Lighting Ltd.; Fig. 126, setting designed by

Rencio Mondiandino; Figs. 126 and 127, lighting by Franco Zeffirelli and William Bundy; Figs. 129, 130 and 132, The National Gallery, London; Fig. 131, M. Georges Leblanc, Paris, for obtaining the photo, and the Musée du Louvre, Paris; Fig. 153, lighting by Wallace Russell, Toronto, set by Lawrence Schafer, production by Stephen Ford; Fig. 154, Ossia Trilling for obtaining the photo; Figs. 159 and 165, information supplied by Charles Bristow; Fig. 170, Reiche & Vogel, Berlin; Fig. 182, Siemens-Schuckertwerke, Berlin, Erlangen.

Contents

To the members of my department over the years,
without whom Strand Electric and the 'I' of this
book could not have done what we did.

1 Setting the Scene

IF we survey the theatre in Britain by far the largest concentration of buildings for that purpose is in London, but this is not to say that London represents all the forms of theatre. There has been little modern theatre building there and to see a good thrust stage or theatre-in-the-round one must go to, say, Sheffield for the one and Bolton for the other.

The very fact that London has so many picture-frame theatres in such a variety of sizes has rendered much special theatre building unnecessary. The picture-frame theatre is curiously adaptable; one can choose anything from the little Ambassadors, with 450 seats and a 24 ft 6 in. proscenium, up to say the London Coliseum with 2358 and a proscenium of 50 ft. It is when a town has got down to only one theatre or none at all that new building becomes urgent and the form or forms it should take become a very serious matter indeed. In fact the British Theatre Directory[1] lists some eighty-three theatres under London. Of these, fifty-three are in the central area, the West End more or less and forty-six of them are easily recognizable, the sort of place one traditionally thinks of as being a theatre. In addition there are listed twenty-four smaller club and lunchtime theatres and eight concert halls. Cinemas are additional to this.

Outside London there are 315 theatres. Eighty of these are new buildings and a hundred and fifty-two are civic owned. Eighty-three are repertory theatres. When it comes to type only thirty-six have no proscenium and of those but twelve are in-the-round. As an insurance even these few have, in some cases, a built-in adaptability to another form.

Eighteen are multi-purpose halls but we do not really possess any equivalent of the American auditorium, nor do our new theatres have the seating capacities of theirs. We have come to think that a thousand seats is large for a modern theatre, whereas they can describe the University of Iowa's new theatre

---

[1] British Theatre Directory, 1975, published by Vance-Offord (Publications) Ltd.

with 2680 seats as having "flexibility and intimacy." Contrast this view with Richard Pilbrow's impression of a new theatre in New York with 800 or so fewer seats: "The Uris is too large and spacious for my taste." However, he comes to the conclusion that we here think to the other extreme and muses, "Let's have many more seats in the theatre, but let's cram them in as snugly as we can!"[1]

This is just what the Edwardian theatre managed to do but it is also what our insistence on a high standard of comfort and democratic sightlines tends to undo! In particular one must look hard at the prevalent practice of long, uninterrupted rows of "continental" seating, which is necessarily spaced deeper back to back. The rows in London's Mermaid Theatre are actually 3 ft 4 in. apart; six inches off each would have reduced the distance of the present back row from the stage by nearly 10 ft.

We in Britain still await the opening of our equivalents of the common German large-production-area/small-auditorium relationship. Primarily an Opera House form, this arises from the preoccupation with spectacle—the creation and movement of scenery, some of which may actually be "live" in the form of crowds. The new National will be our only theatre built for handling scenery on this scale, though the Royal Opera House hopes to annexe considerable space for this purpose in Covent Garden's now departed vegetable market and build an extension there one day.

It comes as a surprise to learn that the, to us, vast backstage areas of the Cologne Opera House complex, for example, can be criticized by its technical director as being "so cramped."[2] Yet there is a logic to this and it arises from the duty to service that particular size of stage and the production policy thereon. In a theatre originating its own productions there is a case for designing the stage to suit the workshops and storage space. It is no good having a large stage if one has not the means to fill it. Far too many of our new theatres arise complete with an auditorium and stage but virtually no offices to administer the place or else no space off the stage itself to store things. And a theatre has lots of things to store (and to assemble)—most of them awkward.

We have to realize that our theatres remain obstinately scenic theatres. Whatever may be said of the power of the spoken word, every time a stage is designed, there we have a space clamouring to be filled with scenery. The better the sightlines from all the members of the audience to all areas of the stage, the less easy it becomes to say that, "We shall mask that part off permanently because only some will see it." The result

[1] *Tabs*, Vol. 31, No. 2.
[2] *Sightline*, Autumn 1974.

is that the action spreads and production costs rise. Benjamin Wyatt, the architect of Drury Lane Theatre who opted for a 33 ft proscenium, pointed out in 1811, "For every additional foot given to the width of the stage opening . . . a great many additional yards of canvas must be used in every one of the Drop Scenes and Flats as they are termed; and the size of the Painting Rooms, Carpenter's Shops and other Appurtenances to the Stage. . . ."[1] He could have added—with similar effects on the machinery needed to move it and on the number of actors needed to people it.

Scenery may once upon a time have been just painted canvas and wooden frames. Today it can be any product of our industrial technology. Designers can no more resist plastics than architects can concrete. You could say they all belong to a mouldy age. Directors, instead of getting tough and saying they do not want things they do not understand, give way and in comes another specialist—another "expert."

Of all the technological manifestations, lighting is the most all-pervading. The one form of theatre which cannot use scenery, theatre-in-the-round, manages nevertheless to use masses of lighting. True, we *have* to have some of this lighting to see, but that does not apply to the technical runner-up, amplified sound. A good actor or singer in the right-sized theatre does not have to rely on microphones and amplifiers. It is perfectly possible to put a show over, whether a musical or a drama, in the 2300 seat Drury Lane Theatre auditorium without such aids. Likewise we do not need musique concrète, abstrait, or distrait —call it what you will—and all those sound effects. There came a time when we learned to scorn the background music and heavenly choirs of Hollywood, yet we still seem perfectly prepared to put up with a commentary of puzzling bruits electroniques.

A corresponding visual bewilderment often goes along with the settings of today. At one time the curtain went up and at a glance the audience would gain an immediate impression of a royal palace, the dense wood, the castle or the drawing-room, and if, as in at least one play, the scene had to be played on top of a roof—then that is how it appeared. I said "impression" deliberately because this type of decor does not have to be naturalistic but it does have to be direct in its message; we must know where an actor is supposed to be. In 1924, when I was a boy of twelve making his first encounter with Shakespeare, Basil Dean's *Midsummer Night's Dream* had me firmly placed, whereas with a half century of one Will and another behind me, it came as a surprise when in the 1972 RSC production of *Coriolanus* Virgilia kicked up all that fuss about "not out of

[1] *The Development of the English Playhouse* by Richard Leacroft (Eyre Methuen).

doors." I had assumed from the open spaces and the lighting that they were already out in some Roman equivalent of Trafalgar Square—but no, "Not over the threshold 'till my lord return from the wars," she declared.

It is said that the trouble springs from the type of training given in Art Schools. Instead of working first to the strict disciplines imposed by traditional materials and techniques students are encouraged to do their own thing. This criticism comes moreover from their elders who will themselves shove perspex, stainless steel tubes, vacuum-formed polystyrene—anything which can possibly get past the fire authorities—on to the stage.

It has of course been customary to think of the "traditional" picture-frame theatre and the opera house as designed around scenery. There is the stage tower with flying grid to hang the stuff from and, if we are lucky, wing space and dock space together with a workshop to store and make it in. The sightlines are usually based on a fan in plan and any balconies contrived so that at least some width and height of backcloth can be displayed. What is not realized is that theatres virtually without any facilities will also use lots of scenery and that the shape of these other theatre forms, designed to get the actor out from behind the picture-frame, may create a need for larger and still more elaborate scenery.

The very fact that there are no orthodox facilities for changing scenery will lead to ingenious but, because they are special, necessarily more expensive solutions. Open staging begins with the theory that the actor and his audience should occupy the same room. If his stage is at one end of the room then what is going to be done with all the rest of that end—the wall behind him? It has been customary to declaim against the fourth wall as represented by the proscenium of a picture-frame theatre but what of the fourth wall when it expands to become that of the auditorium? Forty-eight feet is the width which cropped up in the first of our modern theatres to popularize the open end stage. Like Stephenson's adoption of 4 ft 8½ in. for the railways, simply because it was a gauge that happened to be around, so 48 ft happened to be the width between the walls of the Puddledock warehouse into which Sir Bernard Miles and his architect, Elidir Davies, had to get the Mermaid. Since then some new open end stage theatres have been deliberately built to that dimension. Suppose the warehouse had been 60 ft wide, what then? They would probably have built a proscenium of 30 ft. Not only would the scenery have been smaller but there would have been 15 ft either side as wing space—at least some of which would have been available for stacking when scene shifting.

To do Sir Bernard justice, it may not have been wholly a case of *force majeure*—or rather *force interieure*—because in the previous incarnations of the Mermaid in his own garden, and later in the Royal Exchange for the 1951 Festival of Britain, he opted for an open stage with a permanent set behind. There is the problem. Who is prepared to put up with a permanent set and for how long? For one play only, for a season, for ever?

A recent example of another type which is worth close study is the Sheffield Crucible.[1] There we find a thrust stage with a grid over it and an almost regular stage behind it. It is worth considering why such a stage, which thrusts its actors among their audience, should rate the scenic background as of any importance.

The trouble with this type of stage lies with the shape in plan. This presents the actors to one third of the audience as against a background of pictorial and illusionary scenery. These members of the audience inhabit a different type of theatre from the others. Seated in the centre, the evocation is of an orthodox presentation except that there may be a lot more background than is usual. Most people automatically covet centre seats, yet to Sir Tyrone Guthrie, "One of the most pleasing effects of the performance was the physical relation of the audience to the stage." Describing the original Edinburgh Festival performance in 1948 of *The Three Estates* on the first fitup thrust stage in the Assembly Hall, he went on:

"The audience did not look at the actors against a background of pictorial and illusionary scenery. Seated around three sides of the stage, they focussed upon the actors in the lit acting area, but the background was of dimly lit rows of people similarly focussed on the actors."[1]

It is obvious that this effect is seen at its best by the two-thirds who sit at the sides. What is more, the more of this effect they get the less the impact of the scenic background from their angle.

The architectural design of auditoria of various sizes and their stages, whether "closed" or "open," forms the subject of Chapter 2. My concern here is to comment upon general trends. It is strange that the true form to get the audience-as-background effect, the transverse stage, has gained so little acceptance. This may represent hedging of their bets on the part of the timid or a more noble desire to unite the audience as one. The people in the centre seats are a bridge—quite literally in fact, because we have to tunnel under them to let the actors enter or exit at that end.

The solution to the problem of scenic limitation is, I am convinced, to ensure that the hall itself makes a stronger contri-

[1] *Theatre Quarterly*, Vol. 3, No. 2, or *Tabs*, Vol. 29, No. 4.
[1] *A Life in the Theatre* by Tyrone Guthrie (Hamish Hamilton); a rather more detached view can be obtained from *The Producer and the Play* by Norman Marshall (Macdonald).

bution. This is virtually what happens in an Edwardian picture-frame theatre. It also happened in the Georgian where the actor played on that part of the stage which was actually in the auditorium. Of course a modern hall coated with black paint or something equally gloomy and self-effacing (especially when lit by downlighters) can make no such impact. With skill, particularly in the conversion of an older building of merit, we could use parts of that building as a permanent set and infill with scenery here and there. The only theatre that comes to mind where this has perforce been the practice for years is the Open Air Theatre, Regents Park. There, temporary scenic structures are planted among the trees and bushes which are a feature of the park. Indoors I would not be above faking a few permanent features, taken from any attractive bits the original building happened to have in the wrong place!

When the Royal Shakespeare Company's Barbican scheme was launched, the model made much of a semi-permanent set of screens. Little has been heard of these since and there is as yet no sign of them in the National where again John Bury is now in charge of design. At Stratford-upon-Avon under the Trevor Nunn/Christopher Morley regime, giant permanent masking has been used from 1972 on. This has been refaced and otherwise altered for each season and within the masking there has been elaborate scenery, often with a lot of specialist machinery, including multiple lifts and funicular railways.

This kind of machinery is not there to shift one scene or production out of the way and allow it to be replaced by another but to allow the design to become a kind of jumbo mobile. The automated ramp/flight of steps of Stratford's 1972 *Romans* is likely to receive less use, if that were possible, than the general purpose lifts and rolling stages of 1932. It is said that the giant hydraulic piston of Covent Garden's 1974 square *Ring*, which replaced the 1963 round and screw-jacked one, will be "used for other things." I have never found a designer yet who had much time for the works of another—in public. Anyway to judge by the tilting, bending and staircasing that is going on in the hands of Svoboda there won't be a gyration left to be invented for it by anyone else by the time the Nibelungs have finished their cycling. Perhaps "all undone by mirrors" is a fitting epitaph when it is realized that those singers who are thrust below stage to achieve certain visual effects, do then have to use microphones!

Sooner or later the discipline of the budget may intervene. Except in our major theatres, there just will not be the money for all that scenery and lighting, and we shall really have to concentrate on the actor and his audience. It is trite to say that this is the most wonderful thing in theatre. Anyone who has experienced this rapport, whether as donor or recipient, can testify to this, but it does seem to become obscured. The basic principle is simple, yet to design a theatre for it can be so elusive. At Stratford-upon-Avon they have been trying to get their theatre "right" ever since they opened it in 1932. We discuss the lengths to which they have gone in the next chapter. One cannot help wondering what the interior of the Olivier Theatre in the new National on the South Bank will see over a similar forty-year period.

Do we want our great houses treated as if they were studio theatres and pushed around to test the theory of whoever happens to have control of the place at the moment? The present auditorium of Drury Lane is the fourteenth and, though not typical of its date (1922), surely we shall no more wish to see it pulled about and changed than we would the other parts (such as the Rotunda) which date from 1811 and *are* typical. So too the Royal Festival Hall of 1951 must remain. We put on a show in a particular theatre or hall; ignore it the audience may, but we who do the job should not. Perhaps in the age of conservation we are just entering, we shall be less prone to let people literally wreck somebody else's will.

Conservation may arise not only from the desire to preserve a building for its architectural merit but from sheer economic necessity. It used to be claimed that it was less costly to put up a purpose-designed building than to convert or refurbish an existing one. This is increasingly doubtful. There have been a number of attractive modernizations and redecorations. The top tier can be cut out, the front-of-house replanned to give more spaciousness for the lesser number of people, an annexe built on perhaps, and improvements are always possible with the equipment backstage. When it comes to the less orthodox forms of staging, considerable stimulus may be derived from an existing building whether originally designed as a theatre or not. It is more difficult to begin from a blank sheet of paper.

Scale is another point at issue. If there really is a turning in varying degrees to the "Small is Beautiful" idea then should not the theatre be in the vanguard of such a movement? Mixed up with this is the question of whether the theatre industry could not be labour-intensive instead of following the labour reduction policies practised by industry. People are said to like theatre work. Certainly with so many actors out of work there would appear to be no shortage of the principal ingredient of theatre. Thus, instead of pilgrimages to large shrines in the great city centres, theatre could become more parochial. It then belongs to a community small enough to recognize that it is a community! There is no substitute for your own theatre, even if your standards have to be much lower. There is nothing to be apologetic about in being a small theatre. In the Theatre Directory at present there are seventy-three theatres seating under 400 outside

London. A theatre of four hundred seats or so can be quite a compact affair to run if the stage is not too large or too demanding of scenery—either of which means that the backstage areas must also become large.

It is worth repeating that, given normal scenic aims, a stage is only as effective as the workshops and storage alongside it. Some of our new theatres economize in the very directions which go to make a practical working theatre. They concentrate on the auditorium and the audience facilities front of house and say that this and that will be added backstage as "stage II." This no longer means that the stage itself is made too small; in fact the stage itself, as we have seen, is often made too big, but outside it there will be too few service rooms, dressing rooms and above all offices. Thus in the new Key Theatre at Peterborough, one dressing room has to be used for the wardrobe, another for the administrator and as soon as a show of any size comes in these people have to move out. There is an orchestra pit for twenty musicians, but where do they go when they are not in the pit? In a compact plan like this they cannot haunt the corridors, nor is there the friendly neighbourhood pub next door as was the case with so many of the older houses; this particular theatre stands isolated in a park.

There is little sign of economy in the installation of equipment. This could with justice be hotly denied by the Key Theatre staff; they have a 3-preset, 60-channel control with but forty dimmers fitted. At the Redgrave, Farnham, however, with the same size stage but fewer seats (356 compared with 399) there is a 3-preset control with eighty dimmers all fitted. What do we make of that? The first thing to be said is that the Redgrave had a theatre consultant, the Key did not. The employment of a theatre consultant is advisable (I am one myself!) but they must not be put in a situation, as often happens with architects, where they become divorced from the ultimate management and that management's budget. It is not the money for building the place —one way and another this usually turns up—but the money for *running* the theatre that is really important.

If one sits down and tries to cover, technically speaking, everything which a given theatre may be called upon to do, the result can become extremely elaborate. How many lighting channels do you really need? My Light Console of 1949 at Drury Lane had (at my suggestion) 216, but the full set of dimmers was not required or completed until 1972 for *Gone with the Wind*.

Whether all this lighting really is necessary is the question that comes up time and time again. There are very good reasons for the Olivier Theatre in a great architectural complex to have 622 dimmers. The outlay is financially to scale. But should we always think of the equipment we put into our theatres in terms of "as much as they can possibly afford?" Might there not be some theatres where it could be said, "We don't want to spend all that money" rather than the usual, "We can't afford all that?" Some years ago I wrote an article about my ideal lighting installation. With tongue largely in cheek, it proposed only two dimmers: one for the auditorium decorative lighting and the other for the stage lighting. One could decrease the audience lights somewhat or completely and raise the stage lighting to be bright or dull to suit.

Nonsense perhaps, but just think how free the director would feel to get on with his true job with no experts around. There would be no sound equipment of course—the human voice would have to do its own work unaided, as I must confess I prefer to do when lecturing. I hate being at the mercy of the chap on the sound control and detest mikes even more for discussion. If they are needed then the hall is too big, and if you need that size of hall to get everyone in then your conference is too big!

Of course this is not to say that *all* theatres should think small. But those that do should *think little positively* and without shame: "We haven't got one of those" need not be uttered with head hung down and prefixed by "I'm sorry." It is simply that we neither need nor want one. Some of those touring companies could be told to leave all that lighting behind. A recent National Theatre Mobile tour took a special rig of forty-eight spots and forty-eight dimmers merely to provide white light for a standing set of white curtains. Yet when at one of their whistle stops they had perforce to use the existing set of black drapes and lighting rig of the hall instead no-one found it particularly surprising that Juliet and Romeo continued to live for their audience until Act V, Sc. iii.

Of course if a show is built around a giant Moog Synthesizer, then a jumbo-sized Moog Synthesizer you have to have. Let no one think I don't like scenery and lighting. I sometimes think I like a scenery and lighting show best of all and in my own work, as the appendix on Colour Music shows, I have found the real way for me to express myself on the stage has been to use scenery and lighting only.

Some years ago now Richard Pilbrow used the expression "a multi-lantern complexity" to describe techniques he and his colleagues were using. This is the equivalent of the great orchestra, but what of lighting of the nature of a string quartet? No deeply woven texture but each instrument (and that *is* the American stage lighting term) standing out clear and defined—just for a change. Why need this only happen when the rather familiar symbol of our time—a power cut—reduces 100 kW or so to 5 or 6 kW on a standby generator?

2 Auditorium and Stage

GETTING down to elements, a theatre is a building to enable a number of people to see and hear a performance. A lot is implied about mystic contact between the actor and his audience as if there were some extra-sensory link, but in fact this contact follows from being able to see and hear. In Britain, at any rate, it is advisable to put a roof over all and when this is done artificial light becomes essential.

Assuming for the moment that the lighting is correctly positioned to illuminate the actor, the task is to position the audience so that the result can reach their eyes. There are two ways of doing this: one is to stand him high in relation to them (the soap-box technique) and the other is to put them on a steep slope (upon a hillside). What happens in both cases is that each person is able to look over his neighbour's head, or at least his shoulder. This does not mean that, as the designs of some of our theatres would lead one to suppose, the two methods are interchangeable or can even be used in combination. The effect of the two is quite different.

The soap-box look-up technique is only suitable when one or two people have to be seen at a time. The priest at his altar, the political speaker, the Field Marshal at a prizegiving, or a pair of boxers at a prizefight. As soon as what these people are doing in relationship one to another becomes important, we run into trouble over what is known as masking.

The front edge of a table can mask what is placed on it and one actor completely eclipse another unless they are strung out in a single uninteresting line across the stage. Indeed, if we are looking upwards they might as well be strung out that way for the principal means for establishing relationship in depth, the floor, cannot be seen. To tilt the stage floor to remedy this requires such a steep rake as to be impracticable except as a special effect. And this effect will give a diminishing result, towards those at the back of the house anyway. Where the stage is encircled to some degree by audience, raising it also produces problems in lighting because the front rows will find themselves looking up into the lights belonging to the other side.

This looking up can be a nuisance even in an orthodox proscenium stage, for considerable trouble is likely to be necessary to mask or otherwise draw attention away from overhead areas which have no relevance to the performance anyway.

If the show is seen in its correct perspective as beginning with the actor, then he and the floor he stands on are of paramount importance. Once everything is based on the assumption that he should, when standing normally on the stage, be viewed from an angle not lower than that of a person seated in the room with him, the rest falls in line. No question arises of how high the stage floor should be, for obviously it must be at the same level as that of the floor carrying the lowest row of seats. Beyond this, the seat rows have to be stepped so that the occupants of each look over the others to have a complete view of the stage floor. In theatre-in-the-round this is precisely what happens, on all four sides—a truly round stage being unusual outside the circus. The stage floor is at the lowest level so that everyone can see it and all that happens on it. Both on the count of lighting and to minimize the risk of one actor's masking another, the stage is usually (and certainly should be) one complete riser below the first row. It is then surrounded by five or six rows each on its own riser. This form of theatre relies on intimacy, and Stephen Joseph, its great protagonist, stated 18 × 24 ft as an optimum size of stage. With the 700 seats round the 32 × 28 ft stage of the Washington Arena Theatre, acting going on in the far corner can seem too far away. Living in the room alongside the actors, on the other hand, can make up for the absence of scenery and other aids—at any rate for some people. Another essential feature of this form is a sense of regular encompassment of the stage—the audience must hang together. At its best, each side should have exactly the same number of seats and rows. An odd row out will pass, but to have a great block on one side destroys the feel by reducing the encompassment to a mere token—a fake.

This also applies to another form of theatre which is glibly thought of as derived from the ancient Greek theatre. Since that theatre was conceived in terms of four to ten thousand seats with the show viewed in daylight, this ancestry had best be ignored. Much the same can be said of copying Shakespeare's stage. Apart from the fact that if Leslie Hotson[1] is to be believed we do not know with any exactitude the way it was used, once again this was seen in daylight. Let it be said here and now that there is no way of lighting that raised stage in modern terms without dazzling most of the groundlings crowded in that small space. Of course, they can be moved farther away and the theatre become larger, but that will be by no means the same thing. A correct reproduction will have to avoid stage lighting and use something like fluorescent lighting from high up to give the diffusion equivalent to daylight. It is of interest that Nugent Monck's Elizabethan experiment at the Maddermarket, Norwich,[2] seems to have spent most of its long career as a stage unsuited for but using scenery and even house tabs of a necessarily incomplete sort on occasion.

To renounce modern stage lighting is something only the late Sir Tyrone Guthrie was prepared to do. Others who followed him began to express discontent at being restricted to white light, as was then the case at Stratford, Ontario. Other criticisms then arose and thus we who knew this theatre only as brilliantly successful (rightly so) were treated to tales of woe by the users at theatre conferences—much to our surprise. Treasonable desires were expressed about wanting to get rid of the Stratford balcony sometimes and to use coloured light; to change the scene, perhaps substitute one permanent set for another by revolving the centre section. At the time of writing this is said to be going ahead and the ceiling has already been altered and an extensive new stage lighting system went into action for the 1972 season.

At the Tyrone Guthrie Theatre in Minneapolis, Minn., things are better, as the back wall is not permanent and scenery can be shifted in and out, but overhead clearance in this off-stage area is insufficient. It does not appear that it was ever the intention, contrary to what is sometimes stated, to use this back area as a proscenium adaptation. At least I hope not, for it could not have worked. It is quite otherwise at the Vivian Beaumont Theatre, Lincoln Center. There the thrust stage is

[1] *Shakespeare's Wooden O*, by Leslie Hotson (Rupert Hart-Davis).
[2] *Tabs*, Volume 19, Number 3.

backed by a fully equipped stage, grid, cyclorama, and all; the justification of this being adaptability in which either part or all of the thrust stage is mechanically removed and replaced by seats. It then becomes an ordinary proscenium theatre—but does it? I am afraid that, in spite of the very wide proscenium and the fact that the seats embrace less than 180 degrees, the side seats under these conditions give a poor view. Nor is this fault encountered only in strict proscenium work, for other productions, such as *The Caucasian Chalk Circle*, which I saw there, are tempted to use the full stage depth combined with some degree of apron. Also the seats which replace the thrust stage itself tend to constitute an isolated community in this form (this also applies to the much smaller Questors at Ealing under similar circumstances). In addition to gangway separation, these seats alone of all the seats require their occupants to look up to the stage.

Most open stages seem to use scenery. When I was in Minneapolis at the beginning of their third season, there was a lot of scenery about, much of it hanging over the thrust stage itself, which emphasized the need for suspensions there. This use of scenery on open stage has been explained by Donald Mullin who has worked a lot in-the-round at Tufts University, Massachusetts. His thesis[1] is that a proscenium gives "a sense of proportion" to the stage space concealed behind in contrast to the "roofless appearance" of open-stage examples. He says, "Few plays are so universal or grand in theme that they can expand their environments indefinitely. Limitations are a psychological requirement for any play." The shape of the floor and the presence of something overhead, whether scenery or lighting frame, can prevent this sense of infinite abyss.

[1] *Tabs*, Volume 23, Number 2. "Some Guidelines for Theatre-in-the-Round."

The use of a shallow scenic background with a semi-circular arrangement of audience around a projecting stage was pioneered in Britain by John English, who toured it as a tent theatre. In a full development, this obviously sets a severe limit to the degree of encompassment by the audience, for at the extreme sides the actors are seen backed only by audience and the scenery is nearly edge on. Even where 180-degree encirclement is not practised, there is still the need to continue the spirit of the set out on to the stage: hence the importance of being able to see the stage floor and to hang something overhead. Incidentally, it seems difficult anywhere to persuade audiences that side seats are as good as those at the centre. I remember at the famous "Circle in the Square" theatre off-Broadway a real feeling of disappointment at being led to side seats as honoured guest. Yet in that theatre, shaped vaguely like the British House of Commons, with its very long, narrow projecting stage, the seats on either side were definitely the best, the centre block being far away at one end.

The shape and proportions of any open form of stage are very important. If one is not careful, the actors get involved in very long walks to get on and off, there being no possibility of building scenery to cover their comings and goings. A stage the shape of the Greek orchestra with semi-circular seating seems to ask for trouble, this geometric figure being twice as wide as it is deep. All in all, it seems that it would be rash to go further than the advice that the term "peninsular" or "thrust" gives the best hint to a successful open-stage shape, and that "arena" should not be applied as it is a complete misnomer for theatre except on pageant scale, and invites confusion. Maybe the American use of this term for theatre-in-the-round with its evocation of gladiatorial combat is what has led Washington astray in size. Another method of tackling the matter of theatre form is to refer to "enclosed" or "unenclosed" of "x degrees encirclement." As we have seen, thrust stages are less easy to design than those in-the-round. Both in their architecture and in the staging upon them lie more ambushes. Curiously the most famous of the thrust stages—that at Stratford, Ontario—is the one with by far the largest seating capacity (2258), and is the most successful in its audience relationship. An example on a much smaller scale, The Questors, Ealing (360 seats), also appears to work well in this form (Fig. 3).

The important desiderata seem to be: keep the acting area as a tight square tending to rely literally on thrust—rather than width—and then step the seating sharply. This poses the question of whether the rule about the stage at the lowest level as in theatre-in-the-round applies here also. Personally, I believe it does, and this in spite of Tyrone Guthrie's very much raised and stepped stages at Stratford, Ontario, and Minne-

apolis, and his own writings on the subject.[1] It is not possible to be dogmatic here as far more experiment is needed, but one thing is certain: whether raised or not, the acting area must err on the side of being too cramped rather than too open.

Guthrie is said to have put his stage high because the stage in the Assembly Hall where he worked for the Edinburgh Festival had to be placed over the pews. Whatever the reason, it suits Shakespeare productions at Ontario, and this probably extends to anything on a heroic scale. At The Questors, however, in the thrust adaptation the modest raised stage of 1 foot high is often forsaken for floor level with even a sunken front portion to reduce masking hazards. No matter if the stage, whatever its form, is at floor level, it must maintain its separation from the audience. The feeling must be of privileged eavesdropping but not of actual participation. Except in a "fun palace," whatever that may be, the audience do not take part. Nothing they do can alter destiny as represented by the plot, as distinct from the possible run of the play. Whatever the actors on their part gain from intimate contact (and far from all admit to gaining anything thereby) the last thing they require is physical assistance from the audience. Should a cigarette lighter fail, one proffered from the audience would be the reverse of helpful. When, as actually happened at The Mermaid, Long John Silver fell accidentally but a step or two away, it posed the problem for us in the front rows whether to lend a hand or not as he struggled to get up on his one leg. We all sat tight, but speaking for myself it was agony and we should not have been faced with such a decision.

[1] *A Life in the Theatre*, by Tyrone Guthrie (Hamish Hamilton, 1959).

The stage and its action must appear close, but not so much part of the auditorium that the audience use it for access or to park their coats and boxes of chocolates on its edge, as is said to happen at Guildford. Likewise, the actors should not borrow the audience's entrances and exits but should have their own. John English has expressed the two elements as the "theatrical world" and the "real world." To what extent the occupants of this latter, the audience, are or should be deceived by the former is of little importance here. The more difficult task is illusion and this should be the aim, for we can easily opt out of it. If the means to provide moonlight are so good that the producer believes that, contrary to his intent, the audience will believe it is real, there is always the well-tried "This lanthorn doth the horned moon present," or in another school the spotlight can in its naked glory be exposed.

Personally, I can only say that in a heavily charged scene no amount of reminder that this is only "theatre" works for me. Further, it is the inarticulate who pull my heartstrings, which may explain why the characters in Shakespeare and opera have never moved me as much as the young girl in the Grand Guignol, *Three Old Women*, a one-act play during which I endured a physical pain every bit as real as having a tooth out.

Illusion surely requires sufficient concealment of the means by which it is carried out so as to deceive the audience. It is true that we can accept the convention of dancing in ballet or of singing in opera to work out a plot, but there is another level of theatrical experience which partakes of the art of a conjuror. We know there is no such thing as a magician, that the girl is not sawn in half or that she does not vanish in fact; but, carried out in a polished manner, the illusion is complete. The slightest fumbling and the spell is broken. For all our sophistication, there is still much that can be enjoyed at that level in the theatre. In stage lighting this means that the architect must make provision for complete concealment of the lanterns and, furthermore, that they should not betray themselves when in use by scatter on light-coloured neighbouring surfaces.

In a theatre of this kind, apart from the auditorium decorative lighting perhaps, not a single lighting unit would be in sight. The stage would become, as if by magic, suffused with a glow of light. The musical equivalent is the giant, but concealed, Wagner orchestra at Bayreuth. The school of the visible stage lighting is the equivalent of the visible orchestra of most opera houses. Some people prefer this orchestra at any rate for some operas, and likewise some not only do not object to seeing spotlights and their rays of light, but positively enjoy doing so. There are undoubtedly two distinct effects here, but what cannot be done is to mix the two. Either one sees the lanterns or one does not, but to expect to combine the two and still have an illusion is unreasonable—as unreasonable as the common practice in opera houses of lighting the stage with all the sublety possible with a Bayreuth orchestra pit when all the time there it is—a vast illuminated barrier over which the audience has to strain its eyes to perceive the happenings in what, in consequence, appears as Stygian gloom beyond.

This can be summed up by saying that a large number of the smaller halls and theatres, particularly open stage and other experimental ones, will not be able to conceal their lighting equipment anyway, but other theatres should be designed with proper concealment; in these latter, it being simple enough to expose when necessary. Lighting manufacturers for their part should make their equipment as neat and well styled as possible. Incidentally, concealment does not imply placing lanterns in clumsy boxes; it means that the locations spring naturally out of the architecture and are not just applied bumps and blisters. If lighting and its positioning were regarded by the architect as being as important as the fenestration in a church or any other building designed for daylight, then real inspiration could be derived from it. In no place does this opportunity offer greater challenge than in the area immediately in front of the proscenium in that type of theatre. A number of problems are posed and it might almost be true to say that all problems meet there.

The first point to make is that the proscenium opening arises only because of the need to seal the stage fire risk from the auditorium by dropping a fire curtain into an aperture. All temptation to define or frame this aperture, to make a feature of it, should be resisted. If a prominent frame is needed, the theatre people can build one for the particular production. At one time it was the practice to make quite a feature of the proscenium but this, "the picture frame," is what producers today find most objectionable—the sense of having to see the show through a hole in the wall. The Nuffield Theatre at Southampton University, opened in 1964, with Sir Basil Spence's emphatic statement of a thick wall between stage and auditorium is most unusual. Far more in keeping with the feeling of the time is Peter Moro's proscenium in the Playhouse, Nottingham (Fig. 4), opened the previous year. The walls of the auditorium curve round to embrace the stage and any sense of framing is broken by bringing the horizontal top of the opening forward of the verticals at the sides. A further cunning device is the use of a floating lighting drum to mask the great height of the auditorium at this point.

Traditional picture-frame theatres in the past when confronted with this height problem have relied on a deep pelmet and a decorated tympanum over the opening incorporating angels blowing trumpets or the city coat of arms or, in the case

FIG. 4 Playhouse, Nottingham, proscenium with adaptable forestage/orchestra pit

of the S'Carlos, Lisbon, the large dial of a real clock, of all things.

Another method of reducing height which became common between the wars, especially in cinemas, was to run the ceiling down to the arch, sometimes in conjunction with a pelmet, as at the three-tier Cambridge, London, or without one, as in a more recent example, the Yvonne Arnaud, Guildford. The ceiling descending unbroken can be troublesome for reasons which are considered later. In consequence, when I tried to indicate something of the sort in my book of 1950, I made a virtue of the necessity and incorporated a large cyclorama-type overhead cove with a lighting bridge in the main ceiling beyond. The word "cyclorama" was deliberate: it was not just a cove, as it was intended that the surface of this area was sometimes to be lit evenly as a feature with or without the stage or a show—a feeling of openness being created thereby. Another point about the design was the use of free-standing wings either side of the proscenium opening, to mask entrances and side lighting to the forestage.

There is an awful trap here which the first rebuilding of the Old Vic proscenium, immediately after the second world war, fell right into. Forestage entrances and overhead lighting positions can create a second frame. Thus, there are two prosceniums, one behind the other—two barriers instead of one. There followed at the Old Vic a Georgian modification, then Michael Elliotts oval proscenium, and now Sean Kenny's wooden proscenium with a festoon curtain right down on the front edge of the forestage; but two prosceniums still remain. Rather less obvious, perhaps, in this last version because of the greater width at the forward edge.

I think the welcome for The Mermaid, London, and its

successors, the Hampstead Civic and Phoenix, Leicester, springs largely from the absence of frame. The show extends to the full width of the auditorium, thus giving a wonderful wide-open feel without any sense of barrier. This, according to some, arises from the fact that the auditorium walls continue on to the stage itself. To my mind this idea, even if it is not nonsense, should not be pandered to, for wing space is essential. These theatres, open or not, use a lot of scenery. Taking everything in and out at the back only and making all entrances upstage is a terrible handicap. The first demand in the case of any proscenium stage is wing space, and why should this become unnecessary simply because the thing is called an end stage? If the auditorium walls really are required to extend on to the sides of the stage, they can be made to do so when necessary by painting scenery for the purpose. At Pitlochry in Scotland, where there is a very wide opening, they have found all that is necessary is to extend the feel of the walls by making the scenery follow this line.

There can be no doubt that, once a sense of framing is overcome, a fully equipped stage, wings, flys, and all, can be tacked on to a good auditorium without loss of the open end feeling. This is especially so where an orchestra lift arrangement allows formation of further stalls flooring or a forestage extension to the main stage.

There is in fact a better way of doing this, mainly found in Germany. The orchestra pit or forestage is formed out of the stage itself. The proscenium frame, in their case complete with the usual lighting bridge and tower structure, either moves upstage somewhat or a second one is flown in. The value of this arrangement is that the conformation of the auditorium seating remains unchanged. The fire curtain falls in effect on the orchestra rail. Of course a large stage to bite out of is needed but at least one avoids the circumstance that every time a large audience is essential—as for most musical shows—the seating capacity is reduced.

Special entrances for the actors to the forestage are required where this is in front of the fire curtain. They should be capable of concealment. When required to be stressed, flame-resistant scenery would be used. Figures 4 and 5 show two good examples of such proscenium arrangements. It is essential to avoid any impression of double frame at this point—one to the forestage and another inside it to the stage itself.

A design of the auditorium begins with the height of the stage floor. First of all, it is to be hoped that, for reasons stated earlier in the chapter, this will not have to be high simply because the audience on their flat floor will otherwise not be able to see. Stepping of each row of seats is essential as the maximum permitted rake is 1 in 10. At the new Abbey,

Dublin, the rake is 1 in 7 and some experience discomfort from the angle their feet makes to the floor when seated. Even in a multi-purpose hall with a preponderance of flat-floor activities, folding "bleachers" and other such devices of varying degrees of mechanical elaboration are possible.

A complication arises in that now and then an actor will proclaim that he must have height in relation to his audience. It is difficult to see how this makes any sense since even in the most traditional of theatres such a large part of the audience looks down on him. It is probable that this arises only where the audience is insufficiently stepped at stalls level and, in consequence, the actor feels he cannot be seen properly. Another reason could be the lack of physical separation referred to earlier. The way to overcome this is not to raise the stage but to give an effect of height by a moat immediately in front. Thus, the first row of audience is one full riser up. Below them, two steps down, is the lowest level which serves purely as a gangway; and then well out of reach comes the stage itself, two or three steps up. In a thrust stage, the low-level gangway belongs wholly to the stage and the actors use it whenever they exit in the direction of the audience. On no account should they share the audience entrances. Not only is the mixture of the theatrical and real quite wrong in theory, but it also is quite impracticable and leads to train catchers and other "of necessity" room leavers crossing the path of the actors.

The best way for the public to enter the auditorium is at a high level because then the object of the whole visit is seen at once and approached. Entering at the lowest level one has to turn one's back on the stage and walk away, every row that is passed stressing thereby a sense of distance. Of course, in a very high tier it will be necessary to have vomitories or something of the sort halfway. The question then arises, should those destined for the rear seats then turn their back on the stage and climb to their seemingly remote eyrie? I consider that, if possible, they too should enter their division from the top.

There follows the question that, if in fact there is a division of the audience into two halves, is there anything to gain in having the whole on one floor? The answer lies, to my mind, in the number of seats (up to 500 should not be difficult, given a reasonable width of stage) to accommodate on one tier.

It would not follow that above this number a balcony is essential, and there is something to be said for the stadium form of theatre in which the back part of the auditorium is raised sufficiently to accommodate a cross gangway under it or a row or two of seats. Assuming we are still considering an end stage, the actor continues to see his audience as one, but the fact that the members of the audience themselves do not may be an advantage. Much is talked about community spirit, the sense of a congregation crowded together sharing an experience, but it is noticeable that whenever given the chance the preference is for sitting towards but not in the front, and in the centre at that. It is lovely to know all about the rows behind and at the sides provided that they really are behind and at the sides and you yourself are not there. This levels itself out in the traditional horseshoe opera house, as the tiers of boxes served a useful purpose for those who went to be seen. In any case, if the view was bad there was always the music, plus a chance of a snooze in the corner behind the box curtains, whilst for others there were compensations for a side view of the stage in a a better view of the orchestra. As to a sense of crowd, not everyone enjoys the sight and smell of his fellow men to the same extent. Do we really not know, if there were areas with seats crowded together and others wider spaced, all available for the same price, which would go first?

Packing them in is all very well but this can be a misery for the long-legged, and there will be more of these about in future, not less. All in all, I should have thought 2 ft 10 in. to 3 ft ideal back-to-back seating especially if centre gangways can be avoided thereby, because of the greater clearance between the rows. Beyond 3 ft there does seem to be a sense of the audience's not hanging together. Care must be taken over the amount of padding to the seat back. More comfortable reseating of the Princes Theatre when it became the Shaftesbury produced cramp while the old centres were retained. A raised stadium or balcony, by putting part of the stalls seating out of sight, can lessen the feeling of distance, which a vista of all those rows between the back seater and the stage gives. The great problem, however, when a balcony is included, is to avoid pushing it too high and having to rake it too steeply. The first is bad for the actor who may get the impression that he is addressing two theatres at once. The second may invoke a very real feeling of nausea for the audience.

Large theatres inevitably lead to balconies and it may well be that two shallower balconies with stalls largely in the open are preferable to a very deep one. From this arises the possibility of shutting off part or all of this top balcony when a normal smaller audience is required. An excellent example comes from Limoges in France where Pierre Sonrel's auditorium has a ceiling which can be lowered by electric motors to fill in the area above the top tier front in four minutes. By making the decorative lighting move with the ceiling, all impression of makeshift is removed. The upper area really does vanish. Where a moving ceiling is considered a complication, it should be possible to provide the same visual effect with lighting arranged to act as blinders. A large, rather remote, upper balcony would seem to provide the only solution for theatres which have to expand from time to time, to take a large audience for opera, ballet, or music, or for a festival. Both the type of show and sense of occasion may make these remoter seats useful. There are times when it is a case of better any seat than no seat at all. "Anything rather than miss it" becomes the spirit.

Very much bound up with seating capacity and sight lines is the width of the proscenium opening. I picked on 40 ft when writing for my 1950 book about a theatre which might have occasionally to stage opera and ballet, and see no reason to change my mind. Forty foot reduces very nicely to 30 ft and a production coming from Covent Garden's 43-ft opening should not feel unduly cramped, provided there is sufficient wing space and the fly tower is wide enough. Backcloths at Covent Garden are 60 × 36 ft high. As to stage depth, operating on a strictly practical economic level, it does not seem unreasonable to say that a 40-ft opening should mean a working depth of 40 ft, fully covered by the grid of course. It is not necessary to go much further in a book on stage lighting than to repeat Basil Dean's advice: "The stage requirements are really very simple; plenty of space and height, with walls at right angles to each other and free of all obstructions above and on and beneath the stage level."

Obstruction of the stage can be a terrible nuisance. What constitutes this is a matter of opinion and for this reason a lighting bridge just upstage of the proscenium, if adopted, should be demountable or arranged to travel up to the grid. When in this position, it must be possible to arrange some substitute suspensions in this area to compensate for the blockage of the grid. The grid referred to is the normal arrangement of counterweights to lift scenery clear of the stage. A height of two and a half times the working proscenium opening is usually recommended. At one time hemp lines manually lifted the backcloths and other scenery, but these were replaced by counterweight lines in the twenties and, improvement though they are, they are in turn overdue for replacement by power-assisted lines. The trouble about counterweights is the extra labour called for in putting the weights on or off, and the obstruction in the wings represented by single purchase pulleys. Yet stage people rightly object to double purchase to reduce counterweight travel on the grounds of insensitivity and the extra weights to be put on. Power assistance seems obvious to me, but it will have to be well designed and easy to maintain.

Another device I firmly advocate is a cyclorama, and nothing shakes me in the belief that any properly equipped theatre should have one. Indeed, I would put it before the acquisition of a paint frame if I must make a choice. Taken in conjunction with scenic cut-outs and ground rows, also scenic projection, it saves a lot of painting. In a small theatre or a stage in a hall, a flat plaster cyclorama on the rear wall is a must. A large passage to cross the stage should be arranged beyond, it being a pity to take up tower space for this. In a full-sized theatre, a cyclorama must be larger and more encompassing, and then the rule about obstruction operates. Under these circumstances a roller-cloth cyclorama running around a track high in the grid is the usual way to do the job. But the cloth must be properly made for the purpose, and Germany still seems to be the only place to obtain one. A real cyclorama cloth has an opaque filled surface which reflects the light and wastes little in transmission. There are some dreadful substitutes about, which look just what they are—material hanging there, puckers, creases, and all.

While a grid with full flying height is an essential for large professional theatres, it should not be assumed that the expense is always justified. Little theatres would do so well to put their first preference for plenty of stage space on the level. Even where flying is not intended, there must be sufficient height over the stage to minimize the need for borders. Always extract the maximum height a building is capable of over the stage. There must be a framework over the stage to take pulleys and to allow suspensions to be made off. Behind the proscenium a fire curtain may no longer be insisted on in the smaller schemes, but it has other advantages than fire resistance. It makes a reasonable sound barrier, for example, allowing the stage to be used while the orchestra rehearse in the pit. An orchestra pit should always be included in any scheme if there is the slightest chance of its being needed. A pit is a most difficult thing to add, or to enlarge, after a building is complete, so make it large enough. A time-honoured way of doing this is to provide for extension of a moderate size by making a couple of rows of stalls seats and the flooring under them removable, but the merits of taking the pit from the stage, described earlier, should be considered.

We are now back in the proscenium area and it will be appropriate to consider its design in rather more detail, especially in relationship to that proportion of stage lighting which has to be accommodated in front of the house tabs.

The positioning of this lighting is complicated by the expanding angle of the walls and ceiling of the auditorium in relationship to the proscenium opening. In this respect, the situation is analogous to what happens in the case of sight lines, and may be summed up as trying to look round the corner. A proscenium opening has to be limited in width and height: otherwise the scenery and the facilities for handling it become over large. It is obvious that some people used to working on a small stage do not sufficiently consider the jump in production costs represented by what seems a modest increase of one-third in the dimensions they are used to. This means a cube of over double. An increase of 50 per cent gives a cube over three times as large, scenery almost on opera-house scale, and a heavy burden in labour and running costs, to say nothing about the initial building outlay. In the great theatre-building age, a 30-ft opening was very commonly chosen as practical enough for opera, musical comedy and drama. Forty foot or just over was reserved for a very large theatre, for example, Drury Lane (42 ft 6 in.).

The need to keep the opening relatively small falls foul of two requirements: the sight lines and modern wide open production. In this technique, sometimes referred to as space staging, a composite set of, for example, a house, a garden, and perhaps part of the street are presented at one and the same time. The action runs from one to the other without intervals for scene changing but, of course, the bars still demand their tribute. A warning has to be uttered, however, for any really wide stage technique can increase the chance of making action intimate to some and remote to others, thereby setting an insoluble problem in playing. The best solution is to rely on the fan of the side walls, when used with a forestage, automatically to increase stage width. Thus, at Nottingham, an opening of 32 ft becomes 45 ft or so at the front edge of the forestage when both lifts are up. Then, again, so long as access to this area is through openings not obviously doors, then there is a sense of space beyond them; and also some scenery representing a house front, for example, can be stood there and so widen the stage picture.

Lighting does not fit into this scheme so happily. The trouble is that the purpose of lighting positions in the proscenium area is not just to provide side lighting on the forestage, but to light the downstage area of the stage proper. None of the over-head lighting immediately upstage of the proscenium becomes effective there because the angle is too steep. The more remote lighting in the auditorium, although useful, cannot fulfil properly the modelling and more intimate duties required in this important area because of its more flat-on angle. What is needed is a direct repeat of the No. 1 lighting position behind the proscenium, but this time in front. Unfortunately, just at this point the walls run away and the lighting is dragged away with them too far to the side or, in the case of the ceiling, to a lofty height. Another defect is that because the walls and ceiling fan hornlike they turn towards the audience and catch the light scatter and betray the sources.

Overhead the answer is reasonably simple, although seldom adopted. Height to the auditorium ceiling is no handicap provided there is a floating lighting frame overhead. This can take the form of a Royal Festival Hall style of acoustic sound-board or a structure like the lighting drum at Nottingham. In spite of the brickbats it has received, this latter remains an excellent idea; it fails only because decorative consideration insisted on a circle, and of too small a diameter at that. A lighting frame needs to extend nearly the full width of the auditorium over the area of forestage and front stalls. It must, of course, appear to clear these walls so that no suggestion of another proscenium frame results—indeed, it may well assist in the break-up of this area. Access to the frame is very important and it must be considered as a lighting bridge no matter whether it is an acoustic or decorative feature as well. There may also be merit in clustering stage lighting together as for example in the case of the four vertical features which hang from the main ceiling of the Olivier Theatre.

In positioning a lighting frame vertically, it obviously must not interfere with sight lines or follow spots and projectors which may be high in the auditorium, but otherwise it must be as low as possible. This is because the object is to get well inside the proscenium opening, and even if this itself is high it is bound to be reduced for many purposes by a proscenium border to a working height of 16 ft. If the overhead position is wide and low enough, the side-wall lighting position here will become less important, being reduced mainly to side lighting when the forestage is in use. The lighting slots can, therefore, be combined with apertures which open for use as side doors, windows or Juliet balconies.

In a small theatre without a fire curtain, the lighting frame notion can conveniently be combined with the No. 1 position, and thus this moves out and the other moves in to the extent that they become one bridge above the ceiling just in front of the house tabs. It is still important to keep this low and essential then that the tabs should be trailers moving sideways and not flown. Even if they did fly clear above the bridge, the delay in bringing in this important lighting while they got there would be intolerable. Out in the auditorium there must be a further ceiling lighting slot running across and situated roughly halfway down. The slot also returns vertically partway down the wall to give a masked side position.

At the Leatherhead Thorndike, Roderick Ham has made a feature of the lighting slots. The wall swings round not only to provide concealment for the lighting—accessible from outside the auditorium—but to form two verticals either side to break up the surface and give it height (Fig. 5). The walls themselves also curve to embrace the rear of the auditorium and ensure that the longest rows of seats are not at the rear of the theatre. Peter Moro at Nottingham used a circular auditorium to the same effect.

FIG. 5. Thorndike Theatre, Leatherhead; vertical lighting slots as architectural feature

There remains the housing of the lighting control, and this is best accommodated in a room at the back of the auditorium where it can be together with sound and production control. The rooms should be capable of separation and it is convenient if the window to the lighting control can be opened. The lighting control room can be quite small, 10 ft wide × 7 ft deep; the main thing is to include ventilation as the operator has to breathe. Access without passing through the auditorium is essential, but a visit to this room should not involve too great an effort, which suggests the back of the stalls in a large multi-tier house. There are excellent positions in most new theatres. Backstage positions and bad rooms are becoming the exception; the two worst known to me for size, but not for location, are the Royal Opera House, Covent Garden, and the Royal Festival Hall.[1] The first is a triangular leftover from a ventilation shaft, and the second is only 3 ft back to front.

In a theatre where staffing could be a problem and it becomes necessary to have the control near the stage so that the operator can lend a hand there, or check his own lantern setting, a stage-box type of position can be used. There are several good examples of this. The operator still gets a front view, if one-sided, but at least unobstructed by scenery. Also he can easily get backstage, or when, as at the Aldwych and Queen's Theatres, the box is at stalls level, walk out there to clear up some point visually. Care should be taken to give a good finish to all technical areas as otherwise they become second-class and

---

[1] This has been replaced by cutting into the concrete structure rear of the stalls twenty-three years after the hall's opening to facilitate the replacement of my Light Console by a MMS memory system. It is rather sad that a 1974 control should demand more space than a 1951 one.

degenerate into slums. There can be a tendency to take up too much space. At the King's Edinburgh a veritable bungalow has been built to take over the right-hand rear stalls for lighting and sound control. By the time the front stalls have been removed for the full opera orchestra only seven rows remain on this side of the house.

Although much that has been written in this chapter so far applies to all theatres, whatever their form and size, it must be obvious that the main slant is towards the orthodox proscenium with forestage adaptability in front. This still seems to me to represent what most people want and need when they set out to build a theatre. It is extraordinarily adaptable when full use is made of such devices as optical illusion. Its main drawbacks are the chance of a too distant seat and an expensive mechanical set-up in the stage area. The first is not serious now that so many theatres are intended for capacities of between four and eight hundred. Beyond this capacity, the type of show, opera (ballet and musical) makes a demand for a good view rather than intimacy.

As to the second drawback, end-stage forms based on The Mermaid have shown the way to pioneer theatres like the Leicester Phoenix, without mechanics at all, where low initial cost is all-important. In this connection, I still consider the small Hampstead Civic would make an ideal school theatre instead of the echoing spaces of a multi-purpose hall. School suggests the modern movement with Drama spaces, and thence to the larger enterprises of teacher training colleges, like St. Mary's, Strawberry Hill, Twickenham. This is an adaptable theatre—in its smaller forms justifiable as studio and experimental theatre, but in its larger forms representing indecision, an inability to make up one's mind and the word "adaptable" pressed into service as insurance cover.

One of the sadder aspects of adaptable theatres, as seen in the United States, is the expenditure of a lot of money to jerk an auditorium into its strait-jacketed caricatures of the few forms it unwillingly represents. This does not provide a source of innocent merriment, however, because it means more important matters, such as lighting and stage equipment, have to be curbed by a tight budget to make up for the extravagance. Thus, to quote an actual example, two hundred circuits are patched to only thirty dimmers, a mere twenty being fitted now—a pitifully inadequate allowance for one form of theatre, let alone the several supposedly awaiting rebirth at a touch of a button.

The name of George Izenour usually comes up in this context. There are two main uses to which he puts machinery. One is to change the form of the theatre, as with the Loeb Harvard in 1960 and many since; the other is to change the capacity of the one auditorium, as in the case of the Akron

University, Ohio, where the Edwin Thomas Hall can be adjusted from 894 seats for drama to 2321 for opera and musicals or 3008 for concerts. It is—to quote *Theatre Design 75*[1]— "the *sine qua non* of variable visual and acoustical auditorium volume, variable absorption and adjustable seating capacity and could well be the most sophisticated multi-use building for performing arts in the world." I have not seen that particular one but I have seen another recent piece of ingenuity— namely the Modular Theatre of the California Institute of the Arts—both for a performance and during part of the conversion to another form. Designed by Jules Fisher, it needs comment because, with a seating capacity of about 400, something of the same sort of idea might turn up over here. The floor is based on 348 4 ft square modules adjustable over 10 ft vertically by compressed air. The inner walls of the place also consist of 4 ft squares which move or remove. The whole set-up perfectly illustrates the snares. Firstly, for all the mechanics, adjustment cannot be infinite; everything is confined to squared paper, so to speak. Diagonals and curved lines have to be specially constructed. Next, the question arises as to how long it can all go on working. Already—after a couple of years—there are signs of the floor rams jamming and wall panels distorting and not lining-up. Finally, when you have assembled your new conformation it is just that—new—and has to be inspected and passed by the licensing authority.

It is now generally admitted that full adaptability of form is best confined to small seating arrangements of not more than 200 or so. Every theatre nowadays expects to have its studio with at least a few rostrums and lights to push around while others are expensive affairs. The latter may, I feel, represent playgrounds for the ingenuity of the architect and his consultant in trying to anticipate every contingency rather than a stimulus for the imagination of the user who later has to take over *their* toy. It might also be borne in mind that contrary to expectation it is much easier to let your hair down in a formal room than in a black box studio where everything is lying around waiting to be put into some sort of order even if it is only the order of disorder. It was simpler to stage fancy dress balls in the days when we all wore formal dress.

Much the same can apply if we are not careful to Drama Studios in schools. Here the first thing to remember is that they are only occasionally, if at all, used as theatres. They are said to be "primarily a place where children can work out their own ideas without recourse to the use of the conventional and inhibiting pencil and paper."

---

[1] Published by USITT, New York.

The multi-purpose hall can pose as many problems as a large-scale adaptable theatre: indeed, it is difficult to draw a distinction. It is true that one remains a theatre while the other is only a theatre for some of the time and may have to turn into a ballroom. But both have to rely either on large amounts of labour to move things around or on expensive machinery for the purpose, and this means large inflexible chunks and costs which are likely to make it more sensible to build two theatres in the one case, and a hall and a theatre in the other. In the multi-purpose hall, the difficulty is not so much the combining of dance hall and stage, of flat and raked floor, but of reconciling large-hall purposes with small-hall ones. In a line, it is NODA versus BDL. The operatic and musical requirements of the former for large volume and an audience of nearly one thousand on the one hand, and intimate drama of the latter with an audience of 250 or so on the other. Personally, I see no way but a small end-stage theatre with stepped auditorium, and a high-stage flat-floor hall with balcony for the other purposes, distance and angle of view being no longer so important with drama out of the way. Some alleviation for the back rows is possible with terraced seating partly folding. Only when the seating comes down to about 500 can the combination of the many uses be attempted with reasonable chance of success. Whether there is a chance of success or not, and whatever the size, the following rules for multi-purpose halls still apply. Windows must be minimal so that a blackout can easily be arranged. There must be decorative lighting other than the workaday high level fluorescent for the auditorium, and there must be positions for stage lighting there. On stage there must be plenty of wing space and good access to it when bringing a production in. Also, while a grid and fly tower in many cases would be an extravagance, there must be suspension facilities over the stage. Finally, at every turn the architect should remind himself that he is building this multi-purpose hall because his clients can afford only one hall for the present. In one such hall known to me, the dock doors to the stage were made to present such an appearance of civic splendour that they cost more than the stage switchboard used to light the show whose scenery they admitted. Lavish and special finishes are not playing fair: save the money for the proper theatre that will have to be built one day.

To sum up; by 1976 we now have such a diversity of new theatre buildings or revisions of the old in Britain, that it is necessary to concentrate on just those which proclaim their special features. Taking the thrust forms first, there is the contrast between the establishment's model—for all its modern architecture—the Crucible Sheffield and the rebels' Young Vic in London. The latter has a fixed thrust with the audience on

FIG. 6 Christ's Hospital, Horsham; as adapted to "courtyard" theatre by closing off the end stage with mobile towers which match the auditorium

three sides and a main stage across the other end. Any adaptability comes from the simple inexpensive framework spirit of the place which encourages a free style of production. The Crucible, although in fact much better equipped technically to allow variety in staging, does carry a more restrictive atmosphere; in any case things done on that scale and style will cost more.

An important exercise in this context is the theatre at Christ's Hospital (The Bluecoat School) Horsham (Fig. 6), designed by the late Bill Howell who was also the architect for the Young Vic. The auditorium for 500 to 600 seats has a very strong and individual personality—so strong as to render scenery unnecessary though one can readily use the stuff should it be needed. A sloped, nearly square, floor area is surrounded on three sides by timber galleries in three tiers, each holding one row of seats—evocative of the inn-yard of times past. The fourth side has a raised full-sized stage area. This may be framed or masked-off completely by four mobile towers, square in plan. When used across the stage opening the galleries and decorative lighting on the towers join and match exactly to continue the enclosed courtyard effect of the auditorium. Within this the floor can be levelled off using rostrums to provide thrust or other forms of open stage.

A particularly interesting feature of the towers is that they can be used anywhere on the stage as scenery. Wherever they are placed and however they are angled they dress the stage and provide useful acting levels into the bargain. They are not merely structures to mask-in or to carry lights. It may seem paradoxical but their strong yet simple character and colour, conforming exactly to that of the auditorium, provide them with a neutrality denied to more utilitarian and less visually interesting "structures."

With Stephen Joseph's Scarborough and Stoke-on-Trent theatres-in-the-round still going strong in their converted premises, we have as yet only one full-scale public theatre built for this form—the Octagon, Bolton. Even here, however, by putting a large part of the seating on retractable stepping, this

FIG. 7 Key Theatre, Peterborough, end stage at low level: wide proscenium

form can be destroyed to adapt to end and thrust stages—
whereupon scenery tends to be used in quantity, although the
building design made no real provision for getting it in and out.
Another scheme which is also based on theatre-in-the-round
convertible to other forms but this time encircled by a series of
narrow balconies, is Michael Elliott's theatre structure which
has been built in the centre of the Royal Exchange building in
Manchester. Peter Cheeseman, however, says he intends to
remain faithful to the one form when at length he gets a chance
to leave the converted cinema for a purpose-built theatre in
Stoke-on-Trent.

The end stage either in its open or closed forms, frequently
with a token of a thrust on the front edge, seems to be what most
people opt for. A good application of the open end stage
principle is shown by Greenwich where conversion of a tight
narrow site has provided a stimulating theatre in place of what
could have been a cramped proscenium one with inadequate
wing space. In the case of the Key, Peterborough and the
Redgrave, Farnham, the two theatres, though very different in
architectural style, have such similar plans and seating capacities
(nearly 400) as to have almost the same theatrical feel—and
this although one theatre claims a proscenium of 43 ft width
and the other an open stage of 40 ft! The full stage width of
both is 68 ft.

The conflict between the claims of these two theatres is
repeated elsewhere, notably in the case of the Olivier—said to
be the open stage in the National Theatre in contrast to the
proscenium of the Lyttelton there. Except that there is no
curtain at the Olivier and the audience is spread in a wide fan,
there is little to justify this term when compared with the thrust
stage of a theatre like the Sheffield Crucible. Alfred Emmet has
suggested that "the significant dividing line is not so much
between a proscenium and no proscenium as between a stage
which presents a *multi-view* to the audience and one which
presents a *single* view." This observation is based on many
years' experience with both forms in the adaptable Questors
theatre in Ealing. A simple test is whether members of the
audience have other members in their line of view. Applying
this test a true thrust stage, a transverse stage and a centre
stage do come into this category—they are "open" and "multi-
view" right out among their audience.

The end stage "single view" theatres are probably better
examined in terms of their backstage space and facilities rather
than whether they call themselves open stages or not. Is there a
tower with a grid or not and wing space—rather than is there a
proscenium opening? The Aberystwyth Theatr Y Werin has
in fact a tower and wings but is obviously an open end stage
48 ft wide; yet the new Birmingham Repertory is and feels like a

FIG. 8 Olivier Theatre (National, London), wide fan auditorium confronting large stage for scenery: elaborate mechanics for in-show and repertoire changes

proscenium stage although the opening of this latter is 49 ft wide. It is not just the fact that it has a safety curtain that is responsible; it seems to me that what the architect *thought* he was designing at the time comes through. Birmingham with its 919 seats on one tier should be compared with the 530 at Leatherhead. There is little doubt in my mind that it represents too great a number for this format. A stage should be judged perhaps not so much by its nominal width as by how much of the backstage area is exposed to the audience, for this is what will require masking or filling with scenery.

There are three theatres which well illustrate this tendency. The first is the Haymarket, Leicester, which opened in 1973 and the second is the Olivier in the National Theatre complex which is now complete enough to be able to get the feel of the place although it will not open until spring 1976 at least. The third, the Barbican, is as yet a project only but its basic form was shown as a model in December 1966, one year before that of the National appeared. Although the Barbican, as the future London home of the Royal Shakespeare Theatre, was prepared so to speak by a rival team headed by Peter Hall and his designer John Bury, a certain amount of cross-fertilization must have gone on, due to the comprehensive nature of the committee (everyone who was anyone at the top) advising on the National

Auditorium and Stage 33

Theatre brief. Nevertheless what has resulted is an architect's theatre; Denys Lasdun is its creator. And this is what was so advanced as to be beyond alteration when Peter Hall succeeded Lord Olivier as director. However, he and John Bury will not find the stage arrangements all that different from those proposed for their Barbican Theatre. There is the same reference to actor's point of command (the mystic spot, favouring the old school of the actor-manager as Alfred Emmet has pointed out,[1] from which he is supposed to have the eye of every member of the audience) and more or less the same lavish means for handling scenery.

It is out in the auditorium where the differences lie, although seating capacity is roughly the same. That of the Olivier is bowl-shaped—a stadium-like affair of terraces with the largest block of seating sweeping round with an unbroken balcony effect. The Barbican, however, is intended to go in for Peter Hall's "papering the walls with people" effect with a number of very shallow balconies along the back and sides.

Whatever the sightlines, and in the Olivier at any rate they are very good, one thing is certain: the audience are confronting a large empty space, all of which is on view and waiting to be filled with scenery. This space has no character without it. The auditorium architecture ends in a very wide and high irregular proscenium, although there is no fire curtain.

At the Leicester Haymarket there is a three-sided fire curtain which falls on the front edge of the thrust stage, the grid covering the whole. The seating (703) takes an interesting conformation of three stepped blocks downstairs with a balcony broken into five blocks above with the minimum of clearance; the opposite effect to that in the nearby Nottingham Playhouse.

It is necessary to keep the dimensions of such theatres firmly in mind while examining their stages. What looks like a proscenium at Leicester is 48 ft wide and nearly 20 ft from the front of the thrust. At the Olivier the two heavy prongs backed by German-style pros. perches are 26 ft back and form an opening approximately 52 ft wide. A whole theatre world is encompassed by these, yet it is but part of the stage on view. Downstairs the grid tower walls are seen to soar while from upstairs the stage floor spreads far and wide. Something has to mask all this and it cannot be just black drapes. In the famous Bel Geddes project of 1922 it would have been a giant cyclorama dome but either way we are brought back to Donald Mullin's remarks quoted earlier in this chapter.

The actual handling of scenery, whatever the size and amount, presents no difficulty at the National. The Lyttelton Theatre has, behind its adjustable proscenium, a side stage and

[1] *Sightline*, Spring 1975.

FIG. 9 Royal Shakespeare Theatre, Stratford-upon-Avon: scenic invasion of auditorium 1972 and after, also extra side balconies and lighting bridges in ceiling

rear stage with built-in wagons and revolve to run on to the main stage (which is in its turn divided up into lifts, modular flooring and the rest of those things one has come to expect in a German theatre). A mechanical rake can be applied and the whole is topped with power-assisted flying. The revolve of the Olivier is in fact an enormous drum with lifts in it while three wagon stages wait, each behind its own fire curtain, to take over the square confined within the periphery of the revolve. The intention is to facilitate the playing of giant sets in repertoire and the corresponding arrangements for lighting are discussed in Chapter 8.

In the meantime, under Trevor Nunn and his designer Christopher Morley, at Stratford-upon-Avon the last traces of Elizabeth Scott's 1932 auditorium were removed in 1972. As the photograph shows (Fig. 9) the side walls are now occupied by balconies, the ceiling taken over by lighting bridges and giant scenic flats occupy the forestage. The whole philosophy of some of the playing taking place in the auditorium and some in the scenic stage has changed. Everything now has a scenic background. One thing obstinately remains—the proscenium

(29 ft × 20 ft high) of 1932 just upstage of those flats. This is part of the structure and cannot be removed. Rail against it again and again as they undoubtedly do, this opening continues to restrict the size and amount of scenery that can be used beyond. Perchance one day, to keep scenic costs in check, some sort of artificial barrier will have to be erected to discipline the claims of the Olivier's open space!

3 The Development of Stage Lighting

MODERN stage lighting could be said to have begun when, in 1881, Richard D'Oyly Carte opened up his new theatre—the Savoy in London—with Gilbert and Sullivan's *Patience*. The programme announced "This theatre is lighted throughout by electricity," and it is notable that dimmers were used from the beginning. There were six in all. Four were shunt regulators acting directly on the theatre's own generators, and two were series resistances. It would be interesting to trace the intermediate steps which led to the control of 52 dimmers installed when the theatre was rebuilt in 1929, which was replaced in its turn by a remote preset of 120 dimmers in 1960. The first installation in 1881 was by those pioneers of early electric days, Siemens Bros., then based in England, and the last two by Strand Electric.

Stage-lighting switchboards, like the organs in our cathedrals and churches, have interesting histories of enlargement and replacement at irregular intervals. They do not last for ever. The Savoy Theatre installation does not represent the first use of electric light in the theatre; the emphasis was on "lighted throughout" and on the use of the Swan incandescent carbon filament lamp. Fortunately, a fine contemporary technical account is extant.[1] Prior to this arc lamps had been used for special effects in the Paris Opera. Gas lighting had a very long run before electricity and had provided in the limelight a useful pointer to the possibilities to come. Electricity did not have things all its own way and one detects a touch of the defensive in the writer of the account referred to above. Irving at the Lyceum, who was noted for his artistic use of stage lighting, stuck to gas if not for all his life then for a considerable time after electricity had been tamed. There is some doubt on this point, and those interested are referred to the account given by Miss St. Clare Byrne.[2]

The reason why electricity and the incandescent lamp mark the beginning of modern stage lighting is, to my mind, not

[1] *Tabs*, Volume 20, Number 2. Reprint of article in *Engineering*, March, 1882.
[2] Lighting, Stage, in *The Oxford Companion to the Theatre*.

because the change represented any visual improvement on what went on before—I very much doubt that it did—but because the essential ingredients began there and only had to be built on. Modern transport began with the steam locomotive, although the most splendid services by mail coach and canal undoubtedly preceded it. Gas had its dimmers in the shape of taps assembled together at the gas plate, and there survives alone in today's practice, rather strangely, the 2-in. gas barrel as a means to suspend our electric lanterns. Limelight is preserved only in the language of metaphor and a trace of oil lamps lingers perhaps in the "floats" of the theatre's own vocabulary.

The early incandescent lamps were low in power and had perforce, like the gas jets, to be arranged at close centres in the long rows known to us confusingly as "Battens." The Americans more logically chose the name "Borderlights." Unfortunately, however, this fine start was spoilt as soon as a series of individual compartments, each fitted with a reflector, lamp and gelatine colour, began to be used, when they called these "X-rays"—a terminological inexactitude if ever there was one! The latest expression over there is "Striplights," which is better, but in England means a small wattage lamp with a line filament used at one time, at any rate, in jewellers' showcases.

In England, the compartment batten was made popular by Adrian Samoiloff who used many for his colour lighting stunts, which hit the headlines in the early 1920s. Prior to the compartment batten, colour was obtained by dipping the individual lamps in lacquer but, as soon as the early vacuum lamps were replaced by the more efficient gas-filled or half-watt lamps (see Chapter 5), the lacquer spoiled rapidly because of the higher temperature of the bulb surface. Coloured glass bulbs absorbed too much light and a china glaze sprayed externally or internally was developed, and both these methods had to be employed during the actual lamp manufacture. Theatre people who had been used to a range of lacquers in three dozen or so colours could not be expected to make do with only half a dozen colours. The prevalent, but difficult to explain, need for many colours is examined in Chapter 6. Nevertheless, the three things—a more efficient lamp, a reflector to make good use of its light, and better colours—represented a big step forward. Light was much brighter but it still had the same overall effect coming as it did from rows behind the borders overhead and from footlights along the front edge of the stage.

Saying that the light was much brighter is a claim that can be appreciated only when one sees the comparison for oneself. As part of Strand Electric's Golden Jubilee celebration in 1964, I staged a demonstration beginning with a multiple gas-jet wing flood and limelight, then to vacuum lamp open battens, and thence to compartment reflector battens. Each time the increase of light was remarkable, and yet the intensity of this new lighting of the 1920s was as nothing when compared with what modern equipment provides, which was used in the Royal Shakespeare Company's *King Lear* of 1963, full up and open white, as moonlight! The truth is that an abundance of artificial light is a comparatively new phenomenon. In the gas-lit Victorian and Edwardian ages, the theatre was a place of bright lights though we, who scarcely know what darkness is, would not find it so. All this extra light poses a problem in restoring old theatres: for example, the Georgian Theatre Royal at Bury St. Edmunds. The elaborately reproduced period painted decoration may look garish rather than stimulating lit to our modern lighting levels. At Drottningholm, in Sweden, the lighting in the eighteenth-century palace theatre is today carefully scaled down and distributed in the manner of the period—no strident spotlights there for the performances of today.

So far the stage lighting considered in this chapter has been floodlighting supplemented by some spotlights of the hand-fed type or by limelights. A favourite position for these was perch platforms on the stage side of the proscenium wall and also at the ends of the upper circle or gallery. It is here that the tray, so long insisted on by authority to go under all spotlights over the audience, began. It was essential to catch the bits of discarded carbon.

It should not be assumed that, because arcs needed an operator, they were always moved as follow spots. An obvious use kept steady was as moonlight or sunlight. Another use was for optical effects projection and this remained for a considerable time. The early arc spots had bodies made of teak lined with asbestos and a shutter was fitted to the arc lamp itself, between the source and the lens. This served for black-outs, but also with a great deal of skill it was possible to get a rudimentary dimming effect. In the heyday of the arc, all arrangements in London were in the hands of Thomas Digby,

FIG. 10 Digby's Patent Stage Arc

who would sometimes have as many as forty of his men in a theatre operating the hand-fed arcs (Fig. 10).

It would be a great mistake to read this short history as if each technical development represented a wave of change sweeping over the theatre and wiping out all that went before it. It was more a matter of edging in here and there, bit by bit. Thus, a theatre would have ancient and modern lighting units mixed up together. This is still true today. Certainly, when it came to switchboards, the ancient lingered long. Sometimes by actual survival, but more often by revival. Many a switchboard of the 1930s was simply not new when new, because of the principles its design was based on. As to survival, the original liquid dimmer board in the Aldwych of 1905 was still there when this theatre was taken over by the Royal Shakespeare as their London home in 1960. Across the Atlantic there is plenty of museum material still in the portable "piano boards" of Broadway. Much the same could be said of the electrical arrangements for lighting in film studios.

Basil Dean has written of his experience with lighting and scenery over the long period he has been active in the theatre[1] and the history of Strand Electric, *Fifty Years in Stage Lighting*,[2] represents my own investigations in 1963 into this period of development. The oldest firm in stage lighting seems to be Kliegl Bros. of New York. Founded in 1896, their only possible rival would be Siemens of Germany, but this latter firm is not a specialist one dealing with all items within this field. The big name there in lighting equipment, as distinct from dimmers and control, was Schwabe, of whom the firm of Reiche and Vogel is the direct descendant. The French firm of Clemançon in Paris, founded in 1828, has a long record in stage lighting as one of its activities. As far as London was concerned, something of a contest occurred during the 1920s between the German Schwabe lighting system and the Strand Samoiloff system.

In Britain, victory went to the latter but on the continent the former won hands down. It would be over-simple to say that the battle was between localized spotlighting on the one hand and all-over flooding on the other, for by this time a batten installation would also include some simple spotlights with tungsten lamps of 400 watts. These had originally been imported from the United States in 1917 for Gilbert Miller. A few years later they settled down as the simple plano-convex spotlights often known as focus lamps (condenser spotlights in U.S.) in 500-watt and 1000-watt sizes. Britain was handicapped by the lamp-makers who insisted on using the large glass bulb of the 1000-watt size for the smaller wattage as well. Real baby spots actually had to wait until 1952 in consequence.

In 1923, Basil Dean opened at the St. Martin's Theatre with

[1] *Tabs*, Volume 20, Number 3.   [2] *Tabs*, Volume 22, Number 1.

a Schwabe installation, and as typical German practice this featured a cyclorama. In this case, it took the form of a Hasait cloth hanging on a track at grid level running round the entire stage. These true cycloramas presented a much greater problem in lighting when compared to the normal border and backcloth set, however opened up. One of the features of Schwabe lighting was projection on to the cyclorama, particularly of realistic moving clouds for which very elaborate tiered machines with sets of individual cloud slides were used. Whether these were used or merely plain coloured light, especially deep blue, the elimination of stray light from elsewhere was vital. Lighting of the acting area took on quite a different quality and depended on accurate positioning and focusing of the individual spotlights. This feeling for precise placing of the few rather than the rough bash of the many, still persists in Germany to this day. To provide the necessary accessibility, the lighting units were and are located in German practice principally on a bridge and tower structure just upstage of the proscenium. (See Fig. 13.)

The majority of stages in this country were unable to do this system justice. There was insufficient grid height to allow flying clear of the cyclorama and inadequate storage to allow alternative means of scene changing. It is not, therefore, surprising that the compartment batten and spot bar system was more popular, especially as it represented a more natural progression from the earlier stage-lighting practices. Apart from Mr. Dean's activities and a valiant attempt by H. Lester Groom of the GEC to equip the 21-ft deep stage of the Plaza Cinema, Regent Street, with a full Schwabe-Hasait system in 1926, the best-known cyclorama installation of the 1920s was that of the Cambridge Festival Theatre. Harold Ridge devised for Terence Gray there a hybrid mixture of German and English practice. In this experimental theatre the lighting came to mean really something—some would say "too much"—to those of us interested in stage lighting. Yet the installation of 35 dimmers was comparatively small and its period of activity a few years only.[1]

In the late twenties and early thirties, stage lighting came to mean in Britain and the United States a number of compartment battens, the inevitable footlight, a twelve-way spot bar and a few similar spots out front in the auditorium; but it would be exceptional to have more than half a dozen of these latter and not unusual to have none at all there. Special equipment would be hired for particular productions, especially by men like David Belasco and Basil Dean, who took their lighting really seriously. Incidentally, both of these producers had an affection for a form of indirect lighting. Lighting was important

[1] *Tabs*, Volume 20, Number 1.

FIG. 11 Bank of six indirect spotlights with bowed reflector discs as used by Louis Hartman for David Belasco

in all C. B. Cochran's productions, and Komisarjevsky is another name to conjure with in this connection.

Technically, in stage lighting as in stage machinery, Germany was way ahead with vast cyclorama stages pretty nearly as well equipped as those one sees there today. Sir Oswald Stoll made another attempt to show Britain what could be done when he equipped both the Alhambra and Coliseum music-halls with cycloramas and mainly German lighting in 1930. The latter installation came into its own with the success of *White Horse Inn* in 1931.[1] This production, like Cochran's revival of *The Miracle* at the Lyceum in 1932, made much use of an extensive apron and scenery built over the stage boxes. Cochran always used Strand Electric equipment and the same firm had to replace the German lighting at the Alhambra when Hassard Short's production of *Waltzes from Vienna* was staged in August, 1931. This show went in for light in a big way and represents the first use here of what could be termed batteries of spots, both on towers in the wings and out on the circle front. This was floodlighting, but using masses of spotlights to aid the more normal battens and footlights. Except for the fact that the general level of brightness was lower (but high for those times), it would not differ greatly from what was to be inseparable from the great post-war American musical invasion of London, of which *Oklahoma* formed the spearhead, in 1947.

German stage-lighting development was in the 1930s to stand still while America and Britain got under way. In the

[1] *Tabs*, Volume 21, Number 3.

United States, the ellipsoidal, better described as a Profile, spot dates from this time, being introduced on a large scale in a whole series of sizes using special prefocus lamps burning cap-up made by General Electric. We could not compete over here as our lamp manufacturers were not to make a suitable lamp until thirty years later, and the American voltage of 110 prevented importation.

In Britain, however, there had already been in use since 1929 a spotlight system known as the Stelmar (Fig. 12), which represented a more scientific approach to the problem of increased light than the German large-diameter lenses and big wattage lamps, "Linsenscheinwerfer," still prevalent today. These latter were very versatile, though inefficient, units because, with an extra lens added as an attachment, profile shapes, slides or optical effects could be projected. Size was never a problem there because of the large scale of the German stages. The drawback of the Stelmar was its expense and its length: £50 was a lot of money in 1936 for a 1000-watt spotlight. It did not take much invention on my part to provide a solution, a profile spot, which I called the Mirror Spot.

There followed a period in which stage-lighting equipment in Britain struck out on its own and became very individual. For this, two lanterns, called the Pageant and the Acting Area, were responsible. The Mirror Spot could never be used extensively while it required so much setting up each time a lamp was replaced. Any degree of popularity for a precision optical system was out of the question until lamps with prefocus caps became available from the makers, and this did not happen properly here until the 1950s. Bright beams of light had to be sought elsewhere and reflector systems provided the answer.

FIG. 12 Stelmar spot optical system

An essential part of a German cyclorama system was some vertical lighting coming from hooded units called "Spielflächen-leuter" hanging within the area bounded by the cyclorama. These units were few in number, but on the assumption that they could be many, used in batteries, I was able to aim for a much narrower beam (24 degrees) and this, plus the use of silvered glass reflectors instead of stainless steel, gave an increase of nearly ten times the intensity for the same 1000 watts. There was also a need for a still narrower beam for certain purposes particularly as side lighting to imitate the rays of the sun, and the result was a near parallel beam reflector unit named the Pageant lantern, after its first use for a pageant in the moat of the Tower of London (1935). Both this and the Acting Area flood had to use spill rings to reduce stray light and, in consequence, they were virtually fixed-beam lanterns. The only way to get more spread was to use more of them which, of course, meant more light.

If compartment battens had been a leap forward in intensity when compared to the previous open types, this was nothing to what happened now. It was Robert Nesbitt who first set the fashion for rows of Acting Areas overhead complemented by vertical booms with Pageants in the wings. Strictly speaking, this preponderance of lighting from overhead should have been bad, but as the lanterns were at close centres the beams overlapped and one tended to catch some correction from the side spread of the neighbouring units. Nor was it only light entertainment which found these units useful: the late George Devine, writing in 1953,[1] said "The more productions I light, the more I become endeared to the "Pageant family" of apparatus. . . . The Pageant is a bold and definite light. It doesn't pretend it isn't there, and why should it? It gives the kind of clarity which the theatre needs as it emerges from the muddy gloom of naturalism." Mr. Devine makes the point that he is not much concerned with lighting drawing rooms. Peter Brook was another producer who made much of the "Pageant family" as his production of *Dark of the Moon* in 1949 testified to good effect. What appealed to these men was the strong beam of light itself rather than the malformed patch at the end of it, and it is interesting to find the Germans getting much the same effect with low-voltage (*Nedervolt*) spots after the war. There had been sporadic attempts to take advantage of the greater efficiency and smaller low-voltage filaments here and there in the thirties, but post-war this became a necessity in Germany. Faced with re-creating theatres in any space which could be found among the ruins, smaller and more economical units had to be found. This was the heyday of the *Nedervolt*. However, now that big stages are back there, so are the big lanterns, and

[1] *Tabs*, Volume 11, Number 1.

relegation to an accessory role has been its fate. At the time of writing, the largest concentration of these lanterns seems to be in the theatres of Prague where almost all lighting is built up of these narrow beam sources. They are even used for "following," which in any case is far more extensively practised in Eastern European countries. "Following" in this sense is not to be likened to the pencil-beam techniques of musical, vaudeville and pantomime, and is discussed in Chapter 10.

As far as lanterns are concerned, we have now reached the modern times of Fresnel and Profile spots, and the relevant chapters of this book can take over, but before this, the historical development of the other half of a stage-lighting installation, the control, which we left in 1881 at the Savoy, must be filled in.

As stated earlier, the Savoy had six dimmers and it comes as a revelation to learn from Percy Fitzgerald, a contemporary writer of the time for whom stage lighting seems to have exercised a great fascination, that "in the French Opera House . . . the controlling *jeu d'orgue*, as it is called, comprises no less than 88 stops or cocks . . . controlling 960 gas jets."[1]

[1] *World Behind the Scenes*, 1881.

Eighty-eight dimmers before 1881! Gas had one great advantage over electricity in that dimming was easy. Compared to the gas tap, electrical dimmers were ponderous and it is only in the last two or three years that the modern thyristor dimmer even remotely approaches it for size. A gas plate could have master cocks feeding groups of cocks and the many batswing jets could, if extinguished, be relit by an electric spark. The bottom end of dimmer travel must have been rather chancy as was the whole installation in respect of fire risk.

The likeness to an organ implicit in the French term, *jeu d'orgue*, still current, is of great interest. Whether this arose from the appearance of the rows of gas piping or from the sense of centralized control of large and dispersed resources matters not. The aims of an organ console and a stage lighting control are alike and this resemblance is peculiar to them and does not extend to anything else. The man in charge of a railway signal box or the central control room of a power or broadcasting network is not concerned with using for artistic expression the many controls over which he presides. Only the organist and the lighting operator have this in common; the actual electricity and mechanics are quite secondary to the main purpose in both cases. We should remind ourselves that in no sense should it be regarded as part of these men's jobs as such to have any knowledge whatever of the sophisticated electrical development that their instruments represent. And both the modern electronic organ and the modern thyristor lighting control are certainly built around circuitry and technology, advanced to a high degree. It is response to the fingers of an artist that we seek but the path has been beset until recently with cumbersome electrical and mechanical contraptions which have not only frightened off artists to other spheres of expression, but have positively insisted upon mechanics and electricians to work them. Design for the future must in no way be based on these and the methods they bred.

The earliest electrical dimmer to become popular was the liquid pot in which the current was made to travel through a partially conducting solution. As the submerged electrodes were separated, so more and more liquid resistance was inserted in the circuit and the lamps dimmed accordingly. This dimmer was inexpensive, but being liquid was large and messy and had to be kept out of the way, usually in the basement. Operation was by tracker wire which travelled over pulleys to a row of control levers, in much the same way that railway signals were then worked. The wire was then taken over a large grooved wheel to get the necessary travel, and a handle was attached. It was natural to pivot these levers on a common shaft, and the idea must have occurred very early that a catch to each could be provided to lock the lot together mechanically for operation from a master wheel or lever at the end of the shaft. Several of these shafts became necessary as installations grew, and the notion of allocating shafts to families of lights, the reds, the blues, and the ambers, was adopted. It was not lighting logic but mechanical logic that originated the idea of dividing up the stage into colour or any other semi-permanent groups. Cross-control between the shafts so that they could all be worked together from a grand master followed. More importantly, in order to satisfy the needs of the German style lighting, it became necessary to devise a means to enable levers to be coupled to the same shaft, but to travel in the same or reverse direction to immediate neighbours at the will of the operator. A neat arrangement of planetary gears enabled this to be done within the circumference of the grooved wheel carrying the tracker wire. At the same time, the need for some slip, to stop the braking effect when the levers got home early, led also to a device which could be drawn over from the top or bottom to limit the amount of individual lever travel. With this, presetting, albeit rather crude, was born.

For some reason, the French, who also achieved all these facilities on their classic control, set themselves a much harder mechanical task by using individual pivots for their controls instead of a common shaft. The wheels were thus edge on

FIG. 14 120-channel remote tracker wire regulator by Clemançon

FIG. 15   52-channel French *Jeu
d'Orgue Classique* by Clemançon

instead of parallel to one another. The French, also uniquely,
went in for master switches to short-circuit the dimmers and
bring the lights up to full or down to levels immediately. This
involved switching numbers of separate circuits simultaneously
and great tram-type controllers were used for the purpose, but
this development left the rest of the world unmoved.

Dimmers first as wire-wound resistance and then as auto-
transformers replaced the liquid pots and the main Continental
development separated completely from the methods pursued
in the United States and Britain. On the Continent they
continued to mount their dimmers in the basement and operate
them by tracker wire. In consequence, when the Bordoni
multi-channel auto-transformer appeared on the scene with
the general adoption of alternating current in the late twenties,
the combination of this with their fine mechanical regulator
put the Germans ahead of the world for many years. By

comparison, what went on in Britain and the United States was pitiable.

Dimmer design, particularly in the latter country, led to the development of individual dimmers, for example the Ward Leonard embedded plate, sufficiently small to allow them to be mounted at the back of the control panel and to be operated by handles on shafting in front. This arrangement immediately became popular as being simpler to construct and install. Everything was together—dimmers, switches, fuses, and all—and could be placed at the side of the stage at either perch or floor level. This particularly suited the type of theatre commonly being built at the time, that is, the large Super Cinema with a stage. The advanced German-type remote control needed the large stage and theatre subsidy approach, whereas in the tight competitive tendering required by most commercial managements the direct-operated manual board was all they were prepared to afford. As far as Broadway was concerned, with an odd exception here and there, they never even got as far as that, productions having to rely entirely on importation of portable boards. The interlocking in the case of house boards in America consisted of a slot on each shaft which, as the master lever was pulled down, collected the required individual levers and reduced the lighting to a nondescript murk overall before finally dimming it right out. Pull is the operative word, for these controls were very stiff and telescopic extensions to the masters were required to get the necessary leverage. It is difficult to keep the tenses right for some of the controls are still listed in current catalogues there and supplied, at any rate for small installations.

In Britain, as in America, the dimmer boards were without refinement, everyone considering they had shot their bolt once they had a Grand Master wheel and slipping clutch "self-release" handles. Dimmer scales to show check positions were an extra. Unlike America, many large installations of sixty or eighty or more channels went into theatres up and down the country and in London; the big inducement in getting these controls into theatres being the supply companies' financial contribution towards the expenses of the change-over from d.c. to a.c. which they wanted to make between the wars. between the wars.

There is no need to go into any detail now of these controls and their variants though the interested are referred to my earlier book.[1] Good and complicated lighting was done in those days, but only by using several operators both on the house board and the supplementary portables. Personally, I have never held Grand Master controls in anything but contempt as a contribution to lighting and, in consequence, as soon as I became active in this field, set about providing an alternative. All engineering was taboo and the instrumental approach of the organ console, particularly in its cinema stop-key form, was very attractive. Fortunately, a means of moving the dimmer was to hand, in the shape of the electro-magnetic clutch, invented by Moss Mansell three years earlier in 1929, but largely neglected. For control the Compton all-electric action was ideal, for unlike most organ builders, including Wurlitzer, they did not rely on electro-pneumatics in the console. The Light Console was born, and eventually in 1935 was demonstrated. Although this is not the place, this (at that time, revolutionary) instrument is well worth study for, as one digs deep, it becomes remarkably like a Grand Master control with colour shafts and all. The inventor, I confess, was too greatly influenced by the practice dictated by the mechanical control of the time. Freshness of approach was only partial. It is, in fact, seldom in the history of stage lighting that re-appraisal in terms of need, rather than of current practice, has taken place and when it has it has always been incomplete.

The Light Console, although invented, was not yet made when the one job in London on which it could have been successfully launched turned up. This was the Royal Opera House, Covent Garden, and it was recognized that remote control could alone provide the answer to the control of 120 channels. If for no other reason, there was not enough room to accommodate two "Grand Masters" in the German-type perch position required. The installation had to be made in a hurry

[1] *Stage Lighting*, Pitman, 1950.

using pairs of the Mansell clutch (to obtain reversal) fed from two-way and off switches with a dial to each channel. The drive was from mechanical shafting from perch to dimmer room under stage. It is quite extraordinary that a motor drive was not attempted, but the distrust then for anything which was not moved by a good solid mechanical link is beyond belief, until, that is, we remind ourselves of the hints and innuendos cast more recently in some circles in respect of electronics and printed circuits while these were being developed. The Covent Garden installation of 1934 was to survive for exactly thirty years and opportunities to use the Light Console system had, in the main, to wait until well after the war. By this time, the system which had begun in advance of its time was in need of fundamental reappraisal. This it did not get until the television studio demand was to stress that if combined with servo presetting the Light Console and its electro-mechanical dimmer banks not only could live on but had positive advantages over all other systems. Only in 1964 was this to become untrue.

To make this point, development of other systems must now be examined. The landmark in American lighting control was undoubtedly the Radio City Music Hall installation of 1933 (Fig. 17). This was not the first of its kind there, but size and comprehensiveness, together with a record of continuous service in this showplace, make it unique. When the time comes for it to be removed, I hope the makers, the General Electric, will take steps to preserve at least part of it. This form marks the first practical application of all-electric non-mechanical dimmers on a large scale. There are 314 saturable reactor dimmers controlled by thyratron valves with feedback. This not only gave good variable-load performance but also made true presetting possible. The Americans earlier had used switch pre-

FIG. 17 Radio City Music Hall, New York: 314 channel 5 preset and rehearsal thyratron reactor control (1933)

setting on some of their direct-operated boards, and although these were referred to as eight-scene preset they gave only snap changes. Presetting in the sense of moving a mechanical dimmer a certain distance through a servo circuit received a certain amount of attention in the States, and some patents date from the early thirties but never got far in competition with the thyratron-controlled reactor. It did not occur to anyone there to exploit the inertia advantages of the mechanical servo, as we, in Strand Electric, were to do much later in Britain.

As it was, we find the Americans embarked on multi-scene presetting at Radio City with five preset levers side by side and a larger rehearsal lever under each of the 314 channels. This, plus grouping facilities, results in a rather large piece of equipment which nevertheless is housed the audience side of the orchestra in a special pit of its own—an early recognition of the operator's right and need to see the lighting effects he is producing. These controls were essentially switchboards to be operated rather than consoles to be played, and examples by General Electric, Westinghouse, and Ward Leonard spread into the large multi-purpose auditoriums which have been for so long an American speciality. Control development was thus an offshoot of the giant electrical engineering companies, which was also true of Siemens and AEG in Germany.

In Britain, the big electrical firms never made any real headway in the theatre. Witness the GEC and their attempt to sell Schwabe equipment, and years later the installation by the BTH of a GE thyratron reactor two-preset fifty-two-channel control[1] in the Odeon, Leicester Square, in 1938. This was a cinema anyway and the only other important installation was in Earls Court Exhibition Hall about the same time. That these things were firmly in the hands of specialist firms here was both a strength and weakness. Technically, they were limited in what they could do, but in knowing what was needed to be done in the strange world of theatre they were much richer than any general engineering company could possibly be.

A change occurred in the United States when the specialist firm, Century, in New York, acquired the manufacturing rights of the control developed for Yale University Theatre by George Izenour and demonstrated there as 44 channels in 1947. It used pairs of thyratrons directly as dimmers controlled from a console with a set of large rehearsal levers and their masters, plus a wing unit with miniaturized controls for ten presets. The system is outlined elsewhere but it can be seen that the Americans were still firmly embarked on a course of multi-presetting. The main snags of this approach were hidden by the small number of control channels required due to their use of large

[1] This was removed in the 1950s and a second-hand Strand Grand Master substituted as maintenance had by then become a problem.

wattage dimmers and patching thereto of many circuits.

In Europe it has been the practice to relegate patching to a minor role and, in consequence, development to allow for the control of a large number of channels was always going to be necessary. The Palladium in 1949 with 152 channels, Drury Lane in 1950 with 216, and the Shakespeare Memorial Theatre in 1951 with 144 make the point, and these are only three examples. The first two were Light Consoles and the last a three-valve electronic preset. The latter was devised by J. T. Wood for Strand Electric and used to be referred to as "the Electronic." The three valves, one per phase, were necessary to control 2 kW with the thyratrons. It was also supposed to provide the bonus that each circuit was balanced over the phases (see page 132). Unfortunately it was later discovered that the total load was flowing back through the lightly cabled neutral. The addition of a static balancer, or preferably a star-delta transformer to redistribute this load, added greatly to the cost. This, together with the wasteful effect of the thyratron heaters described on page 126 and the temperamental behaviour of the valves, led to our dropping the system. Some installations went on to survive a long time; that in the then Shakespeare Memorial, now Royal Shakespeare Theatre, Stratford-upon-Avon was only replaced at the end of 1971. The Wood electronic, like the Comet jet aircraft of about the same period, was a brilliant pioneer effort which suffered from being rather ahead of the technology of its time. With its twin desk it won an instant acceptance with operators which was denied my own Light Console, and a wave of enthusiasm for electronic remote control and presetting spread from Britain to Europe.

This had two results. Both AEG and Siemens in Germany decided to forsake the mechanically operated Bordoni for two-valve thyratron dimmers and magnetic amplifier dimmers respectively. They could not bring themselves to do without moving mechanical levers at the desk, however, and Siemens reproduced the Bordoni levers in miniature at roughly one-inch centres, complete with the usual mastering and preset trips. The AEG used a mechanical cam arrangement to move their levers to a proper series of preset positions instead, but this (probably on account of the thyratron valves) had less appeal. Because Siemens had used electro-magnetic means for mastering their levers, they were able to go on to add a servo system to drive from sets of preset levers (Fig. 187) then punched card and finally ferrite store. It was only in 1974 that they at last announced a new lever of the wheel type (see page 165) "which retains the advantages of the living lever but without movement by a motor."

The use of an electro-mechanically operated desk system to

FIG. 18 Organ console type controls: (a) 216-channel Light Console, Theatre Royal, Drury Lane (1950); (b) 120-channel system CD, Strand Theatre (1962)

control all-electric dimmers was rather incongruous. On the other hand for us in London with Mansell clutch-operated dimmers ready to hand, a polarized-relay servo-circuit was our salvation. I was able to devise for Strand Electric first a twin desk system very similar to that for the "Electronic" it had to replace and then to go on to combine it with the Light Console's stop-key selection (known as System CD; see Fig. 18). The instant setting piston "Group Memory" action which formed part of the Compton console action enabled the advantages of the "inertia" in mechanical systems to be fully exploited not only for theatre but for television.

A short history of stage lighting would not be complete without some mention of the remarkable expansion in development due to the adoption by television studios of theatre-type control with dimmers instead of the archaic electrical methods of the film studios. And this in spite of the fact that so many television production centres were converted film studios, purpose-built studios only coming later.

Catering for television studio lighting became an industry for Britain in 1955, the year commercial television began. Both the BBC and the commercial programme companies embarked on a period of furious activity during which the main lines of what was expected of a television lighting control got laid down. These included dimmers to all control channels whenever possible and memory action to form a minimum amount of fourteen groups and two presets. A considerable amount of cross-fertilization between theatre practice and television went on with the result that both were the gainers and the difference is now only superficial. The most interesting result was the rise of the lighting designer especially where, as in the BBC and ABC television, he has been allowed to work his own control. The development of cameras which can be electronically set up and locked has led to the adoption of the technique known as "hands off" in which monitoring the picture quality is very largely a matter of lighting adjustment. The need to site the lighting control alongside the camera "hands off" controls, in such a way as to give a good view of a complete set of monitors, has necessitated its integration into a suite along with the other items. Where the control of lighting has been allowed to the electricians the development of a "hands off" technique has been impeded. One simply cannot instruct someone else to tweak this or that lever rapidly or precisely enough.

If all the larger theatre or television installations in Britain could be based on electro-mechanical principles, something more compact and less costly had to be used for the smaller ones which needed remote control. We had therefore to resort to saturable-reactor dimmers. Because of the rather heavy control current, these in their simple form were difficult to use as a preset system. The full magnetic amplifier form which had been introduced as a dimmer largely by Metropolitan of New York would have been too expensive for our purposes. The arrival of transistors made a small amplifier possible and System LC, as it was called, had quite a vogue. The introduction of the SCR dimmer (later to be called the Thyristor) in the early 1960's stopped all other development and everyone had to turn to this. Here was *the dimmer* at last; it could not be ignored. To make use of it yet retain some of the advantages of the mechanical inertia,

I devised system C/AE. This retained the Compton Group Memory action but applied it directly to the relay action and indicated what had happened by lighting the internal lamps of luminous dimmer levers instead of moving stopkeys. This had in fact already been done for the larger television controls (System C) for the BBC and ATV but in conjunction with the electro-mechanical dimmers.

In system C/AE the dimmers could be selected individually or by groups and raised on the red (active) master. When this reached full on, they were automatically parked on the white (passive) master—a fact which was announced by the appropriate change of colour in their scales. A 240 channel 4-preset system C/AE with thyristors controlling 1·25 megawatts went into the Royal Opera House in 1964 and a 2-preset C/AE, also of 240 channels, into the London Palladium in 1966. As with other Strand Electric control systems, a number were also made for television studios. However, the real answer was to lie in Dimmer Memory controls and in this field, as we shall see in Chapter 8, the large companies were to have the advantage.

The pace of development since the introduction of the thyristor dimmer has been so fast that everything sophisticated in control earlier than 1972 is history. On the other side, the lighting equipment itself, progress is by comparison so slight that what belongs to history and what is of today are still hardly distinguishable from each other.

4 Light

Light is that part of electro-magnetic wave radiation visible to the human eye, but is nowadays taken to include the radiation immediately beyond this and only visible to a camera—the infra-red and ultra-violet. The latter is used in the theatre under the name of "black light" using fluorescent paints to make it visible. As is well known, what is seen as white light is the result of simultaneous presentation to the eye of many wave-lengths (colours), and this is considered separately in Chapter 6 as it makes no difference to the general principles of illumination with which we now begin.

If an ordinary wax candle is lit, light will be radiated equally in every direction, except where the candle itself forms an obstruction.[1] When this source is placed in the centre of a sphere of one foot internal radius the inside surface will be evenly illuminated. Any square foot of this is receiving the light of one lumen per square foot (abbreviated to lm/ft^2), otherwise known as one foot-candle. A rough idea of this amount of light is given by holding a matt white card one foot square one foot away from the candle. The corresponding metric unit is one metre square at one metre distance and is known as the lux. Conversion of foot-candles to lux involves multiplication by a factor of 10·76.

These units refer to the incident light falling on the surface and are related to the source, not to the surface illuminated. The brightness of the surface as perceived, or rather interpreted, by an observer will depend on contrast with the surroundings and so on but a photometer can be used to measure its "luminance" regardless of such distractions. The metric unit commonly used is the apostilb (asb): assuming a medium-grey matt surface with a reflection factor of 0·5 lit by 10 lux then the result is 5 asb.—decidedly dull!

---

[1] The standard unit of light is not dependent on a source as crude as this. Originally a very special candle had to burn under very special conditions. This is no longer used and the new source produces a unit called a candela, but in practice the difference can be ignored.

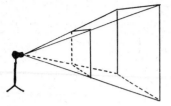

FIG. 19 Inverse square law: intensity decreases to a quarter when distance is doubled

Measurement of light is carried out by instruments called photometers and specialist engineering disciplines (illuminating engineering) have been built up which can provide accurate information both of light sources and lanterns[1] which control the light therefrom. So long as this work is carried out in a laboratory under carefully controlled conditions to give comparative figures of light output and distribution a very useful purpose is served, and recognition of a few of the basic illumination units is helpful to theatre people.

Unfortunately, some illuminating engineers live in a constant fret because light when applied to a job seems so unruly. Inspiration and common sense will win hands down every time. This statement might be questioned in respect of a factory, a street or an aircraft runway, but when lighting places where people wish to live (and this should include a theatre) calculation is not only difficult but also likely to produce the wrong result. One should remember, for example, that for many applications fittings which emit hardly any light may be appropriate. Many, many theatrical lanterns owe their impact to having the optical designer's and the lamp manufacturer's efficient work ruined by feeding them through a dimmer at a low check.

Having indicated where my heart really lies, I hope the reader will take a small dose of simple photometry and optics with rather less than the usual no-enthusiasm.

Photometers to measure reflected light or luminance accurately are more complicated and expensive than those used for incident light, but they are not needed here. The latter resemble the common photographic exposure meter and consist of a cell which responds to the intensity of light falling on it, causing a needle to give a reading on a dial calibrated in foot-candles. These can be called lumens per square foot if desired, the two expressions being interchangeable. With metrication, these units will increasingly be replaced by the lux.

So far the light has fallen on the surface or photometer at one foot distance and the moment the distance is doubled the light falling on the original one-foot-square card drops to a quarter. This—the "inverse square law" as it is called—is a reminder that in light one is dealing with three dimensions: a solid angle of spread or, later on in this chapter, a solid angle of collection

The inverse square law applies only to a single source (Fig. 19). As soon as there are multiple sources, such as two spotlights mounted a distance apart, then as the surface is moved farther away it may begin to receive light from the second as compensation (Fig. 20). This effect would be very marked with a compartment batten fitted with a large number of

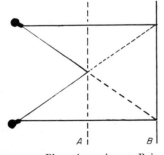

FIG. 20 Plan: intensity at B is only one half instead of one quarter, because of compensation from second source

---

[1] "Lanterns"—I prefer this traditional word for the housing of a light source. See this entry in Chapter 13.

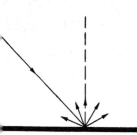

FIG. 21   Diffuse reflection

narrow-beam reflectors. Reference to spotlights and reflectors leads to consideration of the methods whereby the light emitted from a source, whether it is merely a single candle or an electric lamp whose filament gives out the light of "21,000 candles," may be redistributed; this figure being the output of one type of 1000-watt lamp (class *T*) in common theatre use.

Beam Control

As the light is emitted from the lamp in all directions, control involves stopping it from going where it is not required. A primitive control results if the lamp is put in a box with one side open and painted black inside. This is control by absorption, the unwanted light being wasted in heating up the box. Alternatively, by painting the interior white, some of this waste is reflected out of the open side to augment the direct light. A crude reflector like this also gives a divergent light, but it is possible to design one which converges the light to form a beam to some extent. In some cases considered later, the beam from the reflector at the back of the lamp may completely outclass the direct light from the front to such an extent that the latter is ignored.

No optical control system can produce more light than is emitted by the lamp itself. It can only collect and redirect some of the output. The brightest appearing "super" spotlights are inevitably narrow-beam units in which as much as possible of the diverging light has been collected and condensed to light a small area. Ask the optical system to give twice the area and the light must drop, as surely it would have if the lantern had been moved farther away. In point of fact, optical systems can, as will be shown, incorporate some small degree of compensation and, in consequence, to adjust a beam to cover the greater area may be marginally better than moving the lantern farther away. As far as the theatre is concerned, it will certainly be more convenient, and it is almost axiomatic that any theatre lighting units must incorporate variable beam spread.

Reflection

Reflection is a principle which not only can be used to control beam distribution, but also determines the perception of an object. The one-foot-square card earlier mentioned had a matt white surface and would be known as a "diffuse" reflector. Incident light being diffused, the card will appear equally bright at all angles (Fig. 21). A "specular" or "regular" reflector is the surface in use everywhere as a mirror. Light striking this at an angle is reflected at an equal and opposite angle (Fig. 22). Since all light is reflected in the same path

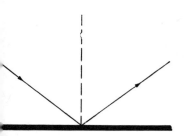

FIG. 22   Specular reflection

Light   59

what will be perceived at that angle may be glare and at all other positions nothing at all, the mirror appearing dark. Water in scenic views plays all the variations according to the angle and nature of the light and the stillness or break-up of the surface at the time.

A flat specular mirror in conjunction with a lamp merely forms a second image apparently the same distance behind it To be effective as a light magnifier, the mirror has to be curved as far as possible round the lamp to collect a large solid angle and at the same time to bring the image forward. This solid angle is important, as an increase of twice the diameter of the collector could mean as much as four times the light. The curve of the reflector determines what happens to the collected light. A spherical reflector is, as its name implies, part of a sphere struck from a centre. If the lamp filament is placed at that centre, light emitted in the direction of the reflector is focused back on itself and a second image is formed there (Fig. 23). A reflector struck on a six-inch radius would be known as one of three-inch focus whatever the diameter of its outside edges. The spherical reflector is useful to reinforce light in the lens-type spotlights described later. The moment the lamp is moved forwards or backwards out of the reflector's centre then the beam crossover point moves in the opposite

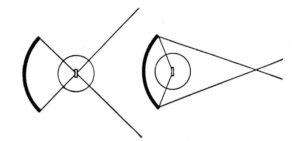

FIG. 23 Spherical reflector: on the left its distance from the source equals its radius

direction and, if intercepted at that point, a crude enlarged inverted image of the filament can be seen. It may be desired to place this image a considerable distance away, to maintain a near parallel beam, and to do this the reflector could be placed with the lamp at its focus or its curve designed to take this into

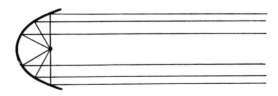

FIG. 24 Parabolic reflector

account. Other forms of geometrical curves used are parabolic and elliptical. The first needs plotting as in Fig. 24, whereas the second can be drawn by the familiar method of two pins, a

FIG. 25   Elliptical reflector

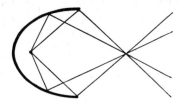

piece of cotton and a pencil. If the lamp filament is assumed as being pin number one, then all the light is brought to a focus at pin number two (Fig. 25). Parabolic reflectors are more often used to project beams over long distances and the elliptical in a truncated form may be used for profile spots, which incidentally are generically referred to in the United States as ellipsoidals, this being the solid as distinct from the plane geometric figure.

Reflector systems used alone in lanterns are particularly suited to beams designed for one spread but with little adjustment either side. Thus, there can be wide-angle floodlight reflector units, medium-angle ones, or even narrow-angle spotlights. What one cannot have is one unit which will cover the whole range. Not only is it difficult to design an efficient reflector to do this but the direct light of the lamp, being diffuse and of a secondary value, is an embarrassment in the theatre. There are various ways of intercepting this light, one of which is a long hood. Alternatively, a blanking disc or a reflector can be used and another method consists of concentric rings known as spill rings (Fig. 26). The trouble is that these devices can work properly only for one beam spread. The moment one tries to expand the beam by moving the lamp out of focus obstruction extends from the unwanted light to the main beam as well.

Hoods and spill rings are never as good as they might be in

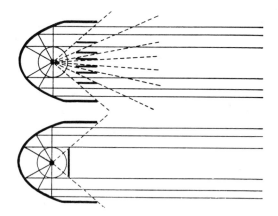

FIG. 26   Spill rings or baffle to intercept direct light of lamp

theory because of the difficulty in providing a completely absorbent matt black finish. However good it may be to begin with, a layer of dust can soon turn it into a diffuser.[1]

Theatre reflectors are nowadays with few exceptions made of super-pure aluminium polished and electro-brightened, and have a reflection factor of between 80 and 84 per cent. Other surfaces such as satin finish can be used to try to diffuse out the lamp filament, especially in the case of the cruder filament shapes, but better control is obtained if maximum reflectivity is retained but the surface is formed as a series of small facets as tangents to the contour of the reflector. Reflectors are usually spun on a metal chuck of the necessary conformation and surface, but where very large quantities are concerned they can be pressed, a process bringing higher accuracy and lower cost once the expensive tools are paid off. The better reflectors are designed with edges thrown up as stiffening flanges and are of sufficient gauge of metal to ensure they will not distort when handled. Where large and/or very precise optically worked surfaces are required in the theatre, silvered glass is still used.

Refraction and Lenses

The other form of light control is by refraction. As a light ray passes from one transparent medium to another—from air to glass, from air to water, or from one glass to another—so it is bent (refracted). This effect takes place at the junction—the surface—of the two materials. As we shall find later, refraction does not affect all colours to the same extent, but for the moment this can be ignored.

A lens is a transparent block of glass shaped to provide a surface which refracts all the light falling on it to bring it to a focal point. The device can be considered as working either way round. Parallel rays of light can fall on it and be focused to a point, or diverging rays from a point source can be placed at the focus and will be condensed into parallel rays; the distance between the lens and this point being known as its focal length. When describing a lens, its diameter is given first, then its focal length.

No lamp filament or other light source in the theatre remotely resembles a point and this, of course, affects reflectors just as much as lenses. However, as the subject is easier to show diagrammatically with lenses, there being no lamp obstruction to confuse the picture, the effect of source size is considered within this optical system. As will be shown later, the neatest lamp filaments conform roughly to a square and if this (represented as an upright arrow) is placed at the focus of a lens as in Fig. 27, then light rays *from all parts* of the luminous arrow

[1] For certain architectural lighting applications a specular black finish on a curved funnel gives the best result.

FIG. 27 Paths of light from
large source through lens

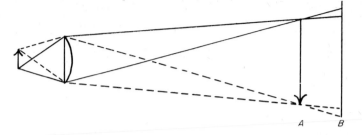

are collected and refracted by all parts of the lens. This arrow
need not be a light-producing source itself. Whether it is a
picture on an illuminated slide of a tree, a mountain or a stanza
of Brechtian verse, the principle is the same. In practice we
need only consider the extremes: the top (shown dashed) and
the bottom (shown solid). When the screen is at *A*, the lens can
be moved to bring all the many paths to coincide and an
enlarged *inverted* image of the arrow appears. But, if the distance
between lantern and screen is increased to *B*, the picture will
become blurred until refocused to bring all the images together.

The lens magnifies the image and the shorter its focal length,
the more pronounced the curve of its surface and the larger the
picture projected. This is then known as a wide-angle lens,
because of the increase in angular width of picture. Both wide-
and narrow-angle lenses can be made to focus the same picture
on either a distant or a near screen, but the picture size will
differ enormously. So also will the distance of lens from slide in
the case of the wide- and narrow-angle versions on both of the
two throws. For example, the short-focus (wide-angle) lens
would probably have to be moved right into its housing when
operating on the long throw, while the long-focus (narrow-
angle) lens would have to be pulled right out of its housing to
focus at all on the short throw.

The diagram (Fig. 27) has to represent three dimensions and
can be taken as showing the behaviour of the rays in either the
plan or section. Often, in a theatre, the screen or surface on
which the picture has to be projected is not at right angles to
the centre line of the beam, which not only alters the shape of
the picture (see Chapter 12) but also renders it more difficult
to focus sharply. Compensation can be made if the slide with
the arrow were angled slightly behind the lens. Provision for
this should be available in the better-quality projectors and the
whole matter of ability to focus shows very well in the professional half- or whole-plate bellows cameras, where the lens
distances and plate angles are so adjustable as to make the
camera at times appear to be looking round a corner!

The simple lens in the diagram might suffice for cut-out
profile projection or for spotlight use (see below) but for scene
or other accurate optical projection more complex forms are

FIG. 28   Types of lens

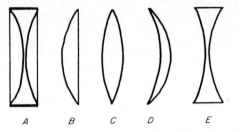

A   B   C   D   E

required. The first step is to reduce the distortion due to the acute lens curve by using a lens curved on each side (bi-convex). The results add together. A simple example of the adding effect of two curves is given when two exactly similar plano-convex lenses are placed one behind the other to give half the focal length. This result is only achieved if the lenses are virtually touching one another (Fig. 28 at *A*). If they are gradually separated one from the other their combined focal length becomes longer and they have to be moved farther away from the slide. This is a primitive zoom and illustrates the two movements—variation of distance between lens components and between the lens and the object focused—in order to get a change in picture magnification.

The design of projection lenses is complex and those of better quality will be made up of many components sealed in a tubular jacket and known as compound lenses. Fig. 28 shows some of the common shapes that can be combined. *B* is a plano-convex, *C* a bi-convex, *D* is a convex-concave known as a meniscus, and *E* with bi-concave surfaces produces a reduced image whereas the others magnify. Unfortunately, while a lens is refracting light it will not be refracting all colours to the same extent, and with a crude lens, particularly a short-focus acutely curved one, this may show up as coloration in the projected image. An achromatic lens employs component lenses of glasses such as crown and flint, whose refractive indices differ, to give the necessary correction. The colours separated by one glass are pulled back in line by the other, so to speak.

All in all, a projection lens will consist of many lenses optically ground to the correct curvature and the larger the diameter the more expensive they are to make. The problem of dealing with a $3\frac{1}{4} \times 4$ in. slide[1] is very different from that presented by an 8-mm home cinema or a 35-mm transparency, though even there a good lens soon proclaims itself in picture quality and in price. The theatre battle, echoed by television, is for more and more light. Fortunately, this is allied to the need for good definition only in the case of scene projection. The amount of light passed by a lens is given by its f/value, the ratio of diameter to focal length. The nearer this approaches to

[1] The Germans prefer a 7×7 in. slide; see Chapter 12 under Scene Projection.

f/l the better. A lens of 1-in. diameter 6-in. focus is f/6, whereas at 2-in. diameter it becomes f/3, thereby passing four times as much light. As has already been mentioned, the refraction of the light takes place at the curved surfaces of the lenses and it has been found that more accurate performance results if these surfaces are bloomed with a special deposit. This, then, is another way of recognizing a high-quality lens.

Once the need for precision of beam control can be put on one side as in the case when a lens is used for a spotlight, then larger-diameter simple types can be used. The aim will be to collect as large a solid angle of light as possible for subsequent redistribution. The most obvious method is to get a short-focus lens as near to the lamp filament as possible, but two things may prevent this. The first is the diameter of the lamp bulb, as only in some lamps can bulbs be made small in diameter. The second impediment is the desirability of being able to move the lamp to and fro in and out of focus to expand and contract the beam. This means that for common spotlights of 1000 watts the focal length must be of the order of between six and ten inches. The solution to improvement of light collection is to increase the diameter of the lens. The method of curving round the source available to reflector systems is out of the question.

The combination of short focus and large diameter produces a monstrosity, a lens thick and heavy, which not only absorbs a great deal of light in the transmission process, but also of course includes the coloration due to the acute curvature. This is the reason why the common spotlight (see focus lantern, page 311) lens used to be 6 × 10 in. or 8 × 12 in. It was not a matter of choice in the past—it just had to be. Lanterns employing these systems were so inefficient that purely reflector units (Pageant and Acting Area lanterns) became popular, their greatly increased light making up for the disadvantages of the almost fixed-beam distribution.

Soft-edge or Fresnel Spots

A solution had been available and in use in film studios for many years, namely the Fresnel lens. But industrial monopoly led to sluggish development in Britain, further aggravated by high price, and, in consequence, poor demand. In 1955 competition halved prices overnight and stage-lighting manufacturers became the pursued instead of pursuers. Fresnel lenses were at last the obvious way of optical control for stage-lighting lanterns.

This lens takes its name from a Frenchman whose basic idea can be seen in an extreme form in the prisms which go together to make the giant lenses in lighthouses. In our application, the Fresnel can be considered as a lens with the back cut out in

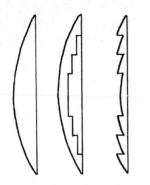

FIG. 29   Plano, step, and Fresnel lenses compared

a series of steps (Fig. 29) to reduce the thickness of the glass. Although some lenses are made this way, the majority have the front curve pushed back as a series of concentric prisms to form a flat lens plate.   Short focus and large diameter no longer means thick glass; furthermore, the lenses can be produced by a moulding process and, provided sufficient quantity is involved, inexpensively.   The risers of the steps can cause slight scatter and where this is undesirable the lenses can be supplied with the risers blackened.   The American term for this is "colouvred."

It should go without saying that for accurate projection these lenses are quite unsuitable, but for spotlight work an accurate picture of the lamp filament is the last thing that is wanted.   The moulding process allows break-up indentations or ribs to be included on the back to soften and obscure the filament image.   The result is a whole class of spotlights giving a soft beam pattern, unrecognizable as the lamp filament except in basic shape and variable over a large range of magnifications by merely moving the lamp back and forward behind the lens.   An advantage of this optical system is that, as the lamp is brought forward and the light spreads, the solid angle of collection by the lens increases.   The rate of spread, however, overtakes that of collection and the spot position therefore remains relatively much brighter, but there is some compensatory effect (Fig. 31).

Precision Projectors

In the spotlight the object focused, the filament, is incandescent and the whole projection process produces an inverted but fogged, out-of-focus, picture of the lamp.   It is necessary now to

FIG. 30   Phantom view of 1-kW Fresnel spot

FIG. 31 Effect of beam spread on intensity

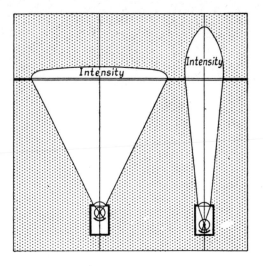

consider systems in which clarity of definition is of prime importance and in which the object focused, the slide, has itself to be illuminated.

The part of the system between slide and screen with its compound lenses has already been considered above and this would be known as the objective lens assembly. Behind it,

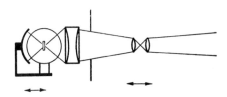

FIG. 32 Condenser and objective projection system

there has to be a condenser lens to collect the light from the lamp and provide a field of illumination on the slide. Thus, there are two distinct parts—the lamp and condenser on the one hand, and the slide and objective on the other. The size of the projected picture will depend on the latter and the evenness of light over the field on the former. Several lenses interleaved with heat-absorbing glass to protect the slide may be used for the condenser. The condenser system is further related to the objective because, while covering the whole slide, as much of its light must be transmitted as possible and not wasted on the inside of the objective lens tube. Some adjustment of lamp position should be possible to enable the cross-over from the condenser to be altered to suit a long- or short-focus objective. It will be noticed the combined optical systems produce two inversions, but these do not cancel each other out so as to produce a picture the right way up because the objective which forms the picture is concerned with the slide only.

FIG. 33 4-kW projector opened
to show condenser system and
heat-absorbing glasses

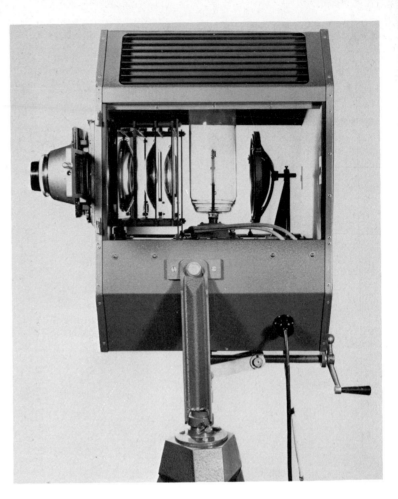

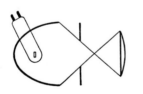

FIG. 34 Mirror spotlight optical system

FIG. 35 Ellipsoidal spotlight optical system

Profile Spots

Where only profile cut-outs are required to be projected, relaxation is possible both at the objective lens and at the condenser; so much so that a reflector system can be used in the latter's place. A reflector, especially an elliptical one, collects a great deal of light which passes through a gate aperture and crosses over to cover a single large-diameter objective. This latter has to focus the edges of the gate whose shape can be determined by a series of masks and cut-outs, or by an iris shutter and four separately framing shutters. The result is a very efficient, comparatively lightweight and inexpensive spotlight known as a Profile type (Figs. 34 and 35) to distinguish it from the soft-edge Fresnel type.

It is difficult to determine who invented the first Profile and when, but to some extent it follows a natural line of development. The firm of Kliegl of New York first introduced it in the ellipsoidal reflector form in a big way in the early thirties in a

FIG. 36   Phantom view of 1-kW Profile spot with ellipsoidal reflector

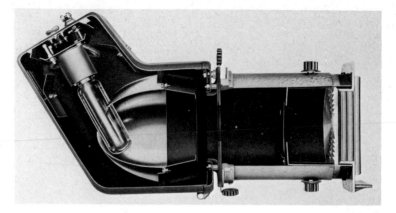

range of sizes, to such an effect that "Kliegeye" went into the language as an eye affliction. Ed Kook of Century claims with his partner Levy to have antedated Kliegl with the Lekolite. Yet between this and the Stelmar of Steel and Martin in England was but a step. Certainly my own experiments which led to Strand's first Mirror Spot sprang from an attempt to make a cheaper and much smaller Stelmar, the American developments being then unknown to me.[1] One thing is certain: it took thirty years for me or anyone else to market the next and obvious step, known and patented as the Bifocal Spot!

For this the poor depth of focus of the type of lens used in a profile spot can be turned to advantage by fitting a second set of shutters separated from the first by an inch or so. If, in addition, these shutters have serrated edges then some sides of the beam can be made ill-defined and vignetted while others are in fact sharply focused. This has two advantages: a soft effect is obtained without the scatter entailed by diffusion at the lens, and hard edges can be combined with soft, greatly facilitating the invisible joining of two or more pools of light.

Classification of Light Distribution

The use of optical control of the light from the source gives a series of distributions of different quality and intensity, and it will be necessary to compare these one with another. This brings us back to the photometric units which opened this chapter. The forms of lamp available and their relative efficiencies are considered in the next chapter and obviously greatly influence light output one way and another.

The simplest method of assessing the problem of light distribution is to put a Fresnel spot on a stand and direct it on to a screen at least twenty feet away which hangs vertically and horizontally at right angles to the axis of the beam. With the lamp forward towards the lens there will be a wide-angle flood

[1] See *Tabs* Strand Jubilee Edition, Volume 22, Number 1, page 62.

FIG. 37 Beam distribution: tenth and half-peak angles for flood and spot beams from 500-watt Fresnel. Vertical axis is in 1000s of candelas, horizontal in degrees

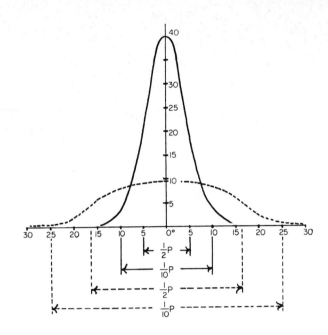

of light and with it drawn back from the lens a concentrated pool of light. Being a Fresnel, the edge of the beam is not well defined in either case (Fig. 37).

If the incident light is measured in foot-candles (or lux) by a photometer in the middle of the beam then the distribution can be plotted by rotating the spotlight gradually on its spigot. It will be found that over the part where the beam varies down to half peak only, the eye will accept this as virtually an even beam. Beyond this the light falls away to a tenth of the value of the centre and then useful light ceases. To provide these variations the lantern traverses the photometer over certain angles. The angle over which the light varies by two to one is known as the half peak angle, and that by ten to one as the one-tenth peak angle. (These are the terms used in the latest relevant British Standards specification and should be adhered to.) At one time, only one angle, known as the "beam angle," was used as covering the 10 to 1 variation inclusive. After some thirty years this definition was changed by the American Illuminating Engineering Society[1] to cover only 2 to 1 and the 10 to 1 became the Field Angle. The confusion which resulted is obvious, and Britain was not left unscathed because Strand Electric in their rush to placate the American continent produced leaflets in 1965 with these unapproved terms. The need to avoid confusion led to the adoption in the appropriate

[1] "Reporting Photometric Performance of Incandescent Filament Lighting Units," approved as a transaction by the Council of the USA Illuminating Engineering Society, October, 1957, and prepared by the joint IES–SMPTE committee on equipment performance ratings.

FIG. 38 Profile distribution: half peak angles from 500-watt Profile spot with narrow (N), medium (M) and wide (W) lenses. Vertical axis is in 1000s of candelas, horizontal in degrees

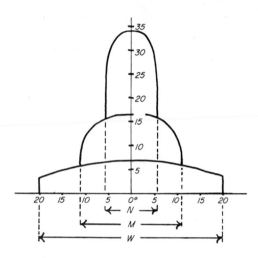

British Standards specification of the descriptive half peak and tenth peak referred to above. Even now at the time of writing it is not certain whether these angles should be judged by rotation of the lantern (strictly at the plane of the lens) or by moving a photometer along a wall at right angles to the beam. As the beam is variable in most stage-lighting lanterns these divergencies are not as serious as they might be, but it is just as well to allow some latitude and not work to the extremes.

Outside the one-tenth peak angle there will be a point beyond which the light is less than one per cent, and this is known as the cut-off angle. The two peak angles are obviously applicable both to floodlights and Fresnel spots, the one-tenth peak angle being useful light which allows blending of one lantern's distribution with another. In a Profile spot only one angle, the half peak angle, should be applicable since this lantern depends on a sharp cut-off with no light outside it. The same applies to optical projectors. Using the curves themselves (Fig. 38) or just the angles a good idea of the relative performance of one lantern compared to another or of the adjustable range of beam spreads within the same lantern can be obtained. It would be a mistake to think the most suitable lantern is the brightest; many factors have to be taken into consideration and there could be cases when a lot of small power lanterns could be preferable to a large efficient one, space or low glare being all important.

5 Lamps

THE common light source in the theatre and in the television studio is the tungsten filament lamp. There are others, arc and discharge lamps, which will be examined later, but the great advantage of the filament lamps is that they can be readily dimmed by dropping the line volts. There is also none of the auxiliary gear which haunts other sources.

The lamp filament is made of fine tungsten wire offering a resistance to the passage of an electric current. The energy absorbed is converted to heat in the first place, and only if several conditions are fulfilled will any part of it become light. The filament wire has to be heated to incandescence and actual combustion must be prevented by keeping it free of oxygen. The original vacuum lamp with the squirrel-cage filament was the result. As soon as any attempt is made to run at a higher temperature, to obtain more light, particles of the filament evaporate, weakening it and blackening the bulb in the process. The next step was to fill the bulb with an inert gas such as argon, the molecules of which offer some obstruction to evaporation. These, however, conduct the heat away and the temperature of the filament drops and the light turns orange. If, however, the filament is wound as a tight coil, instead of as an open birdcage, its heat will be conserved. Often this coil is coiled again on itself and the coiled coil lamp is the result.

Running the filament at a higher temperature still causes the filament to evaporate, in spite of the gas-filling, and this appears on the bulb as blackening.[1] Thus, we see that gas-filling allowed the filament to be run at a much higher temperature and produce more light before evaporation and blackening became inconvenient. Of course this process still goes on to a greater or lesser degree, depending on the temperature at which it is decided to run the filament. In consequence, lamps intended to have a long life must run at a lower temperature than those whose purpose is bright but short. Whereas the

---

[1] Some of the larger lamps have loose granules of tungsten inside the bulb which, by gently rocking to and fro, may be used to remove the blackening to some extent.

"average" objective life, as it is called, for some lamps is one thousand or eight hundred hours, that of the more efficient lamps may be reduced to two hundred or fifty or even less. Lamp efficiency is given as lumens per watt.

Tungsten-halogen Lamps

In recent years a new form of lamp has opened up the possibility of greatly extended life. A small amount of iodine, for example, is added to the gas-filling and this, when it vaporizes in the heat, amalgamates with the evaporating filament particles and redeposits them. As the iodine cycle cannot ensure that each molecule is deposited exactly whence it came, this operation is not 100 per cent efficient and the lamp will ultimately fail. The advantage is still considerable and the choice of what shall be done with the iodine bonus lies once again between greater temperature with more light on the one hand and longer life on the other. Wattage for wattage and life for life these lamps produce more light, but their main importance is the maintenance of light output throughout life.

This does not necessarily mean that this extra light can be efficiently re-used in all optical systems. High running temperature is vital for the iodine cycle to function and, in consequence, the filament is enclosed in a tubular bulb of quartz which is narrow in diameter when compared to its length. This produces in certain of its manifestations a singularly intractable shape for stage optical systems (Fig. 39). In this respect, the fact that our voltage on this side of the Atlantic is twice that of the United States means that our filaments have to accommodate more and more thinner wire and puts us at something of a

FIG. 39 Tungsten-halogen "quartz" lamps: left and right are bulb-encased 750-watt and 1-kW versions. Long horizontal lamp is 1-kW, below are three other types of 1-kW, and to their left are two 500W. (All to same scale.)

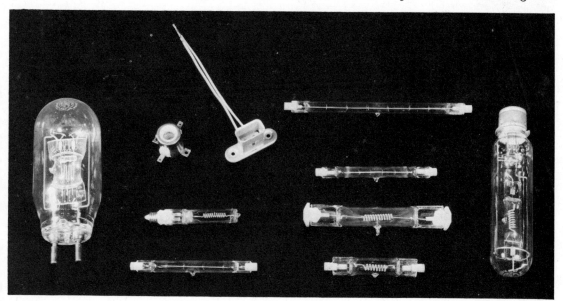

FIG. 40 500-watt General Lighting Service lamp with GES cap

disadvantage. Quartz bulbs must not be touched by hand and should this happen must be wiped with clean water before use: otherwise a fault may develop at the point now carrying the invisible fingerprint. In a few cases the quartz tube is protected in a second ordinary glass bulb and such precautions then become unnecessary. The whole of this class of lamp became known as "tungsten iodine" or sometimes "quartz iodine," but, as is not unusual, the popular catchphrase is inaccurate especially as the filling now is more likely to be bromine and the description to use is, therefore, "tungsten-halogen lamps."

Returning to the main stream of standard gas-filled lamps, we find that their bulb shape and size, their filament structure and life, all vary greatly not only between one wattage and another but within the same wattage. The reasons behind these variations require careful explanation as they vitally affect choice of type for successful use.

General Lighting Service Lamps

The bulb size and filament shape is not critical in simple every-day lighting applications and, in consequence, the lamp tends to get designed for its own well-being rather than for use in an efficient optical system. Examination of a 500-watt General Lighting Service (G.L.S.) lamp shows this (Fig. 40). The bulb is large and rounded so that the glass is kept well clear of the heat of the filament whatever the angle of burning. The weakest part of the lamp is where the lamp cap is joined on and the lead-in wires pass through the bulb—the pinch—so a neck is formed at that point. On the larger wattages a mica disc is included in the neck to form a heat barrier when burning cap up. The lamp cap is a screw type of E.S. (Edison Screw) or G.E.S. (Goliath Edison Screw) size, the British domestic bayonet cap being insufficiently rigid for theatre work and, in any case, little known outside this country. Inside the bulb the filament is constructed with the aim of allowing it to be tilted at all angles without any of its strands fouling each other and so causing a short-circuit. Particularly in the smaller sizes, the bulb may be interior frosted to give a pearl finish or may be given the more pronounced diffusion of a silica deposit. This diffusion is sometimes convenient for the 1000- and 1500-watt lamps used in the television softlights known as "scoops."

Projector Lamps

Lamps for use in optical systems are known as projector lamps and some of the common types of 1kW used in the theatre are shown to the same scale in Fig. 41. These lamps are, unlike the G.L.S. types, to a large extent hand-made and in consequence

it is not surprising that they are more expensive. There are two aims: firstly, to obtain as compact and regular a filament shape as possible and, secondly, to make the bulb small to allow the optical system to come closer and collect a large solid angle of light. These advantages can be obtained only by surrendering the freedom to burn at any angle and severe restrictions may result. These are all a matter of common sense, however. If the filament is housed in a tubular bulb, it follows that the glass is very close to it at some points, and in consequence to burn horizontally instead of vertically is going to cause strain. The bulb will certainly deform especially as more blackening is deposited so trapping the heat. All tubular lamps have to be burnt either cap down or cap up, whichever is specified. Cap down can be assumed in the absence of information, but a new class of theatre lamps, the T4,[1] do burn cap up—a notion of many years standing in United States, but available for European voltages only in recent years. Assuming the correct lamp replacement is used, then the lantern itself provides an excellent guide because any position which allows colour frames to fall out must be upside down. So one would think; but it is surprising the number of spotlights that nevertheless do get mounted the wrong way up, especially in exhibitions![2]

A tilt of twenty degrees either side of vertical is permitted and this ratio can be stretched by pre-tilting the lampholder appropriately. The lantern in Fig. 36 shows this very well.

[1] T12 and others in United States.
[2] Many of the new tungsten-halogen projector lamps do allow tilt in any direction.

A compact grid filament arranged to form a square is especially vulnerable to a tilt sideways. The coiled filament strands, which are tight when cold, expand when hot and as these have to be close together may touch if tilted in that direction. So long as the lantern trunnion is used in a dead vertical position all is well and adjustment should always be undertaken in these terms. The trunnion pivots are the correct place for tilt, and the barrel clamp bolt or stand spigot for rotation. When suspension is required from a vertical boom, then a horizontal clamp must be used and all temptation to clamp the trunnion sideways directly to the boom resisted. This latter should be obvious, but what is not so obvious is that a trunnion slightly out of the vertical will combine with rotation to produce sufficient sideways tilt to shorten life. The modern projector lamp, such as a 1000-watt T4, is amazingly compact as can be seen when compared to its predecessor, the A1, as Fig. 41 shows. Unlike home cinemas and slide projectors, theatre lamps are not permitted the benefit of forced-draught cooling. The noise from a series of Aldis-type projectors with their fans on the circle front or in the No. 1 spot bar position can be imagined. A theatre lamp represents a real feat of technical ingenuity. The rule of no artificial draught has to be relaxed for the big 4-kW scene projectors. In these the actual heat of the lamp is intercepted before it reaches the slide by special glasses between the component lenses of the condenser, but both these and the lamp need the gentle air movement of a slow-speed fan to help remove the heat.

Prefocus and Bipost Holders

A good filament is no use unless correctly positioned in the optical system, and for this prefocus caps and holders are used. In normal lamps the bulb is completely assembled and the cap put on afterwards to take its chance how things line up. In a prefocus lamp, a second shell is soldered on while the lamp is actually sited in an optical jig. In the case of one famous firm, at any rate, the lamp is actually alight on check and the operator lines the projected image on target and then immediately floats the hard solder round the prefocus shell. In this type of lamp the light centre is taken from the top of the two location fins, whereas on E.S. or G.E.S. it is from the centre contact at the bottom of the screwcap. This accounts for the great difference in the published light centres for two otherwise identical lamps. There are two common theatre prefocus sizes, medium and large, corresponding to E.S. and G.E.S. Many other forms of prefocus cap exist particularly among the smaller low-voltage lamps, but more important to

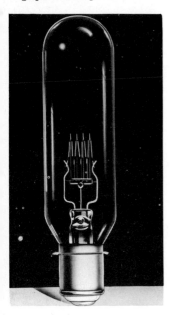

FIG. 42 (a) 2000-watt bipost lamp; (b) 1000-watt lamp with large prefocus cap.

the theatre is the bipost which is used for wattages of 2-kW and upwards. Both film and television studios use it for 1000-watt also, and in a smaller form for 750 and 500 watts. The bipost is not really a cap: it is a fundamental part of the lamp. The whole filament structure is carried on two vertical members which run into two large pins set in a moulded glass dish base. The bulb itself is sealed on to this assembly afterwards, the lamp being not so much "capped" as "bulbed" (Fig. 42). The light centre dimension is taken to the shoulder of the pins. In the latest version, a metal dish assembly with the pins insulated from it is used.

Two holders working on such different principles could greatly hinder the adaptability of certain lanterns were it not for the fact that Strand Electric make a large prefocus and a bipost holder which is interchangeable on the same two fixing holes and automatically lines up the filament centres where appropriate. This bipost holder has a lever clamp to secure the lamp in position and this must be released before attempting removal.

Prefocus-type holders function differently, the fins being inserted in the two corresponding slots, the lamp pressed down against the centre contact spring and turned clockwise through ninety degrees until stopped. Care must be taken to get both fins under their securing lips, otherwise the lamp goes in out of true and may jam as well. The medium prefocus holder has in addition one slot and fin smaller than the other so the lamp can go in only one way round.

Tungsten-halogen lamps have a variety of caps and, indeed, the whole subject is so complex nowadays that one can only touch on basic principles and the commoner forms. Some lamps even use the octal valve base with pins set in glass.

A special 1000-watt tungsten-halogen projector lamp for theatre in our voltage range was introduced by Atlas in 1973. With a GX9·5 2-pin ceramic base it was called the T9 and needed spotlights designed for it and it alone. This *could* lead to a more efficient optical system but more generally popular have been the types developed to be interchangeable with orthodox tungsten lamps. These give the user the choice of buying the more expensive but longer life and brighter lamp or not, both in the case of a lantern he already has or of a new one. If the lamp is only going to have occasional use the extra expenditure will not be justified. These tungsten-halogen lamps are:— T13 (650-watt), T14 and T15 (1000-watt) all on P28 medium prefocus bases replacing the T1, T6 and T4. For the P40 large prefocus holder there is the T16 (1000-watt) replacing the T2. These lamps are intended to burn base down and give three and a half times the life of their equivalents without appreciable fall-off in light output or colour.

The lamp envelope in tungsten-halogen lamps attains very high temperatures indeed and exceptional care should be taken when replacing a lamp which has just failed. With all lamps it is preferable to play safe and unplug from the mains. In the case of some of the latest lanterns the lamp mounting has to be withdrawn for the purpose and does this automatically.

Reflector Lamps

Some lamps include integrally all or part of the optical system required for their efficient use. This is commonly the case with 8 millimetre home-cinema projector lamps, but on a bigger scale a series of lamps is available, the back part of the bulbs of which are silvered. Only metaphorically, however; in reality it is a super pure aluminium deposit. The bulb itself may be of blown glass, in which case the lamp is known as an internally silvered reflector lamp and only rough beam control is obtained. The other form is known as a sealed beam lamp and consists of a moulded back and front (Fig. 43). A number of variations are therefore possible, quite apart from wattage, and either lenses or break-up surfaces are available in what are known as PAR lamps to form the front half. A wide range of beam distribution has been available for some years now in the United States and these are gradually appearing over here. Great efficiency is possible, for each lamp is virtually a complete optical system and when low-voltage filaments or tungsten-halogen sources are sealed in the light output is remarkable.

All this must be viewed with caution, however, as far as the theatre is concerned, for these are fixed beams. In a

FIG. 43 Sealed-beam lamps: top left to right: 1-kW PAR 64 spot, 500-watt PAR 56 spot and medium flood; bottom: 150-watt PAR 36 spot, and flood

narrow-beam spotlight type of sealed beam lamp the optical system is designed for one purpose only. All the efficiency that can be extracted pours out on this one beam distribution; and what chance do the multi-purpose, variable-beam, jack-of-all-trades stage spotlights stand by comparison? Yet it is to these we must inevitably turn as our basic resource in painting stage pictures with light. Variable beam control and distribution, at our behest, are essential. Therefore, beware! If hundreds of sealed beam lamps are deployed as general stage lighting, the orthodox spotlighting is going to take a hard knock. Stage lighting does not have to be bright, it has to appear bright and this is not the same thing at all.

Lamp Efficiency and Colour Temperature

The production of colour begins with the light source, for what is not there to start with cannot be put back later on. The more efficient a filament lamp is, the whiter its light and the better it will function in conjunction with colour filters that depend on the transmission of blue. There are two guides to lamp performance: its efficiency expressed as lumens per watt and its colour temperature in °K (Kelvin units). This last is of more concern to colour photography or colour television. Generally speaking, 3200°K is preferred for that work, but this figure can be achieved only with lamps of 2 kW and over, or very short-life low-wattage lamps such as photofloods. Most theatre projector lamps run at 2800°K when full on. North daylight, for comparison, is 15,000°K.

A lamp of a higher colour temperature may well *appear* to give more light; blueness and sharp edges to a beam are inclined to lead the eye astray. It does not make sense, however, to choose a light by eye for its apparent brightness, which may mean bluey whiteness, and then warm it by using an amber filter or heavy make-up, that is, wasting some of its light by cutting down the blue. For stage purposes it is better to use lumens per watt as a yardstick to judge the whiteness of the light source, provided always this refers to tungsten-filament lamps when comparing one with another.

Efficiency derives, as has been said earlier, from the temperature of the filament. The thicker filaments can be run at a higher temperature than the thinner ones, and this tends to favour higher-wattage and/or lower-voltage lamps. The fact that North America uses 100 plus instead of a 220 plus as a lamp voltage gives them a bonus of 10 per cent more light. In the case of a 500-watt general service lamp on the higher voltage, its efficiency is 17 lumens per watt compared with 19 for the 1000-watt, because of the thicker filament of the latter. Life is 1000 hours and, if a shorter life of only 50 hours is acceptable, the 1000-watt class A1 efficiency is 24·5 lumens

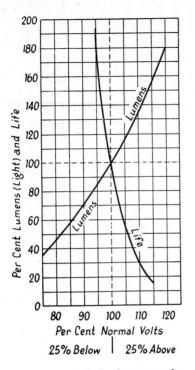

FIG. 44 Relation between volts and lumens (light output) and life

per watt or 26 on 110 volts. Among the projector lamps the round-bulb 1000-watt class B1 makes a poor showing at 16 lumens per watt. As an example of the effect of low voltage, a 30-volt 30-amp lamp in an A1 bulb and with a life of 50 hours gives 28·5 L/W. In spite of a 10 per cent drop in wattage when compared with the mains voltage 1000 A1, this means a total lumen output of 25,650 instead of 22,000—more light from less watts and a more compact filament into the bargain. Tungsten-halogen lamps also show the effects of a decision to opt for efficiency or for life.

Any filament lamp, whatever its designed rating, will be affected by voltage variation. The relationship is shown in Fig. 44. Five per cent on the volts means 40 per cent off the life but 15 per cent more light. Contrariwise, 5 per cent off the volts means 80 per cent more life but 15 per cent less light. Ten per cent down on volts takes the life right off the top of the graph but light is down to 70 per cent. The question of lamp life is fundamental: less than 200 hours could be an infernal nuisance in the theatre. In critical situations, such as spotlights concealed in the auditorium ceiling for some special decorative effect, under-running by ensuring that the dimmers cannot come full up will mean a valuable extension of life well worth the sacrifice of, say, 30 per cent light.

Non-filament Lamps

The filament lamp in its ordinary manifestations converts roughly 8 per cent of the energy it uses into light, and though this is improved somewhat with the latest developments the result cannot be more than another 2 per cent. In the theatre these efficiencies are going to be further impoverished, as we shall find later, by the use of colour filters. It is not at all strange, therefore, that other methods of producing light have been pursued. One of these, the carbon arc, was the earliest type of electric light, but in a refined form these arcs have had a long run and are still used for theatre follow-spots and film projectors in cinemas where great power is necessary. However, the arc has been challenged in these fields by later developments, particularly by the xenon arc and most recent of all by the mercury iodide arc, both of which are metal arcs encased in bulbs. Where concentrated beams of light are not required then discharge lamps, particularly those known as "fluorescent" lamps, have also to be considered.

Carbon Arcs

Carbon arcs, being open to atmosphere, burn quite literally and the carbons have to be replaced, if in continuous use, at every performance. What happens is that two sticks of carbon (Fig. 45), one connected to the positive terminal and the other

FIG. 45 100-amp a.c. arc showing dowser (J) to protect mirror
lowered and positioner (I) to
set arc gap

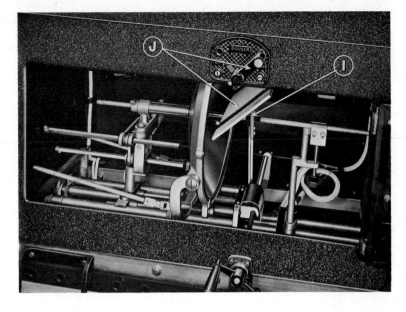

to the negative, are brought together to touch and immediately
separated by a short distance. An arc or electric flame forms
in the gap. A white-hot crater is made in the positive and this
burns away faster than the negative. To keep the light centre
constant while the carbons are fed, until recently by a hand-
operated knob, the positive carbon is made much larger than
the negative, matched pairs being obtainable for the purpose.
Once the arc is struck, the current continues to rise and must
be limited by a resistance in the circuit.

In an a.c. arc the carbons are equal-sized and the source of
light is then both tips of the carbons and a ball of flame between
them. The carbons are cored and copper-coated to assist in
its formation. An a.c. arc, being non-directional, is not so
efficient as a light producer as a d.c. one, but it can make
more economic use of the current by using an efficient form of
transformer-choke, known as an inductor, instead of the
wasteful series resistance. Some idea of the efficiency of the
a.c. arc used this way is shown by the fact that the 90-amp
arc in the large Sunspots used for following in theatres like
Drury Lane require only a 17-amp feed at the mains end.
The bright clear-cut beam is the result of setting the arc in a
mirror optical system which makes it really a Profile spot on
a large scale.

The art of "following" demands concentration and it is not
fair to expect the operator to have to feed the arc as well.
A motor mechanism can be provided, and ought always to be
fitted, which by means of a feed-back circuit keeps the arc gap,
once set, constant as the carbons burn away.

FIG. 46 2-kW Xenon follow-spot with colour magazine

Metal Arcs

The latest rival to the Sunspot Arc in the follow-spot class of work has been nicknamed the "Zenspot" (Fig. 46). The 2-kW Xenon lamp relies on a d.c. arc formed between two electrodes in a quartz envelope with a Xenon gas filling. To start the arc, a high-voltage pulse is used instead of mechanically moving the electrodes. Current has to be limited and one way and another there is a large amount of auxiliary gear. Although the Xenon lamp itself is expensive, if the cost of carbons consumed by the arc over the period of the lamp life is considered, the lamp is marginally the winner. Care has to be exercised when handling the lamp itself for replacement.

A great advantage of the Xenon lamp is that it needs no expert attention when running. It can even be struck remotely and dimmed if, as at Covent Garden, there are servo-operated shutters for this purpose. The Xenon lamp is not particularly efficient taken with its auxiliary gear when compared to other discharge lamps, but as there are no dirty products of combustion it can be placed right inside a mirror reflector system to an extent that an arc cannot. Collection of the light emitted is therefore more efficient and the reflector stays clean longer as well. Xenon arcs have been used in Germany for scene projection and also as large power sources for flooding the stage with light, notably at Bayreuth. Outside the theatre, they have been used on very high mounting poles to flood road junctions and the like.

In 1967 the 400-watt mercury iodide lamp, looking like one of the very small tungsten-halogen lamps, was introduced. Closer examination shows that there is no filament and that it has a short arc gap set in a very small quartz envelope. Although this lamp cannot be dimmed, other than by a shutter or iris, there are a variety of applications of which the follow spot is the most obvious. This field, at one time belonging to the carbon arc, has been taken over in recent times by narrow beam Profile spots using tungsten lamps of 2000 watts. These are of necessity rather bulky because of their optical system. The new source has the high efficiency of 85 lumens per watt which amply makes up for its small wattage. A later 1000-watt version of the lamp, by that time known as the "CSI" (Compact

FIG. 47   1-kW (1000-watt) CSI
lamp follow spot

FIG. 48   4-kW HMI lamp Pani
scene projector

Source Iodide), has become the standard for high power follow spots replacing both Xenon and Carbon arcs in modern stage lighting practice. Some auxiliary gear is necessary and this plus the need for mechanical dimming limits its application. The lamp takes a minute or so to attain full brightness and should it be extinguished accidentally it can only be re-struck when it has cooled down somewhat. A remedy is being sought.

Another stage use for which these new sources are particularly suitable is scene projection. In 1974 Ludwig Pani of Vienna introduced the BP4 HMI projector. This has a HMI lamp, the German equivalent of the CSI lamp. It is 4 kW but owing to its efficiency the compact source emits something like the output of a 15 kW normal tungsten lamp. At last scenery can be projected at a level which no longer sets problems in lighting the acting area adequately. The slide is 18 cm (7 in.) square and with an 18 cm objective lens the BP4 HMI is said to light a 30 ft square screen with 880 lux at 33 ft. Dimming is by neutral density wedges, servo operated by plugging into any thyristor dimmer circuit.

Discharge and Fluorescent Lamps

Another method of light production, known as the discharge lamp, made its appearance in the early 1930s, first as street lighting of "that ghastly colour" and then as crude, if bright, lighting for heavy industry. Just after the outbreak of war there was an outbreak of another kind—fluorescent lighting. These sources have been developed and refined with passage of time and have, although no longer advocated as a panacea for everything, established themselves as indispensable for many applications. None of them concerns the theatre stage or television studio production lighting, outside the workshops that is, except in minor applications, but these are sufficiently important to make it advisable to consider how the lamps function.

The earliest form of this lamp used a high voltage of 6000 or so from a transformer to cause a discharge to take place between cathodes separated by a neon gas in a tube of around 15 mm in diameter. Limited colour variation is possible by change of gas, but the important advance in this respect was the use of mercury vapour and fluorescent coatings which led to a fine range of colours. These are known as cold cathode tubes.

To stimulate the electron flow so that normal working voltages could be used, filaments were later provided to heat the cathodes and the result was the more efficient hot cathode discharge lamp. In the original street lamps mercury vapour discharge was taken neat and the only use the theatre found for these lamps was to age the Gods when the giants ran off with Frika in Covent Garden's 1934 *Ring*—an effect not included in the 1964 *Ring* in the same house. The trouble with the crude mercury discharge lamps is that all the energy is emitted as four lines in the spectrum. The sodium lamp is worse in this respect since all the radiation is in two yellow lines. This has practical results for street lighting, however, because light production is at its most efficient in that area and visual acuity is also at its best. The essential feature of discharge lamps is that there is no path until a momentary surge causes the gas to break down. From then on the problem is to limit the current which otherwise would continue to rise. For this purpose a choke is wired in series with the supply.

In the case of the hot cathode fluorescent tube, the flashing as the starter switch first connects the heater filaments and then causes a firing pulse is all too familiar and one is not surprised that the design of a dimmer to bring the lamp in and out gently was an altogether tougher problem than gradually warming up a filament lamp until it emits light. However, in 1949, Atlas Lighting showed that adequate dimming was possible using ganged resistance dimmers, each way of which fed a pair of 2-ft tubes with earthing strips along the tubes and constantly energized filament heaters. Subsequently, 4-ft tubes on the Continent and 5-ft in Britain have been dimmed using magnetic amplifiers, thyratrons, and now thyristors. Although the situation with the latest thyristor dimmers is much easier, it must be stressed that such an installation has to be designed as a whole and carried out with suitable components, including special Instant Start lamps. There is no equivalent to the easy way in which any one of a number of dimmers can be inserted in series with an existing tungsten-lamp installation and by dropping the voltage satisfactory results obtained immediately. A fluorescent-lamp installation with dimmers is a special which has to be paid for.

Decorative auditorium lighting concealed in coves is the main use for fluorescent lamps in the cinema or theatre, situations where previously there would have been hundreds of small-wattage tungsten lamps to maintain. Sometimes, as in the Royal Festival Hall auditorium ceiling coves, cold cathode lamps may be more appropriate. As stage lighting, fluorescent lamps are virtually useless with the possible exception of a couple of light blue circuits for cycloramas of German type and scale. Except as a softlight like this, the low-brightness long surface of the lamp which makes it so acceptable elsewhere proves a handicap on the stage. Only in one plane does it lend itself to beam control by reflector and, in any case, to lock up special equipment solely for the odd scene with a cyclorama is in most cases nonsensical. Should a long source be required for stage-lighting equipment the high-brightness long type of tungsten-halogen would be more suitable especially as no auxiliary gear or special dimmers are required, and this in spite of the unquestionable claim of a fluorescent lamp to produce certain colours of light more efficiently, by conversion of shorter wavelengths such as ultra-violet into the longer ones instead of by filtering of (i.e. wasting) the unwanted (see Chapter 6).

Ultra-violet Lamps

Certain discharge lamps are rich in ultra-violet radiation and this is what is used to activate the fluorescent powders with which the bulb or tube is coated. If in place of the outer envelope a special glass filter (known as Wood's glass) is used, a black lamp is the result. These are available as a 125-watt discharge lamp with a special three-pin B.C. holder to ensure that it is not used in a non-choked lampholder and as a 4-ft long 40-watt tube. This latter can be used in a normal fluorescent fitting and switches on and off instantly, whereas the 125-watt discharge lamp takes two or three minutes to attain full intensity. Also after being switched off it can only be struck up again when cool—a matter of some minutes' delay. On the other hand, this lamp is of course easier to find concealment for than the 4-ft tube and its distribution can thus be confined to a local area of activity rather than flooding all over the place.

6 Colour

THERE can be little doubt that to a large number of people stage lighting means colour. What colour should we use for this or that is a constant cry. The use of white light or of two or three filters only is regarded as a confession of failure and immense studies are undertaken in order to use as many colours from the colour-filter sample book as possible. In addition, equipment is installed by means of which colours can be mixed and made to flood an area. We are lucky if this area is only the cyclorama: too often this is extended to the rows of battens overhead and a three- or four-colour footlight into the bargain.

Colour is not the principal means of expression; it is merely an adjunct to be brought in when light and its counterpart, shadow, fail. As one in ten of the male audience is likely to be colour-blind and therefore cannot see all colours, it is obviously as well not to rely on it too heavily. If you are a male practitioner in the art, it will be just as well to be checked yourself for colour-blindness before inflicting your colour compositions on others.

There will be times when colour can be indulged in for its own sake and one must not be apologetic about it. The position then is analogous to that of stained-glass windows. The less they are concerned with drawing a clear picture of the particular saint and his story and the more they are a colour composition, the more exciting they will be. It is unfortunate that the obvious answer, namely to get rid of the saint and quite frankly admit we are out for colour, is still far too seldom admitted. In a like manner, there will be times when colour is more important than seeing the actors. Then again, the question whether stage lighting need always be a handmaid to the theatre or the actor arises, and this is explored in Chapter 12 page 272 and Appendix 3.

Colour is a sensation we receive when presented with only part of the visible range of light. This range is radiation of wavelengths from 4000 Å to 7000 Å. The unit of measurement Å (Angstrom Unit) is 10^{-10} of a metre and there is a complete series of these wavelengths which when presented

FIG. 49 The spectrum produced by a prism

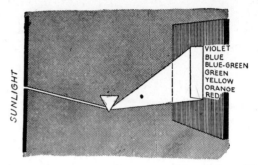

simultaneously to the eye are seen as white light. This light can be refracted by passing it through a very narrow slit on to a prism. What then appears is a series of multiple images of the slit side by side, each in a different colour (Fig. 49). These are the familiar coloured band—the spectrum—Red, Orange, Yellow, Green, Blue-green, Blue, and Violet. In reality there are hundreds of colour lines—saturated hues (pure colours)—but there are so many that they appear as a continuous ribbon.

This sorting of wavelengths by passing them from glass to air is not the only method. White light can be passed through a very fine mesh or grating and a spectrum produced. This method is known as "diffraction" and has the advantage that, unlike the prismatic spectrum, the colours are spaced without distortion and are true to their band widths. Both prisms or diffraction gratings may be made into instruments known as spectroscopes. These range from a small pocket device to large laboratory instruments capable of precise use for analysis and measurement. The small instrument is not to be despised as a toy, however, as an hour spent with one and a set of colour filters will bring home what happens in a way that no mere description can. Instead of a colour change effect, what one sees is whole areas of the spectrum blotted out: thus No. 6 Red held to intercept the light entering the spectroscope will remove all but one end (the red) of the spectrum. No. 16 Blue-Green will do the exact reverse to this, and No. 25 Purple will black out the centre while leaving the ends. Complete removal of areas of the spectrum is characteristic of saturated hues, whereas in the case of desaturated colours or tints the process is analogous to dimming: the whole spectrum is present but some of it not at full intensity. The term colour filter is no misnomer and that coloured light is something *less than* white light now becomes obvious. The same idea must be applied to pigments, whether in man-made paints and dyes or in nature. These, too, act selectively towards light, absorbing some colours and reflecting others.

Beyond the spectrum of visible light there is radiation which is invisible: at the red end, the infra-red wavelengths; at the blue end, the ultra-violet. Both these ranges, though invisible to the human eye, can be photographed; furthermore, the ultra-violet can be used to activate certain substances to produce the longer visible waves, the phenomena of fluorescence. Ultra-violet is not one wavelength but a whole series, and in its shorter wavelengths is extremely dangerous to the eye. Fortunately, these dangerous wavelengths are not required for stage effects and normally are filtered by the glass of the lamp bulb.

Colour Filters

Filters for stage purposes can consist of dyed gelatine, dyed plastic, or coloured glass. Dyed gelatine, although still used extensively in the United States, has not been obtainable in Britain for some time now as the only firm which used to manufacture it in a suitable form for the theatre—John Green —no longer exists. Before this happened, gelatine had virtually been replaced by Cinemoid, a cellulose acetate material which incorporates a self-extinguishing component. What happens is that the material, once alight, generates a gas which promptly puts itself out. Cinemoid was originally made for Strand Electric by British Celanese, but now by Courtaulds Ltd., which simply means that the letter heading and the sign over the works at Spondon have been changed. The process consists in making up a large block of a particular colour and this is sliced into thin sheets of 0·01 in. thick which are then polished. It is, of course, only when the sheets have been cut that the colour becomes apparent; up to that time all that can be seen is dark, nearly black, with only the slightest indication as to colour. This is because light cannot penetrate the block and I mention this because it shows in an extreme form that colour is related to the thickness of the filter material. If the sheet were made thinner, the dye mix would have to be made denser in order to retain the same colour.

This is a matter for the manufacturer, but we can readily use the reverse process and make the sheet thicker in effect merely by putting more than one filter in the beam of light. There is no need for this to be limited to filters of the same colour and the process is considered in detail later on. Suffice it to say that no-one can say he is denied a particular colour, especially as there are more than sixty colours in the Cinemoid range to use as base from which to start to mix. These are added to from time to time for the single sheet is more convenient and is a better economic proposition.

Cinemoid is not the only material of this nature available. There is a British Standard BS 3944 for Colour Filters for Theatre Lighting but this is mainly valuable for its flammability clauses. All it can do beyond this is to specify in detail a few important filters like the primaries and give a schedule of others in current use at the time it was drawn up. The question of how colour may be precisely identified and specified is considered later. Needless to say, it is Cinemoid that I have been associated with over the long period in which we have devised and built up the present range of Strand Electric colours and it was these that formed the basis of the BS specification.

At one time there was more than one series of numbers in Britain so that in asking for a No. 19 one might get a Blue from Strand, a Straw from Digby, or an Orange from GEC.[1] An exact match is impossible between the products of two manufacturers; they naturally do not exchange their formulas in any case. It is difficult enough for one to control his product, but at least both are aiming in the same region.

An important question is the durability of the material mechanically and as to colour. Considerable advances have been made, particularly in what are known as the fade rates. Unfortunately, lamps have tended to punch more light through confined areas and in this way the gains are not as apparent as they otherwise would be. Quite apart from fading there is a tendency of the material to soften under intense heat. Attempts to improve this are bedevilled by the risk of increased flammability and might perhaps require a manufacturing process which could not be adapted to the present comparatively short runs which permit so many colours. Transparent packing material is produced by quantity methods which make our theatre colour filters look like drops of rain in an ocean. At the time of writing a continuous process producing a sheet 0·0075 in. thick has been developed, but as the minimum quantity per colour is 1700 sheets instead of the 400 of the block process obviously this is going to be confined to the commoner colours. The ability to purchase the materials in rolls as well as separate sheets will be useful to those who wish to carry larger stocks.

A far more stable material is represented by coloured glass, but it is not an easy material to use for stage lighting. Speaking for Britain, the colour range available has been very poor; but even in Germany and America, where a much better variety has been available for years, the fact that Cinemoid and even gelatine is so popular tells its own story. Coloured glass is made by introducing small amounts of certain minerals into the mix. The result is then a pot-fused glass which is coloured right through and, in consequence, its thickness will be important. In the second type, a film of coloured glass is flashed on to the surface of a clear glass. The mechanical

[1] We are back where we started! Theatre Projects for example now market the American Roscolene and Roscolor each with their own numbers and there are others.

strength lies in the latter.

The filtering property of glass need not be confined to the visible spectrum; the regions beyond this can be transmitted or impeded by glass filters. To give two examples: ultra-violet which can be transmitted by Wood's glass while at the same time the visible spectrum is not allowed to pass at all; at the infra-red end there are heat-absorbent glass filters such as Chance HA1, which in 2-mm thickness can reduce heat transmission by 86 per cent while still passing 88 per cent visible light.

Glass with its hard crystal-looking surface can deceive. It literally can be a very touchy material. In the case of heat-absorbing filters a finger mark, although invisible, can start a chemical reaction which leads to more and more heat's being trapped with the ultimate result that it shatters. The trouble with passing heat through glass filters is that if the areas are too localized the glass does not expand properly and strain sets in, whereupon it cracks. To obviate this, glass filters can consist of a series of strips in a frame. This allows the centre ones to heat up and expand. They are best used horizontally as, while allowing the necessary movement, their own weight keeps a light-tight joint.

Some glass is known as heat-resisting and one of the ways this functions is by trapping less heat itself. Such glasses are toughened or annealed to perform their function, all of a piece; they cannot be cut. Moulded Fresnel lenses are an example of this kind of thing, but certain coloured glasses are available in the United States moulded as roundels, for example. Although looking somewhat like lenses they have no such properties, being merely colour filters.

Dichroic Reflectors and Filters

When a colour filter is used the energy it intercepts is turned there and then into some heat but the rest is transmitted. This latter will include light of the colour wavelengths required but also a lot more heat in the form of infra-red radiation. However, there are now becoming available what are known as dichroic filters. Glass is coated with an extremely fine chemically stable metallic layer and by using several layers of different refraction a mirror can be formed which reflects only the required wavelengths. The front surface of the mirror is coated, instead of the usual back silvering, and up to 97 per cent of visible light rays are reflected while some 90 per cent of the heat falling on the mirror passes out the back. Much depends on the type of lantern as to how far it will benefit from this kind of mirror. Obviously in the case of a Fresnel spot the principal collector of the energy is the lens, the mirror contributing a relatively small bonus of light. However, the same technique can be applied to the flat back of a lens, i.e. the surface towards the lamp. In this case the coating would be made to reflect heat: the light passing through is relieved of a large part of its normal heat content. Such dichroic lenses or front glasses can be used to go further and transmit only part of the light spectrum. They then become colour filters and already there are on the market in the United States PAR lamps incorporating this type of reflector and colour filter. The colour from these is, however, inconsistent across the beam.

Using dichroic filters the beam of light may in fact feel less hot, but this is important only when very high intensities are concerned; but the heat has still to be disposed of at the lantern. A spotlight pointing down over the stage would have a lens of what the Americans call a "hot mirror" in front of the lamp and a "cold mirror" behind it. The lens would then pass light but reflect heat and the reflector pass heat and reflect light. Heat will therefore come out of the back and light out of the front.

Pigments and Subtractive Mixing

For the rest of the chapter, it is desirable for the reader to have a chart of colour-filter samples beside him for reference. It is not possible to print the colours satisfactorily: in any case, this would not allow the testing of colours superimposed. A rough-and-ready guide as to the performance of a filter is given by looking through it at a white surface to see the colour as itself and at coloured surfaces when one wants to see the effect of light of that colour on these. At this hasty level of appraisal, I would not much bother whether the light was daylight or artificial. For convenience, the colours are scheduled by numbers and names as Appendix 1 in this book.

Just as a colour filter suppresses some colours of the spectrum, so a painted or dyed object may do the same, in this case, by reflecting instead of transmitting. Variation of the angle at which the light strikes the surface of some materials may cause different colours to be reflected and to appear. Most people have their first experience of colour mixing when using pigments in a paint box as a child. There one learns to get green by mixing yellow and blue, and orange from red and yellow. This is not, in fact, a case of adding two colours together but of subtractively mixing them, and the more colours put together the nearer the result approaches black, as a dirty box of paints used to show all too well.

It is important to be clear what is happening when these subtractive primaries were so mixed, for there is another different set of rules for the additive process in light. A yellow pigment reflects yellow and the red and *green* on either side of it, but absorbs the rest of the spectrum. A blue pigment

FIG. 50 Nos. 15 Peacock (Blue-Green), 1 Yellow, and 13 Magenta filters overlapped to mix subtractively

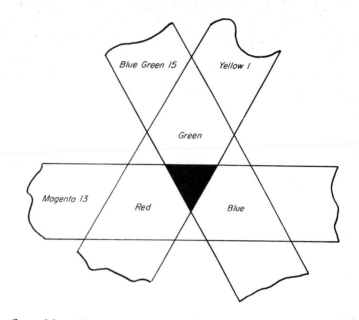

reflects blue, blue-green and *green* while absorbing all the rest. If the two pigments are mixed, only the colour which both had in common, namely the green, can be reflected. In the same way, only the orange common to red and yellow pigments results from a mixture of these two. Exactly the same thing happens when colour filters are added together in the same lantern and a very good demonstration can be made by combining No. 13 Magenta, No. 15 Peacock, and No. 1 Yellow, as in Fig. 50. These strips, when overlapped in this way, can be stuck on a slide glass and put in a projector to be focused on a white screen. At the points of overlap the blue, the green, and the red common to both can be seen. These secondary colours are, in fact, the primary colours of light for additive mixing. In the middle where all three cross, there is a reasonably near approach to black.

This working model represents what happens when two filters or two pigments are put together, but the result is the same if one is a pigment and the other the colour of the light. For example, a No. 1 Yellow spotlight will make a magenta dress appear red or a blue dress appear green. It should be noted that the colour filters used as the subtractive primaries are not, in fact, pure red, blue, and yellow. If the filters were that exact, there would be nowhere for the secondaries to come from. In the same way, the pigment primaries can be taken to be chrome yellow, rose lake, and cyan blue.

A pillar-box appears red by absorbing all colours except the red, which is then diffusely reflected into the eye. It follows from this that the pillar-box must be lit either by white light or red light. A blue-green (No. 16) light, produced by

Colour 93

FIG. 51 Effect of white, red, and blue-green light on red pigment

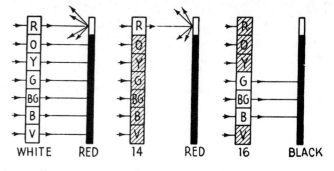

WHITE   RED   14   RED   16   BLACK

removing all spectrum colours except blue-green and its neighbours, will not contain anything that can be reflected by the pillar-box, with the result that it appears black (Fig. 51). Except for trick effects, such as the Samoiloff (see below), we must always ensure that the colours which the dresses or scenery reflect are always present in the light illuminating them. In passing, it must be remarked that the eye cannot see the colour of the pillar-box at very low intensities even if the light is white, as in the case of moon and starlight.

About a quarter of the stage filters are saturated colours which absorb some part of the spectrum more or less completely. The others are the paler colours which merely require a decreased brightness in some parts of the spectrum. No. 36 Lavender (Surprise Pink) reduces the green region slightly, thus stressing any reds and blues it is used on. No. 3 Straw reduces the blue region, thereby giving the light a warmer tone.

Anyone who is particular about his colours, as lighting artists should be, may be far from satisfied with the colours as they come and will combine the filters in one frame. In so doing, the parts of the spectrum not common to both are, as we have just seen, subtracted. Fig. 52 shows diagrammatically how a 26 Mauve passing red and blue may be combined with a 16 Blue-Green passing blue and green, the light resulting being blue. Plotting this mixture it is better to use the minus sign, for example, 26 — 16, as the plus sign belongs to additive mixture (see below).

We can, as with pigments, go on combining colours, but the more we do so the more colours will be subtracted until we obtain black. The joy of these colour combinations is that experiments are easy to do at home without keeping the stage waiting. It is also a chance to express one's tastes in colour; after all, few artists are content to use colour neat as they buy it in tubes. Some suitable mixtures are—

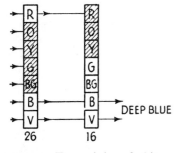

DEEP BLUE

26   16

FIG. 52 Transmission of white light through mauve and blue-green filters

10 Pink — 4 Amber = Sunset (or Flame)
8 Salmon — 2 Amber = Flame
Compare these with Nos. 34 or 35

94   *The Art of Stage Lighting*

19 Blue — 1 Yellow	
16 Blue-Green — 24 Green	Compare these Greens with the Green range taken neat
50 Yellow — 17 Steel	

54 Pink — 17 Steel	Compare these Greys with No. 60
36 Pink — 50 Yellow	

36 Pink — 17 Steel	Compare these with Nos. 36 or 42
36 Pink — 3 Straw	

As a matter of interest, for the Zeffirelli romantic productions of historical operas such as *Tosca* and *Rigoletto* at Covent Garden, William Bundy used 2 — 52 — 3, 3 — 9, 3 — 52, 34 — 7, and 7 — 7. These are responsible for the warm varnish coating of light that these décors seem to thrive on, though it is curious to reflect that in the National Gallery, London, they are busy stripping this varnish off the old masters. In effect, this gets us back to the clear lighting of white, or, at the most, No. 52. I must confess I find rich colour exciting and recommend trial of the colours above if only to keep in reserve for some history play. Costume plays suggest rich antiquity to me, probably illogically, but there is always Tyrone Guthrie's admonition about "elaborate combinations of pale rose pinks, salmon pinks, 'surprise' pinks, gold, pale gold, old gold, greeny-blue, pinky-blue, steel and grey-blue, which is as if the stage were bathed in a weak solution of apricot jam."[1] This colour I have endeavoured to distil as one filter—No. 47—named "apricot" after this reference and providing an instant mix for those who like that kind of thing!

Broken Colour

It is important to realize that the amount of light is reduced by the subtractive method. It is, however, possible to do a kind of additive mixture from the one spotlight, even to combine the additive and subtractive process at one and the same time. This process I call broken colour. This technique consists of placing two or more filters behind each other in such a way that the colour can be seen separately and combined. A circle can be removed from the centre of one filter or triangular filters combined. Some of these are shown in Fig. 53, a sheet of No. 2 with cut triangles of Nos. 4 and 10 imposed and placed in front of a Profile spot give a broken beam of four colours. The broken colour operates as subtractive mixing where the filters are on top of each other but also additively because the light from each part of a lens is concerned with every part of the resulting projected patch of light. Thus, if the top half of a lens is covered with No. 6 Red and the bottom with No. 19 Blue, then the projected patch of light will be

[1] *A Life in the Theatre,* by Tyrone Guthrie (Hamish Hamilton), page 60.

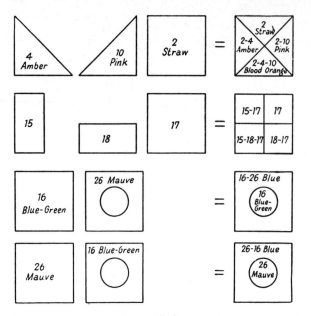

FIG. 53   Broken colour: partial combination of filters for tinting

mauve since every part of it will be receiving red and blue. This will be quite different from the deep violet of the two when completely superimposed.

This behaviour of a lens was described in Chapter 4 and shown in Fig. 27. For the law to work reasonably accurately, the lens must be near enough in focus and, in consequence, it applies to optical projectors and Profile spots. In the case of focus lamps and Fresnel spots, this hardly ever applies as these are mainly used a long way out of focus. This separates the lens paths and only partial adding together takes place, and the patch of light would show the colours more or less purely towards the edges. Either effect takes away from the flatness of the coloured light patches when only a few sources are used. Mixture need not concern colours only but rather dilution of a colour by introducing some white. Thus, the filter could cover two-thirds of the lens only or have a hole cut out of its centre. As the centre of a filter is what fades first, this suggests that colours made up of a stronger hue than one requires and which are diluted by a large hole in the centre might be more lasting. Care must be taken that any filters which are deprived of their mechanical strength by being cut are not allowed to come into contact with the hot lens.

Additive Mixing

Whatever may have been the side effect of the broken colour process just described, true additive mixing requires separate colour sources which are superimposed on each other. If a Red (No. 6) circle of light and a Green (No. 39) circle of light from another spotlight are allowed to overlap, the result is found to be yellow. If the colours are Red (No. 6) and Blue-Green (No. 16), the result is white. From these results it is quite obvious that the laws of subtractive or pigment mixing do not apply; indeed, it would be strange if they did, since we are doing what involves the exact opposite to that process. After all, take the seven principal colours of the spectrum as pigments, mix them together, and the result is black. Do the same thing with seven separate coloured lights and the result is white.

Experiment in mixing coloured light shows that there are three colours which cannot themselves be produced by mixing, and these are Red, Green and Deep Blue. Mixing these three in varying proportions, a match can be obtained for any other colour in the spectrum and, what is more, colours such as mauve and magenta, which are outside it, as follows—

Red and Green = Orange, Yellow, Light Green.
Green and Blue = Pale Green, Blue-Green, Light Blue.
Blue and Red = Purple, Magenta, Deep Red.

This can be checked in a simple experiment that must be carried out for oneself. Three Profile spots are set up and hard-focused so that their beams are superimposed as in Fig. 54. Each spot carries a single filter, No. 6 Red, No. 39 Green, and No. 19 Dark Blue respectively. An even better result is given if the wattage of the Blue spot is doubled (tungsten light being deficient in blue) and No. 20 Deep Blue used. Provided the spots give a good even field where the red and green mix there is yellow; the green and blue give blue-green; and the blue and red make magenta. In the centre, all three come together as white.

The red, green, and blue are the primaries of light, and the yellow, blue-green, and magenta are the secondaries. These secondary colours match, near enough for a rough experiment like this, the strips of filter used in Fig. 50 as primaries for the

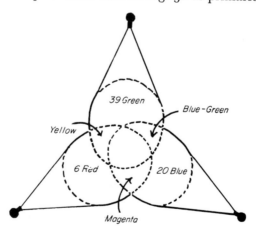

FIG. 54 Profile spotlight beams of Nos. 39 Green, 20 Blue, and 6 Red overlapped to mix additively

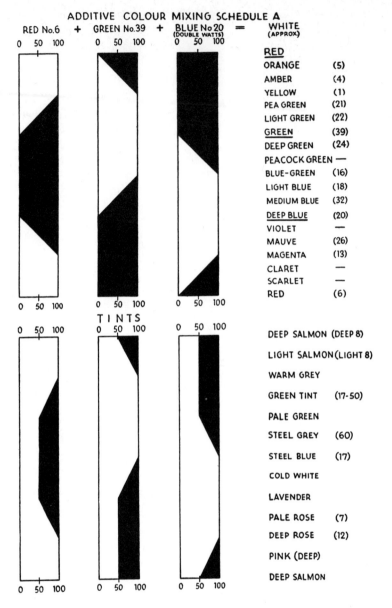

FIG. 55 Additive colour-mixing chart using red, green, and blue with nearest Cinemoid equivalents in brackets

ADDITIVE COLOUR MIXING SCHEDULE A

RED No.6 + GREEN No.39 + BLUE No 20 (DOUBLE WATTS) = WHITE (APPROX)

RED	
ORANGE	(5)
AMBER	(4)
YELLOW	(1)
PEA GREEN	(21)
LIGHT GREEN	(22)
GREEN	(39)
DEEP GREEN	(24)
PEACOCK GREEN	—
BLUE-GREEN	(16)
LIGHT BLUE	(18)
MEDIUM BLUE	(32)
DEEP BLUE	(20)
VIOLET	—
MAUVE	(26)
MAGENTA	(13)
CLARET	—
SCARLET	—
RED	(6)

TINTS

DEEP SALMON	(DEEP 8)
LIGHT SALMON	(LIGHT 8)
WARM GREY	
GREEN TINT	(17-50)
PALE GREEN	
STEEL GREY	(60)
STEEL BLUE	(17)
COLD WHITE	
LAVENDER	
PALE ROSE	(7)
DEEP ROSE	(12)
PINK	(DEEP)
DEEP SALMON	

subtractive mixing experiment. Thus, the primaries of light are the secondaries for pigment mixing, but as there is no colour without light in the first place it is obvious that when the word primary is used unqualified then it must be taken to refer to light.

The experiment with the three spotlights can now be taken a step further by introducing a dimmer into the feed to each and by overlapping all three patches of light completely. Using the spots two at a time with the dimmers in the proportions shown in the chart (Fig. 55), a whole series of colours can be produced. When tints are required, no spot is completely extinguished, as shown in the lower half of the chart. There are thus strong two-colour mixtures or the paler three-colour mixtures to be obtained. Quite how pale these latter are will depend on the level of the third colour. The formula just given is crude and in practice the dimmers can be used with finesse and extremely subtle mixtures produced.

A degree of no-enthusiasm must be introduced at this point. There are two serious drawbacks, namely registration problems and poor efficiency. If an object is introduced between the spots and the screen, the pool of, say, pink light will reveal itself for the composite it is by the vivid multi-coloured shadows thrown. The farther the spots can be taken away and the closer they are mounted together the less this effect will be, but it will remain as colour fringing. If the three colours are used in multiple-source flooding equipment, like battens, this effect vanishes. There still remains poor efficiency however. To produce white with a mixture of all three colours is to produce it in a most wasteful way. A single white lamp will do the job better because the filters in the three primary colour compartments are saturated hues which must therefore absorb the larger part of the output of the lamp. Even if the filters were 100 per cent efficient, they would each have stopped two-thirds of the light of the lamp from passing. Then again, for the sake of an imagined need for many colours, we must have a red, a green, and a dark blue. How often, if ever, in theatre are the first two going to be needed? Even with the most expressionist lighting, the answer will be seldom. It behoves us, therefore, to use the primary effect or the rather less wasteful one in Fig. 56 only when we must have a wide range of colour instantly available from dimmers, and use the simpler arrangements that will be far more appropriate for most purposes.

Consider a sky or cyclorama, for example, as the most likely place for a display of colour; yet in most cases a much more useful variety could be obtained from three different kinds of blue—for example, 40, 32, and 20—or even only two, say 18 and 19, which could be used separately or together. There would be far more punch. On the odd occasion when the blush of dawn or sunset was required, an extra flood or two could be added with the colour required or a projection of some kind could be used. These remarks apply equally to flooding battens over the stage, where used, but of course with less emphasis on blues. Where two-colour battens or footlights are concerned, there is a lot to be said for just white and No. 18 Blue. The white can be used on its own and turned warmer by dimming slightly or turned brighter by adding the blue to improve the apparent colour temperature. Mixtures

FIG. 56 Additive colour-mixing chart using orange, blue-
green (cyan), and blue

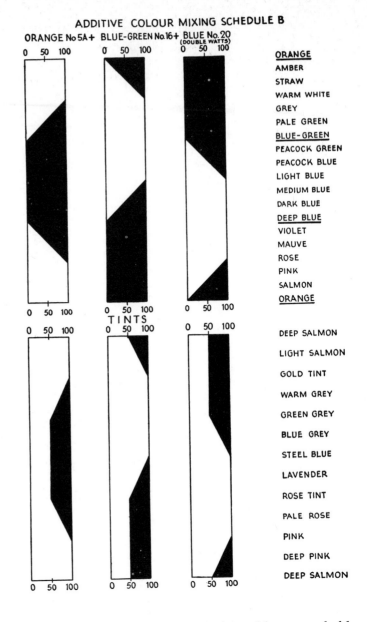

ADDITIVE COLOUR MIXING SCHEDULE B

ORANGE No 5A + BLUE-GREEN No.16 + BLUE No. 20
(DOUBLE WATTS)

ORANGE
AMBER
STRAW
WARM WHITE
GREY
PALE GREEN
BLUE-GREEN
PEACOCK GREEN
PEACOCK BLUE
LIGHT BLUE
MEDIUM BLUE
DARK BLUE
DEEP BLUE
VIOLET
MAUVE
ROSE
PINK
SALMON
ORANGE

TINTS

DEEP SALMON
LIGHT SALMON
GOLD TINT
WARM GREY
GREEN GREY
BLUE GREY
STEEL BLUE
LAVENDER
ROSE TINT
PALE ROSE
PINK
DEEP PINK
DEEP SALMON

of blue with more or less white can give cold greys, pale blues,
and a lot of useful intermediates. If a somewhat more colourful
two-colour combination to mix is needed, then No. 34 Golden
Amber and No. 41 Bright Blue is to be highly commended.
This combination, which I first came across in *South Pacific* at
Drury Lane, should get NODA out of a lot of their troubles in
colouring up their musicals.

Most battens as installed are 3- or 4-colour circuit, but I
would like to see future installations wired for only two, and
existing 4-colour installations could be coloured up for two in

order to get some punch out of the colour. Three- or four-colour battens have often gone in simply to keep the wattage of the individual dimmers down, but there should be less need to insist on this with thyristor dimmers now available.

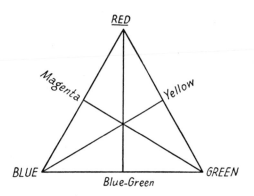

FIG. 57 Colour triangle: additive primaries at apexes

Complementary Colours

If equal amounts of any two colours of light opposite to each other on the triangle (Fig. 57) are added together, the result is white. Any such pairs of colours—red and blue-green, yellow and blue, green and magenta—are known as complementary. Further reflection will indicate that if one of the colours of a pair is a pigment then the result is black, as is also the case if both are pigments. Any pair of complementary colours can be used, but it must be remembered that except in a few instances the stage filters are somewhat impure;[1] No. 1 Yellow actually passes a little blue so it cannot be expected to behave according to the book. The colours that are reasonably pure are: No. 14 Red, No. 6 Red, No. 39 Green, No. 16 Blue-Green, No. 20 Blue, No. 26 Mauve. I can, of course, only vouch for the Strand Electric colours. Anyone who wants to go at all deeply into colour experiments, for their own sake as apart from stage applications, is advised to use the more expensive but accurate Wratten photographic filters.

A warning on sensation matches: the eye can easily be tricked. A No. 19 Blue can be made to look like a No. 20 by adding a little red; a No. 6 Red can be matched to a No. 14 Ruby by adding a little blue; both will pass muster until the blue is used to turn red pigment black, or red to turn blue pigment into black. The slight addition of red in the first instance and blue in the second will entirely upset the result.

An extreme example of the perils of sensation matching when used to light pigments is given by sodium lighting. Most people have seen the sodium discharge lighting used on some streets; it is a lamp which emits its light in a narrow yellow spectrum

[1] Paints are even impurer in this sense; sharp cut-offs are rare.

line. This means only yellow objects will reflect under it: the rest appear grey and black. The pillar-box, referred to earlier, appears very curious indeed. Now, suppose for some peculiar reason we have to imitate this light on the stage. By mixing red and green a perfect sensation match is obtained, but as soon as this light is thrown on to coloured objects not only the yellows will appear but the reds and greens. As a matter of fact, our stage yellow filter will not be much help either, since it passes red and fair amount of green, in addition to the yellow.[1]

Perception and Recognition of Colour

The perception of colour depends very much on the presence of other colours or more particularly white. A stage lit evenly all over in red soon loses its redness and is interpreted as a kind of fatiguing pink. The same red seen as a small contrasting patch on a blue stage will seem to be an entirely different colour. Colour that is to appear rich or vivid must be confined to small patches and highlights. It can be useful on occasion to ignore this rule; there can be instances in moonlight effects or the Samoiloff complementary colour stunts when a lack of colour contrast is essential.

Some musicians claim a sense of constant pitch, but the majority require a tuning fork or some other ready-made note to begin. A patch of white light is our tuning fork, but there are whites and whites! Is the patch caused by daylight, by an arc, a tungsten-filament, or what? Without a white patch at all the brain flounders and can be wildly astray as to what the eye is signalling to it. There seems to be no equivalent to the sense of constant pitch at all. For some years now I have demonstrated this by projecting twenty-four patches of light side by side on a screen. These are introduced as three series of eight and the way colours can change before the audience's very eyes, simply because different contrasts are displayed, is both intriguing and disturbing. Blue-green can be made to look like blue or green and No. 21 Green can appear to be a yellow, to quote but two examples.

This failure to recognize a colour except under very precise conditions—conditions which are seldom met with in the theatre—makes one wonder why we feel the need, as we undoubtedly do, to choose a particular colour filter or pigment so carefully: because when shown on the stage the identification conditions will have changed even for us who chose it and the audience will not know anyway. Show an expert a single blue in isolation in the dark and he is unlikely to get it right: Nos.

---

[1] A much improved sodium street lamp has become familiar in recent years. It has a spectrum from the red to the green and its golden light is far more acceptable.

40, 18, or 32 could be mistaken for one another. By suitable choice of a second colour, the appraiser goes completely out of orbit. In fact, of course, one goes equally adrift when trying to judge brightness levels of white light. It is useless to speculate further in these pages but I mention and demonstrate these matters lest we all get too cocksure.

A Theory of Colour Vision

Deceptions like presenting red and green to the eye for yellow (two very different wavelengths offered as a third), and getting away with it, lead to much speculation on the nature of colour vision. In sound, no two notes can be found in the octave, the simultaneous sounding of which the ear will accept for a third note. There have been many theories to explain colour vision of more or less complexity. As none of the theories really ties up with any physiological findings we may as well choose one of long standing that is simple and accounts for most of the day-to-day phenomena we are likely to encounter.

The Young–Helmholtz colour theory supposes that there are three sets of colour-sensitive equipment (nerves, if you like) associated with the eye. The first is sensitive to the wavelengths in the red region of the spectrum; the second is sensitive to the green region; and the third to the blue. None of these is exactly sensitive to its own region only but tends to overlap, reacting more and more weakly as the wavelengths get into the domain of its neighbour. Thus, a yellow light stimulates the red and green nerves to some extent, sending a message to the brain the same as if red and green light had been employed. Yellow and its complement blue stimulate all three sets, giving white.

The theory also accounts for colour fatigue, a striking demonstration of which can be given on a cyclorama. Put the red and green dimmers to full: the result is yellow. Do this again, but giving the eye a minute of red; the result is a light green. This different colour for an identical mixture suggests that one colour-registering apparatus of the eye or brain gets tired by use, whereas the other two come fresh to the job—probably not tired in a physical sense but rather in the way that a full-up stage seems bright after a half-checked stage but soon loses some of its initial effect on the eye. Colour fatigue suggests a way in which the colour of a stage may be emphasized or not—a blue footlight on the act drop if a very red-appearing stage is required to follow, a red footlight if the red when it is revealed, as for the Samoiloff trick, is not to draw much attention to itself.

Accurate Colour Definition

If there is uncertainty about our powers of colour recognition, there is even more disconcerting vagueness in colour nomenclature: how can there be certainty that the other person's idea of what is meant by a particular colour name is the same? Painters have their own set of names, textile workers theirs, and so on. What is sky blue? Several attempts have been made to ensure certainty that our version of it can be repeated at the other side of the world if need be.

The most obvious way is to provide a chart of numbered samples as, for example, the Strand Cinemoid filter chart, the Leichner numbers for grease paints, or the BSI Colour Chart for paints. A fine example of this kind of thing is the British Colour Council Dictionary of Colours for Interior Decoration, consisting of 220 coloured ribbons of pure silk presenting both a glossy surface and a matt surface. The folding chart with the ribbons is accompanied by a volume of nearly 600 alternative names; thus, Cherry could be looked up and established as ribbon No. BCC 185, Poppy as BCC 97, or Union Jack Red as BCC 210. The ribbons were mainly aimed at textiles and clothing and in 1949 another work was produced with 378 colours shown as three surfaces—matt, gloss and pile fabric—intended for the interior decoration industry. This occupies two fat volumes with a third slim one for the Colour Names and their history. It has been said that the British Colour Council Dictionary is somewhat haphazard, but I must say it appeals to me and anyway, being in no small part responsible for the completely arbitrary range of Cinemoid filters, I should be the last to complain. I shall content myself that among those who like some mathematical logic in their colour work the names of Ridgway, Munsell, Ostwald, and Wilson are highly revered.

Pleasing, useful, and convenient is the *Methuen Handbook of Colour*, which is a compact book and slips conveniently into the pocket. It is both a handbook on colour and a dictionary, the 1266 samples being reproduced by colour printing on art paper. The authors, A. Kornerup and J. H. Wauscher, are Danish and their book gives us opportunity to see how well the eye detects the most subtle changes in colour provided circumstances are right and there is opportunity to set them both against a standard white and to compare one with the other. BS 4800 is a much less ambitious affair which reproduces a series of standard paint samples for building and decoration.

Another method is to use some kind of matching instrument to enable any colour to be described. An early system, still in general use, was invented by Joseph Lovibond for matching the colour of samples of beer. This instrument, known as the Tintometer, employs the subtractive primaries in glass slides or wedges of varying density. The sample to be matched is viewed side by side with the standard glass slides through an eyepiece; a combination of glass slides is adjusted until a match is obtained, and the result can be read off as something like this: Turquoise Blue BCC No. 118 = Y 2·2, B 4·7, Brightness 1·5; or Cardinal BCC No. 186 = R 28, Y 3. There are other instruments—some of which employ purely electrical matching methods. For example, three photometers each fitted with a primary filter so it responds to only part of the spectrum will describe colours as three figures which vary according to the proportions transmitted. These can be plotted in terms of what is known as the CIE chromaticity diagram to show hue and saturation.

By now, readers with memories of an early section of this chapter may be somewhat uneasy. If the eye cannot tell the difference between a mixture of red plus green and yellow alone, any system of colour identification based on matching must surely be more than somewhat unreliable. This is perfectly true, but it is not quite so important for paints and textiles receiving light as for filters transmitting light. Of course, if the Samoiloff effect is being carried out, it is just as important that the costume red dye shall reflect red only as it is that the red filter shall only transmit it.

To specify colour filters an optical instrument known as a spectrophotometer is used. This can provide an accurate record of exactly what wavelengths and how much of each is transmitted. Roughly, the light transmitted is split up into the spectrum, many narrow vertical sections selected, and each compared for intensity side by side with the same section of the spectrum of the unfiltered light source. The comparison can be visual or electrical, and the narrower the width of the sections the more there will be, the more ratio figures obtained, and the greater the accuracy. The result can be accurately plotted, as shown in Fig. 58, and is then known as a spectrophotometric absorption curve. Along the horizontal axis are the wavelengths from 700 to 400 millimicrons; a millimicron is represented as mμ and is 0·000001 millimetre. Sometimes the wavelengths are given in microns (μ) or Angstrom units (Å); the only difference in dealing with the visible spectrum is the number of noughts. However, "they" have just insisted that the familiar millimicron be known as a nanometre (nm).

The position of the principal colour bands of the spectrum is also indicated along the horizontal axis. The exact boundaries between the principal colour bands where, for instance, the red is no longer red and must be described as orange, is difficult to determine exactly. It all depends on what is meant by orange. Likewise, the blue-green band is apt to be ignored, the blue and green bands being by that much enlarged. This

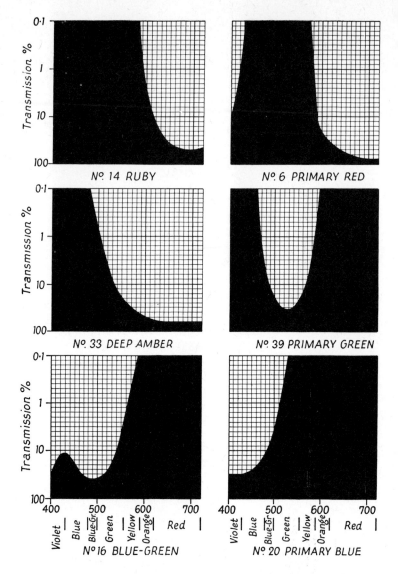

is a pity since blue-green is the complement of red, and it is important to counter the effect of the unfortunate compound name which suggests a mixture and not a spectrum colour band in its own right. The vertical axis gives density of the wedge or transmission percentage. Thus, a perfectly clear filter would merely show a narrow black line along the horizontal axis, the black line representing the slight absorption that results from transmission through even a good transparent medium. The curves of Fig. 58 are easy to understand once it is firmly fixed in the mind that the vertical axis is plotted logarithmically: observe carefully where 50 per cent transmission comes. It will be noticed that a blue filter, such as No. 20, not only absorbs all the red, orange, yellow, and

FIG. 59 Transmission curves
for tints

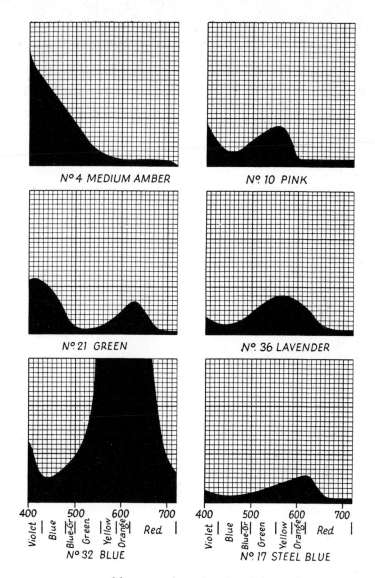

green, as one would expect, but also that it is not by any means
a perfect transmitter of its dominant hue, blue.

It is interesting to compare the curves of the saturated hues
in Fig. 58 with the tints in Fig. 59; the former blot out sections
of the spectrum, whereas the latter act in a more subtle way.
It is easy to see why Nos. 17 and 36, in spite of the fact that
they are very pale, do give such different results.

Colour Efficiency

The production of colour in a stage lantern is hardly efficient:
only 8 per cent of the electric energy becomes light, and of this
14 per cent or so is transmitted by the red filter, 12 per cent by
the green, and 1·5 per cent or 2 per cent by the blue. However,

the red letter-box behaves just as inefficiently in respect of the sunlight which makes it look red, but if the colour obtained gives satisfaction there is no need to worry.

Far more efficient methods of producing coloured light are available in discharge lamps where, first, a great percentage of electrical energy is converted to light and, secondly, the light may be coloured at source or converted to colour by fluorescent powders coated on the lamp. One difficulty is the fact that discharge lamps do not emit their light as a continuous spectrum but in a number of well-defined lines, four principal ones in the case of mercury vapour, and one in the case of sodium.[1] The sodium is a good example of the peril of rating efficiency too high in our present field of use. It is, as explained in Chapter 5, probably the most efficient lamp manufactured, but few derive any pleasure from its monochromatic light.

Effect of Light on Scenery and Costume

The appearance of any pigment to the eye is influenced by the nature of the pigmented material. Thus, a glossy or varnished plane surface will show its true colour only when viewed from the direction of the light illuminating it. At some angles the conditions of specular reflection may apply to a greater or lesser degree and prevent the reflection of any colour except that of the spotlight beam itself. On the other hand, a matt surface will diffuse both light and colour alike. Conditions are usually far more complicated and a set of art silk drapes will behave differently round the folds, and perhaps the visual result will be further influenced by deep shadows in the folds. This uneven reflection is what gives life to the material.

Art silk stretched tight, as a cyclorama, would be impossible to light from a batten in the normal overhead position. From the stalls, a series of blobs of light, the direct reflection of the batten compartments, would be seen; whereas in the circle there would be very little reflected light of any kind and the material would appear drab and unexciting. A bolton twill with a matt surface will be far more satisfactory. If the curtain hangs in folds, these defects are remedied to some extent but the light will still show a reluctance to get down or up the curtain. To obtain even distribution and the life and sparkle absent from the casement cloth, the art silk has to be crushed. A plain matt material can be made to glitter by lighting in different colours from different directions, particularly if the material is translucent and can be lit front and back.

Material can be interesting when it is selective to light —reflecting light from one direction, absorbing that from another. Velvets and velours are best in this respect, their

[1] Two lines close together in fact.

deep pile being very sensitive to direction. Lit along the pile, even black velvet can be made to reflect; light thrown up the pile is completely absorbed. Thus, a curtain which can easily be seen under the light of a batten will become jet black under the footlights. This property makes velvets very useful as a background where it is desired to throw the actors into relief, since the spill of lighting thrown on them may make little impression where it strikes the curtains. In general, materials used for costumes are less critical in behaviour because they are of necessity broken up and no flat surfaces of any size presented.

Effect of Light on Make-up

Stage grease paints and make-up do, of course, behave as ordinary pigments under lighting, and the fact that the heavier coloured light will spoil the make-up is well recognized. The use of make-up to give the face form and colour can be nullified if the stage illuminant is different from that in the dressing-room, and unless care is taken to see that the lighting helps the make-up. The debt of lighting to make-up is just as great, for no matter how much a face may be lit, it cannot be "seen" unless the eye can pick out broad indications which at a distance it interprets as detail. I think it far from true that modern stage lighting requires little make-up. The high intensities and multi-sources used in some professional theatres bleach out everything. Thus, even if one was appearing exactly as oneself, except in the most intimate of theatres, make-up would be necessary to stress facial shape and colouring. No question of character playing arises: it is purely a matter of being seen. We are right back to our painted scenery in which a painted shadow is likely to be less troublesome than a true solid. Actors with fair hair and eyebrows can appear as shapeless ovals devoid of expression, and the more light piled on, the less visible they become. Age can bring its compensations here at least; the face is more formed. The young face is a bland mask on which something is going to be carved as the years pass and you may have to anticipate this as subtly as you can. Unfortunately, painting the face is a job for an artist and the inexpert may swing to the other extreme and plaster the stuff on. What is required is emphasis, by the familiar technique of contrast, of what is there. Close study of one's own features can come as just as much of a shock as hearing one's recorded voice the first time. It is not so much a question of how do you look as how does your face work for you when conveying an idea. There are several books on this subject; one that commends itself as concise is by Richard Blore, of Leichner's, and at its modest price it is within reach of all.

Of course, this present book is aimed at producers and

lighting men, not at actors and actresses, but it is as well to remember that one's concern for a good picture must include the examination of faces. There is so much else to catch the eye on the stage, and indeed the costumes themselves can be great offenders in this respect; thus one can think the job is done and all is well. Closer examination shows that faces are not getting over their message and it could be that the make-up is at fault. What we are then looking for is not the inept, that proclaims itself well enough, but the inexpressive and that will take more finding.

While on the subject of the not so obvious, as said earlier everyone knows that make-up will misbehave under strongly coloured light; what is not so well known is that some tints can be tricky. For example, a colour such as No. 36 will only just be detectable in the beam of light but will bring into prominence reds and blues in a way that may throw the whole make-up out of balance. Vigilance should not be relaxed because the lighting man says he uses the palest colours only.

In certain large theatres a strange situation arises out of the use of high-intensity following arcs, the light of which is so white as to be almost steel blue; in consequence, the players if they are not to look like corpses, must use a heavy warm, almost red, make-up. Now the gain in the illumination from this form of arc is at the end of the spectrum least kind to the red so that the very thing the lantern was put in to light— the face—receives least benefit from the increased intensity. Of course, there is a super-beam, which cleaves the darkness of the auditorium, and also a clear-cut circle of light on the stage, so everyone, from artiste to audience, is satisfied—but for the wrong reason. They merely think they see or are seen better.

Fluorescence

Colours in this chapter have so far been obtained by filtering out the unwanted colour wavelengths or by presenting two wavelengths to create in the eye a sensation of a third colour —the wavelength of which is not present. In the phenomena of fluorescence there is a method of changing the light of one wavelength into another longer wavelength. This effect is usually taken to concern the conversion of invisible ultra-violet rays into visible light, but it is equally applicable to the conversion of, say, blue light into orange colour (Fig. 60). Certain substances will fluoresce in varying colours when lit by the near ultra-violet (UV) rays immediately beyond the visible spectrum; others when lit by the dangerous very short ultra-violet rays beyond that. These latter rays can be stopped by a sheet of clear glass and, as they are dangerous, glass must

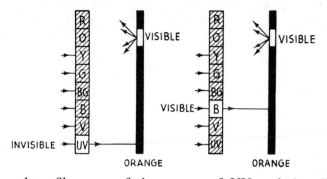

FIG. 60 Fluorescence: ultra-violet or blue filters used to produce a different colour of a longer wavelength

be used to filter any of the sources of UV and the effects confined to those produced by the near ultra-violet. Sources of this light have been dealt with in Chapter 5.

Fluorescent chemicals are usually supplied in solution as paints, dyes, and make-up for stage purposes. Quite a number of colours are available, all of which appear of great depth and intensity under the UV. The two in commonest use are, probably, the Invisible Green and the Invisible Blue. Both these colours have great beauty under the UV although invisible under white light; they are applied as a colourless liquid. Some of the other colours are visible under white light but gain in depth under UV or are transformed from a garish horror into something sublime. Some colours have a slight afterglow when the activating light is extinguished.

Fluorescence is not limited to the special paints and dyes; the teeth (real, not artificial), the skin, and the eyeball also fluoresce. This effect in the latter is what gives the somewhat hazy feeling when under ultra-violet light. However, provided the glass bulb is intact, there is no danger. Since the intro-duction of the "whiter than white" detergents, the commonest example of fluorescence is everything which is washed or laundered in this way. The extent to which these chemicals are retained depends on the material; a few artificial ones are not very good at it, but cottons and linens become vivid indeed. This sets a problem when using ultra-violet for trick effects, for these are bound to depend on being able to choose what shall and what shall not fluoresce.

Another aspect of fluorescence is the efficient and durable production of colour in lamps, and this was dealt with in Chapter 5.

7 Electricity, Dimmers and Distribution

An electric circuit always consists of a complete loop which includes not only the load but also the battery or generator forming the source of the supply. Limitation of the amount of current flowing is governed by the resistance afforded by the various components in the loop. Generally speaking, the electricity supply mains have a negligible resistance compared with that of the wiring added to complete the loop at the consumer's end. If, then, that part consists of a copper wire joining the incoming and outgoing supply, the condition known as a short-circuit occurs. The current continues to rise to the limit of the capacity of the connecting wire which by that time would be red-hot and ultimately melt. The melting would interrupt the loop but a fire might have occurred before this. Worse still, a state of equilibrium might be reached in which the wire became very hot but stayed that way for a considerable time, thereby destroying the insulation of rubber or plastic which covers the wire.

Fusing

The solution is to ensure that there is a link weaker than all the rest of the wiring somewhere in each circuit loop. This, the fuse, will then melt and cut the supply before any danger point is reached. The size of the fuse has to be related to all the wiring it feeds. It is no good having a fat fuse feeding a fat wire if somewhere completing the loop is a miserable thin piece of flex. I apologize for dwelling on what to many readers will seem obvious, but there is something about the excitement of putting on a show which encourages risks. More and more load is put on, backed up by larger and larger fuses, until something has to go, and this may be the supply company's fuse which we cannot get at and which, therefore, cannot be replaced in a hurry. This is no imaginary peril. Before the new 1964 installation at the Royal Opera House, Covent Garden, Zeffirelli's production of *Cavalleria Rusticana*—not once but several times—brought out one of the three supply fuses, thereby blacking out the cyclorama in full view of the audience towards the end of the great dawn sequence!

Another trouble about electricity is that it gives no warning of its dangers. It is a quiet, unseen, obedient servant who at any time, given the chance, will round on his employer and may even slay him. Shock is the *mot juste*. Two rules obviously arise: there must be a first-class permanent installation maintained in good order and, secondly, extensions to it must be kept to a minimum. In the theatre, these extensions are the vital arteries of stage lighting, for they are the flexes which feed the portable and movable equipment. Often they are temporary—for tonight only—and then are forgotten and so become permanent. Like as not, the connections have been carried out by some self-styled "electrician" whose only training ground was his own home. Competent electrical supervision is essential and in a theatre of any size this is a job for at least one man, who must not be diverted to the actual process of lighting or to the pressing needs of blocked drains.

Fortunately, there is a simple test of the standard of electrical work in any theatre. Take hold of a few flexes and examine how they enter the plugs. Does the protective outer sheath of the cable run into and become properly captured by the plug grip, or does it fall short and leave three or, worse still, only two separate wires to find their way in? Anything may follow from the latter carelessness and the actual connections inside the plug must be checked here and at the lantern.

An electric circuit can be considered as an incoming brown[1] live wire which must include the fuse and switch. From this the brown wire proceeds to the load, in this case a lamp, via the live socket and pin (marked *L*) of a plug connector. Most stage lighting lamps use special caps and holders with a centre contact for the live entry, the return from the filament being via the outer shell. Beyond the load the wire becomes the return wire and will be known as the neutral, but its colour, blue, is the important identification.

No interruption in this wire except at the pin and socket (marked *N*) of the plug is permitted.[2] It continues as a blue wire to the fuse box where it is linked, without fuse, to the mains return. The feed and return travel together as a pair and it is important that they are never separated when passing through a metal surround. For example, they must be paired in the same metal conduit or trunking.

Earthing

Both wires are equally insulated but only the live feed is at

---

[1] These wire colours are to the new European standard obligatory from July 1, 1970. Former British Standard was red live, black neutral and green earth.

[2] Regulations for the Electrical Equipment of Buildings, published by the Institution of Electrical Engineers.

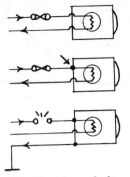

FIG. 61 Earthing: fault at arrow renders lantern body live but does not blow fuse unless it is earthed as in bottom diagram

high potential in respect of earth. Hence the need to make sure this is the only connection broken by switch or fuse, otherwise the lamp might be extinguished, yet remain dangerous. There is, in addition, a third wire—the earth wire—which is green and yellow stripes and has to be connected to the large pin and socket on the plug.

The return (neutral) side of the mains supply is physically connected to earth by the supply authority on their side, but on the user's side it must be kept insulated therefrom. The presence of only one really live wire greatly simplifies switching or fusing, but we must guard against its accidental return to earth, particularly through the human body! In the diagram (Fig. 61 *centre*), the insulation of the live wire has developed a fault through wear or sheer carelessness and the metal lantern housing is live. A man directing it from a metal ladder could provide a path to earth across his body. Depending on the resistance of the path to earth, the effect of this might range the whole way from a scarcely felt shock to a fatal one. The extremes are represented by dry hard wood flooring on the one hand, and damp concrete on the other. The remedy is to make sure of a more direct path for fault current and this the earth wire does. The pin on the plug is larger than the others to ensure that it makes contact first. In the bottom diagram (Fig. 61), the result of this precaution is seen as a blown fuse. Incidentally, never correct a persistently blowing fuse by removing the earth wire, however temporarily.

The precaution of earthing introduces a hazard where not completely carried out right through the installation, for properly earthed lanterns are providing an equivalent of the damp concrete floor. A lantern not earthed may be alongside one that is, and the fault of the former may pass through the body of anyone who directly or indirectly is touching the two. A situation must either be "earth free" or properly earthed throughout, and authority insists on the latter for stages. You have no choice, and at the same time a responsibility.

The Circuit

The functioning of an electric circuit follows in some detail to explain what may be done and to lead to an understanding of how dimmers work and why the various types differ in what they can do.

Returning to the circuit with the lamp: if the mains potential is 200 volts and the lamp is marked as 1000 watts, then the current which flows is 5 amps; this result being obtained by dividing the watts by the volts. A 200-watt lamp takes one amp therefore, and five of these connected in parallel (Fig. 62) gets us back to the original 5 amps. The current in the circuit is determined by the resistance of the lamp, which

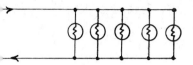

FIG. 62   Five lamps in parallel

is 40 ohms[1] both in the case of the single large lamp and the combined total of the five small lamps. In fact, each of these latter has a resistance of 200 ohms but the effect of paralleling these is to divide this figure by the number of lamps: i.e. $200/5 = 40$. Virtually all theatre lamps are fed in parallel. Just occasionally, as in Christmas tree lamps, they are wired in series, the mains supply to each passing through the remainder (Fig. 63). Twenty lamps of 2 ohms in series adds up to 40 ohms, i.e. 2×20, a total of 1000 watts, although each lamp would be rated only as 10 volt 50 watt and take 5 amps. Note, however, that when the whole lot is connected in series to operate on the 200-volt mains the fact that the resistance of the total circuit increases relative to each single lamp means the total current is still only 5 amps. If the use of lamps in series is rare in the theatre, the use of other forms of resistance in series with lamps is not, for this is what the simplest dimmers really are.

The relation of volts to resistance and current is given by Ohms law, which is stated in the textbooks as $I = E/R$, where I = current in Amps, E = Electromotive force in Volts, and R = Resistance in Ohms. The usual mathematical substitution can enable any one missing item to be obtained. This can be memorized as Amps = Volts divided by Ohms. That the rate of electrical flow is the result of dividing the pressure by the resistance of the circuit to it need cause no surprises; it seems common sense. So also pressure (Volts) multiplied by rate of flow (Amps) seems inevitably to produce the amount of energy (Watts) at any instant in time. Continuing to measure this for an hour produces the watt-hour, such a small amount that it is better to count a thousand of them at a time and the result is kilowatt hour (kWh) which records on the meter as a Board of Trade Unit, and is what has to be paid for. Watts represent energy and it is rather sobering to be told that 746 of them are equivalent to a horse-power. Large lighting loads are described very well on the whole in kilowatts (properly abbreviated kW, but there is a tendency to reduce this in conversation to "K," for example "a 2 K or a 5 K lamp").

In measuring insulation resistance a much higher multiple is necessary. Measurement is in Megohms ($M\Omega$), referred to as "Megs," a unit equivalent to a million ohms. This resistance can be checked by disconnecting the supply completely and substituting a test voltage of 500 (twice the actual mains) from a small portable hand generator with a dial integral to it. The permanent wiring is checked for a leak between the feed and return joined together with all switches closed, also all lamps in their holders and a good earth connection. Portable equipment is disconnected, however, and the dial then reads from

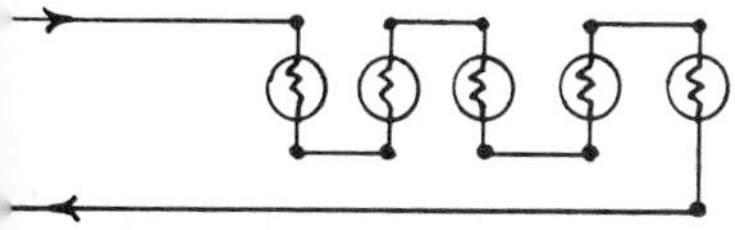

[1] This is the resistance of the lamp immediately it is working; its cold resistance if measured, will be found to be negligible.

FIG. 63   Five lamps in series

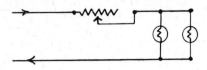

FIG. 64 Two lamps in parallel and resistance dimmer in series

zero through "Megs" to "Infinity." This last is indeed a happy state if it is not caused by the temporary test connection having broken! A reading of 1 megohm is usually regarded as a minimum for the permanent wiring, and 0·5 megohms for pieces of individual equipment. Exact requirements appear in the IEE Regulations and BS Specifications where applicable. Testing of circuits with thyristors (see below) permanently connected therein must be carried out only with a low-voltage tester, otherwise damage may result and a warning should be prominently displayed to this effect.

The suitably fused circuit wired in properly insulated cable of ample size and good conductivity, so as to present negligible resistance to the current required by the lamp load, is now ready to have varying amounts of low-conductivity resistance wire deliberately introduced into it (Fig. 64). By this means the volts will be reduced and the lamps dimmed.

Resistance Dimmers

There are two main types of resistance dimmer. In one, the special alloy resistance wire is wound on two formers mounted side by side and a brush holder can be moved by a knob up and down a guide in such a way as to make direct contact on the wire and bridge the two windings (Fig. 65). A series loop of more or less resistance wire is thus readily included. At the top end there are two contacts to ensure that all resistance is shorted out for full-on light and at the bottom end dead studs ensure an open circuit for blackout. The second type has a set of separate resistance coils, often mounted on a number of element formers, brought out to a series of stud contacts. These contacts are arranged in two arcs as tracks staggered by half a contact bridged by brushes in an insulated holder at the end of a radial arm (Fig. 65b). There should be at least 50 studs a side (100 in all) with full on and dead studs in addition. Stud contact dimmers do not make the squeaks that sometimes emanate from slider dimmers, but are more expensive to make and although very common in Britain are unlikely to survive for reasons that will become apparent as this chapter proceeds.

The crucial amount of resistance to be included in a dimmer is that necessary to ensure the light is virtually extinguished before the brush runs on to the dead studs. As dimmer resistance is introduced in series with the lamp so the volts and the amps drop away. In consequence, more and more resistance has to be put into the circuit until a total value of approximately three times that of the lamp itself, when full on, is reached. A 1000-watt dimmer has 120 ohms in it therefore.

There is a mistaken notion that the full 1000 watts is transferred from a 1-kW lamp to the resistance dimmer, there to waste the energy as heat. No circuit with its current and

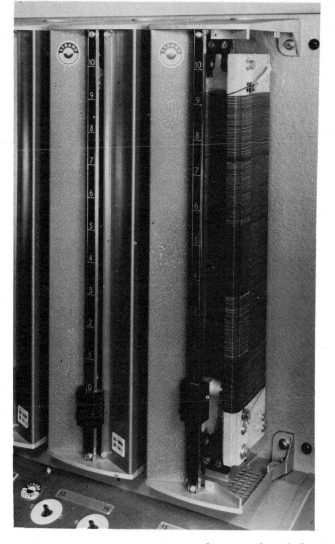

FIG. 65 Resistance dimmers: (a) slider-type, one with a cover removed; (b) stud contact dimmers linked to shaft-mounted levers

voltage reduced by having over three times the original resistance added can continue to take the same amount of power. After all, the wattage is the result of multiplying amps and volts. What really happens is shown in Fig. 66. As the dimmer comes in, the total circuit watts reduce until the loss is almost completely in the dimmer but this amount never exceeds one-third of the original value of the lamp when full on.

The drawback of the resistance dimmer is not really the wastage due to heat losses but its sensitivity to load. Strictly speaking, a resistance dimmer only dims properly the single wattage for which it is designed.

Dimmer Curves

In designing a dimmer, there are two important features to

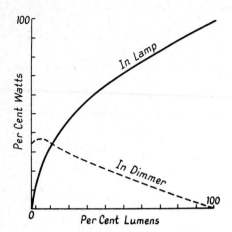

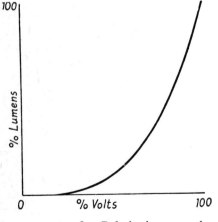

FIG. 66 Relation of light to watts absorbed in lamp and resistance dimmer

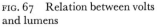

FIG. 67 Relation between volts and lumens

keep in mind. The first is that the lamp filament must have been reduced to a mere glow, which can be seen only by looking directly at it, before it is finally cut. Secondly, the effect of dimming must be spread as a continuous visual change over the whole travel of the control lever. This is not as easy as it sounds because of the relationship of light output to voltage. The curve, Fig. 67, shows that, if the volts drop in a straight line from 100 per cent to 0 per cent, the light falls steeply away to flatten out at about a quarter light, and yet all light is extinguished long before zero volts are reached. In a stud contact dimmer this effect can be altered by changing the values of resistance between studs so long as no single step is so great as to represent a flicker of light. At the same time, the size of wire can be made smaller as more and more resistance is required to cope with the diminishing current. On a good-quality slider dimmer the same effect is obtained by butt-welding a different wire size as the winding progressively gets nearer the bottom end. There are then five gauges of wire used this way, as can be seen in Fig. 65.

With the power to do this, what shape of curve shall be aimed at? Contrary to expectation, a straight line, which would mean, for example, 75 per cent light at 75 per cent travel, 50 per cent at 50 per cent and 25 per cent at 25 per cent, is not in practice popular. As we saw under Light Distribution in Chapter 4, a 50-per-cent diminution in light intensity is not particularly telling, yet half the dimmer travel would be taken getting there. There has been some international discussion in recent years on this subject. What is known as the "square law" has been put forward by the United States and is often specified, particularly for television. This curve can be expressed in the following way—

Divide the dimmer travel scale into ten equal divisions numbered 1 to 10 (full on), then the appropriate light as a percentage should be the square of the position number. Thus—

No.	Percentage	No.	Percentage
1	1	6	36
2	4	7	49
3	9	8	64
4	16	9	81
5	25	10	100

This is an ingenious formula, but of course there is no reason why one should accept each exact step as inviolate. It is a convenient way of expressing a general idea. Georges Leblanc, of Paris, believes that another formula which could be called the "cube law" is nearer theatre needs. The aim of this is to give a slower creep in at the bottom end of travel. The gradual bringing in of the cyclorama pit, for example, on a dark stage is something not encountered in television. In that case, regulation is largely at the top end of travel, the studio never in fact going down to blackout at any time even when the screen represents one.

Controlled tests in which operators had to state their preference from a number of curves showed that the majority of television people preferred "square law" and the theatre people, including myself, preferred a straight-line volts curve with a cut to blackout at 28 volts, that is, where a 240-volt lamp would be virtually extinguished and the rest would be lost motion.

Conversion of volts to lumens produces something very near the cube law, and therefore this voltage curve is obviously the one to aim for in a theatre with auto transformer dimmers. However some have suggested that an S curve with a slow start top and bottom and a relatively steep centre section would better cover the need for a gentle beginning whether dimming in or out. It so happens that this is just the curve that comes most naturally to the simple form of modern A.C. thyristor dimmer (see Fig. 77): in consequence this is another reason for the adoption of such a curve. In saying this, it must be realized that a theatre operator would not find the square law impossible to work with but merely that the bottom end would be to him rather fierce. Whichever is chosen (Fig. 68) it is obviously desirable for every dimmer to have the same curve when forming part of a single co-ordinated light control.

The resistance dimmer, however, is, as stated earlier, dependent on load; halve this and the light will bump in suddenly at the bottom. The solution is to make a compromise winding

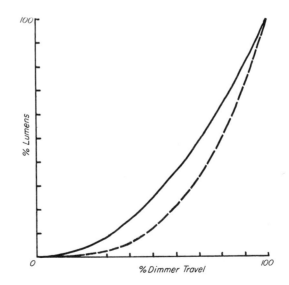

FIG. 68 Square law and cube law (dashed) dimmer curves

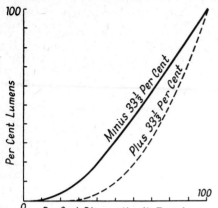

100

Per Cent Lumens

Minus 33⅓ Per Cent

Plus 33⅓ Per Cent

0   Per Cent Dimmer Handle Travel   100

FIG. 69 Displaced curves for resistance dimmer wound to give load variation

with extra resistance to take a 50 per cent load out. These dimmers were at one time known as "plus" or "minus" dimmers but it is now more usual to say "500/1000 watt" or whatever the variation is. The curve is still displaced (Fig. 69). Thus, if two 500-watt spots were connected in parallel with the dimmer, say, at the 25-per-cent light position, then as one lamp is switched off the light in the other would jump up to 55-per-cent light. The lingering on of the resistance dimmer particularly in Britain has been due to its low cost. The money freed for the rest of the control or for extra dimmers has been considered more important than curve conformity.

Resistance dimmers are normally made for "theatre" duty. That is, they must be able to be kept in a check position for reasonable periods of time, as appropriate to that kind of work, without overheating and certainly without the windings glowing. There are two other ratings: the first is known as "master" rating and is intended to be used to provide a collective electrical fade-out or fade-in on inexpensive controls. These processes can be slow, lasting minutes if necessary, but the dimmer must not be left at an intermediate position for longer than that, otherwise it may overheat causing the winding to deform, and the course of smooth dimming will no longer run true. The second rating is "constant" and dimmers to this specification cost more and may be larger, wattage for wattage, in order to allow them to dissipate heat continuously for many hours at a time.

It is important that all dimmers, but particularly resistance dimmers, should be mounted as recommended by the makers and clear of readily combustible material. Left accidentally on check for many hours in an unattended building, scorching and even fire could result if the heat were trapped and not allowed to escape.

Alternating Current

So far the dimmers described could apply both to "direct current" (d.c.) or "alternating current" (a.c.) equally well. If we are allowed to restrict ourselves to the latter, as the virtually universal[1] use of a.c. mains suggests, then several other forms of dimmer, all of which are in common use, become possible and must be studied.

The best place to begin is with the generation of electricity itself. This arises from mechanical motion in all power stations —atomic, hydro, oil, coal, or whatever. A current is induced by the cutting, with the turns of a coil of wire, of the lines of force between the North and South poles of a magnet. The

[1] Many film studios still use d.c. simply because they possess their own early type generators.

more turns employed, the higher the voltage. Continuous movement is essential, either the magnet rotates inside the coil of wire or the coil turns between the poles of the magnet. The current produced alternates rapidly backwards and forwards except in the case of a d.c. generator. Here connections are taken via a commutator which, by alternately reversing its coil connections, cancels out the reversal of the current itself. This d.c. current flows from the positive terminal round the circuit and back to the negative, or so it was assumed. Much later it was discovered that the displaced electrons, which are the reason for the electric current, flow the opposite way. Where a potential difference exists the positive terminal has less electrons and the negative more. However, in the general utilization of power this makes little difference (one cannot see them anyway), but where it is important, as in electronics, then a distinction is drawn between "conventional" and "actual" flow.

Alternating current comes automatically from the generators and in Britain the reversal is locked to a frequency of 50 cycles per second—now 50 Hertz or 50 Hz. (In America it is 60 Hz and the voltage (120) is half that in Europe.) Current flows alternately 50 times forwards and 50 times backwards in a second. This appears on an oscilloscope trace or can be drawn as a sine wave rising to a peak above a zero line and falling an equal amount below. The effective voltage is less than the peaks and is an average known as RMS (Root Mean Square) value. When this is 230 volts, in fact the voltage alternates between plus 325 volts and minus 325 volts. Electricity depends for its properties on potential difference and one should not imagine that a shock of minus 325 is preferable to one of plus 325 volts.

The supply authority is under a statutory obligation not to vary the nominal voltage at the consumers' terminals by more than plus or minus 5 per cent. Quite enough latitude, too, for this swing means a total variation of 26 per cent light. In fact, as many of us know, much greater than this voltage reduction can be experienced—even zero volts are not unknown in cold weather! I wish I could at least state what your nominal, as distinct from your actual, voltage is, but this varies up and down in Britain. There seems to be a lot of 240 volts and an equal amount of 230, but 250 is not unknown, while at the other end of the scale there is some 200 volts. This is quite disgraceful. What confidence can one have in our electrical lords and masters if they cannot achieve a standard user voltage in this little island after over eighty years of producing the stuff? The matter is particularly serious for lamps as the balance between the correct life and light rests critically on voltage.

In fact, all supplies are joined together by the national

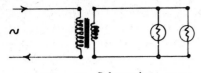

FIG. 70 Schematic: transformer feeding low-voltage lamps

busbars—the grid—and for this alternating current is responsible. Mains cables soon become very large indeed if they have to carry much current. By using the motion in the current itself static devices, known as transformers, can be used to change low-voltage large current into high-voltage low current for transmission over a distance. The uses of transformers are manifold and they come in all sizes and shapes, but the basic principle is the same.

When alternating current is passed through a number of turns wound as a coil round a soft iron core, this latter becomes a magnet in which its north and south poles alternate rapidly just as if it were rotated physically. A second coil of wire in close proximity, although not electrically connected, will have a current induced in it. The ratio of the one to the other being governed by the number of turns in the first one (the primary) coil and in the second (the secondary) coil. Using a large number of turns in one case and a small number in the other and the appropriate gauge of wire, a high-voltage low current can be transformed into a low-voltage high current (Fig. 70) and vice versa. The losses in the process are very small and the only thing on the debit side is that the combination of iron core and coils of copper wire tend to make a heavy device.

Transformer Dimmers

The principles just described can be used in various ways to make non-resistive forms of dimmer. If, for example, a transformer were wound with a core but without a secondary coil a current is still induced, but in an opposing direction to the supply, and in the primary coil itself. This "back EMF" (electro-motive-force) effect is present also in generators and motors, and makes them self-regulating, matching automatically the amount of power used to the amount of work required. It is this property which makes a gear-change box unnecessary on an electric train, for example.

In the present instance, the single coil on a soft iron core can be used as a dimmer by removing the insulation from part of the winding to make a commutator track from which varying voltages can be tapped off by moving a wiper arm. This is known as an auto-transformer dimmer and one end of its winding is connected to the live side of the mains and the other to the neutral return (Fig. 71). The lamp or lamps must be wired between neutral and the wiper contact of the dimmer so that as this is moved any voltage can be tapped off ranging from full to zero. When the lamp is at off, both sides of it are connected to the neutral return. Had the lamp been connected the wrong way round, "no light" could have corresponded to live on both sides of the lamp. Care must obviously be exercised to avoid this.

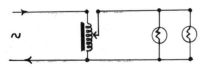

FIG. 71 Schematic: auto-transformer dimmer feeding lamps

FIG. 72 Transformer dimmer
arranged for clutch servo

If the dimmer arm tracks the whole transformer winding
there is a lot of lost motion since the bottom 14 per cent or so
volts produce no light at all. This part of the winding can
be wound on another part of the transformer core and not
tracked (Fig. 72). This conveniently results, as we have seen,
in a curve suitable for theatre. For television, the cut is applied
at 30 per cent volts and this appears to have worked well;
the lumens curve being halfway between square law and
straight line. In the photograph, two separate 2·5-kW dimmers share the same winding and core, there being a track on
each side.

Another form of transformer shares its winding with several
separate dimmer tracks. Ariel Davis in the United States has
had for many years a very compact version with six tracks.
On the continent of Europe ever since the twenties, multiple-
channel transformers, some having as many as forty-eight
separate dimmer tracks, have formed the staple dimming
system for the large subsidized opera house or theatre. These
are generally referred to as "Bordonis." Unfortunately, these
transformers conveniently lend themselves only to mechanical
tracker wire operation. The twin-track transformer shown,
however, is suitable for and has been used in quantity for
electric remote control. The tricky part of a transformer
dimmer is the design of the commutating brush which must
collect current without flicker yet limit the short-circuiting
current in adjacent turns.

Saturable Reactor Dimmers

Mechanical movement can be avoided altogether in a static

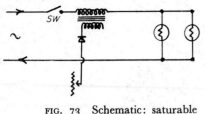

FIG. 73 Schematic: saturable reactor dimmer circuit

device which still basically employs the same principles as the auto-transformer. Roughly speaking, the difference is that the coil winding is put in series with the lamp load. The current emerges at the far end "choked" by its own back EMF. If, however, the iron core could be removed the alternating current would have little effect, there being then no magnet to produce a "rotating" field. It is not necessary physically to take away the core. A second coil is wound on and fed with d.c. (Fig. 73) which saturates the iron and in effect removes it. In practice there are three coils on three limbs of the core. The centre one is the d.c. saturating control and transformer effects between this and the load voltage are avoided by winding the two outer coils in opposite directions and connecting them in series with one another and the load. The choke is said to rely on reactance for its working, not resistance; the actual resistance in ohms of the coil being very small indeed. An a.c. circuit may be subject to both reactance and resistance because of the alternation in the current flow and also the normal resistance due to gauge and length of wire. The two together are referred to as the "impedance" of the circuit.

The form of choke described above is called a saturable reactor and the actual d.c. current to control it is as small as 0·25 amps (250 mA) and this will look after 3 kW of lighting easily. The device is robust and, until 1965, was the automatic choice for an inexpensive remote-control dimmer system. Its main drawbacks were weight and poor regulation with varying load.

FIG. 74 Traces from oscilloscope showing reduction of wave amplitude when transformer dimmer is on check and, on right, distorted wave when using saturable reactor to get the same result

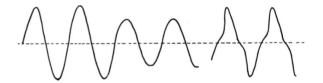

Voltage drop due to reactance varies with load current, thus although load variation of 50 per cent is possible, displacement of the curve still takes place as with the resistance dimmer (Fig. 74). Unlike a resistance dimmer, however, it is of the nature of a saturable reactor to be connected permanently in circuit. This means that there is some voltage drop (about 5 per cent) at the full-on end[1] and some residual voltage at the "blackout" end. These also vary with load and so design has to maintain a rather difficult balance between too big a drop at the top and the chance of light creeping in at the bottom. What are known as feedback circuits, in which the

[1] The voltage drop can be compensated for by using a booster transformer or lamps of a lower voltage but in Britain as the reactor has been used only for the smaller stages the drop has been ignored.

load influences to a greater or lesser degree the control d.c., have been added but lead to a much more expensive system. This was done in the United States in the early thirties using small thyratron valves to feed the saturating coils, the Radio City Music Hall being a famous example. To keep costs down, when transistors became a commercial proposition the British system, known as LC, was devised. This used a small transistor amplifier to improve load variation slightly but more importantly to bring down the control current still further so that presetting networks could be used. In Sweden, the United States, Germany, and elsewhere, a very elaborate variant known as a magnetic amplifier has attained wide use. This last form of dimmer was of necessity expensive but gave a wide range of load variation. The basis was still a reactor but with the output to the load taken through back-to-back connected rectifiers to make the form known as self-saturating. There were also amplifier stages with feedback in the control line.

The simpler forms of reactor ran into difficulty in the matter of time lag even though the device would ultimately bring the load under control. A 2-kW dimmer on system LC could control a 500-watt load but after one slammed the lever down it would take a second or so to respond. Performance on 1 kW gave no trouble. This delay, due to underloading on a single reactor, showed in an extreme form if the circuit was opened by a switch (at *SW*, Fig. 73) before the dimmer control lever saturating the coil had been pushed down. With no load at all the dimmer core remained saturated and retained a memory of the lighting before the blackout. Restoration of the current then produced a very fleeting but perhaps inconvenient reappearance.

Control of all saturable reactors requires d.c. and a potentiometer. A potentiometer is a resistance connected at one end to a common live and the other to a common return while a wiper arm taps off any required voltage between these two. Another term for it is a potential divider and, except that it is resistive, the device behaves rather like the auto-transformer dimmer, but on a miniature scale. The basic reactor with 250 mA of control current had, in order to be really satisfactory, to have a control potentiometer with a series of studs and fixed resistances between. These studs were put opposite the half and full divisions of a 0 to 10 scale giving in all 20 steps and off. The jump between the steps was covered by the slight delay caused by the reactor's iron circuit. In the more sophisticated reactor dimmer forms such as system LC, a wound resistance strip of 10 K[1] sufficed. In better practice a contactor switch was always included in every choke dimmer

[1] In this kind of context K = 1000 ohms.

FIG. 75 Alternating-current sine wave, half-wave rectification centre (dotted wave suppressed) and full-wave on the right

circuit to ensure the dimmer could be open-circuited, otherwise when unloaded mains voltage would be present at the socket outlets.

Valve Rectifiers (Thyratrons)

The need for d.c. saturating current to control an a.c. device like the reactor suggests the availability of a ready means to convert a.c. to d.c. This is known as a rectifier and is well worth some detailing because its principles have led to the development of entirely different forms of dimmer, including the one which, at the time of writing at any rate, is "the very latest."

Reference was made earlier to the electron flow which constitutes an electric current. What a rectifier has to do is to stop either the positive or the negative half-cycle above or below the zero line of the a.c. sine wave from passing. The current is then seen as unidirectional, as shown in Fig. 75, and this would be known as "half-wave" rectification. One way of doing this is to put the simplest form of thermionic valve— the diode—in a circuit. A filament heats the cathode and electrons are emitted which travel across the vacuum and land on the anode. This is where the unlucky guess about current flowing from positive to negative shows up, for the cathode is the negative electrode and the anode is the positive. This flow continues as long as the heater filament is switched on.

Where the flow has to be controlled a barrier in the shape of a grid can be included to make the valve a triode, and this could be used indirectly as a control circuit. The valve we are interested in, however, is designed to carry the considerable current of the lighting load direct. This form of valve is a gas-filled triode (mercury vapour or Xenon gas in place of a vacuum) but is better known as a thyratron. This name is derived from the Greek "*thyra*," meaning a door, and gives a good idea of the valve's action, which is to allow or to prevent the passing of electrons.

This latter the grid does when a negative charge is fed to it. The negative flow from the cathode is held off as like repels like in electricity as in magnetism. Remove the charge from the grid and the valve conducts and an arc forms between cathode and anode. Once the arc has struck the grid cannot take over control but this does not matter as it extinguishes itself as soon as the a.c. current passes through zero to the other half-cycle. The process then begins all over again. If anything less than the full negative charge (required to hold off the valve) is put on the grid, then it is as if the gate had not been made high enough and once the a.c. wave rises to that point the arc strikes, the valve then conducting until zero once more. The whole process is ultra-rapid switching, and the thyratron can be considered as a relay without any moving parts, the gate or switch being opened and closed fifty times a second to let all or only part of the current pass according to the amount of control put on the grid.

When used as a dimmer, two thyratrons are connected in the circuit back to back so that one deals with the positive half-cycle and the other deals with the negative half. In consequence, by regulating the grids of the two valves simultaneously anything from the full a.c. cycle down to nothing at all can be permitted to pass (Fig. 76). Anything less than

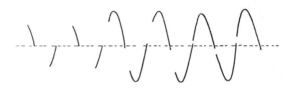

FIG. 76 Traces from oscilloscope showing chopped waveform for three check positions (almost full on right)

the full cycle averages as a correspondingly lower RMS voltage and since dimming is by voltage it is independent of load, the curve remaining the same.

Nevertheless, the thyratron did not make an ideal dimmer because of the need for heater filaments which had to be kept on at the ready so that the valve could be controlled immediately when needed. Any delay like the warming up of a television set obviously could not be tolerated and these large valves needed a longer time than that. This meant that on a large installation some 10 kW or so of valve filaments could be warming the dimmer room and doing nothing except adding to the ventilation problems. Thyratrons were also rather touchy in not liking it too hot or too cold.

Solid State Rectifiers (Thyristors)

Fortunately there is another type of rectifier—the solid state —which was introduced by Kliegl in 1959 as the "SCR dimmer" and has virtually superseded all others. This line of development began with what are known as metal rectifiers. These depend for their effect on the junction between a conductor and semi-conductor. Current flows easily from conductor to semi-conductor but not in the reverse direction. There is no control and the position is analogous to the simple diode valve except that no equivalent of the filament heater is present. Metal rectifiers of this type relied on copper oxide or selenium and the next step was the arrival on the scene of germanium and silicon. Not only have these led to more and more compact rectifiers, but to the transistor and the controlled rectifier or thyristor.

The transistor consists of three sections of semi-conductor material forming two junctions and can be controlled in an equivalent manner to the grid of a triode valve by a connection

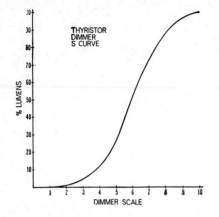

FIG. 77   The "S" curve natural to the thyristor dimmer

to one of the sections. Current can be made to flow in one direction, but the device cannot be used as our rectifier in the a.c. circuit because it cannot cope with high voltages and heavy currents. It is the thyristor that is the controlled rectifier we are seeking for our dimmer.

In a thyristor there are four sections of semi-conductor, one of which forms what is known as the gating control. Unlike the thyratron, however, where the control on the grid prevented the gate being opened, so to speak, in the case of the thyristor it is a control pulse which flings open the gate. On the one hand, control voltage stops conduction, on the other it stimulates it, but otherwise behaviour is the same, the process being repeated every time the a.c. wave has passed through zero. The oscilloscope traces in Fig. 76 could belong to either form of dimmer and were, in fact, taken from thyristors.

As with the thyratron, the thyristor is used in pairs so that the missing half-cycle of the one is made up by the other. A great feature of junction rectifiers is their small size and thyristors are no exception. Personally, I, like many others of an older school of electricity, find what happens inside something that looks rather like an ordinary nut and bolt, quite frankly, incredible. Nothing moves, nothing stirs. At least the thyratron used to glow when ready and light up when actually conducting. As a thyristor is a switch there are no losses when open or shut. Heat is however generated during the 3 micro-seconds when it is changing from one condition to another. The device itself has insufficient surface area to get rid of the heat. Large fins are attached as a heat sink and air must pass through them (Fig. 79). These fins are in contact with the outer case of the thyristor which means they will be live and not as innocent as they look. It is particularly important to remember this, as the metal structure of some types of dimmer module is also made to act as the heat sink. In fact this heat is relatively small and the thyristor is a very efficient device, the loss due to this cause and the clean-up choke together being $2\frac{1}{2}$ per cent or less of the connected load under the worst conditions.[1]

It is one thing to say that a pulse sets the thyristor conducting, but another thing to provide it. Yet another point arises: in theatre, television, and other similar lighting applications, one is concerned with the individual use of, and simultaneous mastering of, many thyristor dimmers at one time. The simple, inexpensive dimmer units sold for use individually to control the lighting of, for example, a room at home cannot be so used. Development of miniaturization hand-in-hand with techniques

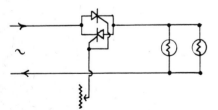

FIG. 78   Schematic: twin thyristor (controlled rectifier) dimmer circuit

[1] Another device, the Triac, resembles thyristors paired with a common gating section in the one unit. The principle of chopping the waveform remains and seems likely to be with us for many years.

FIG. 79   Twin thyristor 5-kW
dimmer

like printed circuits allow such essential circuitry to be housed
on a small card. Thyristors may become unstable when dimming loads of 100 watts or less unless they are of the hard
fired type. This involves increased cost and for stage purposes
an additional (dummy) load should be connected if the need
arises.

The waveform produced by all forms of controlled rectifiers
when used as dimmers must now be examined more closely.
Essentially when the dimmer is not full on the a.c. sine wave
presents a series of incomplete sections, each of which has a
steep front where the missing part has been chopped out by
the delaying effect of the control circuit. These steep fronts
may make their presence felt by pulsing the lamp filament and
supports so that it makes an audible singing noise. This effect,
referred to as magneto-striction, is at its most noticeable when
the lamp is checked down low. The same pulse may be a
nuisance by inducing electrical noise into amplifiers for sound
reproduction in the same room. There are also standards for
the suppression of radio interference to which dimmers must
comply.

Electricity, Dimmers, and Distribution   129

The solution to the problem is to delay the rise time of the pulse front, to make it less steep. The lagging effect of a choke referred to earlier under saturable reactors is just what is needed. A small one to cause delay in the rise time should always be included, but for television and opera, perhaps, a larger delay may be advisable. Delay is a rather inappropriate word for something that can be stated only in micro-seconds, that is, millionths of a second! The effect of this latter clearly appears on an oscilloscope trace as a small slope added to the front of each pulse, but as this is unlikely to reproduce on paper it is not shown. Such a waveform is loosely referred to as "cleaned up."

In most applications where initial outlay is all-important, the lesser clean-up is sufficient. After all, if a lamp is singing (however *sotto voce*) so as to offend an actor, either it or he can be moved out of earshot. If noise is induced in the sound system the offence will lie in accidental crossing of temporary leads and they can be separated. It is quite otherwise with the temperamental *prima donna* in an opera house or concert hall and, likewise, much time could be wasted in a television studio while an offending lead was tracked down. In these cases, time is money and the extra initial cost of the larger clean-up choke is well worth while.

To sum up, this chapter has shown that there are two main groups of dimmer. The first consists of those which need mechanical movement of a tracking arm which actually carries on its brush the current to the lamp. The second group contains the all-electric dimmers in which the current-carrying part is static and relies on either being goaded into action or restrained by a small control current. These latter, the saturable reactors, magnetic amplifiers, thyratrons, and thyristors, all lend themselves to the use of remote-control panels to operate them. On the other hand, the resistance and auto-transformer dimmers need either a direct mechanical link to work them or, if remote control via an electrical cable is needed, then something called a servo drive has to be employed. This group also has the quality which has been loosely described as inertia. Once the dimmer arm has been moved either directly or by servo to any position, it stays there until moved again; whereas, in an all-electric dimmer, removal of the controlling force produces complete darkness or perhaps full light. This distinction between mechanical and all-electric dimmers has vitally affected the design of the control system, as was pointed out in Chapter 3. Indeed many of the control facilities we expect today may be based on no greater logic than that of being easy to do on the electro-mechanical dimmer banks which formed the basis of Strand Electric's larger installations for so long. However, except for occasional historical reference

FIG. 80 Two portable Mini-2 6-way 2 kW dimmer packs permanently mounted but with portable 18-way 2-preset panel Integral sockets are used for patching

and the fact that so many of these older controls will continue to function for some time yet, what follows in this book must assume the use of the thyristor dimmer or some other solid state all-electric equivalent.

There are a number of manufacturers of complete dimmer racks and the racks themselves take three forms: portable with fixed module, permanent with fixed module and permanent with plug-in module. The portable packs (Fig. 80) are usually of six 2 kW dimmers complete with fuses, socket outlets (sometimes as 5 amp pairs) for the lighting loads and connection for mains input. The control levers form a separate small panel which has to be placed on something or hung on the wall. Connection to the packs is by low voltage multi-core cable which plugs in. Extension leads are provided and the packs need not be mounted together. Each can be locally supplied with mains (of different phases if necessary—see below) only the control panel being common to the lot. These panels are usually 2-preset and are obtainable for multiples of six up to a total of thirty channels.

There is no reason why portable packs should not in fact be used as permanent. However, it would be more usual to build a larger installation with multiples of twenty, and the racks for this purpose are more convenient for the contractor to terminate the trunking or conduit at and join up. They also allow larger dimmers of 5 kW to be included. Whether the thyristor modules rely on screws as a connection and fixing or whether they plug in is largely a matter of the money one is prepared to spend; so too is the degree of other sophistication. The thyristor is essentially a reliable device and, except for the odd rogue component in the commissioning period, there should be no reason to have to touch them.

Three-phase Mains

As soon as a stage requires an electric supply of, say, over 100 amps, it is usual for supply authorities to demand three-phase distribution. This is purely a convenience to them and should be resisted as far as possible as an extra hazard to safety. So far the a.c. we have considered in use has been single phase, live, and neutral. This in fact had its origin as one-third of a generator which produced three supplies at once, each 120 degrees out of phase. These are then transmitted on three wire lines and ultimately fed into a transformer, local to the users, with three windings connected as an equilateral triangle (delta). The secondary windings of this are connected in a star, the centre point of which becomes the neutral and is earthed. When the voltage between any phase and neutral is, for example, 230, that between one phase and any other will be 400.[1] This higher voltage is very useful for motors and certain other purposes. However, for lighting purposes a phase wire and its corresponding wire connected to the neutral must be considered as a separate entity, although the neutral is, in fact, common to all three phases. Provided the load on each leg of the star is equal everything balances out and no current flows down the neutral. Even at its worst the neutral will have to cope only with current equal to one phase. This is obviously an economic arrangement and trouble arises only when three phases are insisted on to supply a stage that has a lot of wandering leads; for this increases the safety hazard considerably because 400 volts may be present instead of 230. Where a three-phase supply is insisted on, it is necessary to separate the phases by using, for example, phase *A* in the front

---

[1] The between phase voltage is 1.732 ($\sqrt{3}$) times the phase to neutral volts. Thus, 220/380, 240/415, 250/440.

of the house, phase B for hanging equipment over the stage, and phase C for the stage floor socket outlets. Such separation increases the chance of being out of balance but this is all too likely anyway. This out of balance will, however, never be larger than one-third of the stage load. For the smaller stages, as in school halls and the like, it is usually possible, and certainly preferable from the user point of view, to have a single phase supply; the other parts of the buildings being balanced over the two other phases. The need to use a three-phase supply on the smaller control systems is unlikely to arise.

Electrical Distribution

The main thing to bear in mind when designing an electrical installation for a stage, whatever its size, is the possibility of change, particularly future increase. The cases where sufficient money is available so that an installation can be complete and capable of anything are sufficiently rare as to be left out of consideration here. The more likely circumstance is a basic layout which in time will have to be enlarged. As the distribution point for stage lighting is always the dimmer racks, the fact that modern remote control thyristor dimmers are made up of self-contained racks of twenty and, in some cases, ten dimmers, facilitates the building up and future extension (Fig. 81). Even within a rack the modular form of dimmer allows some to be omitted.

It follows that, once an adequate mains supply has been provided for, the crucial decision lies with the ultimate number of control channels to be specified at the desk or console. Racks and/or dimmer modules can then, if necessary for reasons of economy, be omitted to be added later. In this connection, it is worth while remarking that while a special dimmer room is advisable to prevent unauthorized access it is not essential, and this may be a help in an existing building or where the budget is extremely tight.

There has been some talk of decentralized dimmers, each associated closely with its lighting unit by being mounted either near or even as an integral part of it. This would involve a busbar layout, and while this might be appropriate in a television studio lighting grid it is difficult to see how this would benefit the theatre. However, this notion, which originated in America where owing to the lower voltage there is a preoccupation with copper, seems to have been soft-pedalled of late. It would be rash to predict the future in respect of technical development but I do not see much attraction for decentralization while control lines are still necessary to connect back to the control console. A form of decentralization I am prepared to concede is that dimmer banks need not necessarily be mounted all together, but rather grouped close to the family

FIG. 81 Standard rack with twenty 2 kW or 5 kW Thyristor dimmers. 5 ft high × 3 ft wide × 1 ft deep approximately

of lanterns they feed—front of house dimmer racks in the roof feeding this lighting, fly gallery level racks for the overhead stage lighting and understage ones for the stage floor dip socket outlets. Even this notion needs to be regarded with some caution for these racks have to be visited when channel fuses blow there. Meantime, modular thyristor dimmer units are available for use on such things as house lights, orchestra lights, and so on. These can be given a delayed action so that on pushing a raise or dim button the effect is as if a motor were driving the dimmer up or down, as with the old automatic dimmers, although in fact there are no moving parts.

As well as driving dimmers from variable timing and automatic cycling devices, sound can be used. To quote from a description[1] of such a device "audio signals are passed through a filter system to separate the sound into several channels. These separate channels each control a dimmer feeding a circuit of different coloured lights. Each colour channel thereby responds to a different tone group. Bass notes (bass guitar and drum) connected, for example, to red lights, a middle channel picks up mid-range notes such as the male voice and rhythm guitar operates green lights, and the upper or treble channel which reacts to such sounds as the female voice and cymbal, causes blue lights to operate."

The author of the above goes on to find that the fast response of the light while satisfying the teenage dancer distracts and irritates the older person. His firm can therefore fit a slow/fast switch to smooth things out, and speaking for myself, I hope they turn the volume down more than a bit at the same time!

To return to the control console, the number of dimmer channels greatly influences the degree of sophistication needed in control facilities and this is discussed in Chapter 8. There is a point that is more appropriate in the present context and that is the fact that the cheaper systems do not lend themselves so readily to extension as the more expensive ones. The racks are common to both, but at the desk to keep costs low individual dimmer control levers are not arranged to plug in. Thus, a complete desk of sixty channels might have to be purchased even though only thirty to forty dimmer channels are envisaged for some time, whereas, on another system, levers could be omitted and purchased and plugged in only when they actually become necessary.

Circuit Terminations

Circuits will in British practice be run from the dimmer racks to the socket outlets in the various working locations, patch panels seldom being installed. Occasionally a small part of the installation will be passed through changeover switches or even via some patch plug arrangement. This subject comes up again later on. Meantime, each circuit must terminate in a socket outlet. Even in the unlikely event of some of my permanently fixed lantern theories put forward at the end of Chapter 9 being adopted, the feed to them should still be via socket outlets. Only in very small stage installations should 5-amp 3-pin be used. One size interchangeable throughout including connectors being an absolute rule, the sole exception being suitably larger points for scene projection; but even these

[1] *Tabs*, Stage Lighting International, Autumn, 1974.

circuits should not be permanently tied up to this use.

The 15-amp BS three-pin socket outlet is standard for theatres and rubber connectors to this gauge are available. The 13-amp ring-main type plug with the flat pins should not be used for stage lighting, nor should the three-in-line connector at one time popular and of which there are still too many about. Each circuit termination should at least consist of twin socket outlets in parallel. This is not expensive if done at the time, and lanterns are frequently paired in stage work. At positions like the fly galleries either side of the stage outlets should be grouped together at two or three positions rather than be strung out at equidistant centres. Grouping helps the plugging of multi cores to feed lighting bars hanging over the stage, the number of circuits constituting these for particular productions being unpredictable.

For similar reasons, it is often preferred nowadays to group stage floor plugs together rather than mount them as separate dips under small access traps. Instead, a long wiring trough, or understage wiring tray, extends from upstage to downstage each side and any of the short lengths of cover can be removed as necessary to feed out as required. The appropriate length of flex being laid in out of harm's way, the risk of a set of sockets being put out of action through scenery standing on the trap is also avoided.[1]

Similar flexibility commends the use of trunking to house the permanent wiring because the lids can be removed and extra circuits pulled in quickly without fuss. The electrical engineer should constantly remind himself of this need for flexibility in theatre work and foresight can render makeshifts far less likely later on. Finally, no electrical socket outlet is any use unless someone can easily get at it, and often he needs to hang or stand a lighting unit in close proximity. A fully equipped stage with a grid will usually present no problem in that particular area but in other places and in other halls without a grid there are often great difficulties. Thus, for example, where a series of socket outlets appears over the stage, behind the proscenium, perhaps, there should be a bar conforming to 2-in. diameter OD to take the standard stage clamps which carry lanterns. This will apply in other situations as well and, where the bar is fixed, then it may as well be rigid enough to take a ladder leaned (and I do not mean parked) against it.

Patching

When there are more individual lighting circuits than there are

[1] The A.B.T.T. publish standard layouts for stage lighting installations of various types. These are revised from time to time to confirm to current practice.

dimmers to feed them or more dimmers than there are controls to operate them, then resort has to be made to patching. The term when unqualified is usually taken to cover the first though the prefix "load" avoids all confusion; the second is known as "control patching." Control patching will arise in the discussion on memory systems in Chapter 8.

Load patching had its origin in the need to make the expensive part of a circuit—the dimmer—handle more than one of them. Circuits could be disconnected from dimmers to free them for others or several circuits could be connected to one dimmer. The dimmers are shared out among the circuits and made to work all the time. This had to be the basis of a small low cost control like the Junior 8 (page 322) and in portable thyristor controls such as the Mini-2 it is more economic of money and space to have six 2 kW dimmers rather than twelve 1 kW. In consequence the socket outlets on the dimmer packs are not just there to facilitate connecting up for the show. They can be used for patching—to choose, rearrange and discard circuits (Fig. 80). Alternatively some very sophisticated means are now possible— particularly where a computer-based control system is used (see pages 174 *et seq.*).

Confusion exists in the United States, where the expression "flexible" is often used to disguise the economy measure patching really is. Very many installations exist over there in which a great number of circuits are expected to be bunched together on a few large-wattage dimmers. Not a single circuit can be lit until sufficient thought has been bestowed on how to arrange everything to suit the entire production. Take dimmer *A* for the footlight now and you may prevent its better use as up-stage OP boom or backlight pipe Number 2 later on. This is a strait jacket which the theatre must accept as such when needs must; but to claim an advantage for it *per se* is ridiculous. I rather suspect also that it is used as cover for the inability over there to design a large control. In Europe we have lived with controls of one or two hundred dimmers or more for decades, and this has led us to avoid multi-preset systems of ten or more levers per channel. In the States, until recently these were *sine qua non* for the de luxe installation, but no one had the fortitude to face more than a hundred channels on a ten-preset. In consequence, patching had to follow even in theatres like the O'Keefe, Toronto (500 circuits to ninety-six dimmers), equipped to a high standard in other respects.

Now this patching may be all very well in the right place, the leisurely activity of a college or school theatre, but 200 circuits to thirty dimmers, only twenty fitted now, to quote an actual US example, savours of mania to me—especially as this particular theatre is a fully automated adaptable costing a small fortune for an occasional and dubious facility. In a

FIG. 82 Load patch panel: dimmer sockets above with jack and cords for 2 kW and 5 kW lamp circuits below

professional theatre working at high pressure it is quite out of place. It is, however, warranted in very large installations like Covent Garden, where the bulk of channels are directly wired to their socket outlets on the stage and only certain special circuits for occasional use pass via the patch panel.

It is sometimes claimed that an advantage of a patching system is that circuits can be rearranged in a logical order to suit the operator at the console. To my mind, unfamiliarity of position ("Where did I put that footlight this time?") outweighs this. In any case, the memory groups common to the larger installations here can produce any group at once, be its contents ever so random.

Patch panels usually resemble a giant telephone jack board with cords retracted by weights (Fig. 82). The jacks themselves are often bigger than strictly necessary to make them comfortable to hold and label. It is not easy to insert a jack carrying a long length of cord and a weight into the bargain using two fingers! As far as Britain is concerned, all the large examples are in television studios, and BBC ones at that. It follows from television design that only parts of a studio are in use for a particular production, whereas virtually the whole of most stages would be used at a time. In consequence, 500 circuits to 160 dimmers in BBC TC3, or 800 to 240 as in BBC TC1 are logical. Where a patch panel is not used in a television studio, then the whole of the top surface of the hanging grid takes over this role. Men work up there, lower in the lanterns on monopoles and connect the necessary feeds to the nearest socket outlets.

A modern stage installation resembles this latter with its

socket outlets grouped in salient positions to feed any equipment that may be required. Although a large number of lanterns may have virtually permanent homes, nothing should be permanently wired in. The process is very efficient: a man has to go to a lantern to colour and direct it, so at the same time he plugs it up. There is no question of further plugging elsewhere at a patch panel.

Where cord and jack patch panels are used, the wander leads can terminate in a jack plug (male) or a jill socket (female). Jacks are used for circuits and jills for dimmers, since these latter may be live. Which of the two is specified will depend on whether a lot of bunching of several circuits on large dimmers is intended. The discard type of patching practised by BBC television is better served by jills as, when paralleling is required, "Y" cords can be used. For the majority it is a case of one circuit one dimmer.[1] Cords require more maintenance and take up more room than the fixed sockets. The jill system keeps them to a minimum. When patch panels become very large it is difficult to get sufficient length of lead retracted to cope with those occasions when extreme reach is required. Kliegl in New York has examples in which the jacks retract into a panel overhead and the cord take-up then extends over and down the back and can be very long. Generally speaking, however, it is not a good idea to make a user look up at acute angles. The head just does not tilt back as comfortably as it tilts forward. On the whole, the best plan is to accommodate as much cord as possible by raising the table itself and giving the electrician a raised access platform. Beyond this, "jumpers," which are built-in extension leads with a socket at one end and a plug at the other, are used. I have seen a rather ingenious inexpensive solution in America where the cords hang from terminal boxes mounted high up. The jack plugs dangle by their own weight, nearly touching the floor. This provides quite a reasonable amount of slack to plug up and obviates the cost and complication of weights.

In Australia where they have their own range of 10 amp plugs and sockets with flat pins angled one to another they have a neat arrangement in which the head of a plug also forms a socket. Thus one can insert two circuits one into the other without the need of adaptors. Some self restraint is necessary to avoid building up too great a tree of circuits.

Remote patching systems in which relays or contactors allow a limited choice of paths have the advantage that the operator at the main lighting control can work them for himself. It also

---

[1] Both jacks and jills can be fitted with interlocks in the shape of pegs to keep phase areas distinct when necessary. Using this type, dimmers of only one phase could feed the stage floor but these and any others could feed everywhere else.

FIG. 83 Control patch: pin matrix (top left) to connect 200 dimmers to thirty control levers (below right) as emergency back-up for memory system

allows some degree of preset switching to be incorporated, as at the National (Old Vic) Theatre. It is important not to permit too many alternative paths as this could soon make the equipment as expensive as the dimmer it was intended to replace. For smaller installations there are, not unnaturally in the home of patching, some good examples in the States of cross-connection panels, notably by Ariel Davis. The principle is a series of horizontal and vertical busbars, one for dimmers, the other for circuits, which can be joined by peg, clamp, or switch, the one with the other as appropriate (Fig. 84).

There are examples of limited patch systems on the Continent. One at Hamburg Opera is interesting, as jumpers are used to bridge plug to socket all the time, no single-ended cords being fitted. Generally speaking, as at Hamburg, these patching systems concern a small part of the stage installation only.

As the price of individual dimmers comes down and they become more compact, a process well begun by the thyristor, it will become less and less logical to economize in their use.

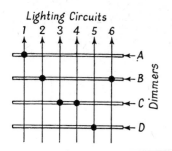

Lighting Circuits
1 2 3 4 5 6

A
B
C
D

Dimmers

FIG. 84 Schematic: cross-connect patch panel

Dimmers, whether decentralized or not, may become as plentiful as circuits even in television studios. What is certain is that there will be more of them under these circumstances. It is then worth while considering patching the control lines to keep the number of channel controls at the console within reason. The most obvious method of control patching is to use an assembly of standard pin matrix units (Fig. 83). These are a miniature version of the principle in Fig. 84. Pins with coloured knobs are inserted and the nature of the pin itself can change the function. We need not be tied to simple horizontal-to-vertical junction. The pin-matrix figures in one application on pages 150–151. It is also almost invariably used to select the channels as the emergency back-up to Memory Systems. In this case a few master levers with a separate power supply can be grouped to numbers of dimmers which are then operated to provide a broad interpretation of the lighting plot in the not wholly unreasonable expectation that the audience will not notice anything wrong and ask for their money back! Another less pessimistic and very sophisticated use of control patching is described under Memory Systems, particularly in connection with the new National Theatre complex.

8 Lighting Control

In the first edition of this book I opened this chapter by saying, "Today it is possible to approach this subject with a freedom from technical restraint never before experienced." I went on to say, "At last a dimmer has appeared which allows even small installations to be appraised in the light of 'what do we need to do?' rather than 'what compromise must we make?'." This feeling of euphoria arose in fact not only from the availability of the thyristor dimmer, then with a history of only four years in the theatre behind it, but from the sophisticated, solid-state circuitry which could be associated with it and do *anything*— even the automatic and instant recording of dimmer levels and their subsequent random playback. Dimmer Memory we called this and, at the time I was writing, we (i.e. the Strand Electric) were making the first of the few which, virtually without test and with but the slightest of demonstrations, were to provoke a growing list of orders.

Of course one knew there would be teething troubles but no one had any idea of the extent of the dire trouble we were to be in. Hitherto I had been able to squeeze in from our own home-grown technology every variant that the inventive mind came up with. In 1968 the inventive mind was still there; what we needed to do was still easy to specify; but the technology to do it came from outside our specialist world. Looking back one can see that even that world was forced into the position of trying to walk before it could crawl. The firm of Sperry—experts in the field—used cabinets full of electronics to fulfil my comparatively simple (in today's terms) demands. All that and much more can now virtually be carried on the back of the operating panel. Certainly to house everything within the control console presents little difficulty in all but the most complicated of systems.

Nor is it just the components—the integrated circuits, magnetic stores and all the rest—that have grown so small (literally "micro," not just a marketing term) but it is the wiring between them. The devices called "integrated circuits" (ICs) already in themselves represent condensation of a number of components which would have had to be joined together.

We now have edge connectors, forming part of multiple push-button and or display assemblies, all of which lock together without intensive panel drilling, mounting and wiring. Perhaps more important than all is sequential multiplexing—the time-sharing of a few wires for a host of signals. This reduces the control cable, which had been growing fatter and fatter, to a small flex of a diameter resembling that for a domestic vacuum cleaner. Only when each circuit leaves its dimmer are we back to electrical normality. We are then dealing with current and at the lamp itself with heat. There, as I have to repeat over and over again, we find relatively little change to report, go back through the years though we may.

There are now a number of firms marketing (and indeed manufacturing) stage lighting control equipment in Britain and elsewhere. Not all provide every type of control from the smallest to the largest but there is plenty of opportunity to shop around the market place. At the bottom end there is probably little to choose between the reputable firms but as greater sophistication is required so it becomes more necessary to take a good long look. To avoid confusion, except for the odd sidelong glance here and there, I shall deal with the systems of today. The rest belong to history and in consequence a brief description of some of the living items of that history will be found in Chapter 13.

The best bargains from the cost point of view are the proprietary systems from the catalogue as the manufacturer prefers to make and sell them. They are also likely to be more reliable, since he will have made or set out to make a number of repeats. A special, to the design and ideas of a consultant, just for you—"custom made" as they call it in America—is bound to cost more and take longer to make and commission. To devise a control incorporating a whole "new philosophy," if that is what it is, without prospect of sharing the cost of commercial repeats, is a luxury that only a prestige project like our new National Theatre may be able to afford. All lighting controls in this chapter assume control by one man to be a *sine qua non*. That he should have a good view of the stage, and that it is only in exceptional cases that this is obtained from other than "out front," automatically follows.

Dimmer Levers

Design of a lighting control begins with the provision of finger-tip control of the dimmers. The fingers are capable of more than two hands. Use of fingers individually and collectively means that rotary knobs, however small, are out; linear levers become a must. Limited span of hand means that control levers must be closed up together. Good guides are the piano key at just under one inch centres and the typewriter ones at three-quarters. Much smaller one cannot go without too great a risk of flicking in an adjacent lever by accident. Even at these centres lever knobs should be carefully shaped and hollowed automatically to centre the finger by touch. A dimmer lever should raise lights full on in the top position and dim them right out in the bottom position. An obvious association one would think, yet German controls work the other way about.

Plotting of intensities for reproduction on future occasions predicates a scale alongside each lever. Low-intensity lighting in the control room and the need for hasty appraisal demands large digits. As one cannot have these if there are a lot to be squeezed in, a scale of only 0 to 10 representing 0 to 100 per cent makes sense. Half divisions can be indicated by intermediate marks, but to show quarter divisions is to confuse resolution. To centre the lever between two clear bold marks is more reliable than to pick out hair-line divisions. This means that forty discrete levels of intensity in addition to zero can in theory be precisely set. No one will need more and I suspect that few will need to plot beyond the twenty half divisions. The requirements of stepless variation at the dimmer lever springs from the need to ensure smooth transition from one intensity level to another, however far apart or close together, when operating a particular lever manually.

A lever moving alongside a stationary scale is essential, as the latter can provide a rest to steady the hand when operating a very slow individual check. Furthermore, movement of levers against a full scale gives a better visual representation of the contour of intensity levels that go to make a particular lighting effect. I consider edge-operated wheel levers particularly inept, not only because one obtains only partial display but also because the finger may have to have "three goes" to clear a lever down to zero. One must be able to bang levers down from full to zero in one movement, like a switch, when necessary. Feel of the lever is important: there must be a sense of some work done, quite apart from the risk of knocking and jerking a frictionless lever.

As both the lever knob and the dimmer scale must be wide, one gets into difficulties over horizontal centres. The French habit of aggravating this by alternating a switch between each dimmer lever represents an extreme which is quite incomprehensible. To keep horizontal centres tight, adjacent levers may be made to share a scale, the odd number on the left and the even on the right. Alternatively, the lever can be notched out so that it covers a small part of the scale. A clear datum mark to read at is essential.

Less important is whether the scale is flat type or a quadrant. In the one type the lever slides along a guide—a miniature of the slider dimmer (Fig. 65) in effect. In the other it is on a pivoted arm; better bearing surface can be given and the general result tends to be more robust. The quadrant type is certainly preferable for masters which, of their nature, must get more use. However, it is more expensive and requires greater depth behind the panel. There is no reason why both types should not be made to be reliable. On better quality systems the levers tend to be plugged in individually or as twins to a single scale. They can be pulled out from the front for service. Where they are not plug-in type they must be carried on hinged panels so that one can readily get at the back.

Yet another form has the electrical and mechanical parts for a number of levers all mounted together as one assembly. A removable comb-like cover with slots and scales alongside is put over this and the levers allowed to protrude. They then have individual knobs pushed on. In choosing a control one must bear in mind that the levers, switches and push-buttons on the panel nowadays usually represent the only mechanical moving parts. They constitute the bits that will wear and will need maintenance. How many screws have to come out, how convenient is this particular type to maintain? How likely are spares to be available in future?

Some dimmer levers have internally-lit scales displaying one or more colours. This is a useful way of indicating which master lever it is fed from and so on. The Strand Electric luminous lever scale also depresses slightly to operate a micro-switch which can be used as a signal or to obtain one. Such luminous levers are much more expensive and should only be used as an adjunct to the really sophisticated controls. Recently, as in the Contel T6, a control has appeared in which such indication is by red and green LED's mounted with a push button above a normal dimmer lever. These initials stand for "light emitter diode," a means of producing a bright signal for virtually no current. The filament lamps used hitherto, though small, have at times represented a considerable drain of current and source of heat within the panel. LED's form the basis for the compact numerical indicators in small calculators. The unhealthy-looking numerals come from their being built up from seven bars—four vertical and three horizontal.

Channel Identification

Identification of each dimmer channel by a single large number is also essential. These should run sequentially from left to right and be mounted over the levers when they cannot form part of the lever assembly itself. To put the number under the lever would suggest a negative rather than positive approach—that one attains the number only when the light is out! Rows of levers must be made up of multiples of ten so that the operator can readily find any number. It is easy to round off to the nearest ten. One wonders how the Mac-Cormick Center Theatre in Chicago managed to arrive at the conclusion that its stage-lighting needs required the patching of 997 circuits to 145 dimmers. Why not be bold and go for 1000 to 150 or sternly sacrifice seven and five to make it 990 to 140?

Information as to location, if really necessary, should be kept to terse abbreviations so as not to detract from the all-important dimmer number. If a control can be made memorably to identify itself without a label it should be allowed to do so. Long descriptive passages belong in the instruction book, but if there seems to be a need for them this should suggest to the designer that a re-think about that particular control might not come amiss.

Colour indication at the dimmer levers can often be made to serve better than elaborate labelling. For example, if forty levers are divided between front of house, fly level above stage and dips in the floor, instead of labelling these F.O.H. 1 to 10, Flys 1 to 20, and Dips 1 to 10, the whole series can run 1 to 40. Then F.O.H. can be picked out as amber levers, Flys as black, and Dips as red. Further subdivisions are feasible for not only can blue and green be used but colours can repeat as it is the block effect that is important. The pattern of the control, not the colour *per se*, is what gives the identification. In using colour, one must avoid dazzle. White, Red, Blue, Green, alternating over the whole panel, would get one nowhere.

Presetting

The first requirement is a second set of levers to allow one lighting picture to be held while a second is preset. When there are only half a dozen dimmers this is not necessary. However, beyond that number it is as well to assume that a change from one complex set of levels to another is bound to arise. A preset is inexpensive and allows complete freedom to decide on the exact balance of lighting that suits each effect. Curiously it is not those dimmer channels which have to change that cause concern but those that don't. These must be exactly matched on each preset. To help in this the levers should, whenever possible, be mounted one above the other, and the manufacturer must ensure consistent behaviour, i.e. 50 per cent is 50 per cent on both etc. Putting them side by side as pairs is a bad arrangement. One needs to clear a preset down to zero and picking out alternate levers for this purpose, or in order to set up a series of levels, is slow work and unnecessarily finicky for the operator. Then again it is convenient to have a preset under the fingers to play or ride the levers. It is worth remembering that it is difficult to do this when they are near vertical; they take it better lying down so to speak.

Simple preset control boards will have two or three horizontal rows of levers with a master fader at the end. Unless a crossfader is fitted, one master must be raised to full before the other is taken out in order to avoid a "dip" where channel levels are common to both presets. If there are too many dimmers to occupy a single row, the levers can be provided with colour identification and the rows interlaced, i.e. White Preset 1–60 and Green 1–60, then White 61–120 and Green 61–120. Where there are too many levers to be accommodated on a near-flat desk, then it is usual to house one preset along with *all* the masters on the desk so that at least these can be played easily. The other presets are then mounted in blocks on some sort of wing unit.

In small installations of up to, say, twenty channels, it will be possible to alternate from preset I to preset II, resetting the levers as required provided they are fingertip type levers. This, plus some manual operations, should do all that is necessary. No switches are required either, since individual levers can always be pushed down to simulate this effect. A cut switch in series with each preset fader is advisable if these are rotary type. Things become complicated when more channels are in question because the resetting time of a preset of forty channels must obviously take twice as long as one of twenty. It is still possible to think in terms of presetting and add another set of dimmer levers. In consequence, a forty-channel three-preset control makes sense with its two changes in reserve in addition to the one in use. Small lighting changes in the nature of modifications to the more comprehensive changes represented by the presets can still be performed manually. I find it impossible to believe that, when given a choice of three presets or of two only with switch grouping in addition, one will not find the former infinitely more flexible. This would be in spite of the fact that a straight three-preset will have only three masters and the corresponding switch grouping system will boast of four or even six masters.

Where the simple preset scores is in its simplicity and in the complete independence of one set of controls from another (Fig. 80). One can set up a preset almost "with abandon" for whatever is done has no effect on the lighting in use at the moment. Switch grouping in contrast can only be used with care, yet we must now explore the various ways of pressing it into service as a switchboard aid.

Grouping

The object of group switching is to avoid expending a whole preset for every change. Consequently, separate groups must be formed within a preset. There is still a large number of controls in existence where it was thought that permanent family groups would do this. Largely this idea sprang from

FIG. 85 144-channel duplicate desk preset. There are twelve row masters to each desk plus grand masters and crossfader in centre section. Three-valve thyratron system in the New Theatre London (1948)

the fact that in very early mechanical manual switchboards a certain number of dimmer handles were pivoted on a piece of shaft between two bearings. It was easy to give them a master wheel of their own and colour masters and other permanent families were conceived, accepted and too seldom questioned. This was carried over to the Strand thyratron presets in an attempt to please those who had been used to Grand Masters. Each row of twelve levers had its local master (Fig. 85). There are many other examples with a large number of permanent group masters, in Europe and America. All these controls had flexible grouping as well, but the fixed groups were an unnecessary complication: something not to use but to confuse. Lighting effects inevitably use a chorus of channels situated here, there, and everywhere.

The only permanent master that has any validity is one for all stage lighting in front of the "house tabs." The footlight, where it exists, need not be on this, but the rest must be, as the object is to prevent an ugly hotch-potch of spotlight patches appearing on the curtain. This one master knob overrides all other controls in respect of those channels. Beyond this, complete flexibility of choice must lie. Any channel on the larger controls should have the possibility of being connected either to Group *A* or to Group *B*. A three-preset desk with *A* and *B* groupings will mean six masters plus an extra one for the front-of-house channels. The simplest way to form these groups is to have a two-way change-over switch per channel. Thus channels are selected to be either on all three *A* group preset masters or on all three *B* group preset masters. Two lighting cues can be got from each preset.

It helps if channels can be selected as common to both groups

FIG. 86 3-preset control with common switches to form A or B or A + B groups

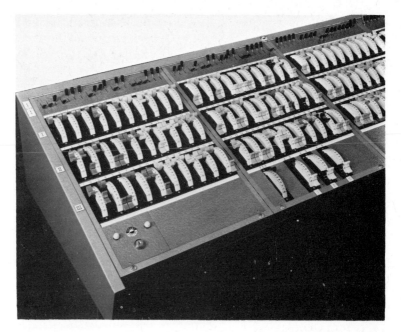

where necessary. Either there can be a pair of push buttons and one depresses both or the changeover switches have a third (centre) position where connection is to both masters (Fig. 86). Diodes ensure that the busbars of the masters are not shorted together.

So far this means that there is one 3-position switch to each channel but two or three dimmer levers. A system marketed by Rank Strand under the name of Threeset uses three separate 3-position switches, one for each of the three presets. In effect

FIG. 87 100-channel "Three-set" control with separate switches to form three groups to each preset

there are three complete switchboards working the same dimmers. The system was devised by Francis Reid and presents some of the aspects of the double desk of the old Strand Electric Electronic.

In the present case one preset with a complete set of levers and switches, together with masters for all presets, is made up as a desk. The other two sets of levers and switches are mounted one above the other as a separate wing unit. Indicator lamps on each preset show which one is live and which group of it. There are in fact three groups to each preset because the centre position of the channel changeover switches, instead of being common, has its own master (Fig. 87).

To my kind of mind the result is rather a fearsome array of switches but this control has proved very popular with its operators. With a methodical approach and the occasional use of a second operator to reset the wing, really complex shows can be successfully undertaken.

In any preset control it is undesirable to use the presets piled (i.e. added together) for long. While this condition exists dimmers are being fed from more than one source and confusion can result. Similarly the forming of three separate groups may mean that some dimmers are not fed in crossfading from one preset to another. Sometimes it will be useful to be able deliberately to ditch channels in this way but at other times very careful matching of the switch positions will be necessary if something critical is not to be lost on the way (Fig. 88).

Of course the usual 2- or 3-preset control systems have a single set of group switches, primarily to keep their price and size down, and the question of matching does not arise. Matching has always been an obsession with me; one system, (known as LP) used luminous levers to allow formation of separate groups per preset or electronic matching of channel numbers at the touch of a master push between groups (see page 331). Such a system would have no relevance today, there being much better ways of spending that kind of money.

Another way of making up and using groups is shown by Thorn's Series PM. Although claimed as suitable for up to 140 channels, I would (as in the case of Threeset above, with which it is comparable in price) limit it to a maximum of one hundred (Fig. 89). The initials PM would, I think, stand for Pin Matrix, for this is what is used to set up the groups—ten of them no less. There can be two, three or four presets known as Red, Blue, Amber and Green respectively. The matrix panel is a miniature affair with a vertical column of ten holes for each channel. These line up as ten horizontal rows, each corresponding to a group master. With no pins inserted, the control operates as a straightforward preset with a single master to each. Pins for the matrix are coloured to correspond with the presets. The

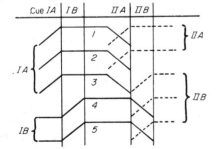

FIG. 88 Unintentional fade-out of channel 3 on cue 11A if groups are not matched on the two presets for the crossfade

FIG. 89 80-channel Thorn series PM 3-preset with pin matrix to set eight groups

moment one is inserted that channel also comes under control of the group master corresponding to the row. It can be inhibited in respect of the preset of the colour of that pin. Its behaviour is similar to the "house tabs" master on page 148. The possibilities of appropriately holding back a whole series of follow-on cues and the combinational effects will be obvious. One jarring note: I wish that Thorn would not confuse things by calling the group masters "memory masters." What kind of memory is it that requires a pin stuck into it? The truth is that the pin matrix is a form of patching but at the control end, and like all patching it requires a certain amount of deliberation and advance planning. Picking out coloured pins and putting them into holes or substituting them for other pins of another colour —perhaps in another place—is no equivalent to the happy-go-lucky "either/or" flipping of a switch. These three last systems can be operated as simple preset systems to begin with but, with familiarity and development of an operational drill in respect of the extra resources, an operator should become increasingly able to use his ingenuity to get round most challenges.

Multi-preset

Past solutions have assumed as many as ten complete sets of preset levers but to get them in the space they have had to be miniaturized in various ways. This is bad practice, because finicky levers do not allow manual "in scene" operation nor easy reading for plotting. George Izenour in his C.I. control employed one set of very large levers for manual and rehearsal operation, while the ten presets (five in the smaller installations)

became small edge-on wheels in a wing unit (Fig. 90). These, already subjected to my strictures above, also make the matching of an effect, which had depended on large gracious levers to achieve it in the first place, very difficult indeed. More important objections to a solution on these lines arise. Firstly, it is one thing to design a ten-preset for sixty channels or so, and quite another for 100 or 200. These latter could mean 1000 or 2000 levers and the sheer size will exercise a veto. Secondly, ten presets do not cover all changes. They have to be reset and a United States report[1] states that such a control needs one man to every fifty channels and some productions can involve resetting ten presets three times.

The use of multi-preset in the United States ultimately led to the whole room being covered with levers in the case of the Metropolitan Opera in the Lincoln Center. We in Strand Electric managed to avoid this kind of thing due to our use of the Compton group memory box and the inertia in electro-mechanical dimmer systems. When faced with the fact that all-electric thyristor dimmers had to be used, a system was devised (C/AE described on page 332) which enabled us to use only four presets for 240 dimmers at the Royal Opera House in Covent Garden, and only two presets for the same number in the London Palladium—in both cases supplemented by forty instant memory groups. However the arguments pro and con belong to history because that kind of money can now be better employed purchasing a dimmer memory system.

Memory Stores

In recent years the term "memory" has become associated with

[1] Thayer, D., "Planning for Lighting Control Systems," *Theatre Design and Technology* (USITT), No. 1, 1965.

instant recording and random recall. Thus the Compton electro-mechanical grouping relay, used for the Light Console and its successors, did qualify for and indeed pioneer the use of the term, whereas punched card systems could not. Although cards stored far more information (including dimmer levels) and could be automatically punched, access for playback was slow. In the Danish Grosman system (later marketed in Britain under the name of "Memocue") which was in some ways the most attractive card system available, there had to be a manual feed into two or more readers (Fig. 91). Some other card controls did provide automatic feed but skipping forwards was cumbersome enough, let alone backwards! One advantage punched cards do have is as long-term storage for repertoire: it is simply a matter of putting a pack on a shelf. Another is that with practice it is possible to interpret the holes and to read the content of a cue directly.

Now that all recording is likely to be done by magnetic means of one kind or another, it is as well to keep in mind that repertoire requires a long-term "Library" or "Dump" store and possibly a means of typing out the content of that store should the production transfer elsewhere. The value of this latter I find questionable. The result is a teaser of a plot occupying reams of paper which is likely to be entirely peculiar to that theatre and to the degree of sophistication of its particular memory system and its operator.

Some magnetic recording systems employ tape cassettes for this purpose, in which case the memory itself is something which can be physically removed and put on a shelf for subsequent repeat, and another cassette inserted to playback or record a

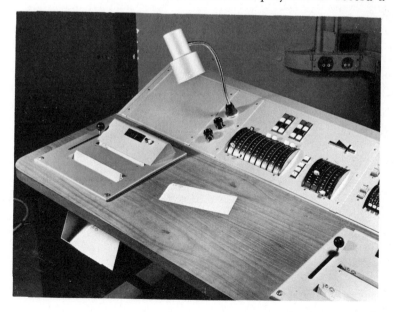

FIG. 91 Grosman "Memo-card" showing a card reader with master faders above

fresh show in the manner now familiar with sound equipment. A cassette of this kind can carry a very large number of lighting cues on its two tracks but of course the tape has to be driven to that part which carries the particular cue we want. Access is automatic, however; the tape moves to the part (or "address") identified by the cue number. The speed at which this happens cannot be compared to the slow motion of sound tapes, even at their fastest rewind; nevertheless there can be appreciable time lapses of several seconds while skipping over widely-spaced addresses—though near neighbours give no trouble.

A very recent addition—the Data Disc or "Floppy disc", a term which excellently describes it and shows a human touch absent from most technical jargon—provides such rapid access as to make it possible to use it for instant playing of the show and store it on the "library" shelf. The disc is about 7-in. in diameter and somewhat like a gramophone record. It conjures up a vision of your favourite lighting designer autographing his latest album! The device has to be kept clear of magnetic influence and free of dust but this is not a bad rule for other equipment whether permissive in the company it keeps or not. (See Fig 94.)

In most first-class work at present a static ferrite store is used to provide instant random access. In the earlier Strand Electric systems, a sealed unit containing a high speed rotating magnetic drum (or in others a magnetic disc) was used for the same purpose. The dump store was then spools of punched tape. Nowadays, however, it is always a case of ferrite only, ferrite plus cassette, or cassette only.

These magnetic stores can be classified as Non-Volatile. They retain their memory until something fresh is recorded there. A Volatile store is normally less expensive and depends on components which need to be energized electrically all the time to hold their memory. They are quite suitable to hold simple information or more complex if it represents a temporary holding point for something recorded elsewhere in the system.

The temporary memory used to hold the group selections on the luminous levers on Strand Electric's system LP was an early example of a volatile memory. However a swing away from ferrite cores is now possible and a volatile memory known as MOS (metal oxide silicon) may come into favour. It is continuously energized from a battery trickle-charged from the mains. This is not as drastic a remedy as it sounds because this memory, which comes in an integrated circuit form, requires very little energy indeed. Considerable advantages are claimed. From the theatre man's point of view this is just another static memory and whatever the form the standard way to store information is to record it as a series of "ons" and "offs." In the Compton memory relay there were "on" notches and "off" notches physically capturing a wire contact. In a punched card there is either a hole or there isn't. There is no question of holes conveying a different message by being a different size. So too magnetic storage in the present context, whatever its precise form, is a matter of energized dots. Five of them, energized in various combinations and counted on the binary system, can give thirty-two discrete steps of level in a dimmer—thirty intermediates plus a full-on and off. To use only four dots (or bits as they are called) gives a total of only sixteen steps which is too coarse and one more bit provides sixty-four! The coding and de-coding into binary represents electronic complication and possible inaccuracy. Unfortunately thyristor dimmers prefer a smooth increase or decrease of control voltage such as comes off a dimmer lever. Not surprising—because this is what they were designed to work with in the first place! The IDM memory system with these orthodox dimmer levers was doubly unhappy as the memory receives an instruction from the lever via an analogue to digital converter. After processing, it then passes on to the dimmer through a digital to analogue converter.

Other systems, for example System DDM (Digital Dimmer Memory), do the whole operation digitally, only converting to analogue at the final stage to operate the dimmer. This in fact means that at that final stage there is a series of numbers which have to be associated with particular dimmer control voltages. One of the joys of computer-style working is that these voltages can be anything we like to make them and thus the irregularities of dimmer curve described in Chapter 7 can be ironed out—always assuming that there are enough steps provided to avoid jerks in the light. Obviously in view of what I said in that chapter about needing 100 steps on an old-fashioned stud-contact dimmer, a memory system functioning in terms of thirty-two steps needs some cover-up for the actual change from one step to another. One way is to add some artificial sluggishness in response—to "slug it" as the jargon has it. It was the natural slowness of response, due to all the iron in the old saturable reactor dimmer, which allowed us to get away with twenty-one studs on the dimmer levers, but we are not now talking of anything of that slow order. Another method is to use more bits for the parts of the systems concerned with action (change) than for storage as a memory.

Dimmer Memory Systems

In tackling a chapter on the subject of memory controls one is aghast at the field now needing to be covered. In a dozen pages of the first edition of this book in 1968 I was able to describe in some detail the two theatre systems then available: Strand's IDM/R (Instant Dimmer Memory, otherwise known as WHZ) and IDM/DL (Dimmer Lever as distinct from the Rocker). The

156   *The Art of Stage Lighting*

Thorn Q-File I did not give much of a run at the time because I regarded its numerical channel call-up as something for television only but nevertheless as a form of lighting control that Tony Isaacs had set out to appraise afresh. In the event not only did Q-File turn up in the theatre in 1971 but other numerical forms from other notable firms, including Strand of all people, have now become available. I still tend to feel this form of call-up is wrong for theatre use, though later in this chapter you will find I do concede it an undoubted role. Still when the historian one day takes up his pen he will have to say that ready acceptance of Q-File for the theatre sprang from the fact that if at that time you wanted a memory system which *worked* you had to have Q-File (Fig. 92). Indeed he should go further because if the BBC had not come to doubt the ability of Strand to produce such a memory system and asked Thorn—in a train of all places—would they like to have a go, they might never have done . . . if you see what I mean.

The first thing to get clear in the mind is why a dimmer memory system. This is not so easy to answer. The quick reply is, "To save time plotting at rehearsal." Experience shows, however, that operators are much more dextrous at this than is usually imagined. For instance, Gill Binks at the Manchester Palace with his ancient Light Console has become a legend for his speed in plotting. Instant plotting can actually be an embarrassment to the lighting designer. It deprives him of time to relax and to think of his next move and the stage management of time to do or note the odd jobs that always crop up at a lighting rehearsal. Not all of us are there just to set dimmer levels.

Dimmer memory is far more concerned with accurate repetition at subsequent performances. Some of these performances may in fact be rehearsals and then the ability to bring back accurately or to combine and modify memories for re-recording can be valuable: one builds on what has been done at earlier rehearsals. These are also the times when the operator is under stress and aids like this, provided the machine is accurate and reliable, can relieve him of anxiety. But if we are not careful the opposite of anxiety may set in—boredom. It is commonplace to hear a salesman today declaim on the merits of the "Auto-sequence" control. With this engaged one merely waggles the crossfader to and fro and one recorded stage picture replaces another. It is just a question of speed pushing the knob. If, as so often is expected of him, the operator does this at a signal from the prompt corner, then one might just as well ask the stage manager to push the thing himself.

Interest in the job or job satisfaction no longer follows, with the result that the pay becomes all-important. There is evidence that I was worried about this aspect of recorded lighting long before we were in fact able to attempt it: in 1950[1] I wrote:

"I feel that there must be the same objection to an automatic board as there is to employing a pianola instead of a pianist in a orchestra of live musicians. The theatre is, except in very long runs, the home of live artistes. In the same way that each night the actors bring to life their roles for their audience, so do the scene shifters bring to life their scenes and the lighting staff their lighting. The inspired rendering of a dawn, or the well-turned cue conscientiously carried out by the man on the board, is a vital part of theatre. It may be argued that most lighting plots are not very inspiring, but often far more could be made of them without transgressing the producer's intention."

The answer to this problem I still do not know. It is true that every now and then a production might come along to tax the operator and his control to their united limit but we can hardly base our lighting plots on a need to keep the operator busy. I find myself thinking that perhaps we should take a hint from Handel, who ensured that there was a solo piece to keep the organist happy between the movements of an oratorio. These organ concertos now stand as concert pieces in their own right, not merely interludes. Should we investigate lighting solos—"colour music"—between the acts!

In the present state of technology, when in fact anything can be done and when the only limit is a financial one—and even that is becoming increasingly ineffective as costs in this particular field come down—all we can do in these pages is to consider the various styles of system available and ignore the particular detail which distinguishes one manufacturer's work from that of another or his work at this time from what he used to do and from what he may do in the future.[2]

One system in particular defies classification in this chapter and that is Rank Strand Electric's MMS (Modular Memory System). This has been designed by their present chief engineer, Martin Moore. The idea behind the MMS system is that the control could be tailored to the budgetry and scale of a particular theatre enterprise by selection of the appropriate set of factory-produced modules. If the needs became greater and more sophisticated facilities were required, the capacity of the control could be enlarged by the addition of further modules; one type of master playback panel could be removed and another substituted. Each module is an integral unit; there is a panel with push buttons or whatever and all the necessary electronics

---

[1] *Stage Lighting*, 1950. Published by Pitman.
[2] Most manufacturers have excellent illustrated sales literature explaining in detail how their systems are laid out and which combinations of controls are used to produce a particular lighting change. Comparative study in depth is readily possible for the enthusiast; to make it complete he ought to get hold of my *original* IDM 12 page illustrated handout of May 1967.

are carried behind it. One simply plugs in. This of course means that a variant or combination of modules entitles the MMS to a place in the often somewhat conflicting lines of approach to the problems of control.

Cue Identification

The action of recording will be much the same in ergonomic terms whatever the system. A number has to be selected and this is used to identify the preset, the memory or the file, call it what you will. Columns of illuminated push buttons have been used for this purpose or even edge-operated rotary selectors but the tendency now is for the standard keyboard of the calculator. Just as in a calculator, there can also be extra keys to qualify whatever one does with the numerical selection and these we shall discuss later on.

The assumption behind use of the calculator type keyboards is that they will become as familiar as the typewriter[1]—even more so because the order of the keys being in this case logical, it does not take so much learning. However, both Thorn and Dynamic Technology Ltd. continue to use the columns of digits for cues (files), it being claimed with some truth that changing from one number to another involves less movements.

There must be some means of displaying the number selected, and when recording is complete that fact must also be indicated by a change in the coloured background to the number or by its transference to another window or by some other signal. Even when, as is usual, there is an auto-sequencer which puts up the next number as each is used, there must be some means to guard against what might be called inadvertent "double exposure." After all one can select any number at any time and it might be "occupied" with valuable material. One method I have used is an audible warning signal triggered the first time one tried to re-record—a chance for second thoughts; then a second pressure on the Record button overrides this.

Channel Control by Lever

A memory system is primarily expected to record dimmer levels and this raises the question of how these shall be set up in the first place. The most obvious way is a complete set of dimmer levers (Fig. 93). Throughout the time there has been electric stage lighting, operators have been used to a lever. The levers themselves may have varied in style, in size, in the physical relationship to the dimmer and in the precise way in which they operated it, but basically when one put the levers up the lights

---

[1] It seems singularly perverse that the keyboard settled on by the Post Office for the telephone is in fact the other way up from that of the calculator on which it is modelled. Some American memory systems use this version as does Datalite here.

FIG. 93 Original IDM console:
120 dimmer levers 2-groups,
record controls top right with
two playbacks C & D below.
Transfer to manual in progress

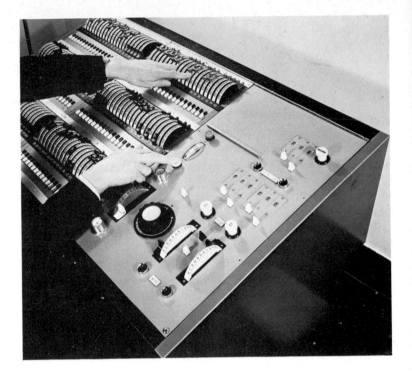

FIG. 94 Thorn Q-Master 2000:
120 dimmer levers, 3 playbacks
centre with a rate regulator to
their right and manual master
to their left. Data disc readers
above on either side of logic card
receptacle

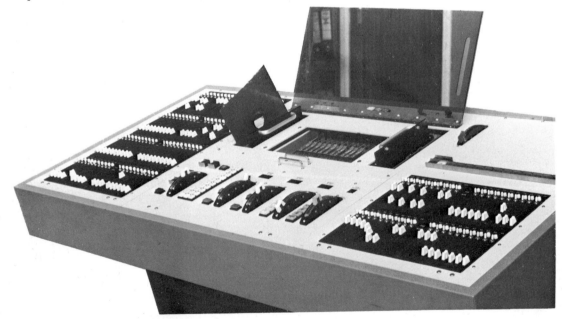

were up and when they were down they were down. A further advantage of levers was the indication of intermediate levels; a rapid glance round could, so to speak, present a visual representation of the contour of the lighting intensities over the stage. Operationally there is the feeling of being able immediately to modify by pushing these levers up a little more and taking those down a bit for example. Now in a full memory system the likelihood of the dimmer lever position resembling anything on the stage is so remote as to be completely irrelevant. Where these have a servo mechanism to move them, as in the Siemens remote control standard for so many years, then the problem that the levers will not display playback levels is overcome. This mechanism is an expensive luxury which the rest of us have not been able to indulge in.[1] My own solution for system IDM was to use Strand's internally-illuminated scales to give a red display when connected for direct, manual operation (responsible therefore for the channel levels) and white when the channel was in playback. The actual level in the latter condition could be read off on a dial by pressing the scale slightly to activate its micro-switch. The lever was moved to match and the "Transfer" mode push[2] pressed.

When a few years later Thorn introduced a memory system with dimmer levers (Q-Master) they opted for a lamp above and below (Fig. 94). When either is illuminated it indicates a discrepancy of lever level above or below that of the memory in use. The lever is moved towards whichever is alight until it is extinguished and transfer can take place. Lighting modification is unlikely to concern single channels only and lever by lever matching and modification is essentially a slow process whatever the system.

Another way of using the dimmer levers is that adopted by the firm of Grosman in Denmark, originally in conjunction with punched card as the recording agent (Memocue) and later with magnetic stores. In this case there is a pair of levers per channel. These can be used as a normal two-preset system; alternatively they can be set to act with one preset in a plus mode and the other in a minus. Thus, should the operator wish manually to modify a channel in playback, the light may be increased by using one lever or decreased by the other. Whether the result is subsequently re-recorded for permanent use is of course optional. No matching is needed but the use of two levers, positively and

---

[1] Thorn do however offer the option of full servo-driven *master* faders. Others have sometimes fitted master faders with motor drive for the slower speeds but this latter is not a true servo.

[2] "Mode" is used to describe a push button or switch which can be used to alter the behaviour, or mode of action, of a control or a number of controls rather than have a second set of them. There is a lot to be said for foot operation of mode pushes.

negatively piled so to speak, can set traps and the truth is that with a memory system we should not use positional levers at all.

Channel Control by Rocker

In August 1964 when trying to reconcile the System C/AE—just installed in the Royal Opera House—to the needs of a new production of *The Ring*, as a relaxation going home in the train I thought once again about what I would do if instead of just a group memory system we had the magnetic dimmer memory that was then thought to be just round the corner. Since the control I had just left possessed 960 dimmer levers it is not surprising that I went right off that type of channel controller. The result was the rocker: press the top to increase the light, and the bottom to decrease it—leave it alone and the light stays where it is. So that the intensity level could be ascertained, a push (originally above the rocker but subsequently in the centre) was also provided.

The rocker proved expensive to make and, since we made it in our own works, not as reliable as something bought from specialists in that kind of thing. In consequence it was later superseded by three standard luminous pushes mounted in close

FIG. 95 240 channels as rockers: the author at Royal Shakespeare DDM during tests. Channel and memory setting on left, twin rate and cut playbacks right

vertical formation on later models of systems requiring this form of channel control. The largest installation of this kind was of 340 channels for La Scala, Milan. Assuming for a moment that one *does* require a separate control to each channel on a memory system, the logic of the rocker (or the equivalent triple push button) is inescapable. Lighting should be set for visual effect and this is just a matter of "up a little, down a little" with each channel until it looks right. Since the memory system is going to record the levels and play them back the operator need not concern himself with them. However, it is nice to know when there is no more "Raise" (or "gain" as the sound people would say) to come, so I opted for a half level of light in the internal rocker lamp which went suddenly to full when the dimmer was full and correspondingly went to out at the other end. This electronic luxury was also subsequently dropped.

More important of course was the centre push giving precise indication of level on a dial, since lighting designers require to know this and indeed often set up their lighting by some such means: "Let's have x at seven; up a point!" etc.

The rocker was first used on the controls for the two theatres of the National Centre for the Performing Arts in Ottawa which went into service in May 1969. This system was known as WHZ[1] and later IDM/R. The rocker was to turn up again in 1972 for the System DDM in Stratford-upon-Avon, and its push-button equivalent appeared on all subsequent DDMs.

Channel Control by Push Button

A number of channel rockers collected together to cover an installation represents a kind of operational mimic diagram. For the more everyday theatre and its budget something less extravagant in the shape of a single push button per channel can be considered. Since a single button can only select or de-select (though its internal lamp can be borrowed for other things) all operation depends on a channel master which may take the form of a dimmer lever.

The channels are selected by touching the appropriate buttons which then light up and any movement of the master will regulate them accordingly. De-selection (and extinction of the lamps in the push buttons) holds the channels at their levels. This process can go on until the complete picture is ready to be memorized. Unlike the rocker system it is not possible here to

[1] Like many of the old Strand Electric identifications the initials WHZ had their origin in lab whimsy rather than logic. For instance system LC was "Len's Choke" and KTV, our punched-card experiment, had its origin in the loud klonking noise made by the automatic card punch—which led to a bogus German portmanteau word "Klonktechnischewerke." Perhaps the worst was System CD, derived from a rigmarole in which the fact that these initials stood for "Corps Diplomatique" played a part. However WHZ was simply the noise the high-speed magnetic memory drum was supposed to make as it rotated.

FIG. 96   Channel selection by
push button and master wheel;
Rank Strand MMS

raise and lower individual channels simultaneously but the
lights in the pushes can be used as indicators to display the
channel content of a memory and so on.

A channel master control is not just for setting but also for
subsequent modification and if, therefore, it is positional the
problem of matching arises. The ADB Memolight system
provides either for using the channel push so that the operator
can find out the level on a dial and then select after matching or
alternatively he can opt for the plus or minus use of the master
lever, already described in respect of the Grosman channel
levers. In Dynamic Technology's Datalite, the master has
pilot lights top and bottom. Matching then resembles Thorn's
Q-Master channels! In Rank Strand Electric's push button
variant of their system MMS (Fig. 96), the channel master
becomes a wheel and is not positional at all.[1]

Thus a channel can be selected on to the wheel and it is then
moved slowly or rapidly until the channel is at say 50 per cent.
De-selection at that point will leave whatever it is there and
something else can be selected without setting the wheel back
to zero at all. The wheel acts much like a rocker. Moved
upwards it increases light and downwards it decreases it but
unlike the rocker a positional and time quality is inherent in it.
When I wanted to give my channel rocker a different rate of
change we had to use a positional master speed regulator, and
when in one mode a specific instant level was needed there had

[1] The parallel between this method and the stopkey selection and key operation
of the Light Console of 1934 is exact.

to be another separate positional lever for that.

Mind you, the wheel tends to take up more space and costs more than a rocker, so it is difficult to use them as individual channel controllers, though in the latest Siemens control this is just what they are doing.[1] Most circles will have to be content to cast the Wheel (sometimes referred to as an "encoder wheel") in master roles. Indeed the need for an individual control per channel of any kind can be questioned.

Channel Control by Numerical Call-up

Implicit in all the systems described so far is the notion that the operator may need, as he can do on all memory controls, to work manually a number of individual channels at once; thus to say to him that he must call up and operate channels one at a time is a retrograde step. This is of course a way of saying that to identify and call up channels by numerical means is a bad thing; yet it does bring advantages. Compactness is one and another, once familiarity with the keyboard is achieved, should be the ability to use that part of the control without looking down. The buttons always lie under the fingers in the same way.

Auxiliary pushes as part of the keyboard format permit a remarkable extension. It was MMS which gave us, in addition to the encoder wheel, the alternative of actually calling up the level. Thus the fingers can for example select "channel 92 at 7" and then go on to modify it by increments "at +2" or "at −3" and so on. A dial indicator, or even at long last a thermometer-style luminous column, can give visual indication of channel level—a numerical indicator performing the same office in respect of the channel number (Fig. 97).

FIG. 97 Keyboard and wheel selection of channels, levels and Memory; system MMS

A further two pushes "&" and "&M" on the keyboard allow a number of channels and memory groups to be collected for combined adjustment. The question of display of what has been collected then arises. After all it might be desired to keep that combination in play for some time and it is easy to forget what exactly it is made up of, or a slip might have been made in the first place. One of the attractions of the individual push button per channel system is that it is its own mimic whereas in numerical call-up a separate one is essential. Thorn's Q-File, the original numerical call-up system, has always provided both a channel mimic and a memory mimic but the whole question is better discussed under "playback."

[1] In the new Siemens Sitralux control (first announced in *Bühnentechnische Rundschau* of June 1974) they are using wheels for the channels but restricting their number by employing "shift." This principle I patented for Strand Electric's experimental system KTV of 1959 and subsequently revived for the stalls control of the Stratford DDM. In the first case I had to have expensive columns of luminous push buttons for the channels and in the second, in order to keep the desk portable, it was necessary to limit the rockers to thirty. With shift keys the 240 channels of the main desk could be covered from the stalls row by row.

Playback

At its most elementary this can be taken as a means of calling up a memory number and crossfading to it from another number. In so far as the operator can bring anything to such a simple process, it would be in the timing to fit the stage action and in any modifications which might arise—particularly during rehearsal when the actual composition of the pictures, which the memories represent, is still going on.

Analysis of my first memory system WHZ which later went into the National Arts Centre, Ottawa shows the dangers of taking this picture-replaces-picture theory to extreme. It also concentrated far too much on the idea that modification would concern individual channels. This thinking was imposed by the extreme difficulty then of combining any memories except by piling two on separate faders at the same or different levels and re-recording the combination as a third memory. The same discipline was imposed on the ergonomics for my lever system IDM. It was not until I met the DDM computer that the key of the front door was handed over to me.

The adoption of channel levers instead of rockers for IDM was not so much to attract operators with the familiar as to simplify the electronics for our engineers. In the event it succeeded wildly in the minor aim and failed on the latter, major one.

In the case of IDM,[1] there were two playbacks only—C and D. (A and B looked after the channel levers in manual mode.) One simply called up memories one at a time on either C or D and pushed one fader up and the other down. There was also a rotary crossfader which could be switched in to replace C and D. What was in use was displayed by white lighting in the channel lever scales. The combined C and D display could be separated by switch in order to check over and modify the incoming memory if need be (Fig. 93).

In the case of WHZ (or IDM/R as it became) the incoming stage lighting picture was displayed as red in the rockers as soon as the cue number was selected, and the content could be modified before use (i.e. before the incoming cue fader was raised) or during use. When this fader arrived at the top, the picture was automatically transferred to the outgoing fader and the display changed to green. This transfer could only take place if the second fader was at the top, having been run down to bottom first to free it of the outgoing memory. During the time that it was occupied by the outgoing lighting the two could be used in a piled fashion. To quote a contemporary account of mine:

"Lighting changes once plotted always employ the same operational routine: in with one fader and then out with the

---

[1] The initials of this Strand system stood for "Instant Dimmer Memory." Our earlier customers must have been tempted to substitute "Irregular" for "Instant."

other. The only exceptions are when an integrated cross-fade is required or a quick cut from one effect to the other. A single control in each case provides these and signals that it is working by changing the display of the cue numbers in use above the appropriate fader. This restriction virtually to two faders is quite deliberate. It is an essential feature of the system that the operator confines himself, once the show is recorded, to timing and emergency modifications only."

This method of working is referred to by de Backer (ADB) in connection with their Memolight ST 150. In the literature under "Procession effect" they say "The large memory capacity enables this particular effect to be easily achieved, although it is seldom used. To achieve this, the whole 'movement' will simply be recorded by decomposing it into a certain number of cues and recording the latter.

"For playback, the automatic transfer (cross fader) system will be used to successively reproduce the recorded cues. The only limitation of this principle is the minimal time to play back each cue of the effect. This timing of approximately 1/3 of a second is perfectly compatible with the requirements of the affect."

The reference to a slight time delay is due to the direct use of a tape cassette as the show memory. Since there are 300 memories each side, it would be easy to record this kind of cue in this manner and a delay of this order is not serious. The real drawback comes when there are longer intervals—as in a slow procession. The trouble with action on a stage is that it is not precise in its timing. Thus one might have to slow down or hurry in the progress of a cue, particularly if a switching cue takes place in the course of a dawn or a sunset. The sky may not have arrived yet at the precise level recorded for it on the memory to be switched-in.

One way of getting over this kind of thing when there is only one playback is shown in the photograph (Fig. 98) of Rank Strand's Compact 80. The right-hand panel can be opened to reveal ten faders with a pin-matrix. Yellow pins provide a pile-on mode and red pins inhibitor mastering in respect of any groups set up. Using such facilities in conjunction with the more usual alternation of one memory with another increases the versatility of what is basically a simple playback system. The actual crossfader can be supplied in the more usual form (Fig. 98b) or as a joystick (Fig. 98a). The latter "is dipless when operated from side to side, but the contour is variable in any arc above the horizontal, for maximum common levels, or below the horizontal for minimum common levels."

Where a full scale memory system is concerned we are back at the fact that manual positional controls for masters are just as much a nuisance as they were for the channels—more so in fact because so much more work depends on them. Now that the electronics allow us to add or subtract memories, it becomes vexatious if this can only be done safely with the crossfader at one end or the other.

Rate Playback

This method allows all actions to be initiated by push buttons. These usually light up while the action is in progress and extinguish to show it is complete. All actions except one, that is—the setting of the rate of change itself. For this something positional like a dimmer lever is used. Along with it goes a "Mins/Secs" switch to alter the range from "Instant to 60 seconds" to "Instant to 60 minutes." Incidentally setting this latter range accurately for repeat is virtually impossible. These slow speeds, when required, are a case for recording. (See the National Theatre Control later.) Instant is dangerous. I prefer one second with a separate Instant push. There is too much risk, when riding the speed, of turning a fast fade up into an inadvertent switch cue. The best control for playback is the encoder wheel. All its advantages already discussed in respect of channels apply even more in playback. The majority of cues are still required to be of a speed readily carried out by hand. Little we do has to be really slow.

An advantage of the wheel is that not only can it be used positionally as a manual master but it can modify a recorded rate of speed if that is what is in action at the moment. One simply pushes it upward to increase speed and downward to decrease.

With a Rate playback there is a Preset store and a Stage store. The more sophisticated the system the greater the number of stores, not all of which need be known as such to the operator. In my view he should not in most operations have to decide where to park things and where to collect them from, so to speak. There is a shade too much of the engineer-likes-to-know in many of the memory systems currently about. We should be talking of an artist operator and the machine should produce the things he wants from out of the air as it were and look after everything he doesn't want for him.[1] The charm of the albeit cumbersome old electro-mechanical control systems was their property of inertia. Dimmers could be driven to their levels and then left without any need for a holding current. The operator could relax and select for *changes* in lighting. Later

[1] There is an interesting comment from Francis Reid, who by chance had not seen my DDM system for more than two years after it was completed. He immediately wrote, "I went into the control room at Stratford and there it was . . . all sitting there waiting to be *played*. It looked cheerful."
Earlier I had found myself coining the phrase "Lovable computer;" it had come as such a surprise that these dread automata could become friendly.

FIG. 98 Manual playback: (a) Rank Strand Compact; channel select left with mimic along top, single playback joystick crossfader centre, manual back-up right; (b) close-up, alternative twin lever crossfader with master fader; (c) MMS in the Round House, London: channel select right with mimic, two manual playbacks left and memory select in the centre

on in system C/AE an attempt was made to give this effect in respect of all-electric dimmers by *automatically* "parking" the dimmer levers on a live bus bar once the cue had been faded in on a master. Developments in electronic techniques make this kind of holding or storage available to any degree of sophistication. However, except for the two special National systems, nobody as I write is using the wheel for playback. There are now a number of systems from various firms which use **Rate** playback, one of the variants of MMS for example, and in fairness it must be stated that this form was part of Q-File from the first.

A number of memories can be added together in the Q-File Preset and other modifications made before that store goes into action and transfers its content to the Stage store to become the lighting on the stage. Any spot readings of channels in it will tell the levels they are going to be. A mimic of the channels is always provided but often it has to be shared by switching from Stage to Preset for preview (an ideal task for a sprung foot-operated mode switch). Q-File can have duplicated mimics. In the case of Datalite there is a twin lamp display—red for those in use and white for preset. In DDM the display is in the rocker of course but we keep the second colour for the second playback and use the mode switch type of preview.

A minimal rate playback must consist of two components: the incoming lighting and the outgoing, each with their respective speed regulators. It is more convenient operationally to associate these latter with increasing intensities and decreasing ones.

In DDM we duplicate the playbacks as Green and Red, each with a pair of speed levers (Fig. 99). Q-File has in addition a

FIG. 99 Rate playbacks with indicators: (a) stage store on left, preset on right, system MMS; (b) two playbacks with the dials and speed regulators right, channel setting left, system DDM

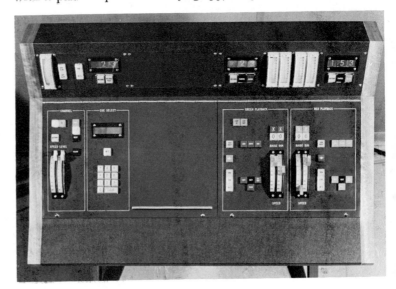

separate master to Stage and Preset. One is very conscious of these two as stores, whereas I hid the preset away under the title "Next." Datalite goes further and the four stores (i.e. the two pairs) each have their own complete set of master buttons. I was very keen on the idea of Next and there was a button called by that name, whereas others use the Cut buttons and the operator either cuts direct into the Stage store for a switch cue or into Preset when it is to be a fade. I had a separate Cut store specifically for switching. Then again the rockers enjoyed a modification store of their own; one just touched them and did not have to decide where they belonged.

There is little point in going into the pros and cons of what one system does compared to another at this level of detail. Each of us as a designer has deployed his considered opinion on the nature of the controls and their layout. Unfortunately there are as many ergonomic logics as there are designers. Thus at the very time when these new systems should make operation easy the differences of detail (and even the names applied to what is virtually the same push button) will confuse. It may be some time before an operator, in going from one theatre to another, can relax and feel at home.

Some other controls are bound to be there in one guise or another and allow memories in the Preset to be either raised to join those in the Stage store or dimmed from the Stage store. The memories have to be put into the Preset store or its equivalent in the first place; a "plus" push will enable a number of them to be added together or the "minus" push will take away (reduce to zero) the channels represented by that memory. "Cancel" allows a fresh start.

Emergency Faders

All manufacturers have to assume that their system may develop a serious fault and in consequence an understudy will be necessary. The usual arrangement is a pin-matrix patch in conjunction with ten or twenty manual faders on a completely independent supply (Fig. 84). It is possible to use these manual faders as an auxiliary device to the main system for certain effects and in consequence they are placed on or adjacent to the main desk. ADB sometimes supply a complete 2-preset lever control as part of the Memolight system and some customers insist on this with other systems. It is important to draw a distinction between such an arrangement and the IDM principle where the levers are used for setting up and memories are recorded therefrom. In the case of Memolight, for instance, luminous channel push buttons—an operational mimic—are used for that purpose. Personally I consider that as one hasn't a hope of reproducing manually the memorized plot in any detail, suddenly and without rehearsal, the large blocks of lighting method is more likely to be effective for an emergency.

Computers

I first encountered this new world in the experiments with Alan Payne, an independent consultant, which led to the devising of DDM (Digital Dimmer Memory). The ultimate DDM as manufactured under David Baker, the then chief engineer of Rank Strand Electric, depended wholly on the use of a standard mini-computer—Digital Equipment's PDP11 (Fig. 100). Other systems such as Q-File and the variants of the MMS depend on a particular assemblage of hardware, devised for and in use in this so rapidly expanding-contracting field; I cannot resist this paradox for every day more and more can be done with less and less. Not only the components but often the actual cost (in spite of inflation) shrinks fantastically.

However, for rapid or special development work the advantages of the complete computer system are obvious. Changes and additions are no longer a matter of work with soldering iron, or any other form of physical connecting up. It is for this reason that the Rank Strand computer-based system, DDM, has been used for the controls in the two National Theatres on the South Bank. I must add hastily that these control systems are, however, quite special and will have to be outlined later.

What a computer has to have fed into it to enable it to become a stage lighting control is its instructions on how to behave as one: the software program. It could be fed with the characteristics of any existing control. To take an extreme case, a program could be written so that it could join one of my old Light Console desks to a modern bank of all-electric thyristor dimmers in such a way that the latter behave like old, electro-mechanical clutch-operated resistance dimmers. The program could either be written to provide an exact replica—advantages, drawbacks and all—or an idealized version. When using a computer for a modern memory system, one can start from zero and reject all that went before. Writing a software program is a long business involving a lot of expert work; it is expensive, not something to be tossed off and changed at the slightest provocation. When completed, it is followed by the solemn ritual known as "de-bugging" in which conflicts or lacunae in detail of the progam are shown up as the machine is put through *all* its paces. Like so much else, one wants a chance to share the cost of at least the major part of the program over several jobs. This part of the computer's memory can be regarded as permanent even though it is itself also put on a cassette—which can be inserted in case of mishap, either in this computer or another replacement one. It must not be confused with the memory for the show itself, i.e. the cues with their dimmer levels and other information such as speed of change.

FIG. 100 Rack with PDP11 computer, logic, memory and power supplies; system DDM

In the present context the main advantages of using a computer are: (*a*) that it is possible to have what is in effect a large number of stores, (*b*) that the change between, or the combination of, two or more of these stores is achieved by automatic computation, and (*c*) that what the original designer of the control wants to do has to be expressed as a logical statement. This last is both stimulating and unnerving. A statement in plain English of *exactly* what you want each push button to do cannot be ducked—even though the programmer is going to turn it into software jargon before the computer can digest it. One is reminded of the difference between writing and typing when it comes to spelling. A touch of illegibility is a cover up denied us by the machine!

To take an easy example: suppose we want to add together two or more memories already recorded. This seems of itself a logical intention, but it is possible that there are a number of common channels on each one, recorded at differing levels. Do we wish to add the highest levels or the lowest levels (in effect to subtract) or to take the levels on the last of the memories —which might also mean subtraction? There could be separate push buttons for each of these functions so that the operator can make the choice. Even this does not wholly answer every need because in the addition process we might want some part of a memory to combine as "add highest" or another as "add lowest." For instance odd numbers might combine in one way and evens in another. Then again if memories are added to a crossfade after it has started, do we want them all to complete at the same time, the later ones going faster, or should they arrive one after the other?

This is the kind of thing that can run away with a lighting control designer nowadays. A lot of time, trouble and treasure can be spent in providing facilities to do *anything* but these requirements are thought up in the small back room—not in the heat of the battle in the theatre. The adaptability of the human operator when his ingenuity is challenged tends to be overlooked.

In the past the mechanics or the shortcomings of the technology we had to employ provided a restraining discipline. A lot of the earlier all-electric controls for which I was responsible do not have crossfaders simply because we found it impossible to design an inexpensive one that would give a true crossover in which common channels, which did not have to change level, would hold steady. In a computed crossfade a more complex logic can be applied; common channels of the same level do not of course change and those which have to decrease or increase do this in a predetermined manner even though the incoming cue is required to arrive at a different speed or to make a later start than the outgoing one. The ultimate destination is examined in terms of level and compared with where it is now, and the calculations constantly "up-dated" as they say. Indeed present systems tend to talk in terms of increasing levels and decreasing ones rather than specifically incoming or outgoing cues and we can set quite different rates for them.

This "up-dating" is no mere jargon. The computer scans all the things connected to it one after the other and at least twenty-five times per second—push buttons, levers, pilot lights, dials, dimmer control lines and all the rest. The slightest change—a contact made here or something touched there—is recognized in just the same way as the magnetic dots of the memory. The computation and action that follow that particular change in that circumstance are the result of instruction previously programmed.

Light Control by Memory (Project LCM)

Earlier in this chapter it became evident that a memory system which does not permit the ready combination of the content of several memories must be classed as elementary only. Both at rehearsal and at special performances (one-night stands and the like) it is necessary to put groups of lighting together—sometimes taking into account levels and at others merely as an identified family of lighting; the blue booms left, ditto right and so forth.

This need becomes more and more apparent the larger the installation becomes. It is seldom that channels are used solo; it is rather a matter of choruses. With the experience of the 240-channel Stratford DDM of early 1972 behind me, I could think on from there. The result was a monograph (dated December 19th the same year) intended for limited circulation inside and outside Rank Strand entitled "Lighting Control by Memory" and it described a theoretical system LCM. Needless to say I had the National Theatre much in mind.

Two main ideas were expressed in this document. One concerned full exploitation of the encoder wheel used as adjacent pairs of playback masters; the intention was to eliminate push buttons for this purpose as far as possible. The second notion was that there should be a dimmer to every circuit even though this could mean several hundred of them. There was to be no patching of any kind but, using the MMS version of the numerical keyboard, one would call up dimmers to form memories. Some memories might hold a large number of dimmers and others just two or three—even one only, if a particular spotlight was required solo. To quote from the document itself:

"It is important to start discussion on any fundamental change in switchboard design by beginning at an ideal level and then work from there, applying such economic and physical limitations as may be necessary. If we do this, then there is no escaping the conclusion that every expressive lighting circuit should have a dimmer—that when we switch it on we must also be able to dim it. . . . We now have to consider the "patching" of say 400 dimmers to the actual controls on the desk and here the fundamental principle is that there need be no patching whatever. Every dimmer or logical combination of dimmers is a memory and this would continue to be so whether we had 600 dimmers or 1000 or even 2000. On this system individual dimmers do not have any controls. The system consists of two components only—Memories on the one hand and Playbacks on the other. . . . The operator is confronted only with the lighting arrangements used in the particular show that is on the stage at that moment. All the leftovers and items belonging to other shows are, as far as he is concerned, not there at all. The programme cassette does not turn the computer into a System DDM or even a System DDM/Nat Theatre I, but into a System DDM/Nat Theatre I/*Hamlet*. There are as many DDM systems as there are production cassettes plus some vamping DDMs for non-rehearsed and non-planned shows— with separate cassettes for Comedy, Farce, Ballet, Discussions, etc. . . ."

The National Theatre Controls

It is of great interest to go on from LCM to examine the actual National Theatre control systems as devised by Richard Pilbrow and Richard Brett (Theatre Projects Consultants Ltd.) and programmed by Rank Strand Electric engineers.[1] As stated earlier, the basis is a special DDM-style software program for a computer. There are two computers, one to each theatre, with the idea that both control systems could share one computer in case of failure.

To appraise the merits of the system it is necessary to understand the reason for such large installations. We are of course dealing with a special case. Just as one needs a much larger and more comprehensive Grand Organ in a cathedral than in a parish church, so too in our National Theatre one would expect a "Grand" switchboard.

The technical equipment of the National Theatres is based on the idea that the use of labour must be kept down. Settings are to be shifted with as little breakdown into their component parts as possible. The theory is that the main purpose of the machinery is to facilitate the playing of productions in repertoire and not just to be used at one fell swoop on the biggest changeable-scenery production you ever did see. So it is said at any rate and the budget may ensure that this view prevails.

Richard Pilbrow uses the television studio term "saturation rig" to describe the nature of the lighting installations. They

[1] A full and illustrated article by Richard Pilbrow on this control appeared in *Tabs Stage Lighting International*, Volume 33, Number 3.

can be regarded as a large-scale extension of the Old Vic principle where the National had their temporary home from 1963–76. The bulk of the equipment is permanently directed and focussed and a small proportion is refocussed between shows. It is incidentally not sufficient in this connection to consider the relationship of productions in the repertoire over just one season. There are cases where a production becomes such a popular success that it may turn up in more than one season in much the same way that certain opera productions become tried favourites.

With all this in mind there will be 498 circuits or rather dimmers in the Lyttelton Theatre and 622 in the Olivier. Of these, 280 dimmers can be in play at any one time but the particular 280 may not only change from production to production but from moment to moment in a production; it is merely a question of which the computer is instructed to activate. The limitation of "any 280 at a time" is enforced by the display system. Just the same situation would have arisen, however, if an orthodox DDM with only 280 rockers had been used for this large number of dimmers.

FIG. 101 Theatre Projects/ Rank Strand "Lightboard" control for Lyttelton and Olivier theatres in the National, London. Palette in foreground duplicated as rehearsal palette far end; two playbacks with twin wheels centre

The National controls (Fig. 101) are entirely based on numerical call-up. The same keyboard is used for an individual dimmer (called a "socket") or for a memory (called a "cue") or for a group, of which more anon. The logic of this approach on so large an installation is indisputable but as we have seen earlier, when individual pushes or whatever are no longer used to activate, they are also no longer there to indicate. The push button that lights up to tell you it is operational, or to tell you something else when under the influence of a mode switch, is an old but extremely handy device. In my system LCM theory, the memories would have been represented either wholly (or at least that proportion which could be considered as "composition" rather than "show" memories) by luminous on and off pushes. This had already been done, among a number of other installations, in the case of the C/AE group memories at the Royal Opera House. One could see at a glance that two or three memories had been added together.

Mind you with full dimmer memory one has to show the level at which one memory is added to another (the proportion of its contribution as a whole) since every composition is built up from memories as if they were single dimmers of a small installation. I am sure I would have found luminous thermometers (columns of LED's) irresistible for this purpose—elaboration though it would have been. Perhaps a rocker to each memory would be appropriate. One could raise it, dim it, and use the centre push to find out the level of its contribution as a whole.

However, we are not concerned here with theory but with what has been made and is being used now. The display system adopted for the National is known as a VDU. This stands for Visual Display Unit and is simply a 15-inch television screen with a read-out of figures (Fig. 101). This kind of thing is quite usual in computer work; in consequence a large proportion of standard rather than special hardware would be involved in providing this kind of display of information. In fact such a device formed the basis for a system known as Autocue which was introduced early in 1972 by CBS of America for television lighting control. The ticking over of the information concerning the individual channels as a crossfade took place was very impressive. I was less pleased with the method of channel modification which involved picking out channels on the screen with a "light-pen" actually placed on the surface of the cathode ray tube. Compared with the VDU and pen part, the rest of the system was curiously unsophisticated.

The trouble about the light-pen was that it suggested keeping one's head down among the figures—in much the same way that one would play a game of draughts or of chess with a computer. Psychologically one's assistant (or perhaps "boss" is the better word) is the computer—a soulless robot who can round on one and issue a rebuke like, "You have fed me an incorrect statement, think again," or even more tersely, "ERROR!" on the screen for all to see.

In the present case the VDUs, of which there are two to each main control desk and one to the lighting designer's stalls console, are solely concerned with display of information—quite literally *all* information: the state of the channels, what cues are on which playback, progress and speed of change and so on. The order in which the "sockets" appear can be left to the computer, or you can issue it with a typed instruction as to what layout is wanted for the 280 which can be displayed at any given time.

All information need not be displayed all the time—it can be localized by push button to an operation under question—and, if preferred, the baleful flickering eye of Cyclops and his twin (and the high-pitched whine of the line flyback) can be put out. However, although the action controls are very comprehensive indeed, we shall without the VDUs lack the information as to what has been called up and where—no numerical indication whatever being provided. This is to keep costs down but does seem to me a grave mistake for, once a show is well into repertoire, the full VDU information may be needed only occasionally.

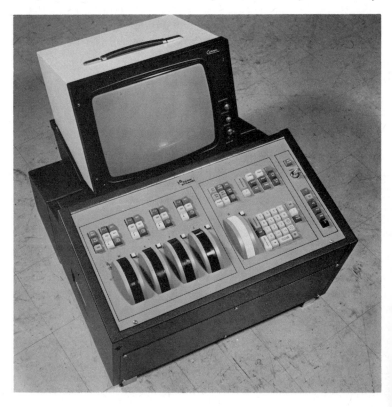

FIG. 102 Lightboard portable rehearsal palette; composing keyboard and wheel on the right, four sub-master wheels left, VDU screen to show all information, as required, at the top

Except that a pair of wheels is used instead of the pair of positional speed levers, there is not a great deal of difference between the two playbacks here and the red and green playbacks of the original DDM, not at any rate in intent. There are, however, no transfer pushes to allow part of the content to be taken from one playback to another, to be speeded up or slowed down for example, nor is the special "Cut" store provided. However, in the case of the Stratford-upon-Avon control we had to make the two playbacks cope with all situations whereas in the present instance there are other playbacks assembled under the title "palette" (Fig. 102). There are five single wheels, each with associated push buttons. Four of these repeat exactly and are known as sub-masters; the fifth constitutes the nucleus of the setting panel. It is here that memories are made up in the first place—composed for use later.

The title "palette" is much more than a handy metaphor; it is a literal description of how it is intended to be used nor need it be restricted to the composing process. Anyone who like myself has tried to make extended use of a memory control, to play the thing rather than operate it, becomes aware of certain areas where "old-fashioned" orthodox controls remain supreme. I tried but never succeeded in playing my well-known colour music interpretation of the first movement of Tchaikovsky's Fourth Symphony when the Stratford DDM was in our Covent Garden demonstration theatre; the mental effort to get everything tied up was too great. Yet I have played that piece on most of my other controls from the Light Console to C/AE, System LP and even on an 18-channel Mini-2.

What one comes back to again and again is the need in certain types of lighting—even with an established plot—to lay one's hands on things and improvise; to ride the controls. This was I think recognized in the Thorn Q-File from the first. A virtue was made of the necessity to have emergency levers and these could be worked alongside the rest of the sophistication.

So it is at the National; individual sockets, memories (whether used as such or as groups[1]) can be transferred to the palettes and kept in play, balanced against each other as need may dictate. This does breed a lot of buttons; because what you do, you have to have the means to undo. Indeed the secret of any instrument is how quickly you can untie it. One can go on piling up and up, coupling this to that, both in the organ and a stage switchboard, and then suddenly the horrific moment comes when you have to

---

[1] I do not like the distinction often made between a "memory" and a "group." They are in fact the same except in the second case the recorded levels have to be ignored. Why should not the nature of the operational push subsequently pressed determine whether they are or are not? As to the problem of having to think up from limbo some level to set the channels to, why not seven and then we can rise above it or sink below it? Most systems have a means of setting to a constant anyway.

clear the board and get down to something simple and quiet. You can get by if you leave out something wanted in the grand climax but the reverse does not apply—something unwanted cannot be left in when you get down to that solo spotlight.

As befits this age, modulation by music, by tape or other automatic means can also be fed into the palettes. Thus the operator need not tie up his left hand to giving an impression of a street sign just round the corner or flickering lamps to suggest flames.

Lightboard

The disgraceful delays in the opening of the National theatres in London have not been echoed in the lighting controls. In the interim opportunities have been taken to demonstrate "Lightboard," as it is now called, and before ever it has worked in either of its ultimate homes, one of 400 dimmers has been ordered by the Vienna Burgtheater. At one of these demonstrations, Lightboard was stationed at one end of the balcony in Strand Electric's one-time theatre (now the ABTT theatre) while my old Strand Light Console—to give it its full title—occupied the other end. There could not have been a greater contrast. The philosophies both operational and technical were, of course, separated by over forty years. In the case of my Light Console the operator perforce received a minimum of information via a few dials, whereas in Lightboard every scrap of information is available at will for presentation, not just digitally but if need be in the language of the immortals.

For a Light Console operator it was very much a question of keeping his eyes on the stage and if it looked right it was right. In contrast the problem with Lightboard could well be how to get him to look up from his fascinating displays. Fortunately in the Lyttelton theatre at any rate the control is excellently positioned dead centre at Stalls level only thirteen rows away. The angle is also just right and in consequence the stage picture dominates the switchboard displays and the correct sense of proportion is preserved.

Control of Auxiliaries

The software program of the National Theatre system will allow remote colour filter change and servo-positioning of the lanterns to be controlled and memorized should the need arise. Too often such things are forgotten nowadays and the control of such things is relegated to crude switch panel afterthoughts. This particularly upsets me because my Light Console could always take these auxiliaries in its stride. There were forty colour-change channels at the Palladium and fifty-four at the Royal Festival Hall for example; the first were controlled individually and the second as twenty-three ways, each exactly conforming with the dimmer arrangements. In these there was no question of occasional use; they were in and out all the time. Many of the most important cues in a show were on the colour changers. The stopkey of the Light Console selected the channel for everything—dimmer, switch full on, switch off, dial and colour change. As the colour change masters were always there (the sets of five black notes) no extra controls were necessary, no matter how many changers there were.

Stalls Control

Needless to say both National theatres will have stalls controls. Each consists of a palette (four sub-masters and a setting panel) and a VDU monitor. It is optional whether what the designer does on his stalls control is memorized at the time as part of the show or memorized as a kind of electronic note pad for consideration afterwards. Incidentally the memory numbering system allows the insertion of nine extra cues (0·1 to 0·9) between whole numbers—nine lives rather than second thoughts, so to say! When not in use in their rehearsal position each stalls control is placed to the immediate right of the permanent desk in their respective control rooms. One can envisage a sort of duet or artistic battle if the designer is allowed in the room on first nights. The claim of the man actually running the show to be in command when the audience is in, is paramount.

Although in the present case the actual playback masters for running the show do not appear on the stalls controls my enthusiasm has dwindled since the first one appeared in Glyndebourne and I regretted that I was asked to devise one for the Stratford-upon-Avon DDM. At Glyndebourne there was logic in such a provision in 1964 because Francis Reid was going to play the main control himself for the show but, where this is not the case, it is now my firm belief that using the device we lessen the role of the operator and deprive him of a valuable opportunity to familiarize himself with the particular production layout. It should be part of the fun of switchboard operation to comply with (and anticipate if possible) every demand. It may have been difficult at one time, in the days of written plots, to make such sudden changes and to interrupt what one was doing at the request of an impatient so-and-so who didn't know his own mind for more than five seconds at a time, but not nowadays. Certainly not at the National where, if desired, any memory can be instantly set to take account of the entire state of the board, where things are, their speeds and *all*. As it is, only costs have vetoed yet another gadget: a radio link pocket calculator for the lighting designer to call up what he will from where e'er he walks. There is an old song of the canal boatmen not inappropriate to the channel switchman, "Keep Yer 'ands Off, She's Mine!"

9 Lighting Procedure

THE most obvious exhibition of lighting procedure is the lighting rehearsal, as this is the time when everything else in this book comes together and is put into its place. It should be a very satisfying time, the act of creation with light—far more interesting than the mere reproduction which follows at performance after performance. The actuality is usually far removed from this dream and for most people a lighting rehearsal seems frustrating and irritating or, worse still, a bore.

The first duty of whoever is conducting the rehearsal is to see that it never degenerates into boredom. The trouble is that a lighting rehearsal seems to involve purely private fun for the few who assemble in the stalls to lash into action at uncertain intervals, with a vociferous electronic bellow, the "slaves" scattered over the often cold and cheerless theatre. No job can hold interest unless one knows what its purpose is. Without this, it degenerates into merely a way of earning money—not all that good into the bargain.

Much of the vexation and strain of rehearsals can be avoided if a few rules of humanity are observed. Keep everyone informed of what goes on, of the cause of any delay, and how long one hopes to take. Avoid all-night sessions even if it does seem the only way to keep "helpful" friends at bay. Remember to allow breaks for food and drink. Nothing makes people more tetchy than when they see drinks at the stalls rehearsal station and there is none for them. There must be a sense of community effort and a great help to this is a break, all together, at the local. In this connection, keep an eye on closing time and, of course, on last trains and the problems of transport.

It is important that there should be enough but not too much time for lighting. With too little time, the last act gets scamped, while with more time than necessary too many second thoughts come in. An actual experience of a few years ago will show what to avoid and illustrate the faults of the wrong kind of pre-planning. This particular case concerned the London production of a New York show, and although scenery was built for the different stage here and Strand Electric lighting units were to be used, instead of the American "Century," it was a condition of the contract that the original lighting layout and plot must be used.

This assumed a precision of pre-planning quite impossible to achieve, and after each cue was called for and put into action, as determined by the American plot, so the stage had to be unlit, taking out first this offending spot, then that. This left a quite inadequate and patchy residue. Lamps were then added by trial and error to complete each picture. Thus far the pre-planning had been only a handicap ensuring, as it did, twice as much work. The task was further complicated by the fact that what each dimmer-controlled circuit and its lamp or lamps produced was so utterly unmemorable. What No. 169 last did, or what it was likely to do out of all the hundreds of units, could neither be recalled nor be predicted.

Eventually, after some evenings, everything was sorted out and the large cast then joined in rehearsals to reveal that the lighting concentrated too much on the scenery and not enough on them. This was not surprising since, except for the odd stand-in, there had been nothing else to direct the light at. The careful readjustments which followed to cope with this were negatived shortly after by the first dress rehearsal. Drab rehearsal dress gives no clue to the ultimate drawing power of a splendidly costumed crowd; the principals did not stand a chance for all that they were picked out by limes. Yet another rehearsal was called for a relight again, but without the cast, so alteration was reduced to guesswork. Further hazards were to follow when the great impresario arrived from New York to vet the result. The ballet mistress and the renowned designer then started separately, each to shove an oar in. When the completed masterpiece finally took the stage, how much of the result was the actual work of the American or British lighting designer, if either, was anybody's guess.

Who "Does" the Lighting?

What should happen is something like this. First of all, who is going to "do" the lighting? This has to be decided very early on. It is no good calling in someone, however distinguished or expert, at the last minute, when everything has got out of hand and "We simply must get it right before we open the day after tomorrow." Even if he knows the play because it is a revival, he cannot know this production of it. He is unlikely indeed to find the lighting layout to his liking, and yet there is no time to readjust let alone rehang it. All the newly-arrived expert can do is to create friction and cause sufficient resentment to ensure that those who at least were doing their best, if unsuccessfully, cease to do even that. The lighting man in a show can be more difficult to change at the last minute than one of the principals in the cast. For this, the essentially clumsy and intractable nature of the lantern end of stage lighting is responsible.

The producer may decide he is going to do the lighting himself with the aid of the electrician. There is no reason why he should not, but he must then take the trouble to learn about the subject—the actual painting with light. Theoretically, he ought to be able to leave the technical mechanics, how lanterns are fixed and fed, to the electrician, but he may be at an awful disadvantage if he does. Not to be able to ask for something, in the certain knowledge that it is possible, may invite refusal to do it, or disappointment with the result.

These remarks also apply to scene designers doing the lighting. Personally, I am more in favour of their doing this work than the producer; for, like playing in his own production, it may demand too much specialization, so interfering with his essential general view. It is quite otherwise for the scene designer. Because not only is the light, that enables it to be seen, an essential part of his set; but also when designing he is able to make due allowance for the physical accommodation and placing of the equipment. He can arrange, for example, that such a spotlight can shine through here or there and that the areas nearby are painted dark enough not to catch the scatter from it and betray the hidden source.

The scene designer who does his own lighting is indeed a happy man, especially if to complete it he does the costumes as well. Why, then, do so few undertake this work? The answer seems to be that they are scared of the disciplines imposed by electricity, optics and illumination, yet the specialist lighting designers are seldom themselves engineers, illuminating or electrical. Lighting is an art and with what this book and others like it provide, all that is needed is inspiration and the ever-growing skill that comes with experience.

Whoever is designing the lighting, he or she is responsible to the producer alone. While the opinions of the ballet mistress, the scene designer, the members of the cast, the friend of the backer, the theatre owner, and perhaps even the architect, who may not like the way those ugly blue spotlights are disfiguring his new theatre, may have to be endured: they can and must be ignored.

Making a Layout

Given the lighting job, obviously one should get hold of a copy of the play or script to study. There should follow a briefing by the producer with preliminary models of the settings. Artist's design sketches in the flat are very unreliable. If I had my way I would ban them from all theatre exhibitions as well. Theatre is three-dimensional and the least that can be expected is simple models; the detailed ones can come later on. It is essential that at the earliest stage the producer should himself be thinking, as I say often in the pages of this book, in terms of light; that his "moves" are motivated by the lighting atmosphere in which the action will have its being and by which it will be seen.

The completion of $\frac{1}{2}$-in. scale plans is a signal that one can really get down to work and make a layout of the lighting equipment. A free hand is unlikely. One's desires are bound to conflict with the hanging plot for the scenery if there are a lot of changes. The lighting bars have to be fitted in and they must have the necessary clearance to enable them to be used. If this cannot possibly be done then one must know at the start and substitute other arrangements before things have got too far. Fig. 103 shows how in *Jorrocks*, at the New Theatre, in London, the serious blockage of overhead hanging space when heavy built pieces are flown was overcome. As can be seen, lighting was actually built into the base of the scenery to become the overhead lighting after being flown. All this is a matter for discussion—in which the stage manager takes a leading part, as the practical man who has to run the show—to make it work. Eventually a compromise is worked out and we have a preliminary plan showing the positioning of the equipment. There follows a struggle to get the layout reconciled to the available dimmers during which some lanterns may have to be deleted and others paralleled two or more at a time.

"Practical" must be the watchword as there is no merit whatever in lighting that cannot be run so that all its effects are realized each night. There is a similarity in the processes of lighting and building scenery. Someone has to do the detail drawings from which the man on the bench will actually make the bits of scenery in such a manner that when they come together they will fit properly. Now whether the designer does all this or whether someone else does, using the original designs, depends on aptitudes, time and scale of the enterprise. So, too, the lighting designer may be his own electrician or have to depend on an electrician for the practical side as to how the equipment is to be assembled and fed. It does not matter which state of affairs prevails so long as it is clearly understood who is doing what, as things do not get done by themselves!

The resulting layout can be directed, focused, and coloured all on paper in the shape of a final plan, before ever one enters the theatre for the first lighting rehearsal. In a simple show

FIG. 103 Lighting fixed into underside of built scenery to compensate for blocked lines overhead when flown. *Jorrocks* at the New Theatre, London

with a straightforward layout there may only be one lighting plan for all purposes. In a complicated show there could be a series of detail drawings, perhaps for each scene. Certainly as far as drawings to be handed out to the electrician who rigs and wires, too much detail on the one drawing may lead to disaster. It may well be appropriate to keep the wiring layout

186   *The Art of Stage Lighting*

quite separate from the lantern setting layout. This is especially so if the theatre is one of those with all sorts of odd circuits masquerading at the switchboard as battens, fly dips OP, float spots, and goodness knows what else.

In the actual drawing of the lighting, the merits of the international symbols which are issued under CIE auspices should be considered (Appendix 2). These are in $\frac{1}{2}$-in. scale Letratape (made by Letraset Ltd.), so that a *clear* symbol can be made without fuss, but they were also designed for freehand drawing. Each symbol ties in with an international definition of general optical performance which has been translated into several languages, including Russian. The more these symbols are used, the more chance one will have in understanding the lighting layouts of other countries, whether from practical involvement or when reading purely as a matter of interest. Against the symbols it has been said they are not detailed enough and recognizable outline drawings of equipment are essential. But recognition at this level would be extremely parochial since such outlines would of necessity be of proprietary equipment. When all is said and done, the actual variants in basic optics and, therefore, beam characteristics are few; it is the wattage, colour filter, direction and angle of spread that make the great differences—not the shape of the lantern. If the commonest lanterns and those which are uncoloured are not qualified except for direction, then additions to indicate change of power are simplified. Thus, on a small stage the principal lighting might come from 500-watt Profiles and Fresnels so only wattages higher or lower need be marked as 1K and 2K. An example of a simple marked-up layout is shown in Fig. 104, and the symbols are used in all the layouts and lighting diagrams in this book, qualifying marks being kept to a minimum.

In deciding which lanterns go on which circuit, the actual operation of the switchboard must be borne in mind. This means one should preferably have visited the theatre to familiarize oneself with this particular control. At this stage the electrician and his operator's opinion should be sought as to what arrangement suits them. This opinion need not be taken completely as holy writ. If for one reason or another it is not possible to visit the theatre, you are entitled to know what the switchboard specification is: the number of dimmers and their wattages, the type, and its manufacturer. This known, then Chapter 13 will help to clarify what may be expected of it. Although in the last resort the operator can make or mar *any* control, one at least has an idea whether what is asked for is reasonable or not. Of course, in some instances the lighting designer may be working his own control, though not all wish to do so or are permitted to do so. As is by now well known,

FIG. 104 Lighting layout by William Lorraine for the set in Fig. 105, showing use of CIE symbols. Simplified for clarity. Booms and Number 1 bar were in fact 500-watt units paired to each circuit, i.e. 16 and 24 not 8 and 12 as shown. Other Fresnel spots were 1-kW and 2-kW as appropriate. Those upstage have been reduced and basic angles only shown. The 12 F.O.H. Profiles have been omitted entirely.

FIG. 105 Set by Neil Hobson for *Power of Persuasion;* Gert Hofmann at the Garrick, London. Particular interest lies in the need to light the top of the set—the roof—separately from the room below. The Fresnels in the flys (Fig. 104) and the cyc battens were used for this

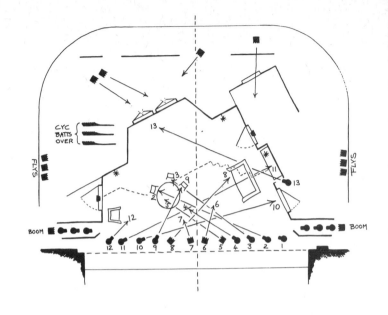

my preference is for designing lighting directly using the control oneself. Not only their design but their positioning front of house, in so far as I have been responsible, has been directed to this end. Such a policy deprives no one of work, for the regular operator has to be on hand to take over for the run, and this can only increase his status.

Lantern Setting and Rigging

Whatever the procedure decided on in respect of the lighting control, one should be armed with a plan identifying every control channel by a number. To ask the operator for something known to him as the "OP upstage green trucks," which by then has been used by you as a flame-coloured firelight spot, is to invite confusion. The control levers must run for the operator sequentially as 1–60, for example. Unfortunately, this may lead to some dodging about on the actual lantern layout as there will usually be more of these than control channels even when patching is not practised. Whether you prefer two sequential series, one for the greater number of lanterns and the other for the control, is a matter of personal preference. No difficulty should arise in two series provided there is a good cross-index with control numbers in one colour and lanterns in another. Not only may the need for clarity in layout demand two sets of numbers, but also replugging and patching, if any, during the show.

Assuming the lantern rig has been completed by the electrician and directed according to the indications on the plan, the next step is to set them as accurately as possible so that when the first lighting rehearsal takes place they are on target. These setting sessions can, if not taken seriously, merely waste so much time for all will have to be set again when the scenery and furniture turns up. But whether one prefers to cut this session out altogether and go in for setting only when the stage is properly dressed, it is certain a proper layout in which one knows what is expected of each lantern is an invaluable time saver. One of my objections to the stage lighting bridge form of access is that it relieves some lighting designers from the trouble of thinking out in advance what they are going to do. This casual play-around approach to lighting can be adopted only when dealing with a mainly permanent installation which one knows intimately from old acquaintance (see "Repertoire," page 197). When well paper-planned in advance, even a new layout is an old friend by the time one arrives in the theatre and we shall see later how important this is.

As an example of how far pre-planning can be carried, the requirements of the Robert Nesbitt production, *Rainbow Square*, some years ago at the old Stoll Theatre, can be quoted. The

FIG. 106 Rigging the equipment hired for a production—the only time it will be readily get-at-able! The Shaftesbury Theatre, London

plot called for almost every realistic lighting effect known to the business—Evening, Sunset, Night, Moonlight, Early Morning with Dawn, then Fine Sunny Day turning to Thunderstorm, and so on. All this fortunately took place on one magnificent standing set (Fig. 161) designed by George Ramon, but as it occupied the whole stage and was to be completely encompassed by a cyclorama carried right up to the grid, virtually all lighting had to be installed in advance, and would remain inaccessible. The bars were loaded and directed at stage level, then taken up to their deads and tested by switching on. Probably we had to lower in and out a few times in some cases, though I cannot remember. Once the scaffolding was built on which the all-too-solid scenery was later to be hung, no further adjustment was possible, not even to change a colour or a lamp. A tower wagon could not be used on the obstructed floor or even got on, and beanstalks and the like had not been heard of. Cinemoid colours were chosen from among those known to have the best endurance and lanterns such as the old Patt 56 Acting Area were used in order to take advantage of long-life (1000-hour) lamps. Our precautions in this respect turned out to be unnecessary, as the show did not run more than a couple of months! However, I still feel a warm glow at the proof that it is possible to avoid all finicky fiddling and light on broad lines yet get a notice—"beautifully lit"—from Alan Dent in the *News Chronicle*. Of course, the very form of set which prevented access greatly facilitated the adoption of the broad lighting theory. Distance lends an enchanting hand, and, although most of our theatres do not permit this approach through lack of space, German opera houses and theatres do.

Lighting Rehearsal

The first lighting rehearsal proper is going to set a problem. Assuming the scenery, furniture, and props are all there, the most important ingredient, the cast, is still missing. Where there are but few, as in a drawing-room comedy, stand-ins will suffice, but in a play with a large cast, or a musical, what is one to do to avoid the disasters outlined earlier in this chapter? Nor, as we have seen, is the chorus without the actual costumes much help either. Yet if we can plan on paper and even set lanterns in advance, surely dimmer levels can be set in anticipation of targets to come. On the other hand, if one decides to cut any sort of lighting rehearsal and start from zero during the first dress rehearsal, there is likely to be a protest at the absence of light. All in all, I am of the opinion that the solution consists of combining in the lighting rehearsal the final adjustment of lanterns and the sketching in of dimmer changes. The operative word is "sketch"; the prolonged "up a little, down a little" to establish precise levels which are then subsequently discarded only leads to friction. The lighting rehearsal is an opportunity to inform the switchboard and others of the lighting plot. It is perhaps the equivalent for them of the first play reading, and it is here that the operator learns of the number of cues, their duration and the time available between them.

One way of going about it, having checked the positioning of the various spots and preferably committed what they do to memory so that only an occasional glance at the plan is necessary, is to call for the contents of the first lighting cue as a series of numbers. There is a good idea here to be borrowed from television. In a scene which is likely to require a lot of balancing, ask for the numbers called automatically to be put at, say, 7 on the scale (say half-light), instead of full, except in cases where you know for certain that you will require, and therefore call for, something very different. It is now possible when finally balancing, perhaps not until dress rehearsal, either to dim or to increase a particular lamp. This will also have the practical advantage of extending life of lamps and colours for later. Never leave projector lamps blazing away hour after hour without purpose. Make sure a reasonable level of lighting, using long-life lamps, is available for non-lighting rehearsals; people are seldom content with just the stage working lights.

As soon as possible complete each cue and tell the operator to plot it. Do not linger lovingly over the early changes of the show for this will lead to a rush later on. On the other hand, do not rush the operator while he is plotting. If he does not get your beautiful lighting properly written down you may never see its like again.

It is important to take a look at the effect of the lighting by moving round the theatre, both now and during other rehearsals, from time to time. A view from the tiers above can show faults that simply must be remedied. On the other hand, there are times when something visible from a few extreme side seats or stage boxes will simply have to be toler- ated. The actual glare from a lamp never can. An early check on the state known as a blackout can be useful in avoiding waste of time chasing mysterious stray lights later on. It is, however, essential to switch on exit signs and orchestra lights (if it is a musical of any kind) when lighting.

When you get the "all clear" from the operator that all is plotted, the next lighting can be set up in the same way, but it will also be necessary to indicate how it is related to the previous lighting. Is it a slow change which begins some minutes after the completion of the first cue, or does it follow on immediately, or what? If it is a switching or a fast cue and the control is not a preset type, do not ask for a large number of existing levels to change to an entirely unrelated series.

It may be possible to bring lighting to one set of levels and then move on to a proportional increase by merely advancing the master fader, but anything more in respect of a lot of channels already in use requires a preset. Maybe the control has not got a master or even a master wheel; then one is re- duced to jockeying a few levers by hand as a token, in earnest of what would have been done—if only! Playing the dimmer levers individually by hand can go a long way in a slow change, but at speed there are serious limitations, especially when one follow-on cue comes fast on top of another. The plot has to be read, the levers picked out to "go" in next to no time. A chance to practise this sort of thing is essential. Never call for a run-through immediately after plotting. Give the operator time to con his plot and decide how best to deploy the resources of his control. I have seen Paul Weston perform wonders on one of the larger examples of my Light Console. Bringing in large numbers of new circuits and moving others to as formid- able an array of Joe Davis' levels as can be conceived. That instrument was invented at a time when such a type of cue and quantity of spots had never been imagined. Yet after some thought and a bit of practice in dumb show—press this piston, then those keys, cancel off Manual I left stops at 5 on the dial, add these stops at 7, knock off those at 8—all in the space of six seconds and the job was done. What is more, night after night! Wonders can be performed, and indeed enjoyed, by a virtuoso operator even on an unsuitable control —but give him time to think things out. We should remember that the elaborate plots of the past were performed on primitive controls simply by use of many operators and these men are no longer available.

Plotting

Reference to plotting raises the question of plot sheets. Established operators have their methods and to ask them to change without a good reason, like a completely new form of control, would be silly. However, since this book has to be all things to all men, a few words on the subject will not be out of place.

I prefer a sheet, preferably printed but anyway ink ruled in advance, on the lines of Fig. 107. Each cue then occupies a *horizontal* line: never make it vertical because being contrary to normal reading it conveys no message at a glance. Theoretically, I suppose a vertical column for each channel number is required, and I have prepared such plot sheets for 120 channels without much difficulty, but, on the whole, so long as there are good vertical divisions to correspond to similar landmarks on the switchboard this will be sufficient to space things out and in many instances allow use of larger digits than otherwise would be the case. Using the control (Chapter 8, Fig. 86) it would be natural to make these divisions between 20 and 21, and 40 and 41, thereby covering the whole sixty channels.

On a switchboard which involves the operator in a lot of

	Cue	1–20	21–40	41–60
1 7s	Raise 5 sec	1/F, 2/F, 6/5, 7/3, 8/3 11/7, 12/F 19/5	21/3, 31/5, 32/F, 35/5, 38/2	41–45/4
2 30s	Raise 3 sec	3/F, 4/5, 17/3, .20/5	24/5, 25/3, 34/F, 37/5	
3 2s	c/F 10 sec	(2/0), 6/F, 7/8, 9/F (12/5)	(31/0) 33/F, 34/3, 36/F 24/8, 27/5	
4 4m	Cut	8/0, 11/0, 17/0	25/0, 38/0	41–45/0
5	Raise 15 sec	2–7/F 14–16/5	21–24/F, 34–35/F	52–56/F

FIG. 107   Example of plot sheet

FIG. 108 Plot arranged to show throw-off at levels

	Cue	1–20	21–40	41–60
7s	1 Raise 5 sec	1, 2, 12/F 11/7 6,19/5 7,8/3	32/F 31, 35/5 21/3, 38/2	41–45/4
30s	2 Raise 3 sec	3/F, 4,20/5 17/3	34/F, 24,37/5 25/3	
2s	3 c/F 10 sec	6, 9/F 7/8, (12/5) (2/0)	33,36/F 24/8 27/5 (31/0) 34/3	
4m	4 Cut	8, 11,17/0	25, 38/0	41–45/0
	5 Raise 15 sec	2–7/F 14–16/5	21–24, 34–35/F	52–56/F

manual dropping off at intermediate levels, such as direct-operated switchboards or even the Light Console, it may be helpful to take several lines per cue so that the related drop-offs stand out, as in Fig. 108. On an all-electric system or any kind of preset board, in most cases the detail work is done before the cue. The levers are set before the appropriate master is moved and, in consequence, the multi-line technique loses its point. One simply circles, preferably in colour, dimmer numbers which have to be manually moved against the main stream as with a cross-fade, where there is either no preset or not sufficient justification to use a whole preset with the consequent resetting it may entail.

In point of fact, on the smaller twenty- or forty-channel, two- or three-preset controls, which the thyristor dimmer is likely to popularize, there is a good reason to make a practice of moving alternately from one preset to another in all except the most obvious finger cues. Under these circumstances, it will be a good thing to make up one's mind and mark the plot at those places where it will be better to clear an inactive preset down to zero and set up from a clean slate rather than merely reset some levers among a forest of static ones.

When plotting a group of numbers, always put them in numerical order even though, as is all too likely, they are not so given. Some rearranging is well worth while when at last one comes to a fair copy of the plot. The left hand of the plot carries cue number, type of cue, "cross-fade," "raise," "dim," and its timing, but there should also be space to write in the appropriate interval between cues. The plot just referred to is the working one and is peculiar to the switchboard, but at the same time it is customary for an ASM to plot each dimmer level for each cue as a record of each lighting picture. This is, of course, what a full dimmer memory-type control records and, in consequence, the working plot then becomes absurdly simple, just the type of change, for example, "cross-fade five seconds."

In writing a plot it is important that the operator should not squander words by using them interchangeably even though others may do so. There are, for example, three verbs which are used in the theatre to mean the same thing. These are "check," "dim," and "fade." They are beautifully short and if the operator disciplines himself to give them each a precise meaning much extra writing can be avoided. I suggest that "dim" is the verb to use in respect of the individual dimmer channel levers. "Fade" should be applied to master controls which otherwise might give rise to confusion by being referred to as master dimmers. There is also the verb "check" which could be used for operations in which dimmers drop to marks but do not go right out. A very normal use of "check" is as a noun for the marks themselves. Thus, dimmer 9 could be at check 7. A very useful shorthand for this is 9/7, always putting the channel number first. Presets can conveniently be indicated by roman figures and groups by letters, commonly when there are two or three as X, Y, and Z. These letters avoid muddle with possible colour symbols, R, B, G, for example. Keep the verb "preset" for its true application and use "set" for adjustment of levers where there is not one or, when there is, for adjustment within a preset. Avoid unnecessary words: "C/F" saves writing "cross-fade" and "D.B.O." "dead-blackout," and so on.

Of course, the switchboard operator will not be the only one to write a plot as those whose duty is "to follow" or to strike and set lanterns will also have to write down what they have to do and when. In this connection, a frequent task is the changing of colours both during the show itself and during rehearsal, due to changes of mind. Colour filters can be difficult to recognize at the best of times, let alone in the half-light, and a clear number written in Chinagraph pencil on the filter itself can be a great help.

Dress Rehearsal or Run-through

The preliminary plot has now been prepared as just described at a lighting rehearsal or on paper as homework by the lighting designer. In either case, there will not be much point in doing anything further, except to keep an eye on movement changes, cuts and additions and all the other changes of mind, until the show comes together, cast and all, at a run-through or at the dress rehearsal if it is a costume piece.

Always remember that at the end of a run-through which has not gone too well, it was probably the operator's first, or at the most second, opportunity to rehearse as a show. Allow him time to rewrite his plots in peace to include alterations, and at least to rehearse again the difficult bits at the control by himself. Switchboard operation is a full-time job with anything like a plot. During a run-through never interrupt unless disasters are likely to, what is now known as, escalate; otherwise take notes and sort out afterwards. Try to avoid "going back" and repeating a lighting change. The switchboard plot assumes going forward and lighting at a particular time can consist of the results of several successive cues; sorting this out to go back takes time therefore.

Rehearsals with cast will tax the communication system so it is worth while considering it now. It should go without saying that to attempt any lighting for a musical once the band is in without so much as a telephone from stalls to the lighting control is sheer lunacy. Yet this is exactly what happened in the case of a new remote control positioned on a stage perch in the West End not many years ago.

Communications

From the point of view of lighting, the most important communication from the stalls rehearsal station is with the operator and this must be quite independent of other sound systems. It does seem that, when there is a lighting designer, the best method is for both he and the operator to wear one ear-piece and a chest microphone. Notice that they are similarly equipped. One-way messages—commands only—to the control do not make sense. One must know that a particular action has been carried out, for it may not announce itself visually. Something may have happened—a fuse or lamp blown, or it could be that the wrong circuit has been called. Contact must be really close between these two. Under certain happy but rare circumstances, as already described, the lighting could actually take place from the lighting control position. The headpiece system allows call keys to be dispersed with and allows verbal communication with the producer alongside.[1] At the operator's end he would be able to take other messages direct from producer, stage manager, and show via a loudspeaker. Reply in these cases is needed, but more rarely used, so a sprung "speak" key meets the case.

Another important special line is between switchboard and dimmer room. This is for testing and trouble shooting. At a minimum it should consist of a battery-operated pair of phones with a very long flex and/or more than one jack position at the bank end. This phone is outside the normal house system which can be used by the electrician, stage door and others to communicate, though there should be an extension on that

[1] A system is being developed for loudspeakers in which reply and call occupy different frequency bands. This allows both circuits to be kept continuously open without a risk of howling round the loop.

system also in the dimmer room. There is a case with the more elaborate control systems for having an extension of the outside phone available in the dimmer room. The manufacturer's engineer may, there and then, need some simple test to be done in order to give the right advice over the phone.

Another important link is with the follow spot positions when they exist and, once again, means to reply other than by shouting through the aperture is needed. Make sure that the call-up is really audible. Four arcs in a room can make a lot of noise. Here again, headpieces have their advantages, particularly when talk-through cueing is practised.[1]

Cueing

This brings us to something else that must be decided at early rehearsal: what is going to initiate lighting changes? What are the cues? At one time, it went without saying that the switchboard, follow-spots, and all the rest went into action on light signals from the stage manager's corner. These lights still must be provided, supplemented in most cases by buzzers (mainly to sound an alert during rehearsals). It is usual to have red and green lights (warning and go), but personally I wish the colours were amber and green.

Working to lights is tricky in a series of fast cues, and cues have a way of coming in bursts, one on top of the other. No matter how well positioned the cue light is, one cannot keep one's eye glued to it when working a number of levers, and it may have been extinguished and come on again. Thus we are into the next cue without knowing it. The best method is to make close cues into automatic follow-on cues corresponding to certain visual happenings on the stage. There is a strong case, which stage managers are reluctant to admit, now that so many controls have a good view of the stage, for the lighting control to take its own cues from the action. The view from there can often be much better than from the prompt corner and also delays are avoided. Besides, it encourages the operator to feel part of the show. The question of lighting-control position was dealt with in Chapter 2.

Layout for Repertoire

It must be apparent by now what a large amount of work and time is likely to be involved in setting up and rehearsing to get the lighting right for a particular production. For a play with a run of a week, a month, or a year, the main work once done, repetition is easy. The situation is similar to that in printing. Once the type has been set up, corrected, and finally put on the machine, extra run-on copies are inexpensive indeed.

[1] The ABTT publishes a pamphlet with details of essential communications arranged to conform with various scales of enterprise.

FIG. 109 Proscenium lighting bridge and fly galleries, Royal Opera House, Covent Garden

Break up the pages and distribute the type and then, although there was an exact record in the shape of previous edition, costs of a reset would be almost as great as before. This situation is encountered in repertoire working for the production is interleaved with perhaps five or six others and returns at uncertain intervals. If the lighting is quite unrelated to the other productions in the repertoire, what has to be faced is something like a re-rig for each. Furthermore, matinées may differ from the evening performance on some days and new productions may be in rehearsal during the morning or afternoon and on Sundays.

It is the repertoire working traditional in opera that is responsible for the insistence on lighting bridges behind the proscenium and elsewhere to allow the necessary access (Fig. 109). Even so, the lanterns will not move themselves and a large number of staff will be necessary to do this work. Leaving on one side the question whether this repositioning will be accurate enough to prevent a poorer performance being given, it is necessary to ask what ought to happen when the stage is admittedly of a size that must not be cluttered with a bridge, or there is insufficient money to provide for large numbers of staff. It is no good saying that the artistic result ought not to be subjected to such limitations; the fact is that nine times out of ten it will be so limited.

The solution to not having time, men, or money to move lanterns between productions is *not to move them*. The result is a layout in which three-quarters of the equipment is locked up solid and never moved. The remaining quarter is made accessible so that it can be suited precisely to the special needs of a particular production. Where a particularly vital lantern cannot be made directly accessible, then remote pole-operation or even motor-servo control should be adopted. The time saved in a repertoire house would soon write off the admittedly large increase in initial outlay.

The design of the permanent part of the stage lighting installation in a new theatre or for a new season of repertoire has to be approached with the notion that some changes will have to be made during the initial productions. The plan must not be deemed a failure because this happens. After all, it would happen even in the most carefully designed special layout matched to a single production so it is all the more likely to happen when trying to serve all productions in this way. The aim must be that before long the resident lighting designer can sit down and light any show *adequately* without touching anything, except the switchboard controls. The adverb is used deliberately; beyond this, the adjustable part of the installation is used to put on the gloss and the special bits of lighting peculiar to that production.

Does this mean that only a resident lighting man can be used? Certainly not, provided the visitor behaves himself and really tries to use the installation. The trouble is that so few lighting designers make a practice of using the control themselves. Every loss in respect of being unable to change direction, focus, or colour pales into insignificance when compared to the ability to use the fingers to call up, modify, blend, or dismiss pools of light before your very eyes. Before his visit, the guest expert can be given a stage plan showing not the usual aimless array of lanterns for him to shift, as he will, but an exact statement of what each does. He can then concentrate on getting the maximum effect from the free area. Without this discipline, he may by chance have spot No. 1 on the circle front adjusted to do near enough exactly what No. 2 normally does. There may be many examples of such unnecessary work for, however special the production and the lighting, a great deal of the latter is going to be concerned with bread-and-butter illumination. Individuality in respect of production and/or creation can be confined to the jam and how it is spread.

This basic or foundation lighting was the one great advantage of the batten and footlight era. It was always possible to get some light on the stage very quickly and work could then be concentrated on the trimmings. Today we have the other extreme. Whether visiting a theatre or the stage in some school hall, a trial operation of the switches produces random and ugly patches of light, each one of which will require considerable thought and work on it before the whole blends as lighting. When this is combined with a complete patching system on the American model so that decisions are required as to which dimmer should be used before current can be applied, then this light task is indeed heavy. There is no "stand easy" condition from which the lighting can be called, with but an electrifying command from the switchboard.

Yet it should not be all that difficult to achieve on the smaller stages in theatres and halls. The lack of space is bound to insist on more or less the same scenic floor plan being used each time. In open staging, especially arena forms, a standard pattern of light should be relatively easy. The layout by Stephen Joseph shown in Fig. 124, page 218, was devised with fixed separate area lighting in mind. In the proscenium theatre intrusive scenery can be a problem, but even this can merely mean leaving certain permanents extinguished and directing a few specials to cover the gap. This is where a scene designer who is his own lighting man scores.

The permanent lanterns also rely on not changing the actual colours used therein. The changing of colours for replacement or even for special effect is, however, never so difficult as disturbing the actual setting of lanterns. Where bars can be easily lowered in, there can be no objection to changing one set of filters for another richer in colour to suit a production, provided the essential beam relationship is not disturbed.

Fixed lanterns should be really fixed—wing nuts and other finger-tight adjustments being replaced by bolts requiring the use of a spanner. On the other hand, the lanterns intended for adjustment should not only be accessible but be of a type lending themselves to adjustment. In the case of a Patt 23 Profile spot or equivalent, the standard internal mask, difficult to adjust, of the cheaper model is a positive advantage for fixed positions, whereas the built-in shutter, readily adjustable, model is essential for other positions. All the adjustable lanterns should have scales giving amount of tilt and rotation so that notes can be taken to simplify resetting next time when that production comes around.

It will probably be necessary to repeat that the ideas for a semi-permanent installation are not put forward for the long-run West End house. They are, however, recommended for adoption to some extent in all repertoire and repertory playing houses and for all theatres and halls with minimal staff, often one man and he not expert. In the latter, the firm supplying the equipment ought to leave it set up (this would have to be included in the contract and paid for) adjusted ready to produce a series of lighting patterns and not just random puddles.

Fixing a large part of the lighting not only saves labour but enables one, through familiarity, to get the best out of old friends, so to speak. The cry for flexibility and adaptability is overdone these days. The constant pursuit of new materials to the neglect of the old may lead scene designers to handicap themselves with improperly learned techniques. By common consent it is agreed that an adaptable theatre furnishes only a compromise version of each of the forms it apes.[1] Too much labour, time, machinery, and money is needed to make changes. Why then should lighting be an exception?

On the contrary, my notion is that where we are working at drama-studio level with plenty of students to provide the labour, chunks of an adaptable theatre may in fact be more easily manhandled around than the lanterns required to light the result. The idea of considering a large part of an installation as fixed is not put forward as being novel. Some have adopted it of their own volition, others of necessity, and yet other sturdy characters will not have anything to do with it. These last prefer to battle on to perfection and fortunately for them do not return to see the variants which the stage manager has had to devise behind their backs to make it practical to fit the show in repertoire.

Resetting

This raises the question of how one resets lanterns, few or many, for each different scene or each different production. It is no good spending time to achieve an accurate switchboard plot if the other end, the lanterns, are not properly positioned and focused. The lighting plans have to be kept up to date and any changes noted as the rehearsals proceed. The re-direction itself can be eased if lanterns have scales fitted and if particularly No. 1 bar can be readily lowered in. Sadlers Wells had a method using targets marked on special presetting stage cloths for each production which were arranged to be appropriate when the bar was lowered in to adjustment height. In 1960, pole-operated Fresnel spots (Fig. 110) were installed in the No. 1 position, this stage being too small to employ the usual opera bridge. The height of 24 ft at which these are used must, however, be considered the limit for this kind of working. A similar arrangement is used for all lights in the studio

FIG. 110   Fresnel spot arranged to pan, tilt and focus using pole attachment

[1] John English is a dissentient voice believing as he does that the large theatre when built at Cannon Hill will be fully and rapidly adaptable. He does, however, state that there will have to be three complete sets of lighting and even in his small first instalment, the studio, there are two complete sets.

theatre under the main Civic Theatre complex at Frankfurt in Germany.

Even where lighting bridges are not used over the stage they will be necessary in the auditorium ceiling, whether in the open or behind slots. The design of these is an extremely tricky business. They must not take up too much room and yet all likely equipment must be capable of accommodation. One has to be able to reach the front of spots to insert colours and focus and there has to be access farther back to the profiling shutters, also for relamping without dismantling. Clearances to give the correct angles of traverse are critical. The socket outlets have to be positioned and flexes to be housed. The thing has to be, and feel, safe, so there is no reason for lighting staff to be acrobats. The floor must be of wood and not of expanded metal or some other torment, in order to be suitable for kneeling on. The ABTT publish recommendations for these auditorium bridges, also vertical wall slots and stage bridges, in the form of data sheets which are more likely to incorporate the latest experience than a book such as this; in consequence, the reader is referred to them.

Another problem is represented by the need to change colour filters during the performance, particularly front of house. Some theatres can face the expense of using motor-driven mechanism for individual change (Fig 174 is an early example), others will be better advised to spend the money on extra spotlights and circuits. A relatively inexpensive substitute is a motor-driven wheel with five colours. These can be accurately selected using the control in Fig. 112, but of course an inscene change may involve passing through unwanted intermediate colours.

Of course, a good visual memory plays an important part in all work concerned with lighting, and it is a good idea to encourage it by not keeping one's nose stuck in one's notes. But notes there must be, and it seems to me more could be done to keep a photographic record, especially as, thanks to the Polaroid Land Camera, this need not be so chancy, or mean importing an expert photographer.

FIG. 111 1000-watt CCT Silhouette spot for the National, London; gate profile is set while in lantern, removed and locked for repertoire storage. Four zoom lenses are also interchangeable to give differing ranges of beam spread

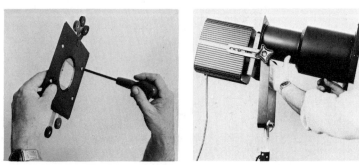

FIG. 112 Push-button box to preset five colours on four spots (see also Fig. 174)

Lanterns can be conducted on to their targets by standing at the various receiving ends. Even so, when all is done, it is still an immense help if the artistes have trained themselves instinctively to seek the light. Professionals, except opera singers, are very good at this, but amateurs not only do not make the best of a bad job when something has moved, but seem positively to dodge the light or make sure it lands on their chest downwards. For this the glare is responsible, but glare means that you and your lamp have achieved your rendezvous in space. As for the opera singers, we should not be too hard on them, as light is a commodity somewhat infrequently encountered in their world!

10 Illumination of the Stage

THIS chapter explores the essential basis of lighting: how do we see, and, because the subject is stage lighting, how can one influence what is seen? The first essential is to repeat once again that, although we talk about looking at an object, the eye is a receiver not a transmitter. Light comes from a source and is reflected, probably only partially in respect of intensity and colour, and ultimately reaches the eye. Once the light arrives there it is automatically focused on the retina and transmitted to the brain. Only then does it become a picture capable of rousing interest and possibly emotion. No light in the first place and there will be no picture. Seeing is a matter of external stimuli.

If the light is poor, then the picture will be so incomplete that the brain has to supply the missing bits, and this may give rise to a continual strain and fatigue. It is not the eye that is strained with too little or distorting light: it is the brain. The eye will carry out instantaneously an adaptation to the levels of light of some eight to one by opening the iris wide to pass more when there is little, and closing it when there is a lot of light. Certain chemical changes also go on at the retina and, provided sufficient time has elapsed, the normal eye can adapt itself quite easily to either the 0·02 foot-candles of moonlight or 10,000 foot-candles of sunlight. At very low levels, like moonlight, the eye cannot perceive colour at all[1] and at all levels of intensity it may be quite unable to perceive form correctly. The fault in the first case is inherent in the eye itself, but in the latter case it will be the lighting that is wrong. The picture may be on the retina but cannot be interpreted by the brain correctly. It is like listening to a conversation in a language in which one understands only some of the words.

---

[1] Black and white vision is known as "scotopic" and concerns rod receptors all over the retina. These are very sensitive to light and one can literally see out of the corner of the eye. Colour "photopic" and fine-detail vision needs cone receptors which are concentrated in the centre. The angle embraced by this vision is very small indeed and the eye has to scan the scene to bring it to bear.

Personally, I consider optical illusion—the deliberate deceiving of the brain—has a large part to play in the theatre, and it is therefore considered later on.

Visual Perception and Lighting to See

Visual perception in the theatre suffers from the serious handicap that members of the audience each get their own angle of view of the stage. In the cinema the picture is presented complete on one plane. It was lit for one viewer, the camera lens, and yet even there, when projected, troubles may be encountered of physical obstruction due to poor sight lines or too distant or too close or too angular a view. In the theatre the picture is three-dimensional, usually as deep as it is wide, and the range of angular view encountered even in the most orthodox of picture frame proscenium theatres is extremely wide and varied. In the circle one looks downwards and sees mainly stage floor, whereas in the stalls the view of the stage floor may be minimal or non-existent. To those in the stalls the actors may appear crisply lit against a dark night sky and the producer congratulates himself on a lack of offensive shadows there; but take a trip to the circle and the actors will be seen against a confused collection of pools of light and shadow on the floor. Of course, one accepts the idea that not everyone will get a view of all the backcloth or of, perhaps, the scenery on one side of the stage or the other, but not to see the actors properly, that is quite another matter. After all, any producer knows that their principal action must be concentrated in that magic, and often all too limited, part of the stage, the acting area to which all audience have uninterrupted sight lines. It is, however, no good doing this if that area is not going to be lit properly.

Where everyone looks down at the stage floor only from one side the problem is eased, but in the old multi-tier house the reluctant conclusion may well be that only the flat lighting from the days when they were built—the battens and footlights—is really appropriate. This is an extreme statement but has more than a grain of truth behind it and may explain the multiplicity of spotlights, the very negation of spotlighting, encountered in West End theatres.

A very good place to begin our study of seeing is with the geometric solids of the art school. In drawing either the cube or the cone, for example, one would not expect them to appear solid without some shading on one side. This seems obvious when trying to reproduce these three-dimensional objects on a flat two-dimensional sheet of paper (Fig. 113), but applies equally well when trying in fact to draw the same picture on each of the two-dimensional retinas of the eyes of the audience. It follows, therefore, that any lighting of these solids must be

FIG. 113 Sketch of geometric shapes with shading

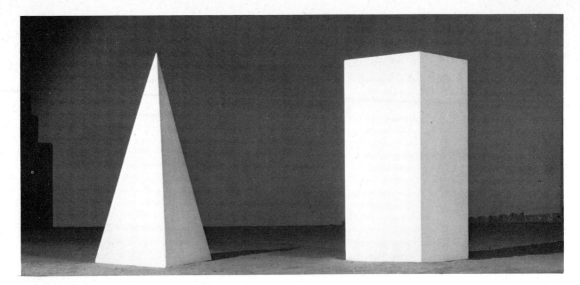

FIG. 114 Geometric solids lit from side angles (LH dominant) but viewed flat on

arranged to cast some shadow. Too heavy a shadow could become confusing if (Fig. 114) the objects are seen against a dark ground. All becomes well again in the illustration (Fig. 115) where the camera angle provides a view of the baseboard and the shadow of the object gives a further clue. This angle is deliberately chosen to emulate the ideal theatre angle of view, the baseboard becoming the stage floor.

Essential key lighting is obviously that from the left side and a second source (fill) from an opposing angle has been used to

FIG. 115 Geometric solids as in Fig. 114 but, viewed from above

FIG. 116 Geometric solids as in Fig. 115, but lit from one angle with softlight from the other

lessen the contrast. The two shadows on the floor might then conflict, particularly if sunlight were supposed to be represented, and therefore one would try to use a softlight type of source (Fig. 116) throwing little or no defined shadow at the second position. On the other hand, if shadow-free soft light from all directions was all that was available, then shape could be put back in the cube by painting one of its sides in a darker colour. The next step is to make the cube two-dimensional only and paint in the perspective and shadow. Under certain illumination as in the second photograph (Fig. 117), the eye would not only be completely deceived but might take the two-dimensional painted object as appearing more solid than the solid itself.

However, the principal target for stage lighting, the actor, is a solid and a very complex one at that. Lighting him, as for a portrait, the key light would be placed to the left, but, as heavy eye-socket shadows and nose shadows would be undesirable, this light could be neither too high up nor too acutely to the side. Even with the most skilful placing, however, light is not going to turn corners and light the other side of the face, so a second unit of less intensity will be placed at the opposing angle. For photography, a third unit, a backlight directed in reverse, would help separate the hair and shoulders from the background. Thus, for one position and one member of the audience, we have three lighting units (Fig. 118), and if the floor were seen, as it must be in the theatre, then there would be three conflicting shadows.

FIG. 117 Top, two geometric solids and two flat-profile painted cut-outs viewed flat on, but lit from side angles (LH dominant)

Bottom, the same, but lit flat on; only the painted profiles on the right now appear really solid, but are in fact flat, as can be seen from their bottom edges

When, in addition, one remembers that there are in the theatre several hundred other cameras all at different angles—the eyes of the audience, so to speak—and that acting is not static and usually involves several characters, an insoluble problem appears to be presented. Fortunately, the eye of the playgoer is only as perceptive as his brain and, generally speaking, the latter is only capable of giving full concentration to one visual idea at a time. Thus, if lighting provides some acceptable dominant idea, the rest of the information gets pushed into the background. The brain even seems to swallow the

notion of moonlight coming from two equal and opposing directions at once—the wings—as in most productions of the ballet *Les Sylphides*, simply because the scene is painted as a moonlight glade and the light is conventionally blue. Provided the show is suitably gripping, many, but not all, of the various defects, conflicting shadows and so on will pass muster. I have absolute faith in a single dominant idea and no faith in lighting with several ideas, for this will be interpreted as none. Lighting whose sole purpose is to make the actor visible is vulnerable to attack. The audience start subconsciously attaching their own interpretations to what they see, and as in fact there is nothing to interpret they are bound to find something to criticize.

Lighting an Open-end Stage

Now let us consider the portrait lighting blown up to cover the whole stage. It might be assumed that, if the three lanterns giving key, fill and backlight are moved farther away and made to cover the stage, this would be all that is necessary. To some extent this is true and for end-stage work, the third unit, the backlight, can usually be omitted. Colour denied to black and white photographs or television may well provide the necessary separation, so this brings the minimum number of lamps for an end stage down to two.

This really does work out; a spotlight out front either side flooded to cover the entire acting area can provide a pleasing effect, especially if one is a *slightly different* colour from the

FIG. 118 Left, one key light only; right, key light, fill light and backlight

FIG. 119 Plan: end stage lit by
two lamps only

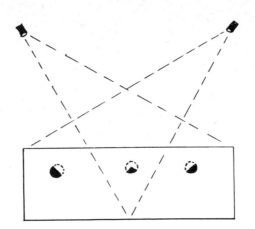

other or somewhat less bright (Fig. 119).

Of course, reliance on only two sources imposes limitations even on an open-end stage, but on a picture-frame stage with scenery it would make a nonsense of the setting. For this, like the actors, requires lighting and what suits one is unlikely to suit the other. However, it is worth while to pursue the study of the "two source only" lighting rather further. Assuming no scenery, the limitations would make themselves felt as an addition to the movement problem well known to producers already as masking. An actor might all too easily block the light which should illuminate his neighbour. To some extent this could be overcome by placing the lights relatively high so that the beams would pass overhead, and by ensuring that actors did not get too close to each other—rather troublesome in a courtship scene! A further problem may arise in revealing the actor's features as he moves away from the centre of the acting area. It is going to be extremely difficult in practice to light all his positions on the stage from the essential minimum of two angles. Further, these two angles must not just be any two angles; they must be the correct two angles for proper modelling from the audience point of view.

It will be noticed that when considering the lighting of an end stage with but two lanterns two important principles arise. The first is that the lanterns are automatically placed "out front" and the second is that the beams are crossed. Each of the two lanterns is directed to light the farther side of the stage while lapping over the other in the centre. This provides an effective compromise since action, being concerned with the relationships of one character to another, tends to turn inwards. One could say that the on-stage rather than the off-stage aspect of the actors is lit. Furthermore, any shadows tend to be projected to the outer edges of the stage where they are less distracting. The light itself comes from the direction of the audience and this helps its redirection back to their eyes and

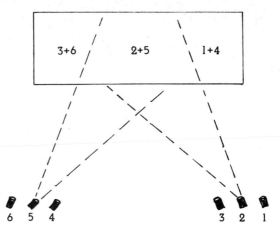

FIG. 120 Plan: end stage lit by six lamps

allows them to see as much as possible with such slender resources. There is a further bonus that, as the two spot beams lap over each other centre stage, this gives rather more prominence to this important area.

When more lanterns can be placed at the two side positions this will not only increase the amount of light but improve the general pattern of illumination. Because spotlights basically give a symmetrical beam they become wasteful when spread to cover a wide area. As the width of the beam is increased so is the height, and this latter may not be needed and, indeed, may have to be intercepted by a shutter or barn-door flap.

With three spots a side, the beams can be arranged as in Fig. 120, which not only is going to make more efficient use of the lamps but will allow lighting to be localized into areas, left, centre, and right, each being illuminated by the requisite two sources: 1 plus 4, 2 plus 5 and 3 plus 6 respectively.

Continuing with the simple open-end stage, in other words a rectangular platform at one end of the hall with an audience on one side only, the next step is to consider increasing the number of locations for the lights. For example, instead of one vertical boom each side there might be two, one farther from and one nearer to the stage, allowing another set of three areas upstage. But in this form of theatre, both booms would still be in the auditorium area rather than the stage area. Another method would be to use two horizontal bars at differing heights on each wall instead of relying on vertical booms (Fig. 121). The next step is to put a bar or two across the ceiling (still in the audience area) for frontal lighting and to help light to get over to the far sides in a very wide hall. Indeed it may be that the overhead position is essential to get the correct illumination.

All these arrangements allow a great increase in flexibility since lanterns can be positioned at a variety of angles and, if for no other reason than that scenery[1] often obstructs beams from some positions, such provision will be justified. However, these extra positions demand greater skill in choosing which to use, and if one is not careful the more lanterns and angles that are employed the less the visual impact.

This paradox arises from the loss of the essential modelling and contrast without which the brain cannot interpret the picture on the retina. So long as heavy painting of both scenery and of actors' faces was the rule, flat lighting from all directions did not matter, since shadows and lining could not be destroyed. Today real materials and little make-up are the rule and this, coupled with too many lanterns from too many angles, means that although the picture is many times brighter, we see it less well; it becomes bleached out. There is an exact parallel in sound. Speech in an echoing and too resonant room becomes unintelligible no matter how loudly the words are pronounced. Clarity is essential to lighting as well as to speech and to see better it may be necessary to switch something off rather than to add something.

I think the open-end stage an essential beginning, before all others, to training in the use of light. A proscenium provides greater opportunities but too many temptations for the beginner, whilst thrust stages, or arena stages, with a large amount of audience encompassment, demand so many disciplines as to discourage him at the outset.

Working on an open-end stage it will soon be discovered what a small proportion of lighting is actually placed over the acting area. This arises not because there is no provision there (The Mermaid, London, and Phoenix, Leicester, both have excellent arrangements for this) but because these positions are primarily not useful for lighting. To take an extreme example, vertical light except for some deliberate distortion effect is virtually useless. Stand a character under a vertical light and the result is not only unbecoming but areas such as the eye sockets, under the chin, and so on, are so shadowed as to become invisible (Fig. 122). A hat brim may remove the whole face and a bald head or blonde hair may, by presenting excessive contrast, do the same thing.

It is true that this extreme effect will only be experienced in the centre of the beam, for when set to diverge even slightly its edges will be at an angle and the result in these positions may be somewhat less objectionable. However, for every one of these positions there will be an equal number where the light will come completely from behind. Vertical light is something to shun on the whole, but there is one application

[1] Contrary to popular belief, a lot of very solid scenery is often used on end stages—open and ill-equipped to receive it though they may be.

of stage lighting where it cannot be avoided. Concert musicians insist on lights pointing straight down in order to avoid glare in their eyes. The only solution is to make sure beams lap over each other, then each lantern automatically provides some angular correction from the edges of its beam in the area of its neighbour.

There is a further objection to overhead lighting on the open-end stage in that many halls suitable for this form, particularly those of historic interest, are lofty, and lanterns hung on wires or frames would look singularly ugly. In saying this, one is all too conscious of the variation in sizes and shapes of halls, historic or otherwise.

It is one thing to declare "hang nothing overhead" and advise the use of the wall position only to find in fact that the hall may be excessively wide. I can only say that by choice of long-range spotlights it is possible to achieve the desired

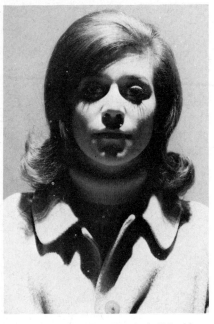

angle positions more often than one would think. It is necessary to add that objection to lighting hanging overhead in the field of view applies mainly to the usual temporary mess. When it comes to a designed frame containing the equipment within a boundary, there may be positive visual advantages as was discussed in Chapter 2, but as a lighting position it can be overrated. The one thing that defeats side-wall positions or their equivalent at the ends of an overhead cross-beam is the acutely hipped roof, for this brings the lanterns too low. In consequence, ugly shadows become visible on the stage and, worse still, the actor masking by shadow referred to earlier will be aggravated.

Vertical Lighting Angles

Several references to lighting angles not too high or too low have already been made in this chapter, and it is time to be more precise. I am a little reluctant to quote exact figures because when I got the ABTT to propound this as a requirement several experts became scornful and refused to be tied down (Fig. 123). What in fact I had been doing for years was to declare that lanterns must hang at 45 degrees and, at the same time, point my arm dramatically in the air at probably 35 degrees proclaiming "up there." This, possibly, when all is said and done, is about as accurate as one need ever be. When set out as in the ABTT diagram it suggests to people incapable of reading drawings a degree of rigidity that in fact will not be there. Even if every hanging position were sited to give only the exact 45-degree centre line a considerable variety of lesser angles will be available because we are working in three dimensions. Angling a lantern from one side of the stage to the other could bring the original 45-degree centre line angle of the diagram effectively down to 35 degrees or even less.

The truth is that the 35-degree or the 45-degree angle provides a useful and memorable formula—a beginning, to prevent people from positioning lamps too near vertical or too low near horizontal. An added advantage if we stick to the 45-degree image is that it also applies to the plan view as our key light diagrams showed. Overhead lighting positions at these angles are a must, and this particularly shows in the case of audience encompassed stages, but other angles are, of course, desirable when possible. In fact, as the proscenium stage is the only one which allows an unlimited variety of angles, at any rate backstage, this may prejudice some lighting designers in favour of it.

The great need in considering lighting angles for illumination, for visibility as distinct from dramatic effect, is to avoid the common trap of imagining that because a beam of light

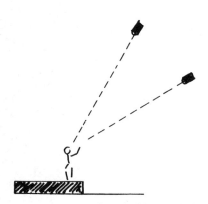

strikes an actor he can be seen. The fallacy was pointed out at the beginning of this chapter, but it cannot be repeated too often. It can literally be the case that an actor cannot be seen as lit in certain positions on the stage—not that light of some sort will be unable to reach him, but that having reached him it cannot present any intelligible message to the eyes of the audience. In these circumstances, the producer must alter his moves; there will be no alternative. He would do so, one hopes, if he found one actor masking another by actually standing in such a position as to present a physical barrier. This being so, why allow a long scene to be played in pitch dark except for a beam of light from off-stage picking out little more than a man's left ear?

Opera is the worst offender in this respect—yes, even in Germany. There is too much token lighting—a shaft of light, probably a stage bridge follow-spot—coming from a random direction to proclaim: "Yes, I haven't forgotten. I know he is there." Except for his voice, the singer might as well not be there, for his face cannot be seen.

One reason for this kind of thing in opera is a preoccupation with gauzes and transformation effects. One overhead spot per Norn just because they are to appear in some sort of limbo is not sufficient for the twenty-five minutes' introduction to *Götterdammerung*. Nor is Hagen's prompt-side shoulder and half Alberich's cheek good enough for their goings-on some hours later, even though it is supposed to be moonlight. Of course, where these latter two were actually positioned in that particular production, right downstage with a permanent gauze stretched immediately in front between them and the audience, no other means but a pin spot from the nearby wing was possible to keep dark the rest of the set that was to be revealed later. But, Herr Direktor, these characters need not have been so positioned—a few extra feet upstage would have made all the difference.

Never let it be thought that bad positioning for lighting applies to opera alone. It behoves every producer to understand sufficient about the behaviour of light and its relationship to seeing to appreciate the need to alter a move or to shift the whole scene a little more upstage. This does not mean that the lighting designer should not try his best before making such a request. Indeed, if he was on the job early, as he should be (see Chapter 9), he might have been able to point out the particular difficulty long before the show arrived in the theatre.

With the above warning in mind, one has to consider lighting for seeing first and then dramatize the scene with lighting for the dominant effect, what the Americans call "motivation." This does not mean that the first stage takes place in isolation and, once completed, some thumping super lighting is produced and poured on top of the rest. In positioning every light for illumination, one should have the ultimate dominant idea in mind to such good effect that the final motivation lighting is almost unnecessary. This is a counsel of perfection, requiring great skill. In the world of compromise that is stage lighting, even if attained, it will all too likely become lost in the mêlée later on.

Lighting the Acting Area

Let us consider a specific treatment over an entire acting area but divorced from the problems imposed by any particular form of theatre. In addition, the audience is still regarded as being one side only. In effect, every important area of action requires the minimum two spotlights of the original portrait lighting. To what extent this is strictly localized to one area or shared with several or neighbouring areas will depend on the importance of the action there; but one thing is certain— any character, wherever he or she stands, should be lit from the requisite two directions. Only thus can a suitably rounded portrait be presented to the eye. However, knowledge of the ultimate motivation can even at this basic stage begin to exert an influence.

To state an extreme case: if in one scene the dominant effect is to be sunlight from the OP side and, in another scene, moonlight from the P side, it might be logical to warm all the spots angled OP to P side with No. 52 Pale Gold and chill those angled P to OP with No. 17 Steel. This does not mean that all the illumination on one half of the stage is warm and on the other cold, but rather that there is a sense of direction in the lighting for each of many areas. Now this effect can be overdone and scorn can be poured on it.[1] Nevertheless I still think that Stanley McCandless, who probably made the first authoritative statement of the principle (as distinct from inventing it), was right to do so. Like my 45-degree angle referred to earlier, one is provided with a bendable formula which in this case acts as a reminder that modelling is not achieved by equally balancing the lighting on both sides of an object; also, that, where daylight is supposed to be concerned, the whole stage is under one influence even though for practical or dramatic purposes it is divided into a number of separate areas.

[1] "In theory the actor will be seen from the front as having one side warm, one cool with the facial configurations shadowed in the opposite colour. Features are modelled or made plastic and three-dimensional in appearance, and colour differences echo natural light, which is half direct and half reflected light. In fact, members of the audience seated close to one source will see an actor primarily in the colour tone of that source and those close to the other will see that colour tone. Almost half the house, then, will see pink actors while the other half will see blue ones, if those colours are used."—Donald Mullin in *Tabs*, Volume 23, Number 2.

If later in the same scene one has to deal with an impression of artificial light, for example, the supposed sources of light being electric brackets on the two side walls, then the distinction of No. 52 from the OP direction and No. 17 from the P direction in each area would prove an embarrassment. This is because all the separate areas no longer have to appear part of a whole; they are each, in fact, under the influence of the local motivating source. Cold light may be wholly absent; in consequence, the effect of modelling will be more appropriately obtained by putting a still warmer colour on the other angle, say double No. 52 or a pinker colour such as No. 54. This is all very well in a standing set for a run with a limited range of changes and plenty of lanterns. For most of us these theoretical questions will not arise; it will be a case of one colour throughout and use of dimmers to reduce the intensity to obtain the modelling and distribution appropriate to the particular motivation at that time. It is a question of accenting some spots by dimming the others somewhat.

Thus far, illumination has been considered with only half an eye on a dominant effect. This latter subject will have to be considered in the next chapter which describes how to paint the stage with light. Suffice it to point out here that, provided the illumination of the acting area does not quarrel with it, motivation is easy and may largely be confined to the scenery or props. For example, if there is now a dark sky outside the window the same spotlights which served as daylight for the acting area, when the sun's rays shone through the window, with but a slight shift of emphasis on the dimmers become perfectly appropriate to this very different time of day.

Lighting in the Round

Up to this point, lighting for perception has concerned end staging with or without a proscenium but with the audience always on one side. In staging with a large degree of encirclement, lighting would appear to present difficulty. How can modelling be indulged in if the actors have to be lit from the four points of the compass equally at once? There is no doubt severe restrictions are put on lighting in these open-stage forms. However, there is one compensatory effect which results from the fact that the distances are much shorter. As theatre-in-the-round relies on its intimate effect, no one is farther away in a good example than five or six rows. Obviously seeing is going to be much easier than in theatre where twenty-eight rows or more are not uncommon.

The usual practice in theatre-in-the-round is to consider four lanterns as absolute minimum and then repeat this formula in four separate areas or six areas or more, depending on circumstances and funds available. Spots for special effects

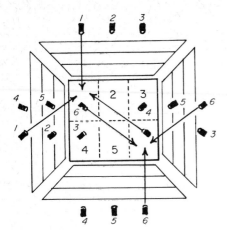

FIG. 124 Plan: minimum three-lantern area illumination of theatre-in-the-round

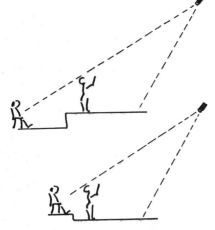

FIG. 125 Sectional views of raised and sunken stage techniques showing need for no-man's-land in one and raised seating in the other

would be additional to this. Stephen Joseph, who should know, declares that three lanterns per area will suffice if absolutely necessary, and Fig. 124 is based on one in his book, *Planning for New Forms of Theatre*. Whatever the number used, the angle is going to be important to avoid glare and a stage at the lowest level is essential when the aim is to keep the audience as close as possible. If, however, the raised Guthrie form of stage is used, then although the stage itself still continues to be intimate in area it has to be separated from the audience by a no-man's-land or moat in which the beams of light terminate (Fig. 125).

Following

Some unkind words crop up here and there about the simplest form of illumination—the follow spot. Just because this is basically so simple, it is used without imagination. The main idea is a lot of light from the direction of the audience to pin on the star and then hang on, following at all costs. This, when used in light entertainment on a variety act, a comedian or singer, is the equivalent of a close-up. There is a real place for these hard beams stabbing the darkness at the London Palladium and a strange beauty in the pursuit of the skaters by the discs of coloured light in an ice show. This kind of thing is out of place in any kind of serious work but this does not necessarily put the follow spot out of court altogether. Sometimes it may literally be the only way of getting the actor, singer, or dancer lit in that particular part of the stage or of making them tell.

Except that someone is moving a spot, this kind of following has no relationship to the other. The beam must be kept soft-edged and at relatively low power. The pencil beam is of itself no more important than the beam of any other spotlight; it is the result at the end of it—the subtle lift in light—that is important. When such following is properly done the operator must have a means of regulating intensity to hand, preferably as part of the spotlight itself. He can then match his follow intensity not to tell too much against the level of the area of the stage he traverses and, in consequence, the spot will not draw attention to itself. All this can be done, as also can the Palladium type of following, with great artistry. If the skill is not available, it is better to leave following out. A follow spot blundering after the dancer as he leaps into the air or wandering around looking for the target before opening up or steadfastly aiming at the star's middle instead of his face is no help at all. It is a not uncommon fault to centre the beam on the chest, or even waist, instead of the face. As the beam is at its brightest in the centre and the reflection factor of the face may be much poorer than that of the clothing, expression can come off fourth best in these circumstances.

There is another use of manned spots which is still very common in Eastern Europe and Italy, namely their use steady, with only the slightest movement for correction when lit but when each man's spot is dimmed out he promptly re-positions it for its next entry. I saw extremely skilful work of this kind in the National Theatre, Prague, recently, which reminded me how impressed I had been in 1934 with the six Stelmars on the perches in Covent Garden used in the same way. This is very much a carry-over from an earlier skill derived from necessity but not to be despised even now. Having said this, I must in truth confess it would not suit me, for I have always liked to be master of my own console, whatever form it has taken, and moving spots are therefore out.

Optical Illusion

So far we have been considering how to help the eye to examine a plastic three-dimensional shape and to light it to appear as the solid it really is. It is now necessary to think in terms of downright deceit. The weapon most easily used for this purpose is perspective and its concomitant, painted shadow. With certain remarkable exceptions, these two essentials of the scene painter's art have been curiously neglected in recent years. It is significant that amid all Sean Kenny's scenic complications for *Blitz!* at the Adelphi the sudden appearance of a perspective cloth of Victoria Station was able to capture applause.

Scenically, there seems no limit to the deception that can be practised. I defy anyone, when it is properly designed and carried out, to state what is painted and what is constructed. Indeed, it may well be that, as the late Ernst Stern relates of Max Reinhardt, the wrong choice is made.[1] In *Mister Roberts*, at the London Coliseum in 1950, the battleship was so well painted, rivets and all, that the deception was complete even when standing on stage. I had literally to go up to a hatch cover and take hold before it betrayed itself as the framed painted canvas it was.

Fortunately, *My Fair Lady* is a stage production which almost everyone will have seen. It presented a remarkable exhibition of perspective scene painting. In the main, only the Higgins' study scene was built in relief. Even then, a large part of it was in fact foreshortened and was made to look much deeper than it really was by perspective. The big Covent Garden Market scene was created entirely by clever perspective cut-outs. The apse in the "Why can't women——" dressing scene was perfectly flat. Several times during rehearsal I had to go on stage to convince myself the stuff was really flat. Per-

[1] *My Life, My Stage*, by Ernst Stern, Chapter 9 (Gollancz, 1951).

FIG. 126 Perspective painting
and foreshadowing, *Tosca*, Act
I, Royal Opera House, Covent
Garden

spective enabled an apparently lavishly built scene to appear
like magic as Mrs. Higgins' conservatory near the end of the
show. Just drop several two-dimensional cut-outs in and add
real furniture and the result was absolutely convincing. A
permanent example of this kind of shaping by paint and
perspective is to be seen any day behind the altar of St. Brides,
Fleet Street, and this is viewed in daylight.

The Royal Opera House, Covent Garden, has some excellent
perspective sets, particularly for its Zeffirelli productions. Of
these, Fig. 126 of the first act of *Tosca* is a fine example. This
set consists of a mixture of built pieces, notably the altar and
the dominant pilaster, actors right of it. The rest where built,
for example the pews and ironwork screen, is constructed in
perspective greatly to increase the feeling of depth. The whole
scene from setting line to backcloth was only 42 ft deep—no
great depth for the Opera House. The backcloth itself hangs
parallel to the footlights—the appearance of sloping away is
entirely the effect of painted perspective. The archway overhead is a simple cut cloth and both its appearance of solidity

and of changing direction, of being bent through an angle, are wholly the effect of painting.

Of course, we all know some painted cloths which look just like the painted cloths they are. Many, especially those painted as ballet décor, are not intended to look like anything else, but others set out to deceive and yet they fail. Why? There is a number of reasons, of which the most important is the treatment of the edges. These must not appear as a floppy piece of cloth. Either the vertical edges of a painted cloth must go right off stage or they must be framed and profiled so that the mouldings appear in correct silhouette. Another method is to run the unframed cloth behind a built piece. In such cases great care must be taken that light does not show the joint. Not only this, side lighting must be avoided on the cloth otherwise the bowed folds running from top to bottom towards the sides of the cloth will show. These are quite invisible under other conditions of light but this fault spoilt the effect of the library cloth for *Love for Love* at the National Theatre when I was there. It may have been an accident in positioning that night, but it was there.

Another tell-tale area is where the perspective cloth meets the floor. Not only may an actual line show there but the change of direction is too sudden. Built pieces foreshortened and constructed partly in perspective are helpful in bridging the gap between the reality of the actors and the world of paint. A steeply ramped floor (Fig. 127) or steps (Fig. 126) are also a great help. These two photographs should be compared with Fig. 161 (page 294), where the whole set was constructed in three dimensions, film or television fashion.

The next deception that has to be practised relates to apparent size or scale. In a way, perspective painting is concerned with increasing size, certainly depth, but there are other means available. Scale cannot be judged without some measuring rod, and in the theatre this is provided by the actor, and it might seem that as he is always present little deception can be practised. However, it so happens that to use him as a measure of scale we need to know exactly where he is in relation to the object whose size we are seeking, probably unconsciously, to know.

The principle involved is never to provide a complete frame and this applies at the proscenium opening just as much as in the case of any archways or doorways which have to look larger than they really are. At the proscenium it is highly desirable that there should be no complete frame, not only to avoid the barrier effect but also to prevent an accurate assessment of size. (There may be cases where a frame is deliberately required, but these are outside this discussion as it can easily be provided when necessary. It is abolition that is difficult.)

FIG. 127 Ramped stage and
perspective with cyclorama:
Cavalleria Rusticana, Act I, Royal
Opera House, Covent Garden

If the vertical sides and the top of proscenium opening never actually join but merely cut one another and at the same time the stage floor runs through without a joint to form an apron, it is going to be extremely hard to judge the exact position of our human measuring rod in this area.

Another curious optical illusion arises from the fact that any line which is not actually seen to terminate seems to be automatically interpreted as continuing when it goes out of sight. This is an effect well known to both film and television producers where judicious cutting of the edges of the picture is all-important. A fireplace, part of a wall and a door becomes a whole room; the brain automatically assumes the rest is there. No effort is required to make this assumption; the effort comes if one wants to remind oneself that there is little beyond the edges of the picture but studio impedimenta, cameras and lights.

It is the use of lighting that can help us to achieve somewhat similar results to the cameraman's choice of shot. "Stage lighting must conceal more than it reveals," I wrote in 1948 for my first book, and this has become rather a trite observation through over-use since. However, it still exactly conveys the main force behind the use of spotlighting, the ability to put light just where required and thereby draw the eye away from something. Under certain circumstances, one may be quite unable to see beyond a pool of light. Without the contrast of light there will be no darkness.

Perception of intensity and, as was described elsewhere, colour is absolutely dependent on contrast. The eye adapts itself over a period of minutes to accept new levels of light but cannot do this when both are presented simultaneously. If a

FIG. 128 Setting without a frame; *The Caretaker* at the Mercury Theatre, Colchester

scene is to appear really bright, it is no good piling on more and more light in the entire field of view. The true overwhelming of the eyes we get in nature requires thousands of foot-candles where in the theatre we deal in tens. Suitable contrast can overcome this difficulty and, as a beginning, there is the darkened auditorium. The design and colouring of an auditorium so that it will appear dark is obviously important. An extreme use of contrast in the theatre are "blinders," a row or cluster of low-power lamps facing the audience, beyond which what is happening cannot be seen. This substitute for a curtain might have its moments in open staging.

Today's "island" sets, without a frame on a wide stage, as for example in Fig. 128, may bring an unwanted isolation. Irving Wardle, describing *John Gabriel Borkman* at the Lyttelton, says ". . . the indoor scenes are played on a central pocket handkerchief acting area which reduces their scale and pushes them away into the distance."[1] I can confirm this as seen both from the front row of the stalls and from the back rows.

This effect is the result of the use of black in the audience's field of view. There is a common fallacy that to paint an object or some area black is to make it vanish. It is true that there will be little if any significant light reflected back to the eye but the interpretation will be to see a hole, gap or chasm. The more perfect the black the more the effect is aggravated. Of course there are times, as in the Royal Shakespeare Company's *Macbeth* at the Aldwych theatre, 1975, when to play in a limbo created by unlit black drapes gives a fabulous detachment from dependence on scenery for time and place. In a normal scenic context, however, to frame in with black legs and/or black flooring is to detach the show visually from its audience. This can even happen on a thrust stage. At the Crucible, Sheffield, they have found, for instance, that brown serves the purpose much better. Keith Green, for some time technical director there, points out: "Without an architectural feature similar to Stratford Ontario the designer at the Crucible has the problem of how to cope with the gap up-stage. He can either fill it up as if it were some kind of remote proscenium —which is not an answer—or effect a "blend" with the auditorium wall on either side to achieve a union of set and building. In my experience this is rarely achieved. However, with all vertical surfaces of the auditorium painted the same dark brown one is not unhappily aware during performances of this problem or of a point when the auditorium finishes and the stage begins. Scenic elements are usually masked behind by a kit of dark brown felt-covered flats. The choice of this colour is admirable and infinitely preferable to black."[2] An

[1] *The Times*, March 12, 1976
[2] *Sightline*, Autumn 1975.

extreme example of the lengths one has to go to, so to speak, is the way the mobile towers in Christ's Hospital Horsham (Fig. 6), painted a strong red—of all colours—can remain neutral because that is exactly what that particular auditorium leads you to expect. However, red happens to have been the undoing of the excellent Guthrie-type stage in the Octagon theatre, Perth, Western Australia. Unlike the Crucible there is actually a proscenium behind the thrust and all would be well were it not for the fact that they have been landed with a fine set of *red plush* tabs, simply because they were second-hand and going cheap! These tabs unfairly rivet the gaze and declare "proscenium" where otherwise it would not be noticed.

In conclusion, another remarkable optical illusion—the cyclorama—should not be forgotten. At the moment, this device, like the use of house tabs, seems rather under a cloud, but this does not mean it might not return. The trouble is that so few people have seen a real cyclorama. The essential is a perfectly smooth surface designed to reflect the maximum light. It need not be a fixed affair of plaster, as I pointed out in Chapter 2; cloth will do, but not any old cloth as most theatre people seem to think. Provided the edges are masked, the effect, properly lit, is of limitless space: there is nothing by which the eye can judge distance. This is a true optical illusion, every bit as convincing as good perspective painting in its field and just as right and proper to the theatre.

11 Painting with Light

ASSUMING a layout exists to provide illumination, as in the previous chapter, it is now necessary to consider what to superimpose upon it to paint a particular lighting picture. To do this, it will be both necessary to add something to suggest a reason or motivation for the dominant effect and also to mould the sources already existing for illumination, mainly by the use of dimmers and/or colour filters to back up this effect.

To keep the whole exercise within simple terms, the basic illumination layout of Fig. 134 on page 235 is used throughout to illustrate a series of naturalistic examples. This does not signify a preference on my part for naturalism or that this layout is suitable only for, or is the only one suitable for, that kind of work. The variables are so great as to size and type of stage and amount of equipment, to say nothing of the show and style of production that only generalizations can be used with safety. This means a vagueness which is not helpful to the beginner, and to avoid this the specific layout is shown producing a number of naturalistic effects while the text ranges somewhat wider afield. This is lighting at the five-finger-exercise stage, and no one should be content to remain there. I remain nervous, however, because it is a fact that, when I queried on one occasion some years ago why an entire theatre project had been drawn to $\frac{1}{16}$-in. scale, the answer was that the scale was the one I had used for the theatre plans in my own book. It simply had not been realized that my scale was enforced by the size of the book page and not by choice!

The whole basis of using light to convey a dominant idea or to provide motivation, call it what you will, is observation. Once one tries to go beyond mere illumination, the lighting for perception or deception, the position is analogous to the process of memory drawing. In that case, instead of sitting down before the actual scene with pencil and paper, the image is first committed consciously or unconsciously to the brain. So too with lighting there must be a picture stored somewhere

in the head as to what sunlight itself looks like and what it does to its surroundings before one can set about producing sunlight on the stage. The whole time it is a matter of observation, keeping the eyes open and storing for future use. What does a night sky really look like? One thing is certain: it seldom looks like the conventional No. 19 or 20 dark or deep blue often used in the theatre. In the suburbs of a big town, a night sky may often look brown or grey-pink, not blue at all. Likewise a fine day sky may present difficulties unless it is realized that the particular grey-blue often seen looks summer-like only so long as some building, some scenery, is brightly lit in the same picture.

Observation and the Painter

A short cut to this eye-training is to do some of it second-hand by visiting art galleries to see things through an artist's eyes. The Dutch painters, for example, knew all about light. One among many, the Pieter de Hooch interior (Fig. 129) shows how stage lighting could have been used in the fifteenth

century had there been any. Rembrandt's "The Woman Taken in Adultery" (Fig. 130) is a perfect piece of dramatic lighting—spotlighting from the left side, with full value made of contrast and of the scarcely seen. Of course, if the producer were to make the characters play out that big scene down-stage left, or on some infernal apron, instead of on the altar steps, then it could not be lit that way. But then, if he knows how to use lighting effectively, he will realize the much better result of playing it up-stage. The notion that principals must be brought down-stage with the crowd in the background seems to arise from the lack of realization that down-stage can be the least important area if it is not lit—provided always the various levels are arranged to avoid masking. Many crowd scenes of this kind would gain if no front of house lighting were used at all. We should then get the dark foreground figures silhouetted against the others. Georges De la Tour, the painter of

228   *The Art of Stage Lighting*

Louis XIV's time, often uses this effect in his obsession with artificial light in the latter years of his life (Fig. 131). Stage lighting from the front of house is vital, but try leaving it off sometimes. Hogarth is a painter whose pictures seem to be the very embodiment of stage scenes. Constable can be compared with Canaletto to find the distinction between English and Italian light. The latter's habit of putting half the scene in shade to stress the sunlight is particularly instructive (Fig. 132).

All through this chapter, light and shade to give contrast is going to come up time and time again. Without it the lighting is going to be mediocre—just illumination, and not very good illumination at that. As we saw in the previous

FIG. 131 "Saint Joseph as a Carpenter" (Paris, Musée du Louvre) De la Tour's treatment suggests that illumination might sometimes come from within the stage action rather than always be projected at it

Painting with Light   229

FIG. 132 Venetian Scene:
Canaletto
(*Reproduced by courtesy of the*
Trustees, The National Gallery,
London)

chapter, flat lighting does not assist perception. To use lighting dramatically is *to position the characters to suit the light*, not the other way round. Only the producer can do this—which brings us back once again to the fact that he must see the lighting in his mind's eye when working out any moves at even the earliest rehearsals. "He, elated, goes over to lean against the pillar (mid-stage left) in the shaft of sunlight, while she, depressed, moves over to the shade (down-stage right)." The alternative will be: "He and she leave pool of light centre to arrive at their respective pools mid-stage left and down-stage right." This will light them right enough, but without a message for anyone because the producer himself had none to convey—he was just "doing the lighting."

Some of the commoner forms of lighting found in real life must now be examined in relation to the means open to us to reproduce them on the stage. This assumes a proscenium stage, there being too great a limitation on angle and distribution in audience-encompassed forms. However, adaptation may be possible in some cases, admittedly with some compromise.

The first thing that will be noticed is the large diffused component in all lighting, and particularly daylight. Outdoors the source is obviously the sky. The light from this enormous surface is soft and absolutely shadow-free. This does not mean that there is no variation in intensity, no light pattern over the earth. There is less light under the spreading chestnut tree, for example, but the boundary is not defined at all. To take an extreme case, there is of course less light in a room, the amount depending not only on the size of the window but on the amount of sky by which the window is backed when seen from the various parts of the room. Diffusion not only involves the original source; but everywhere the light strikes there is further diffusion to a greater or lesser degree depending on the nature and colour of the surface. This kind of light does, in fact, turn corners; not nearly as well as sound, but in much the same way. Even the most defined and parallel ray of light —sunlight shining through a chink in the shutters—still introduces diffusion for the odds are that the ray will strike a diffusing surface and scatter back into the room. Even if by chance it impinged on a mirror, the diverted beam would land up on a diffuser eventually.

Nor does this diffusion apply only to daylight. The chandelier hanging over the table is supplemented by its own light returned from the tablecloth, and shadows in the eye-sockets and under the chin of the diners are softened thereby.

Softlight

A serious problem is posed by all this diffusion in the world we are to imitate for we have to keep light in its place and cannot permit it to reveal everything. What, therefore, is the answer? Before giving this, some methods of providing diffused or softlight might be examined. The first and commonest in the theatre is the compartment batten. Some forty or so lamps of 100 or 150 watts hang in a line as close together as their reflectors allow. Subdivided for colour, one is reduced to using, say, every third lamp and this puts up the centres. However, using diffusers or frosts the apparent area of each light source can be increased somewhat and the result becomes tolerable. What, however, cannot be tolerated is the way this light behaves if used as the principal source of illumination.

The trouble can be summed up as going all over the place and lighting the top of the scenery to a brighter level than the acting area itself. This latter can be overcome to some extent by suitable reflectors or even by using sealed-beam PAR lamps. These latter do, however, involve extra weight and expense which seriously limits their field of use. Nor is a narrow angle beam reflector or the concentrated beam of the PAR, which is necessary to get the light down on the acting area, really

FIG. 133 Compartment battens, with 500-watt spot bar

equivalent to diffuse light; rather it equates to a series of close centred spots. Instead of every character receiving some light from all the compartments, from, if not one large surface at least a number of small surfaces, in fact only some are actively concerned. On the whole, while these PAR battens have some special applications, I think they had better be disregarded in the present context and battens should be taken to mean a wide-angle light as soft as possible (Fig. 133).

In these, it will be the object of the reflector to prevent waste of light which otherwise would not be used, and thereby to back up this effect. To prevent the top of the wing scenery receiving a splash of direct light from one or two close-range compartments, these can either be killed or never put there in the first place by keeping the batten shorter; all the rest receives an amalgam of everything. Such a system has the advantage that although there is some drop-off with distance the drastic inverse square law does not apply.[1] These battens should never be hung close to and in front of the borders except for special effects, as in some light entertainment where these are featured as part of the décor. In other applications one would hope that borders, if necessary, would be few and retiring. A batten may be required immediately behind the proscenium to make softlight available and on really comprehensive adaptable installations not only would this be essential but it should be supplemented by the traditional rows at intervals up and down stage though these are found only in opera houses nowadays.

[1] The inverse square law and the effect of multiple sources was described in Chapter 4.

Before the reader rushes off to buy a complete set of these things or accuses me of going back on the doctrine of spotlights I have preached for years, I shall remark that, while this is the inevitable logic of trying to imitate the principal light in nature, it is a paradox that this kind of light is only of secondary importance in stage lighting, being used for accompaniment and seldom for solo work. Another piece of accompaniment equipment which should never get a solo role is the footlight.

Footlights

This source of lighting has got itself a bad name in the past through being too bright. Thus, more lighting was ruined by its use than was in fact aided. On small stages all the money was squandered on battens and footlights first and one was lucky if any spots were included at all. To counter this, the conversation was kept on the other essential equipment and any reference to the floats was omitted. It was to redress the balance that the Junior footlight, a simple open trough of one circuit of silica-sprayed lamps, was introduced. It just clips on the front of the stage without any special trough, has no great power and occupies only one dimmer, but a touch from this can make all the difference to those shadows in the eye sockets, under the chin and the hat brim. Where do these shadows come from? Why, from the spots described in the previous chapter.

Impressionism and Naturalism

How does one justify the use of these sources so different from the diffuse light of nature? Simply by the fact that this is Theatre and to use the words *imitate* and *reproduce* a few pages ago was quite wrong. It is our job, even in the most naturalistic play and setting, to give an *impression* of the light of nature. This involves discrimination to select what is important and discard what is not. It also puts our lighting in an interpretive role for it is our own impression that is put over.

It is possible to argue the philosophy of naturalism versus all the other "isms" in the scenic side of the production, for real rooms can be built and, even if real live trees are not used (and they have been), then passable imitation ones with fabulous individual plastic leaves and all the rest can be made. With stage lighting the situation is different: we cannot even remotely approach nature. Intensity and distribution is completely wrong, so it is Hobson's choice—impressionism or nothing. Just take intensity: real daylight is 100 times as bright as the most optimistic level we might achieve; real moonlight is 100 times lower than the level we can put up with in order to sit through a scene.

So it is that the question which has to be added to the needs of illumination is: "What impression do we wish to convey?" The answer should be capable of being written down and may consist of a long or short sentence, or even a single word. It is interesting that this dominant idea is not necessarily tied to naturalist phenomena. The answer may be "hopelessness," even though it is a fine sunny day in a garden like that of *A Month in the Country*. On the other hand, the reverse could easily apply. Some farces have depended on bad and gloomy weather for their comic situations. "Is the sunlight kind or hurtful?" is likely to be a far more important question than: "Does sunlight really behave like that?" So one is launched on a deep sea of psychological lighting without a single violet or green spot or other expressionist aid—merely the afternoon light gently caressing the curtains at the open french window.

Scale in Lighting

In composing lighting, a scale has to be determined first of all and then all work is tied to this. It is just as likely that the lighting will be ruined by an overbright unit as by something too dim. The designer who builds his layout from zero can keep everything in scale, whereas the majority who take over a stage for a night, or a week if they are lucky, are faced with what already exists. Additions to this should be made with care. Import some super units and the rest of the lighting is dwarfed. I often think the most important step that can be taken towards brighter stage lighting is to dim auditorium lighting. Even with the most vicious fluorescent installation, the lights can be taken out early and the eyes of the audience rested by something gentle on the curtain. We need an over-ture and an entr'acte just as much for our eyes as our ears. It is most important to have a specific curtain effect available on one dimmer, to be brought in when necessary. The footlight used to be able to do this but it is not often available and the spots set for the show make such ugly patches that they are left off. The consequence is that the audience are either left sitting in the dark or pitchforked with a jerk into the act. Even on an open stage there can be some interval and entr'acte effect; quite mad things go on in these anti-curtain days. For example, I saw a production of *Arms and the Man* on a thrust stage with the scenery set on the main stage at the back. The curtain was closed to change the scene there but opened once this was done to reveal the new set in the house lights. These dimmed later to darkness in order that Louka and Nicola could take up their opening positions. The stage lighting was then raised to reveal the complete scene: the impact of the change of set had been completely lost. A rather similar misuse of the house tabs occurred in *The Devils* at the Aldwych. Although these had been used during the show they were

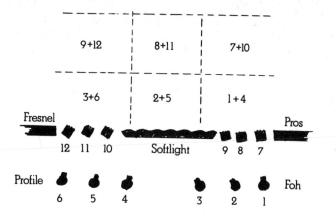

FIG. 134 Plan: basic layout. For diagrammatic purposes the No. 1 bar is shown in the pros. opening and the FOH spots at half their normal distance

not allowed to open it or close it.

In setting a scale of lighting, it is just as well to begin some-where. Stanley McCandless said in 1947 that "a little as ten foot-candles of general illumination on the stage conveys the impression (of daylight) adequately."[1] It could still pass, provided the audience had time to get dark-adapted, but I think today this should at least double—20 foot-candles. The professional West End theatre probably uses at least 50 foot-candles. What does 20 foot-candles look like? Well, a 500-watt 6-in. Fresnel spot flooded to cover 12 ft at 20 ft range gives about 20 foot-candles at the centre of the beam. This falls off to one half over the centre 8 ft and then diminishes to one-tenth at the edges. Taking Fig. 120 on page 211 and 134 above, bearing in mind that each area has two spots on it and that the spots lap over each other considerably, we are not too wide of our target. The front of house spots would be throwing farther but their beam spread should be adapted to suit by choosing the right lens. Thus, a 500-watt Profile spot covering 10 ft at 30 ft gives 20 foot-candles.

The next matter that arises is what wattage to use for high-lighting effects, such as sunlight. This, of course, may be light put on top of light, but on the other hand such light is often directed at scenery only and this could be dark painted; accord-ingly, double wattage will be more appropriate—thus, 500-watt Fresnels for acting area illumination, 1000-watt for direct sun-light. In a larger theatre, the wattages are doubled: 1000 watts for acting area, 2000 watts for sunlight. Personally, I consider that in most cases the extra wattage for highlighting will be better obtained by using a larger lantern rather than two smaller ones.

Basic Layout

For the purposes of the discussion on lighting that follows, a basic layout (as Fig. 134) is assumed. It consists of six acting

[1] *A Method of Lighting the Stage* (Theatre Arts, N.Y.), 1958 reprint repeats this.

Painting with Light   235

areas with spots paired to each and a change of colour is not provided to these. When essential, specials will be added as they are also for any special effect, dominant or otherwise. Of course, if the stage were deeper or there was a forestage, then extra areas and spots to correspond will be needed. All spots are fitted with No. 52 Pale Gold and the areas lap well over into each other so that at head height of a standing actor there is no sense of division. The squares are diagrammatic only. The spots would be in the order required to get the correct angle and are shown in numerical sequence only for the sake of clarity.

The softlight is shown as compartment batten immediately in the centre of the No. 1 bar just upstage of the proscenium (Fig. 134). It points vertically downwards and there are two circuits: No. 51 Gold Tint and No. 40 Pale Blue, all with heavy diffusers. Twelve feet of this is imagined for a 24-ft opening, making eight compartments warm in colour and eight cold. On very small shallow stages with little overhead height, the softlight circuits might have to be made up of a lesser number of baby floods interleaved among the spots. This would negative the softlight effect to some extent but would allow individual angling and masking with hoods when essential to correct bad shadows. It might be argued that extra spots would be better in these circumstances, but these simply do not have a wide enough spread, nor does the lens have sufficiently large a surface area to serve the same purpose on a small scale. When compartment batten is used, the two lengths may be separated at the centre to allow spots for special effects to be introduced at that point. A useful extra spot position is that known as the perch, at one time actually a platform, nowadays often only consisting of brackets high at the side of the proscenium or even just a boom as far down-stage as possible. On much larger stages, the spots and the batten can hang on separate lines and a lot more of the former can be accommodated and a greater length of the latter (Fig. 133).

There has been a great tendency to say one can do without softlight, particularly when discussing open stages, but it is of interest that Donald Mullin, who has a lot of practical experience with theatre-in-the-round at Tufts University, Massachusetts, even uses two batten lengths pointing vertically down (side by side) over the centre of the acting area, and this in spite of a layout which uses some 56 spots of various sorts. He explains that these in the context of the proscenium theatre "serve to wash the acting areas and the setting, removing unwanted hard edges and neutralizing spill. They also add a colour tone to the entire stage, as opposed to specific colour requirements for individual areas."[1]

[1] "Lighting the Arena Stage," *Tabs*, Volume 23, Number 2.

No lighting is shown upstage on the standard layout as this will be special to the type of scene.

Interiors: Natural Light

Assuming it is the direct rays of the sun, stage left, that are doing "the caressing" of the french window curtains referred to earlier, the stage picture can be shaped accordingly. Spots Nos. 2 and 3 and 8 and 9 in the basic layout become accented by dimming the others slightly (Fig. 135). Spots 1 and 7 cannot be accented as this side of the stage would receive less light from the window with the sun in that direction. If the window were assumed to be in the fourth wall, then they could be so used or, of course, if there were a window in the wall stage left. Since this is daylight, some softlight from the warm circuit, perhaps both, is required. In this minimal working it will probably provide sufficient light for the walls of the room and help to blend in the beams of the acting area spots where they strike them. If, as the diagram suggests, there is only one window upstage, then two things must show there: the diffused light of the sky and the direct rays of the sun. Any sky, backcloth or cyclorama, may require softlight from an overhead batten but it is unlikely that the blue needed will suit the upstage acting area beyond the window; in consequence, this sky light must be kept off that area. This would also apply to any Linnebach (see Chapter 12) or other effect used to give a broken sky. Once it is admitted that the light for the sky is not going to be used on the acting area and be allowed to throw multi-coloured shadows there, then the way is open to discard a batten for this purpose and use a few individual floods of, for example, 500 watts each, hanging well clear and throwing as flat on to the cloth as possible to minimize wrinkles.

The acting area upstage of the window is likely to be a

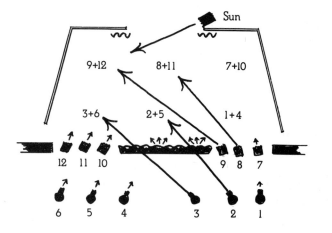

FIG. 135   Plan: afternoon interior

FIG. 136 Behind the windows: (left) *The Mousetrap* at the Ambassadors, (right) *The Three Sisters* at the National (Old Vic)

problem to light, because of the lack of space on the kind of stage we are talking about. Though softlight would be more correct, the only things that can be kept under tight control are Profile spots hanging at the sides, possibly on the same bar as carries the backcloth softlight. If this brings the latter too close, then a boom would have to be used. Provided these side spots are high, actors will walk on facing them, turning out of them only to enter by the french window. These spots are for illumination but may need to be accented by dimming one of them slightly. Whether this will be necessary will depend on the decisiveness of the sunlight. This must register on something, otherwise it will be useless, so it is a matter of working back from the objects which one wants to be gilded by the sunlight and thence to the position outside the window which will allow this to be done. It may well be that two lanterns will do this better than one, since they can then be pinned down and not only directed to tell at the points required but at one and the same time be kept from straying out of bounds. In any case, the nearer the beam approaches parallel the better it resembles sunlight. With two sun sources, one must avoid too obviously conflicting shadows. If, however, one is regarded as the actor's sun and the other as belonging to the scenery, the risk is lessened.

A boom pipe off-stage at the correct angle is the approved

mounting, but this can be used only if the lanterns can be placed high off-stage and yet enter the window to some extent. In extremely cramped conditions, it may be necessary to treat this sunlight purely as a local decorative effect, smaller Fresnels being put close to the off-stage edge of the window frame.

The wall of the room, actor's right opposite the sun, should be brighter than the others and it may be necessary to provide supplementary lighting for it from the spot bar or left perch position, if there is one. Other additions would be specials if one wanted to draw particular attention to a centre of action or lift an important entrance. It is going to be a nuisance if either of these has to take place stage left as this should be less brightly lit than the right. It must be if there is to be any sense of motivation at all. A second window in that wall would provide the excuse to put extra light that side, by accenting spots Nos. 1 and 7 in addition to 2, 3, 8, and 9. This is, in any case, an interesting exercise for it raises the question of matching the backings of two separate windows. The first piece of advice is try to prevent the audience seeing directly out of this second window as matching is seldom possible under ideal conditions. Where, as is all too likely at the side, the backing is cramped close to the window frame, because of lack of wing space, the result is stagey in extreme. Whenever possible, lace curtains or muslin or something of that sort should intervene. Even when the window concerns an office or factory, the actual opening can be filled with gauze, linen, or even just Cinemoid that can prevent the sense of open frame with a view beyond. Other backings to watch will concern doors, and unless something splendid is going on off-stage, like a ball, then it is just a matter of providing some light and it will be a better fault to have too little rather than too much. In this context, a baby flood with diffuser over the door should suffice. Never use a flood on a stand directly downstage of the doorway so that one sees the actor's shadow on the backing. This is bad enough as he makes his entrance, but may betray his presence while waiting for it.

Overhead Masking

The set as so far assumed has been vagueness itself, but it is necessary before going any further to become specific in respect

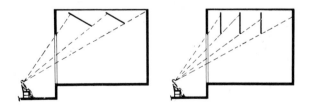

FIG. 137 Sight line for over-head masking, floating ceiling pieces versus borders

of one thing and that is overhead masking.

At one time it was possible to say with conviction that every interior should have a ceiling rigged over it. I think I still believe this if full height scenery is used and there is any pretence of naturalism at anything resembling domestic level. A complete series of flats terminating at borders which cut across their tops looks terrible. On the other hand, cut-down scenery is open to no such objection. This principle has been much advocated by Percy Corry with amateurs in mind, but it has been commonplace to see sets of this type on the West End stage. For example, those of Abd'Elkader Farrah for the Royal Shakespeare Company's *Cherry Orchard* at the Aldwych. This type of scenery is low and set in front of dark, preferably black, drapes. Light is concentrated at acting area height and the rest is ignored. The line of the top of the scenery can be broken by profiling or by the extra height of a window or chimney-piece. The important thing is that there is never any suggestion that the overhead masking borders belong in any way to the set; they must keep their distance and be forgotten.

Another form of masking consists of floating ceiling pieces which do not belong at all to the drapes or scenery. They are quite frankly there as masking. The object is not to mask by filling completely the space overhead and blocking all lines of sight but to mask by blinding. If the off-stage space overhead is black and the floating ceilings are grey, then it will be impossible to see past their edges.[1] It is not necessary to light the ceilings; they will pick up sufficient scatter from the stage lighting to provide enough contrast to suggest a black abyss beyond. The fact that these ceiling pieces can be made to leave gaps all around and break back to form slots to take intermediate curtain tracks and lighting bars greatly increases lighting angles available for special effects. On no account should the ceiling be permanent. An item over or on the stage which cannot readily be removed, however worthy, is an obstruction.

Ceiling masking problems are greatly lessened when the stage floor is low and the audience tend to look down on it. Whatever is used up there must be retiring and certainly should not be lit. Many stages have a light set of "silver grey" borders and this, plus a high stage floor and a low flat one in the auditorium, makes them draw the eye. Borders and overhead masking are there, with few exceptions, to prevent the audience seeing something even less desirable. Thus the overhead regions, as they are, have to be weighed in the balance and the decision

---

[1] This kind of ceiling has its points when used over the auditorium as well. The floating architectural shapes are often referred to as "clouds" and may also function as part of the acoustic design.

taken to mask or not and if so how much, will depend on the amount of height available and other such factors.

In practical terms, lighting becomes much easier once the proscenium position can be used without the need for another batten behind a border at mid-stage, and so forth. If there are a number of borders fixed in position, then try to keep direct light off them. Certainly never be tempted to use the edge of a border as a cut-off upstage for unwanted light from a batten, a kind of curtain barndoor, for this means the border itself will be lit. The proper thing to use is a hood to each compartment or to make a metal flipper to attach to one edge of the batten so that the up and downstage spread can be restricted. This is where the individual baby floods may be better than a continuous batten since then they can be angled and masked more readily. Unfortunately, for reasons discussed earlier, these do not constitute true softlight.

Evening

It would seem inevitable in our drama for the sun to set and thereafter night must fall in the room already discussed. The simplest and most effective way of conveying this would be to cross-fade the sun spots for a sunset glow lower down and preferably, but not essentially, at a different angle in the horizontal plane as well. The sunset spot should be less powerful than the sun it replaces. The sky darkens, of course, and it is here the value of a Linnebach comes in because apart from the opportunity it gives to make a sunset it lessens the risk of its being marred by stray light. Associated with evening there may have to be a sense of the coolness, but, as all the illumination spots are No. 52 Pale Gold and will get warmer and warmer as they dim down, this is where the cold circuit of softlight can be made to dominate to cool the shadows.

Artificial Light

As the sunset proceeds, it will be necessary to switch on the wall bracket stage left, then the table lamp right, and finally the chandelier centre. Each of these artificial sources must have its own field of influence so that they can be used separately or combined in any order. Artificial light cues are very common and are worth consideration in detail.

In J. B. Priestley's play, *The Glass Cage*, it seemed to me that the characters spent most of their time going from one fitting to another and turning them up or down. An artificial light source must give an impression of local distribution otherwise little distinction can be made without a change of colour and that cannot be permitted in elementary exercises like this. The bracket on the wall primarily demands spot No. 7 as the

FIG. 138 Plan: interior lit by
wall bracket

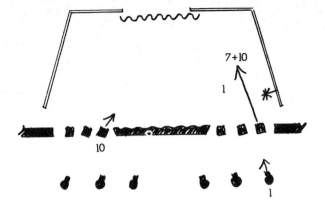

one giving least conflict to the direction of the light. On the
grounds of modelling and visibility, we must add spot No. 10
but No. 7 is the accented one. In point of fact, unless the room
is supposed to be enormous, the light from the bracket would
have struck all the walls including the fourth one, so some
return light from that direction is legitimate albeit at low
intensity. This would certainly allow spot No. 1 to be added.
Thus, the wall bracket consists of No. 7 accented plus 1 and
10 on check (Fig. 138). Of course, to get the right level for
feel and not to spill on the sky, all may be on check; the
accenting being relative to the others of the group.

The actual level of light from the bracket will have to be
sufficient to register it as alight but not to draw the eye. A
particular thing to avoid is that sense of bloom on the lamp
shades which comes when they are overpowered by the spot
that has to represent their illumination. There is also sometimes a tell-tale shadow *under* the bracket. The solution is to
allow the bracket to give off quite an amount of light but not
in the direction of the audience. This is best considered in the
case of the next source—the table lamp.

A table lamp, being of necessity low down, is going to suffer
most if the illumination it is supposed to be giving comes
entirely from high up. Whenever possible, therefore, it should
be permitted to act as a source of light but not in the direction
of the audience. The interior of the shade in that direction
can be lined with neutral filters, like Nos. 55, 56, and 60, or
that side of the shade covered with darker material. The light
will then escape from the far side and on to the table top and
thence to correct eye-socket shadows which might appear from
overhead spots.

All this may seem finicky and likely to lead to disaster,
especially in those cases when the action requires the lamp to
be brought in and stood on the table, but, if the fitting is given
the right feel to the hand, then one is asking no more than

that the actress shall pour the tea from the pot out of the spout and not the handle. It is particularly important, especially on a low stage, that light from these prop fittings shall be prevented from going upwards and throwing a patch on the ceiling or borders. A disc of card or metal set in the open top of shades will prevent this. On the subject of prop. fittings, it should be remarked that Strand Electric publish a catalogue which enables these to be selected by post for hire. In London, not only their large collection, but the even larger collection of J.M.B. Limited, another member of the same group, can be seen together in Shepherds Bush.

The table lamp, unless it is situated right downstage, will, like the wall bracket, require an accented spot plus two others, in this case Nos. 12, 9, and 6 respectively. I referred earlier to De la Tour's use of light with darkness downstage so to speak, and one cannot help feeling that it would be nice to be able to leave out FOH spots Nos. 1 and 6 for this effect. Nowadays, it is possible to go even further in local light for a miniature 100-watt Fresnel spot is available which is only $4\frac{3}{4} \times 3\frac{3}{4} \times 3$ in. in size. This represents a reasonable source which can be concealed in furniture and other props, and thereby opens the way to lighting that grows locally from within the actor's world rather than being projected upon it.

The chandelier is an obvious case for spots Nos. 8 and 11, but, as it hangs in the centre, both would be equally accented and 2 and 5, if added from the FOH, well checked down. It is now possible to set out a plot for these three distinct effects and it could be imagined as something like this—

Wall bracket: No. 7 Full, Nos. 1 and 10 at $\frac{1}{2}$.
Table lamp: No. 12 Full, Nos. 6 and 9 at $\frac{1}{2}$.
Chandelier: Nos. 8 and 11 Full, Nos. 2 and 5 at $\frac{1}{2}$.

When added together, the twelve spots (Fig. 139) would be as follows: No. 1 at $\frac{1}{2}$; 2 at $\frac{1}{2}$; 3 at 0; 4 at 0; 5 at $\frac{1}{2}$; 6 at $\frac{1}{2}$; 7 at Full; 8 at Full; 9 at $\frac{1}{2}$; 10 at $\frac{1}{2}$; 11 at Full; 12 at Full. Quite apart from the fact that two spots are not used at all, the distribution will appear very different from the day scene described earlier, which would probably turn out more like this: No. 1 at $\frac{3}{4}$; 2 at Full; 3 at Full; 4 at $\frac{3}{4}$; 5 at $\frac{3}{4}$; 6 at $\frac{3}{4}$; 7 at $\frac{3}{4}$; 8 at Full; 9 at Full; 10 at $\frac{3}{4}$; 11 at $\frac{3}{4}$; 12 at $\frac{3}{4}$.

The daylight also included some softlight at full, whereas for the artificial there would be none, or only a touch, so it can be seen that the spots which are there for illumination of the acting area can be blended to provide considerable motivation as well. For clarity, I have used the same check levels for unaccented spots. Unless the room curtains are drawn or there was an interval in which something darker was put as backing behind the windows then it would not be possible to use the

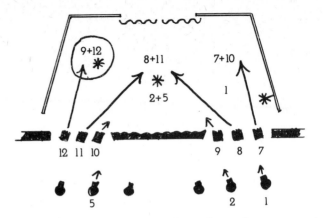

same levels. Light would scatter from the acting area on to the night sky. Under these circumstances, the accented spots are not likely to be at more than $\frac{1}{2}$ check and the others at $\frac{1}{4}$ check. Once again, this is a simplification, there being no reason whatever why check levels should be all alike; they will each take the level at which the eye tells us the correct balance has been achieved and which lessens the more objectionable shadows in the sky.

Where a lower lighting level such as this would be inappropriate to hold for long, a production detail like closing the curtains after the table lamp has established itself is obviously a great help to the further lightening of the stage, particularly with the centre chandelier. Whether or not the closing of the window curtains is permitted, there must be something across the window frames. This has already been alluded to under daylight, but at night this is essential for under most conditions of artificial lighting we do not in reality see out very well even through uncurtained glass. Thus, any attempt by adding light on backings to overcome scatter and shapes of window frames being projected thereon is doomed. Too much light is added to light. If the french windows have to remain open, then the conditions resemble open air and this comes up later. In the present context, grey gauze stretched across any window that has to remain uncurtained will prevent us seeing too well into the night beyond.

The introduction of lighting fittings as a supposed source of illumination opens the way to positioning of special spots to light, for example, corners other than from the spot bar behind the proscenium, and thus gives a chance for some interesting back lighting. If the stage represents a large ballroom lit by a series of wall brackets across the back and down the sides, it would be legitimate to assume that at least some of these brackets hang on the fourth wall so great freedom in choice of lighting angle becomes possible. It is a matter of lighting for glitter and excitement and, as in real life, this is

244   *The Art of Stage Lighting*

achieved by patchy contrasty light. On the stage this means lighting from the sides, as described later under Ballet.

An extreme case of making the lighting fittings actually work is given by the use of 2-kW Fresnels hanging vertically to represent them in John Dexter's production of Arnold Wesker's play *The Kitchen* at the Royal Court Theatre in London (Fig. 140). These sources had also to serve the purpose of making the actors really sweat as they mimed the frenzied activity of the lunch service.

Moonlight

From the point of view of lighting, the drawing-room box set is more confining than ever castle or dungeon. Lighting phenomena there are familiar—the audience are on home ground. In lighting for another age, problems are eased but even then so long as there is some suggestion of naturalism in the sets then rules like one moon only or, at any event, from one side only must prevail. Which side? Well, if the sun has just set stage right, a full moon is not going to rise shortly after on the same side just to allow us to use the same lantern and merely change the colour. The departing sun is the source of light for the moon which means it must be positioned on the opposite side of the stage.

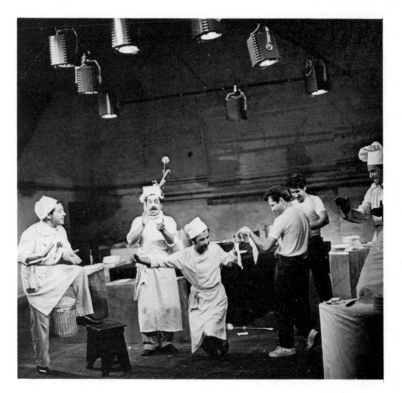

FIG. 140 Jocelyn Herbert's set for *The Kitchen*

We are now settled in the room by the fireside, with the moonlight streaming through the windows in much the same way as the sun did but from the opposite side and using a tint such as No. 40 or No. 18. It is a romantic scene and at least part, if not all, the room lighting is extinguished so the problem arises of sufficient light to hold the interest. The excuse for this is the moon itself coming in from the right, but even assuming the only windows for this to stream through are upstage, some faking would be permissible by adding a spot in the same colour from perch or extreme right-hand end of No. 1 spot bar. Such a change of angle, if diffused and carefully set, need not strain credulity. Remembering that where the moonlight strikes there is some diffusion, this can even permit a slight token light in the reverse direction if absolutely necessary. These moon spots would be additional to the twelve acting area spots unless as might be the case out front there is some means of changing colour. Even so this might not work well, because a switch cue in or out of the moonlight effect might need to employ the self-same spot to represent artificial light and a colour-filter change would catch us on the hop. The safe method is to regard the twelve acting area spots as sacrosanct, both as to colour and positioning, and regard the rest as specials. Sure enough, if we are tempted to move one a little now it will spoil its use for another scene to come or possibly one already lit. The agents for expression in respect of these spots are the dimmers and they should have one each.

Firelight

Firelight is useful both to aid the moonlit scene and to add interest to a scene with the lamps lit. Anyway, some plays specifically mention the fire and direct some business therewith. Generally speaking, what sits in the grate is of little importance —hardly anyone sees it anyway; it is the light from the fire that must be our first charge.

There are two important things to remember about firelight. Firstly, its light is not red and, secondly, when active it is a sheet of flame and this is a large source. A good ready-made colour for a fire is No. 34 Golden Amber, but if the fire really blazes it gets yellower. As a good fire is a sheet of flame, a floodlight is a better representation than the usual baby spot. One would expect firelight to go over everything including the ceiling of the room. Where more control is needed and we simply dare not allow light upwards, a Fresnel flooded wide will be a good compromise. An arrangement of two or three 100-watt miniature Fresnels might be more convenient than a single larger one.

Morning

There remains the morning after. It is reasonable to assume the early light is cold and, as the softlight has the only cold circuit, this will have to be used. This is by no means a bad thing for early light is diffused light anyway. As early light increases it is going to become necessary to introduce the acting area spots and it is here that a colour change out front could be very helpful. The loss of spots in a cold colour will be more serious out front as the softlight is only effective upstage of the proscenium. It is easy to see that on a really flexible installation, each acting area spot should be duplicated by a cold spot, making twenty-four in all. In this way one could put down warm or cold light or a mixture of the two from each direction and position.

In present circumstances, I can only allow myself two well-diffused cold spots on check out front positioned to cover the whole stage to fortify the cold softlight (Fig. 141). As soon as the sun rises, the warm spots can be brought in. As the sun sets behind the upstage window, we had better leave that alone for dawn and give an effect up there of a brightly lit exterior as the day advances. The sun is assumed to be out beyond the fourth wall among the audience. This does not, however, permit all spots to be put on full. They should be accented; in this case Nos. 4, 5, 6, 10, 11, and 12 would be the ones in question. While talking of upstage windows, it should be remarked that for a part of the year the sun travels more than 180 degrees in azimuth and, in consequence, it would be perfectly possible for the sun to enter the window at dawn, travel right round past the fourth wall and make a sunset appearance through the same window but in the opposite direction. This is precisely what happens with my kitchen window at home in Ealing.

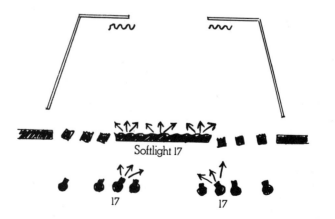

FIG. 141   Plan: early morning interior

Softlight 17

17

17

Operating the Changes

Before passing on to an exterior scene, do any of the lighting changes during the twenty-four hours to noon described above present any difficulty at the switchboard? A slow sunset can be "played" by moving first this dimmer a little, then that, on any board. Even if there is a preset it would be better to keep it for the more complicated things later on. As it falls out the artificial-lighting cues require three groups in addition to the natural lighting represented by the approaching night. Two groups are usual on good controls and, if there were a preset in addition, these facilities could make these changes easy. However, in the context of our installation, there may not only be no preset but no kind of interlocking either. Analysis shows that each switch cue consists of three spots, plus the light source itself. If the spots could be cut in on switches the dimmers already having been set to levels, to work four switches at once would not seem to be difficult if they are reasonably close together and push buttons rather than the usual lever type. However, it is more likely for artistic reasons that these spots cannot go right out before the switch cue; that *all* acting area spots have been worked down to levels to give an impression of twilight and that these have now to be cut in to a new set of levels imposed by each artificial light source they now have to represent. It is here that a preset control can help and it is easy to see that the layout and the cues expected of it should not be planned to outrun the potentialities of the control; unless one is prepared to call in extra operators. An effect just possible to operate by hand with only three spots, might, in the case of a more lavish setup, require six or sixteen spots. Then better control facilities become essential.

The answer in the present instance, however, is to patch spots and lighting fitting to occupy a not unmanageable number of dimmers and this means two in the case of slider dimmers and four where there are fingertip controls. A control with slider dimmers implies a few only; therefore, two to each of the three lighting fitting effects is probably all that can be spared—seeing that there are outside window effects and other backings to look after as well. The quick running of dimmers from one set of levels to another set is an acceptable method of obtaining switching cues when needs must. Where some grouping facilities exist but not sufficient for all parts of a follow-on cue, keep them in reserve for the later parts. One can get poised for digital dexterity to begin but it is comforting to have something easy like a master fader or switch to complete the follow-on.

Where one is working on an absolute minimum of dimmers, not only can spots be paralleled to the same dimmer and if necessary repatched to be grouped differently during the interval for the next act, but also the lighting fitting is connected to the same circuit as the spot representing it. For example, the wall bracket requires No. 7, plus 1 and 10 on check. If needs must, the wall bracket is paralleled with No. 7, its accenting spotlight and the 1 and 10 spots go on another. It is not inconceivable that necessity would insist on a dimmer being avoided altogether for the first pair and they could be switched on directly, but the wattage of the wall bracket would have to be watched and neutral filters pressed into service to keep its brightness down. This done, severe limits would be set on what led up to this. No dimmer would mean No. 7 spot could not be used in the sunset—not serious because owing to the position of the window, this is one of the darker areas. Alternatively if there is a dimmer it has, unlike the rest of the lighting, to travel right out, then have the wall bracket joined to it before coming back in on cue. This is all very elementary to anyone who has worked a lighting control; but I put it in so that any producer who has not will appreciate that there can lurk very real problems in a cue which seems on the surface to be simplicity itself. Indeed, it is often the case that a spectacular lighting change is much easier to operate than subtle changes only requiring quick alteration of lighting balance.

It must be stressed that the switchboard has control of the lighting fittings, not the actor. He simply puts his hand on the appropriate switch and keeps it there until the lights change. In the case of an imitation oil lamp which has to be carried on and subsequently lit, there is no escaping the independent battery source. A rheostat rather than a switch should be fitted. The gradual turning up of this will not only give a better imitation of lighting a lamp but also enable the switchboard to follow up the light reasonably well. There remains the problem of lights carried across the stage. With a complete traverse, our three groups would have to be raised and taken down in a lap arrangement. The first thing that would be discovered is that actors can move very quickly about the stage—something some designers of automated switchboards are inclined to overlook. By the time the lights came up in each locale he could have passed on. Such cues have to be anticipated. After all, if our stage represents part of the castle hall, the coming event would have cast its light before. Thus, the light is on the way up before the entrance is made to the acting area itself. This will be much better than a risk of the light's suddenly appearing on the place just vacated.

Another case for anticipation is when a character alludes to a lighting change. Dawn must have begun to tell before Horatio's line, "But look, the morn, in russet mantle clad"—

always provided it is the kind of production of *Hamlet* which allows us a dawn and somewhere to display it discreetly.

In changing effects, such as are implicit in dawn or sunset, it is very important to keep the cycle of change smooth. A 1000- or 2000-watt lamp for a sunrise will need very careful dimmer operation. The thick filament takes some appreciable time to warm up; when creeping the dimmer in, one is likely to overdo it and the light will come either with a rush as too much light or so slowly as to miss the cue. Lighting changes must always flow, and any suggestion of bringing up the sun in a couple of minutes at the behest of a cue must be avoided.

Exteriors

An exterior, when compared to an interior, demands a much greater softlight component by day but much less by night. The first state is accounted for by the sky over all and the second by the fact that at night when artificial light is used not only is the reflection factor of grass, outside walls, and so forth, much poorer but these surfaces are less in number and much farther away, and there is no equivalent at all to the ceiling. Point a torch vertically upwards and indoors some light, perhaps a great deal, will appear over the floor, whereas outdoors the ground will remain as dark as before.

Although by day so much light descends from heaven in nature, we do in real life spend little time looking up there and where the sun is concerned, in fact, automatically dodge looking at it. The eye sees in detail and in colour a very narrow angle indeed. Beyond this vision is a matter of being aware of rather than seeing. If we want to take a good look we have to turn our eyes and perhaps our head to do so. Thus the eyes scan the centre of interest and one could walk for a considerable distance without consciously taking in the sky overhead. It follows that as with interiors so too with exteriors the borders, or whatever the overhead masking is, should not be directly lit.

The angels and cupids of an Edwardian theatre interior do not vanish: they merely retire when the house lights are lowered and no difficulty is experienced in forgetting them. If, however, some of them were picked out by lighting, then they would obtrude. So it is on the stage: masking, if reticent, is easily accepted. Masking problems in exteriors very often extend to the sides of the stage as well as to the borders overhead, for it is not convenient always to have houses, tree trunks, or icebergs lining the wings!

The Curtain Set

This seems as good a place as any to consider the curtain set and roundly condemn the use of "silver grey" for this. I think this colour arises from the misguided notion that it will take coloured light well. What is wanted is something that will hang well but take light badly, that is, absorb a very great deal. A dark charcoal grey or black is my recommendation. Ideally a velour or velvet hangs and looks well but cost often rules it out. I am always hoping to find a less expensive good-looking material; but this needs weight, and this kind of weight cannot be provided by a chain along the bottom, necessary though these may be. Cheap materials might be given a feeling of weight by making them up to include a grey gauze in front as a kind of front lining, thereby giving them the surface texture that is otherwise missing.

It is sometimes argued that a dark or black set of drapes is too funereal for some shows. To avoid this, curtains, particularly legs, are made reversible and hang on a short length of track which one pulls down slightly to unlock and pivot. The curtain leg can thus be made to present either silver gayness or sombre obfuscation at will. But at whose will? The tendency is for the wretched curtain to twist at the edges at the slightest provocation, thereby revealing that every curtain has its silver lining. Gaiety can be achieved in other ways, and these are dealt with under Ballet, later on, while for gay plays it is the job for such scenery as there is to provide this.

I dislike the mounting of drapes in such a way as to form a box set. To be fair, a good case has been argued, especially at amateur level, for the boxing of the stage by strips of curtain which are rolled up and put on top of the inserted doors and windows.[1] I much prefer that the curtain set be treated solely as masking and hung so as to do this and impede neither lighting nor actors entering anywhere up or downstage. This is perfectly satisfactory with cut-down or token scenery. This latter goes the rest of the way, following the notion that, if we do not need the top half of the scenery to get over an idea, we may not need all the actors' surroundings at ground level either. This principle is extremely useful in exteriors, great chunks of scenery being omitted and those areas left to take their chance with the curtain set or some other form of permanent masking. This is quite accepted in the professional theatre and if it is good enough for the Royal Shakespeare company on the one hand and glossy Broadway musicals from *Oklahoma!* onwards, why not for us? The photographs (Fig. 142) give two examples of the combination of permanent masking (in this case, curtains) and partial setting on a very small stage. The difference between the two is simply a matter of black or silver-grey drapes. Another version of the same set

[1] *The Curtain Set*, by Frank Napier (Muller).

FIG. 142 Token exterior in moonlight with grey and black alternative drapes

but with a cyclorama or plain backcloth appears in Fig. 143, opposite.

Lighting Exterior Scenes

This set will make a useful one on which to base an examination of the principles of exterior lighting. In fact, the stage in the photograph (Fig. 143) has only a 13-ft opening between the front curtains, which means lighting can only be divided into left and right. I have accordingly, in making a diagram for analysis (Fig. 144), enlarged the width to allow the same standard three area side-by-side layout to be used as was the case in the interior discussed earlier in this chapter.

FIG. 143 As Fig. 142 but with cyclorama and cloud effects

To aid the direct comparison, the sequence is assumed to be the same with the sun coming from stage left and running into evening and night. To begin, acting area spots Nos. 1, 2, 3, 7, 8, and 9 are accented by being at full, while a slight check is taken on Nos. 4, 5, 6, 10, 11, and 12. To this the softlight is added. It is possible that on an open set like this all twelve spots could be full up and the accent come from side lighting high up on the stage left in each opening. This would give a sense of direction to the sunlight, which should on no account be spoilt by falling into the temptation of duplicating it on stage left, to make things look brighter or enable the audience to see better. It is the job of the twelve acting area spots to provide illumination so that the audience can see, and if they do not do this well enough then the wattages should be increased by using larger spots or by doubling them up by twin spots close side by side at each position.

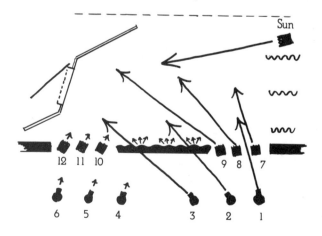

FIG. 144 Plan: exterior daylight

Painting with Light 253

The sunlight from actors' left is purely there for motivation and this relies absolutely on light from one direction, making one side of each object on the stage brighter than the other and even, perhaps, one side of the stage brighter than the other. This would all depend on whether it is assumed that the black curtain masking the non-picture area is supposed to be occupied by open landscape or by trees or a building, which would cause stage left to have a shadowed area. The impression given would simply depend on whether the sunlight spots are kept high only or whether some lower power sources, notably floods, are added lower down.

Mounting and general principles of side lighting are dealt with later on, so for the moment let us assume we are still working with minimal equipment and return to the twelve acting area spots, six of which (1, 2, 3, 7, 8, and 9) are accented. As was the case with the interior, the effectiveness of the dominant idea—the sunlight—is going to depend on what it is going to display. In halls where the bulk of the audience sits low in relation to the stage this amounts to the scenery and actors, since the floor is unlikely to be seen. Of these two, it is likely that the scenery is a safer bet to get the message over as it is there all the time and does not move anyway!

In the present instance, there is not much scenery and one can only be grateful that the sun is permitted to shine from stage left. It is a very obvious example of the interdependence of light and scenery. The lighting of the building is important because it is this rather than the colour of the sky which is going to convey the impression of what kind of day it is. Once the building is brightly lit as sunlight a wide latitude of colour is permissible on the backcloth. In the present scale, two Fresnels, one for the part of the wall which backs the actor and therefore to light him also, and one purely for the top of the house and pinned down as bright as possible, will do the job. No question of conflicting rays of sunlight comes in as they do not overlap and the rays of the two beams will not be seen against the light sky anyway.

The sky itself will require some floodlighting at the top and this could come from a batten or a few wide-angle floods, as described earlier. The most important item is some kind of break-up in the shape of clouds. Various methods, elaborate and simple, are considered in Chapter 12. An archway, as in Fig. 144 stage right might seem to suggest that this does not lead directly into the house but rather into a patio. Now, although the sunlight would not reach this, the shady side of the house, and although the masking overhead is black, it is supposed to be open to the sky and would receive diffused light from that source. A backing flood over the top of the arch is therefore essential to give an impression of this. On the other hand, if the arch leads directly into the house then the backing will not be lit as an interior is by contrast dark against the exterior.

Unwanted Shadows

The archway can be troublesome because it may well display conflicting shadows from the various acting area spots. Just as the best way to ensure a positive shadow where one is essential is to paint it on, so the best way to avoid an unwanted shadow is not to have anything to throw it. We cannot do without the many spotlights though sometimes a particularly offending one can be taken down a point or two on the dimmer. What can be dispensed with is the setback that interrupts the light and causes the shadow. Thus, if the backing is hard up against the vertical of the arch, that particular shadow is reduced to a thin line. The alternative is to take the backing a long distance away. Of course, the curve of the arch will spring away from the backing, but this top shadow is not so serious as the backing flood can be introduced on check to soften it.

The point can be taken a little further in respect of the cyclorama. Should a profile ground row be required to show a middle distance city with a church spire, there are two methods of treating it. Either the ground row is sufficiently distant that separate lighting is used for cyclorama and the profile piece and no shadow can be thrown; or where, as is all too likely, there is little space, then the profile is put as hard against the cyclorama as possible, even to the extent of putting any stiffening on the front and disguising it in the painting instead of, as is usual, on the back. Under these circumstances any shadow is at most a thin line.

In complaining of the other type of shadows on backcloths or backings, those thrown by window frames and the like, it is not the shadow that is the trouble; it is the line between what is shadow and what is not that is the nuisance. A complete shadow right across would be excellent and this is what is achieved when one changes the position of an offending acting area spotlight. The bright patch is still there but is out of picture in the wings or beyond the window frame. This repositioning of the spotlight casting the offending beam is often not possible or desirable. For example, it may owe its position to the needs of an earlier scene. Assuming a substitute spot is not available then the solution is to put something in the foreground to intercept this light. Beyond the french windows a garden trellis, pile of dustbins, dumped motor cars or whatever is appropriate, has to be placed just the size to intercept the light hellbent on spoiling our backcloth only a couple of feet or so beyond. Under all conditions, even with a pitch black night outside, it would be quite proper for that trellis or whatever to pick up light emanating from the room.

The scene designer can anticipate some of these difficulties and arrange his set so as not to ask the impossible. Where an unsuspected trouble of this kind arises then some extra dressing of the set in this way may be an easier solution than moving the offending light.

While reinforcement of light under a balcony is possible with auxiliary sources, such as 100-watt mini-Fresnels for example, it can never become the principal source. Quite apart from the unnaturalness of this by day, there is the room neither to house nor to spread major sources. Thus a deep balcony, such as that which was featured in the original permanent set at Chichester, ensures that an actor makes his entrance feet first from under it. The majority of the lighting resources being placed high, as they must, create a deep shadow. If a large second acting area is required up aloft, keep its actual overhang of the main acting area to a minimum. Incidentally, do not forget that light may be in trouble on the top deck, too—not in its incident path but in the return journey to the audience. Looking up at deep balcony from the wide range angles of an encircled audience may lead to an unwelcome amount of no view for some; the balcony itself getting in the way of action on the far side.

Sunless Daylight

To return to lighting proper, it by no means follows that the stage directions will insist on a sunny day but it may simply be added as suiting the mood we wish to obtain. There are bright days without direct sunlight but it is far more difficult then to show what one is at. Lacking the dominant idea, the conflict of the various acting area beams could become more apparent. On the other hand, a grey or overcast day or an early morning has to be faced and these, in nature, would be the result of the sky only. There is nothing for it in such cases; the acting area spots must play second fiddle to the softlight, both circuits of which will be at full giving a cold white light. The problem of colour of the spots has already been dealt with under Interiors. A suggestion of cold light could be added by a Fresnel spot flooded on the building from No. 1 bar or from the perch position and set high to avoid actor's shadows.

Whether the day is grey or overcast is a matter of the effect put on the cyclorama, and in case a feeling of guilt should creep in when using effects there, it is important to remember that in the context an even sky may be more eye-riveting, especially as it usually has to be much brighter to drown the results of stray light, whereas these get lost in an uneven background.

Dawn and Sunset

It is necessary to be very clear where the actual sunrise or sunset is supposed to take place before starting to paint the stage with light. If the sun is behind the cyclorama ground row, then objects in the foreground of this do not pick up the pink light except in the case of water. Thus, a mountain range remains stark and contrasted—dark blue to violet. To get the effect of pink mountains, the sun would have to be going down in the audience somewhere. In mountain areas, other mountains can cause a cut-off effect, whilst the pink, especially on snow, is very pronounced as to colour and location. The acting area could not be pink; on the other hand, in open country all will be bathed in a diffused pink glow. However, I do not need to stress in a book published in Britain that not all sunsets and dawns glitter or are in the pink. A cold grey light crawling up the cyclorama can be the very embodiment of dawn. A lavish three-colour ground row is not necessary to represent the sun when down low; a single flood lying on its back with strips laid across the top or soldered up to make a giant gobo will make a good sunburst with a suggestion of radiating rays. Where much more light or a stylized effect is required, the same thing can be done with three or more spots set radially.

Night Effects

Outdoor night effects are very troublesome as the usual lack of depth makes it impossible to keep the cyclorama as dark as one would like. To drown the scatter from the acting area too much blue has to be brought up. One solution for a really dark night is to draw black drapes immediately in front of the cyc and leave them unlit. This works equally well for interiors. Another solution is to remember that it is a feature of a dark night outdoors that it is really dark. On top of this, diffusion in the shape of returned light is negligible. It is likely that concessions as to actors' movements will have to be won from the producer. This enables areas supposed to be lit by a local source, be it street lamp or camp fire, to be more starkly defined. In a scene of fairground gaiety, the sky can be made to appear darker by using the blinder effect of fairy lamps strategically placed. Usually a sky can be made to appear blacker by adding just a touch of blue, Nos. 19 or 20, checked right down. Another form of blinder that can be used to make the sky appear darker than it really is, is a star slide tinted with No. 17.

The whole point about giving an impression of darkness on the stage is that we shall, as pointed out earlier, be working to levels much higher than those in nature and the only way open is to locate darkness to certain areas and make it tell by contrast with lit areas.

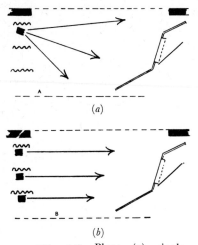

FIG. 145 Plan: (a) single-source moon and (b) multiple-source compared

Moonbeams

Outdoor moonlight effects are best conveyed by directional rays superimposed on the setting in much the same way as in the case of sunlight, except that the appearance should be hard and contrasting, little or no blending softlight being used. For large theatres, a 2000-watt Fresnel spot can be used, sometimes hung in pairs in special frames from the flys. Smaller stages will find a 1000-watt or 500-watt Fresnel spot very suitable. A flood cannot be used, nor can a spot be wide-focused as the shadows will then radiate from this source. The only true solution, where large coverages are required, is several lanterns each set to give narrow beams. For example: if our setting has a series of wings stage left, each wing will have its moonray lantern instead of a single 5-kW Fresnel flooded well off-stage which would throw the shadows of the wings in widely conflicting directions (Fig. 145). At one time the parallel-beam lantern known as a Pageant would have been used for moonlight and sunlight, but in these rationalized days they are difficult to come by. The German Nedervolt lamp is another suitable unit. In all these cases it is a matter of a number of units throwing parallel rays to different positions on the stage. In a television studio, the technique under these circumstances would be to have a high-power open arc in a distant corner of the studio putting a dominant hard key over all else. There is still a case for something of the sort in a theatre provided a really distant throw is possible. Of course, an arc would not be used as it could not be dimmed, but a single Fresnel could be made to work provided too high a level of light was not demanded and the set was suitably open. Take out the lens, and the hard shadow effect is so evocative that the audience will overlook the radiating shadows from the single source.

The multiple parallel source method outlined previously suits a glade, ruined castle or even a cloudy night. All in all, people are not dead set on finding inaccuracies and some very strange levels of light and colours have been used. In Peter Brook's production of *Lear* with Paul Scofield, about sixty foot-candles of white light represented moonlight and it passed. However, I personally drew the line in *Uncle Vanya* at Chichester when to suggest an interior on the open three-sided stage a moonlight-coloured pattern of windows was projected from the direction of the audience as well as from the two windows actually present as scenery upstage left and right. Seeing that this kind of theatre is designed to abolish the fourth wall convention, it seemed somewhat irrational to invoke by the conflicting directions four moons to suggest three walls that were not there!

The colour of moonlight needs some thought and it can be

stated here and now that the No. 16 Blue-green, at one time labelled "Moonlight Blue" in some colour charts, does not in the slightest degree resemble moonlight. Direct moonlight is, under normal conditions, a very low-intensity cold white, and its characteristics are the hard shadows giving stark black and white lighting. This white would be best imitated by one, or at the most two, Steels (No. 17) were it not for the fact that we can scarcely perceive colour at these low intensities in nature. From this it can be seen that the best moonlight effects will be obtained from black and white scenery, costumes and make-up, lighted through double No. 17 Steel-blue filters. If this is not done, then reds and colours show up in such a way under this light that the brain automatically says this is not moonlight but cold daylight.

Such a complete change of pigments for one act or scene will seldom be possible, and we are faced with the job of spoiling colour with our filters as far as possible without conveying the effect of a riotously blue stage. The thing to avoid is any contrast that will emphasize the blue. A No. 40 or 45 Blue, or better still 40–50, will be effective enough to suppress most colour and at the same time will not look particularly blue, unless deliberately contrasted with amber to red lighting. Thus, if the scene is the moonlit village with the glowing lights behind the windows, the temptation to make these orange must be restrained; they must be steel-blue, or at the most natural, white. The camp fire must err on the cold side for similar reasons; fires are always too red on stage, anyway. The problem of showing the image of the moon on the sky is treated in the following chapter.

Non-representational Lighting

In the early part of this chapter, I suggested that stage lighting when it was trying to give an impression of sunlight should be more concerned with the mood of the sunlight rather than the actual behaviour of the stuff in nature. Yet page upon page of lighting technique has followed in which a pedantic concern has been expressed not to offend against the laws of nature as if it mattered twopence to a good play how the sun goes down. The preceding pages were exercises—the piano scales of the business—and only simple ones at that. A dawn or a moon-beam is universal, a datum from which we can all work. A mood is too personal to build an exercise on. To some people, green light means the terror of a plague or of a ghost; the only mood it inspires in me is one of laughter. Terror is a subtle affair in which one is conscious of something unnatural but cannot put one's finger to it. In cinema, this can be done with a slightly "off" choice of camera angle. To take a particular play would be to pick a very strange one, if it is going

to have all these lighting exercises in it. Will the play endure, and what about the style of staging and the kind of theatre? Dramatic lighting may be so much a part of a production that, as in Fig. 146, it is impossible to conceive of one without the other. Little of what has been said in this chapter can apply to theatre-in-the-round where stage lighting is mainly concerned with illumination. No, for a wide range of painting exercises it is back to naturalism and the proscenium stage.

For a glimpse of emotional or psychological powers inherent in stage lighting, the reader is advised not to be put off by the title of Appendix 3—Colour Music. The pursuit of that art, even if one disagrees violently with the aims of providing a visual accompaniment to music, is deeply involved with the emotional powers of light when used in the abstract, completely detached from the representational. There is another form of non-representational lighting which must be divorced, as far as I understand it, from emotion as well. Brecht's *Life of Galileo* is a good example. The faithful do not always apply the alienist rules as strictly as they should. One set of rules must apply, however, whatever the play and its style of staging and those belong to Chapter 10 on Illumination, for the players must still be seen.

If the lighting has other jobs than the representational, so too have the lighting changes. These can be used either to suggest a change of emphasis or to act as a kind of punctuation. The most elementary example of this is the lowering of lights to denote the passing of time, but a change from one lighting effect to another can be used to convey the distinction between the imagined and actual. Good examples of this occurred in the plays, *Ten Minute Alibi* and *the seven year itch*. This is a case where one cannot afford to be subtle and a change of colour over the acting area spots to, say, No. 18 instead of the No. 52 or to No. 42 if the effect is supposed to be light-hearted rather than serious, can call attention to what is going on just as effectively as a change of typeface on the printed page.

Musicals

Nowadays the distinction between the musical and the straight play has become less and less marked. The staging and lighting for *West Side Story* or *Oliver!* to take but two examples, have little in common with the *Desert Song* or even *Oklahoma!* Yet in amateur theatre, the latter are both very much current and, indeed, musicals and operettas of a much earlier period are still around.[1] For NODA members, a popular musical never dies. It is, however, likely that a change of staging will be forced upon societies for the simple reason that the kind of full stage sets that went with such productions are becoming increasingly difficult to hire. Scenery will use the techniques implied in the earlier pages of this chapter and this will mean the same lighting principles. No longer will it be a question of flooding the stage with light depending mainly on battens, footlights, and wing floods, with spots reduced only to the role of fortifying the light on the acting area. I am not saying all amateur musicals are staged in this way, but a great deal of it still goes on. Probably the fact that so many have to perform on stages, such as those of cinemas, in which the staple lighting is three or four colour battens, is responsible.

It would not be logical for the lighting of musicals to lag behind for they have always been in the vanguard of any development. It was the musical that first made popular the massed batteries of lighting units now common in straight plays. As was pointed out in Chapter 3, *Waltzes from Vienna* was the

---

[1] The top ten musicals in 1971–73 were according to NODA: *Fiddler on the Roof, The Merry Widow, The Mikado, My Fair Lady, The Gondoliers, The Sound of Music, Iolanthe, Oklahoma!, Carousel* and *H.M.S. Pinafore. The Desert Song* was in fact number eleven on the list while *West Side Story* was very near the bottom—*Oliver!* was moderately popular with 45 productions to *Fiddler's* 118.

landmark as far as Britain was concerned. As time has passed, the individual lighting units have become more powerful but, in turn, their numbers have multiplied. Spotlights in this quantity partake of some of the quality of softlights and, for example, the twenty-six spots on the circle front at Drury Lane have largely moved as one and remained as flat-on front lighting. At the time of *My Fair Lady*, the number was increased to thirty-six and two vertical booms of spots were added up the audience side of the proscenium. This idea was carried even further for *Blitz!* at the Adelphi when these spots were carried along the top of the proscenium also. Another common auditorium position now, but not originally, is the 45 degrees or so one represented by the point where upper circle runs into the top tier boxes.

On stage, the power of overhead lighting was first increased by adding rows of acting area floods pointing straight down or later by Fresnel spots mainly directed at the area of the stage opposite to which they hang. The American musical introduced backlighting in a big way, often with several flood battens and spot battens directed from upstage to down—the former for lighting backcloths as transparencies from the back and the spots to throw the cast into relief, which was all the more necessary in view of the strength of the light from the front. Along with this goes side lighting, on booms and ladders, of corresponding power. These methods I call lighting by chorus. Two hundred spots are not unusual and constitute a great choir sometimes all shining together in unison and, at other times, in lesser combinations as altos, basses or whatever

(Fig. 148). To call up a particular resource, direction or colour is to bring in a multiplicity of sources, and a solo spot, when it is used, must be very powerful to make itself heard at all.

All this is very different from the chamber-music type of lighting we have been practising. Even if there is an apron or a very deep stage the acting area spots for the nine areas would only number eighteen. Allowing the luxury of two colours to each makes thirty-six and doubling that for all other contingencies—softlight, motivating lights and specials —works out at seventy-two controlled circuits. Even in this lavish (for us) version, we still do not approach the chorus either in numbers or method. The inevitable conclusion has to be that whatever Broadway or the West End may do, in the present context it is as out-of-reach as the stars they employ.

Ballet Lighting

Lighting for the dance shows interesting differences from lighting for drama which will help when trying to design a lighting layout for an intermediate form such as the musical which uses both. The first thing to bear in mind is that there is an orchestra and no lighting should be undertaken without this switched on so that due allowance is made for the scatter therefrom. The relationship of conductor to stage is important and, whatever the lighting, he has to be seen by performers, though I wish they would not make this so obvious sometimes. Another point dancers like to be aware of in the darker scenes is where the front edge of the stage is and, in the absence of a

FIG. 148 The spotlight chorus: *Gone with the Wind*, Theatre Royal, Drury Lane

footlight, some small blue marker lights spaced out there are essential. The notion of a possible fall into the orchestra pit, which I have seen happen, does not help relaxed performance. With some of today's lofty scenic structures, it seems that a head for heights is another essential for the actor.

While opera and many musicals have lighting which is essentially dramatic and therefore little if at all removed from that for drama it is quite otherwise with Ballet which is stylized within a rigid framework as its means for expression. Of course the boundaries are ill defined; there is stylized opera or drama and a musical incorporates a large element of ballet or at any rate dance, but it is ballet with its décor of wing scenery and back or front cloths which operates to the most rigid discipline. As a result it is possible to make a lighting layout for ballet as such rather than for a particular ballet with a hope that all will work out reasonably well whatever is put on. At least there will be nothing that cannot be remedied with a special unit here and there plus a change of colours. The basic intent behind a lighting layout for ballet is shown in Fig. 149. The stress on lighting from the side is apparent and this subject is treated under its own heading later on. Suffice it to point out that the main drift of lighting is as shown by the arrows. On the overhead bars Fresnels for the acting area tend to be gathered at each end and may even as is shown in the diagram be directed exactly sideways across to the opposite side of the stage. This is also the case with the lighting actually in the wings. Indeed the one can be regarded as an extension of the other and it may be appropriate to angle those hanging overhead somewhat upstage. This is certainly so with number 1

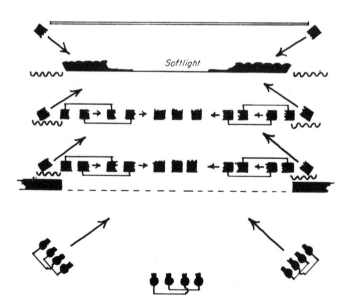

FIG. 149 Plan: basic layout for ballet. Bulk of lighting is angled from side even when overhead

bar to prevent light wandering outside the stage frame. The nature of and positioning of the side masking and borders also exercises critical influence.

Direct side lighting has some of the advantage of back lighting in respect of those downstage of it. Backlighting is so important that it rates its own units for the purpose as shown upstage. Colour change is also important and the notion of grouping for colour is shown in this case for two colours, a pink and a light blue—not too blue or it will not be suitable for moonlight. Three colours allowing the addition of a gold would increase the range of effect. Ballet is one case where contrasting colours or at any rate deeper shades of colour from one side than the other come into their own. The unattached lanterns in the centre of the hanging bars and out in the front of house can be used for special lighting particularly of the scenery. Some FOH units can be set to lift the centre of the large cloths which are so characteristic of ballet décor. These can be used not only on the special act drops that some ballets employ, for example *Petrushka*, but on the cloth upstage. Even though a batten (softlight) is usual in that position it may not get right down and does not give the essential emphasis to the centre of the cloth. The correct insistence on FOH spots high and to the side for lighting artistes and three-dimensional scenery should not blind one to the fact that spots on the centre of the lower tiers can be very useful when a drop-cloth type of scene turns up. This is certainly so at the London Palladium, for example. It is usual to employ a footlight for ballet but the effect is much nicer from the stalls when there is no sense of obstruction. The Royal Opera House has a footlight specially made which does not come above stage-floor level and at Drury Lane it has been the practice to lower the footlight out of sight and dispense with it during ballet sequences in some American musicals,

Coloured shadows produced from low down can be used to great effect. Fig. 150 shows the basic method. The sources required to throw the shadows must be few in number and wide spaced if they are to tell. On a shallow stage the effect will have to be done from the footlight position. As low-powered coloured sources are insipid, a bright and therefore larger source than the usual float spot will have to be used. If necessary, rigged in the orchestra pit for just that number and struck immediately after. No one who has not tried the shadow effect for himself can realize the wonderfully rich variety of multiple colours which results, given a suitably intense source.

The use of spots thrown directly on a plain backcloth as décor is worth considering. A few clear-cut circles of light in different sizes, for example the Patt 23 Profile spot with its three lens angles, makes real composition. Add other shapes or gobos and a range of bright décor is possible without the

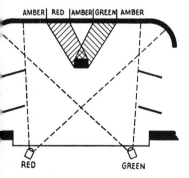

FIG. 150 Plan: coloured shadows

expense of painting scenery or slides. These spots are used direct front on, perhaps from the No. 1 bar position with the borders kept high. Where this is impossible, other methods can use the effects of the spot beams at close range from below or above *along* the cloth. This can also be done from the sides if the cyclorama is a rigid one without folds; not that folds are to be despised—the most splendid effects are possible on a curtain lit from the sides in contrasting colours. These are at their gayest and most colourful on light or white curtains but at their richest on blacks—especially on black velvets, which officially do not take light at all!

Among all the talk of colour and the dance, those whose sole opportunity to practise this art is the local dancing school annual display should remember that obscurity, however colourful, is not the way to popularity with mothers. No matter who Sylvia is, where she is can be a matter of great moment: beware the artistic shadow in these circumstances.

Stage Floor

What colour should the stage floor be for dancing? The whole subject of finish for floors is left decidedly on the vague side. To begin at the beginning, should the stage floor be flat or raked? The immediate answer nowadays is flat; the rake should be in the auditorium not on the stage, and dancers do not like much of a rake anyway. Yet in opera a very steep rake is very frequently used and greatly aids both dramatic and perspective effects. The Royal Shakespeare Company uses a pronounced rake on the apron half of the acting area but allows the rest to remain flat. This has point since the original Stratford-upon-Avon forestage was lower by three steps than the main stage and the slope covers the awkwardness of having to have these steps across every scene. The flat area allows for use of wagons, periaktoi and other legitimate scenery machines. John Bury, the designer responsible, gives it as his opinion that the stage should be flat but adds that this is because it makes a better sub-floor for him to base his different built-up and raked levels on.

A raked floor, and indeed any stage floor in any theatre where the bulk of the audience look down, plays an important part—maybe the only part in the composition of the scene. A lot of trouble is taken over the floor in the Royal Shakespeare productions. Sections are taken up and exchanged for others. Sometimes to get the right sound from that particular place— the grating of swords, for example—expanded metal is let in. At others, to get the feel of marble paving in a way that painted floor cloths could not achieve, large plastic treated sheets or black formica are used.

While Stratford has been busy on its floors, the dancers of

the Royal Ballet prefer to forsake stage cloths and dance on the wood floor whenever possible. This floor is medium in tone and is a nice compromise and I think it is the one I would commend to architects. Heavy brown lino resembling the Corkoid flooring of television studios is often used over old floors. Black lino has its advocates, but I was once told very firmly by Lydia Sokolova that the feet should not be too prominent in ballet and my black floor had to be covered with a stage cloth. Whatever the floor colour, it should not be given a specular polished finish as light will have an unhappy way of turning up where it is not wanted. A light-coloured floor is essential in theatre-in-the-round in order to obtain some corrective diffusion from the lighting overhead which tends to be mounted at too high an angle in order to avoid glare.

Side Lighting

Side lighting conjures up for many people a telescopic stand in the wings with some unit, probably a flood, mounted on top. Easy to position and feed from the dip plugs and easy to get at to change the colour. It dispenses a rich variety of lighting with little trouble. Here lies the trap, for the easiest way to use side lighting is the worst way to apply it. It is scarcely an exaggeration to say that, if any lantern is on a telescopic stand, nine times out of ten its light is being misapplied. The trouble is that such a stand in its common form neither goes high enough on the one hand nor low enough on the other. What it does best is to position the lantern at head height, a level from which lighting is never advisable and seldom required. It is not the lighting effect that needs it there but the convenient stand that insists on it.

The vast majority of side-lighting effects demand really high positions so that the light can get across the stage without being intercepted on the way. This is a practical reason but it is also valid for any evocation of natural light. Sometimes the main stream of light directed from aloft at the other side of the stage can be supplemented by a flood lower down to suggest a continuously lit area offstage, in the wings, but this will rarely need to be a shaft of light. This is because the illumination of what is supposed to be off-stage—a passage, a room or another part of the wood—is almost certain to be diffused light. Even if the time is sunset and our woodland glade happens to be situated on top of a hill, the light that filters through the trees, implied by most forms of wing masking, would be fitful indeed. The condition is even less likely as seen through the window of a house for there are almost always obstructions to the low-lying sun in the shape of other houses, trees, and bushes. This is all to the good for when sunlight approaches the horizontal it is very much on the move and to

FIG. 151   Incorrect low position
of side lighting (a) and correct
high position (b)

hold that effect for a whole scene is out of the question.

This will seem like more pedantry, for all sorts of natural
laws besides this one will be broken to dramatic effect. This
is true, but one must know them in order that when broken
they shall be effective. It so happens that, as well as being
correct in what we are trying to give an impression of, it is a
great aid to lighting to mount units high. Rude flares from
artistes standing near the wings and receiving on their posteriors
a shaft of light at point-blank range are then easily avoided,

as is also the effect of standing in one another's light (Fig. 151). Strange effects, like an actor exiting into the dawn and increasing the intensity of light on himself twenty-fold as he does so, are no longer a risk. This is of course the inverse square law at work. The real sun being an infinite distance away presents no such effects.

The best way to use side lighting is in most cases from vertical booms. This not only gives high mounting, but when securely fixed allows access by climbing up a series of extra clamps positioned to form a rudimentary ladder (Fig. 152). Another form of mounting is known as a "ladder" but, although there is a vague resemblance, it is a frame hanging high and one would have to be an acrobat to use it as such. The advantage of these frames, on the other hand, is that when hanging and fed from the flys they keep the stage entrances clear. The fly rail itself is also an excellent position for side lighting but I think it would be even better if a special lighting gallery were provided just below it, as at Drury Lane for example, as this would prevent the inevitable conflict between electrical and flying requirements particularly on the working side.

FIG. 152 Lighting from the wings: (a) spots on a boom (b) spots on ladders

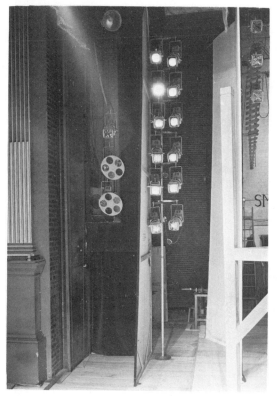

Visions and Picture Effects

Reference must be made to the properties of theatrical gauze. This gauze has the faculty of appearing solid when lighted from the front and of vanishing altogether when scenery or actors are lighted behind it. The secret of success in these vision effects is that the fogging front lighting must be so placed that it does not pass through the gauze to light the regions beyond; similarly no light on the vision must be allowed to strike the gauze. A common mistake is to use a magazine batten and footlight to fog the gauze; naturally this light penetrates and no end of difficulty is experienced in getting the vision to disappear. Except on large stages it is essential to use narrow-beam floods and spotlights for both the gauze and vision.

Properly done, the gauze and vision will, in their turn, vanish absolutely. The best general-purpose colour for gauze is grey, and this can always be painted with a design. Sometimes gauzes are used one behind the other, the second being a few feet up stage of the other. The second should be white to make up for transmission through the first; a different size mesh is needed unless watermark effects are intended. Gauzes may be hung in folds, though these will not vanish altogether. Ethereal effects are obtained by side-lighting the folds of one gauze behind the other with a blue-lit cyclorama at the back. It is as well to remember that, though a vision may be perfectly "disappeared" when still, an actor taking up his position may, by his movement, betray his presence. To be absolutely safe, a black velvet curtain should hang behind the gauze until the revelation is to take place.

By using a slightly fogged tight gauze down stage of the actors a two-dimensional effect can be produced. The eye is deceived into considering everything beyond the gauze as on its plane. This tight gauze, whether framed by a picture frame or by the entire proscenium frame, is used for tableaux vivants or to bring a picture to life. Gauze used in this way can also be an aid to pin spotting for head and shoulder scenes. A single spot, for example, is sharply focused on someone using a telephone. We see him clearly through the gauze but the light itself is thrown back to diffuse over the rest of it, causing slight fogging. This helps prevent the rest of the stage from being seen and can increase the effect of isolating the character. Mention of fogging is a reminder that this is one way of producing an impression of mist on the stage.

Fluorescent Effects

Visions, ghosts, and the like can easily be produced with the aid of the invisible ultra-violet rays on fluorescent paints and make-up. However, such effects tend to become, by their close resemblance to the accepted ghost, a burlesque rather than a horror. The spectre with his head tucked underneath his arm and a rapier through his chest (possible under UV) is far less likely to terrify than a normal being, slightly abnormal in a way that the mind can only feel but not recognize.

When illusions are contemplated, the stage must not be flooded with a high level of ultra-violet as this may bring into prominence the natural, if low-intensity fluorescence of many materials. The skeleton that dances, throwing away his bones, one by one, until he vanishes will require a black-draped stage and black tights to which the fluorescent bones are hooked. One 125-watt lamp in the footlight for a small stage and two for a large one may be sufficient. The skeleton's routine must be arranged so that in no circumstances does a limb from which the bones have been removed pass in front of those that remain.

Another illusion is the reverse of the preceding effect: in this the scenery is treated but the actor is not. For *The Golden Toy* at the Coliseum before the war, the setting included a great fluorescent archway flooded by lamps in the footlights and overhead, and backed by a black velvet sky. In this instance, Lupino Lane ran on stage in a pool of ordinary spotlighting, climbed up a fluorescent rope, hanging from the arch, out of the pool of light and thereupon vanished. The Indian Rope Trick! When arranging these effects nowadays one has to be very careful of the unwanted result of the "whiteness" added to detergents. Almost everything fluoresces bright blue. The impact of the ghost loses more than somewhat if the sheets of the bed, nightclothes of its occupants, and even the bedroom curtains also take on an unearthly glow. Beware the laundry!

Fluorescence need not be restricted to the supernatural; as a decorative effect it can be very striking. The treated surfaces, appearing as actual coloured-light producers not reflectors, give extraordinarily rich luminous colours. For these decorative effects, the higher the ultra-violet intensity the better— three or four lamps in the footlights and UV floods overhead. Ice shows always feature at least one high intensity ultra-violet sequence of this kind.

Ultra-violet and fluorescence can have practical value as well as stunt value. There are times when part of a scene or a prop has to appear to be lit though in fact it is quite impossible to get light there without spilling over something beyond, thereby wiping out part of a projected scene, for example. At the Adelphi, London, in the revue *You'll be Lucky*, the UV was used to light a built sailing boat standing immediately in front of a screen on which moving optical waves were back projected. The boat and sail were treated with fluorescent paints and appeared to be sailing on the water by moonlight. Had any normal spotlighting been used on it the inevitable spill on the screen would have killed the wave effects. The artiste in the boat was picked out by an accurately located Mirror Spot. On a larger scale, in *White Horse Inn* at Empress Hall, Bernard Bear projected wave effects on the ice by normal tungsten-lamp optical effects lanterns while fluorescent boats activated by ultra-violet sailed thereon.

A subsequent production there used ultra-violet to light the chorus while they skated over a splendidly colourful carpet made of separately projected slides to join on the ice below.

The Samoiloff Effect

This relies on the use of complementary colours and is so called after its inventor. As we discussed in Chapter 6, a lantern fitted with a blue-green filter does not transmit any light wavelengths that can be reflected from a red surface; it therefore appears black. Under the red light there will be little colour contrast, and so the reflected colour will be interpreted as a reddish-white. Now, suppose an actor is made up in red and wears a coat of black and blue-green stripes; under the red light he will appear as a white man in a black coat; under the blue-green as a black man in a striped coat.

Any pair of complementary colours can be taken from the colour triangle in Fig. 57, page 101, but the filters and pigments must have perfect cut-offs. There are other factors to consider. For example, at first sight, yellow and blue complementaries may seem to be more pleasing, the yellow being more nearly white, but under the blue light the black effect does not get a sufficiently strong contrast. Powdering on top of make-up must be in the same colour.

Of course, the colour change need not be sudden; the changes from winter to spring or summer are easily performed on dimmers. The backcloth must be painted with black tree trunks, red flowers, green leaves, and so forth. Beginning under blue-green light, the scene appears in black and white, colours being spoiled either by absence of their colour in the light or by absence of contrast. As red is gradually added to the blue-green, these defects are remedied and spring arrives!

Solo Lighting

Time and time again in this book and elsewhere I find it necessary to stress that lighting and lighting changes must not be overdone—less is more likely to be effective than more. Yet this is to put the lighting designer and the operator at his control in, at times, an intolerable bondage. Any of us who have attained some degree of mastery over this medium have savoured and know something of its power of artistic and emotional expression. Today, more than ever, I feel there is a dire need to take account of "Light" as a solo medium; not as a gimmick, nor as a safety valve to prevent lighting men going berserk, but as imaginative capital for the artist to use to the full—capital locked away in the instrument that a great modern stage lighting installation represents and which can so seldom be released in the service of theatre as we know it.

Compared with lighting controls, those concerned with sound are primitive but it is sound which has been able to branch out—to break with tradition. What is more, as sales of discs and tapes show, sound finds a large audience for its advanced technological experiments. This is not service to music, nor does it do anything but irritate me, but the imaginative freedom it represents is something we in lighting can only admire and envy.

Have we got to sit around waiting for the occasional play, opera or ballet with exceptional demands, or succumb to the temptation of putting in too much lighting or too many changes because subconsciously that is what we *have* to do? I can claim to have come under this temptation much earlier than anyone else, but I came up with a solution which has kept me satisfied over the five decades of my active career. This solution was the playing of light to interpret music in terms of form and colour—lighting variations upon a three-dimensional setting as theme (Fig. 167). Here were all the opportunities to tease the imagination at very low levels—normally denied by the need to light actor, singer or dancer—followed by build-ups to a final climax. Here was a chance to use light to create beauty or mood in a language of its own.

On April 24th 1936 Bernard Shaw, who was among the audience for a recital on my brand new Strand Light Console, said—amid much else—that my lighting would be distracting to his plays; my retort that "his plays would be distracting to my lighting" was not intended to be flippant. Although it got a laugh, I meant exactly what I said. It is still my belief that what I prefer to think of as Colour Music—rather than a Light Show—not only provides an opportunity for the expert to stretch his technique but is also a valuable exercise for the student or trainee (see also Appendix 3, Colour Music).

Finish in Lighting

Although some productions make a feature of the lighting equipment by hanging it in full view, the majority still prefer concealment. On the stage this means exactly what it says, but unless care is taken the lantern may be hidden but still proclaim itself by scatter on to nearby scenery or even by being seen through the canvas of a flat that has not been backed properly. Out front in the auditorium it may not always be possible to provide complete concealment but an unnecessary give-away comes not from leaks from the lantern itself so much but from catching the illuminated surface of the colour filter in the corner of the eye (peripheral vision of the eye can be very sensitive). It may be desirable to use a blue filter on a lantern during a day scene in order to help bring out colour somewhere in the set or costume, but the incongruity of the blue lantern itself jars. Another reason for it being there could be that the cross-fade into the night to follow insists on it because the control has no preset. In certain critical side positions, if the lantern really cannot be hidden then a barndoor or lens hood should be fitted.

Another common fault is that the crossing beams of light intended to stress important areas may lap over each other so that a great accent comes in between. As characters walk across so they flare up into prominence for no obvious reason. Much the same can happen when a character is wearing a colour particularly sympathetic to the colour of the light at that position. Thus, someone comparatively minor can take on undue prominence. This could happen if a member of the crowd wearing a blue dress found herself standing in the blue spot referred to earlier.

Another serious trouble arises from the amount of stage lighting used in the auditorium. I am not joking when I say that in a recent production at the Haymarket the level of light in the auditorium was brighter when the house lights were out than during the interval when they were on. This was mainly the effect of scatter from the twenty-two spotlights mounted on the upper circle front and is all the more worthy of comment for the particular auditorium decoration is low in tone and ought to be quite capable of self-effacement. Whatever one may think of the picture frame, there can be no doubt that, if, as in this case, the production is entirely behind the proscenium and there is no apron or forestage, the auditorium should be dark. To avoid scatter, smoking should never be permitted in the auditorium and lenses and colours must be kept clean. The beams of light should be angled well clear of their housings for if part is intercepted not only does that mean less light on the target but also extra scatter. Also, frosts and diffuser glasses are great spreaders of ghost light. If there is one merit in my bifocal spot it is that it has removed the diffuser hazard, as instead the soft-edged shutters can be used.

12 Optical Projection

THERE are many ways of using optical projection and many purposes for which it may be used. The great thing is to make up one's mind what one is really trying to do. "One" should be understood to mean "two" for if the producer's notion is at variance with the intent he may call for more light than can be reconciled with a projection for that particular purpose. As I write there is a noisy production in London in which the whole of the décor consists of a series of slides, very good twin projections on the background, but because the acting area is too bright these are overwhelmed. This happens because both of scatter and of contrast and will be considered later.

Yet in the same theatre, the Saville, three years earlier the Czechs were able to do much the same thing, with the added hazard of film projection, with no such problem. This was simply because they used less than a tenth of the light on the acting area.

In Edward Kook's study on this subject[1] time and time again quotations appear about lack of power. For example, Peter Hall is quoted as saying: "The power and variety of equipment available in Britain is not sufficiently strong to make it possible to use it with adequate full stage lighting." It is commonly believed that German projectors have more power but in point of fact the contrary is the case, though not to any great extent worth making a fuss about. In any case there are complaints about intensity in the same study from the Germans themselves and, one may add, the Americans as well.

Another association of projection, which comes up pretty frequently, is with a dreamlike or insubstantial quality; or again, a lack of blending with foreground scenery and therefore with the action is complained of.

It needs to be said here that neither of these two qualities is inherent in optical projection as such. Projection can with some equipment be as sharp as you like and, secondly, a good slide of a design painted in perspective can look just as effective as the corresponding backcloth. There is no difference what-

[1] *Images in Light for the Living Theatre*, by Edward Kook (Ford Foundation, 1963).

ever between the two. Both are attempts to deceive the eye into believing that a flat surface, in one case the cloth or in the other the screen, is in fact solid. Now just as paint can do this so can projection. Assuming the light is properly balanced and the edges of the screen are masked, then if the projection does not succeed it is because of the style of the slide or its execution.

This is why one must decide at the outset what the aim is. After all many a painted cloth is not intended to do more than act as a décor—a painted backing—and no question of deception need enter into it. A slide of the same thing will not deceive either except in so far that the audience may believe it is a painted cloth. Likewise a projected real-life photograph may be intended to look just that—a slide on the screen. Many designers do not want their set to look naturalistic, but the question arises—can it be done anyway? Is it possible to take a colour photograph on location, whether of architecture or natural scenery, make a slide and then project it at the back of the acting area and take in the audience?

Now in television this happens time and time again. Viewed as a two-dimensional black and white picture on the TV set at home, slides appear blended perfectly with a certain amount of solid foreground scenery in the immediate neighbourhood of the actors. Even on the studio floor where one sees the set-up for oneself, back-projection screen and all, a glance at the monitor and deception takes over. This even happens where the projection represents middle distance, though in certain changes of camera angle there could be a tendency to get suspicious since the angles represented by the two-dimensional area would remain identical. However, the viewer is ready, as we have remarked elsewhere, automatically to assume that life continues beyond the edges of his picture and can be brought back to earth only by something like an intrusive mike boom.

So too, in the theatre, members of the audience are only too ready if not to believe then at any rate to suspend disbelief—a fact which seems to upset some directors. It has been claimed from Düsseldorf, to quote *The Times*, that "Sets are built accurately to scale in model form and then photographed in colour. The intensity of light used for throwing the slides on to the cyclorama and the possibility of gearing it to that of the stage lighting, preserve the projected image intact and make it impossible to tell the flat scenery from the solid with the naked eye. The three-dimensional illusion is perfectly sustained throughout." While too much importance should not be attached to a photograph, it must be admitted that Fig. 153 looks very convincing. Personally, I can see nothing which would prevent achievements of this kind, granted the open spaces of the German stage, for where they would un-

FIG. 153 *Die Kluge*, Carl Orff, multiple projections at Macmillan Hall, Toronto

doubtedly score is in keeping adequate distance between acting area and projection. The use of true photographs for projected backgrounds would have to assume a similar treatment for foreground built scenery so no jarring change of style was involved. The difficulty and undesirability of using this photographic type detail in the foreground, where the actor moves, is what in the end will rule out for the background the use of photographs taken on location. If, however, photographs of this sort are contemplated then great care will be needed to keep live objects out of the scene. I remember one photograph taken in St. James's Park in which we managed at last to keep all humans out only to forget the birds, which remained obstinately frozen in the slide which ultimately resulted.

Painted perspectives not only obviate these troubles but are far more likely to set a standard which can be kept to in the case of the built scenery, and thus a marriage between foreground and background becomes credible.

So we see that, if naturalism is the aim, projected backgrounds have just as much chance of success as painted backcloths—and this in spite of the fact that, in both, their perspective can only be composed for a limited number of seats in the centre and is really phoney for all the rest. Success is a matter of the painting of the design and it does not matter whether it is realized in the enlarged version by the scene painter on a backcloth or by photographing the design as a colour slide and projecting it. In both cases the positioning of cloth or screen so that the edges are masked by a broken frame will be important. Almost equally important in both cases will be the lighting. Everyone knows a slide can lose its effect if the lighting is not carefully done, but in fact a painted backcloth is pretty nearly as touchy in this respect and too much light on it can give it a bleached effect which greatly reduces its power to convince.

The principal forms of projected effect are—

(*a*) Naturalistic scenery,
(*b*) Impressionist scenery,
(*c*) Slides and films (as themselves),
(*d*) Naturalistic moving effects (clouds, etc.),
(*e*) Impressionist moving effects,
(*f*) Patterned or abstract lighting.

Some divisions tend to spill over into each other; for example, the boundary between Naturalism and Impressionism could be described as "fogged" where the representation of a misty morning is concerned. Nor can all painterly activity be summed up as either Naturalism or Impressionism, but from the point of view of optical equipment it certainly can. The essential difference is between those cases where the artifice lies in the slide itself and those where it lies in the manner of projection. When all is said and done, it is simply a matter of sharp focus. Some projectors can and must, others can and often must not, and yet others cannot and need not.

These types may be classified as follows—

(1) High-definition optical projectors,
(2) Low-definition optical projectors,
(3) Profile projectors,
(4) Shadowgraphs.

The main difference between (1) and (2) is the quality of the objective lens though, as the only way to get high definition is to use one projector on any one part of the surface at a time, light will be important and this presupposes a larger and more elaborate machine. In contrast, in low-definition work superimposition from several projectors can often be practised and therefore light is being added to light. In both the above cases slides can be stationary or moving either to provide a between-scene change, which is not seen as such, or to form an in-scene effect.

The profile projector of (3) is any profile spotlight though usually with a special cut-out slide (known in America as a "gobo") in the gate instead of relying on the usual masking shutters. The shadowgraph is not an integrated lighting unit but consists of a very large slide with a light source in a housing somewhere behind it. This source might well be any handy lighting unit just pressed into service. Where, however, some purpose-made assembly is concerned, then it is usually referred to as a Linnebach Projector. There are some self-contained shadowgraph units which provide movement, for instance a water ripple.

As high-definition projection of scenic slides is the most difficult proposition it will be better to begin with a description of that process. With this over, the rest is by comparison easy.

FIG. 154 Projected scenery at Düsseldorf

Scene Projection

This entails more than usually close co-operation between lighting and scene designer; therefore these two should certainly make a thorough examination, at the outset, of the machine they propose to use. Although there are several types differing in wattage and size, the basic optical system is as outlined in Chapter 4. The stage itself may impose severe limits on the use of the machine and there is no escaping the fact that in many cases it simply is not going to be possible to use high-definition projection at all. The next thing to realize is that projectors are costly mainly because of the lenses. A reasonably good (f/1·8) 4-in. objective alone costs £140 (1976) and this will be required even with some of the lesser 1- or 2-kW projectors. The largest wattage commonly employed in professional theatre is 4-kW British or 5-kW German, but there is also a 10-kW German. Wattage is not everything as we saw in Chapter 4, Light, and as these bigger wattage lamps have large bulbs the optical systems may show relatively poor efficiency.

The size of slide is another complication. In Germany, artists like to paint direct on the slide and, in consequence, prefer a large one, 7 in. (18 cm) square. This means an expensive condenser system of large-diameter lenses to cover it with a suitable field of light. For general purposes a slide $3\frac{1}{4} \times 4$ in., known as the American standard, is used, and I imagine that for many readers of this book a 2-kW projector (Fig. 155) will represent the limit in cost, even if hired, and certainly in physical size. Whatever projector is used, there is a limit to the spread obtainable even with the widest-angle short-focus lens, but of course the larger 7-in. square slide does offer a bonus in extra spread for those prepared to pay for it. Projected scenery in its higher manifestations is not so much a cheap substitute for scenery as an easy method of providing a large number of rapid scene changes. Another way of looking at it is that effects are possible which are not obtainable in any other way. In either event, a lot of care, patience, and practical experience is required to get good results.

Just as important as the projector is the surface on which the light is to be thrown. This is often neglected and yet it is vital that the reflection factor be of the right kind. Since neither the projector nor the audience is likely to be positioned flat-on to the screen, the more or less specular types used for home cinema are out of the question. On the other hand, untreated canvas results in considerable waste. The surface needs to be loaded with several coats of matt paint. This results in a crisper, brighter picture. Of course, a solid surface like a newly painted plaster-faced cyclorama is best of all.

FIG. 155   2-kW optical projector with cloud disc

This side of the thing needs to be taken seriously; after all, it is not much good complaining about the need for more light from the projector if the incident light is squandered recklessly on a screen with a reflection factor of less than fifty per cent. Never use gauzes and scrims for this purpose unless absolutely essential for some other effect. A good guide to the efficiency of the screen is to stand behind it. The more that comes through the poorer it is, assuming of course back projection is not what is required.

Back projection is not a good idea anyway in most cases, because the screen material has to be very special and, in Britain anyway, the stage is unlikely to be deep enough. Such depth as there is should be taken up in keeping a no-man's land between the screen and the acting area. The situation is much the same as occurs with a night-sky cyclorama and it may, in fact, be the cyclorama that is used. Colour is important as we are trying to get the brightest picture back to the eyes of the audience. Both screen and lenses have to be kept clean all the time. This means *no smoking*, for, as the cinema owners know only too well, this can spoil the screen. It also spoils the crispness of the picture, both by obstructing and by revealing the projection rays. White is best for the screen as it reflects all colours equally well, and who knows which colours the slide may be composed of. This leaves the problem that a screen that is good for reflecting projection in all the directions required is also very good at reflecting scatter from the acting area.

The main thing that can be done to discourage this is to use a dark floor cloth on the stage. Direct light on the projection must be avoided, the situation being much the same as obtains in peninsular staging or theatre-in-the-round where stage lighting has to be kept out of the eyes of the audience. This is certainly so if the cyclorama encompasses the major

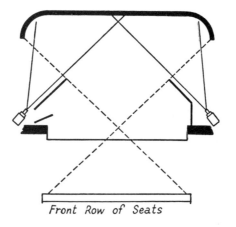

FIG. 156 Plan: scene projection from the perch position with centre overlap

Front Row of Seats

part of the acting area. In the projections more commonly used there is only a flat cloth upstage to contend with; built scenery then masks the sides down stage (Fig. 156).

In positioning the projectors, the need is for as long a throw as possible in order to get the wide spread usually required and this has to be combined with the most gentle angle obtainable. It is true that pre-distorted slides which correct themselves when projected can be made, but acute angles distort the actual field of light available for projection. This means that on the one hand light may have to be wasted by being masked out on the side farthest away while there is not enough spread on the near side. This is known as keystone distortion; another form is called pin-cushion distortion and is something to which wide-angle lenses are prone.

When one adds the necessity to avoid interception of the projection beam by foreground scenery or actors, then it can be seen that the best solution is a couple of projectors either at a perch position halfway up, one each side of the proscenium, or on a bridge over it. Two projectors may be directed so that their pictures join more or less at the centre of the cloth. It is not essential for the projectors to be symmetrically placed to the screen though it is obviously easier if they are, but this and the making of the distorted slides are dealt with later.

The moment we say that two projectors of 2-, 4- or 5-kW are to be used to cover the whole of the backcloth, we have usually set a standard of lighting level which cannot greatly be exceeded on the acting area as well, or at any rate on the built scenery surrounding it. This does not arise from the need to avoid scatter or the chance of direct light from spotlights hitting the cloth but, assuming these are under control, is purely a matter of brightness levels.

Imagine a street scene which has to continue upstage as a slide projection. Any sunlight on the foreground will be added in the usual way by side lighting units on top of the rest of the lighting. On the projection however, the brightest that can be obtained to highlight any building there is clear glass on the slide. Thus, in the case of two 2-kW projectors there is only 2-kW spread wide-angle over each half of the backcloth and probably not particularly efficiently at that for this is a failing of scene projectors.

Inevitably this means that the acting area must be lit down if not to the actual highlights on the slide then much nearer to them than today's stage lighting levels usually provide. Every narrow-angle highly-efficient spotlight used on the foreground is lessening the chance of a marriage with the projection. It is this, rather than angles of light on the actors, that constitutes the problem. Under certain circumstances, loss of brightness in the background will be interpreted subconsciously as heat haze or distance, but this cannot apply when the projection represents the middle distance where the same sun or moon has to shine both fore and aft, so to speak. One solution is so to design such slides that on just one small part a narrow-angle extra projection can be superimposed to represent just the highlights, for example, on a church tower and the upper part of tall buildings, if any. In rural scenes, part of the horizon might be emphasized in this way or by adding separate projection of some clouds at the top of the cloth. Let no-one imagine that this will be easy and great care would have to be taken to ensure that the effects are in register.

Another point to watch is to try and ensure that the light on the foreground and acting area carries conviction. It can never be a happy sunny day if characters are wandering about in the fitful shadowy glim and all the built scenery is dark where it approaches the projection area. There is no excuse for this as Profile spots allocated to the scenery can be made to cut in exactly. There is also the possibility of using ultraviolet light in these areas as described on pages 271–72.

However, I think one can be too pessimistic as to the effect of relatively low levels of acting area light on the audience. Both when in London and in Prague, Laterna Magika manage to put on a gay show while working to low intensities to match their use of cinema film. Incidentally, the way this is combined is an object lesson as to what one will accept. One of the film projectors has to deal with the backcloth but it is sited with the others in a projection room out front. The angle has to be virtually flat-on to get under the borders and fill the full height; in consequence, the artistes are duplicated as shadows on the backcloth. However, after the first shock, these small scale shadows become so easily accepted that one does not notice them. A particularly interesting effect is the way that the stationary stage with the live actors on it can be made to appear to rise or fall by moving the camera appropriately while shooting the film. This is a special effect that could be achieved to some extent with an optical-effect disc when a simpler means is required.

Laterna Magika takes on a role something more than mere stunt in their full-length opera production of *Tales of Hoffman*. There are not more than half a dozen live characters, the rest, including the orchestra, being excellently recorded on film. One of the people responsible for Laterna Magika is Svoboda, now well known as a shining example of a designer who believes in the imaginative combination of scenery, lighting and projection. He is said to manage on a very tight budget, his sets consisting "of trickery rather than solid matter," to quote Peter Moro.[1]

[1] *Tabs*, Volume 24, Number 3.

This I have been able to see for myself in Josef Svoboda's famous *Romeo and Juliet* of 1964 at the National Theatre, Prague or *The Three Sisters* at our then National Theatre—The Old Vic—in 1967. In the first case, the mechanics were a matter of a simple track and a push from a stage hand or two, while in the second case stretched ropes literally vanished into small boxes easy to strike and store for repertoire. However, as money has become available he has shown equal ingenuity in using it and the current *Ring* cycle—already referred to on page 6—must bring into question whether such a large outlay is justifiable for mechanics special to a production.

Optical Effects

Scene projection, and indeed any optical projection of what are generically known as "effects," has two completely different roles it can play. In one case, these things are there to proclaim themselves in the same way as a striking décor or costumes may do. No one attacks Cecil Beaton's costumes in the Ascot scene in *My Fair Lady* on the grounds that they stop the show, for this is just what they are designed to do. In the same way optical effects, or indeed any kind of lighting effect, need not be condemned always to a secondary accompaniment role. Even in serious productions there may be times when they can be given a flourish before being retired to the background. The main thing to remember in the case of moving effects is that the mechanical action being regular becomes wearisome. Opera offers splendid opportunities for optical effects to show how they can excite, but too often they then go on to outstay their welcome. Opera acts can be very long and the relentless march of clouds in *Valkyrie* gives the visual equivalent of what would happen if the opening bars of the famous ride were repeated over and over for an hour or more.

Optical effects must be confined to where they belong. It is better to project them on too small a patch than on too large. There are two reasons for this. The first is that when they slop all over the place they may change direction in a disconcerting way. The trouble is that this may not be seen from where the show is rehearsed in the stalls. This is another reason for a tour of the theatre during rehearsals.

A water ripple can do most peculiar things where it leaves its ground row and runs on the stage floor or off-stage if it strays on to masking wings. Fleecy white clouds may be fine up on the sky cloth or cyclorama, but when every now and then one strays elsewhere it gathers speed and resembles newspapers blowing away in the wind. Flame effects can look decidedly odd when they are allowed to run wild along the floor and over some of the scenery instead of in their appointed place. Flame effects also suffer more than any other from lack of intensity. Flames are intensely hot—they burn and light up the place with their glare. One optical-effects disc with a mere one or two kilowatts behind it simply does not stand a chance to convey this unless strictly confined and even then two is a minimum. Confining effects to restricted areas then avoids conflicting directions and gives a brighter picture. A flame effect on half the area of the backcloth will be four times as bright as one spread all over it. Not only this but it will appear brighter still because of the contrast with the dark areas. Richard Pilbrow's use of flame effects in *Blitz!* at the Adelphi Theatre in 1962 was magnificent. When the bombs dropped and the sheet of flame went up among Sean Kenny's changing scenery I wanted to cheer. One was even reconciled to the utter tedium of the scene which had preceded it. These flames looked real (my wife actually took them for such) and for this their burning brightness was responsible. In contrast, neither Brünnhilde nor Tamino ever seem to run any risk whatever in their fiery ordeals.

Effect Projectors

These are known in America as "sciopticons," and both there and here there are several sizes. In Germany, as well as the special projectors dedicated to this purpose, a number of the spotlights in the one, two, and three kilowatt sizes also convert to projection by means of an extra condenser in an attachment which slides into the front runner. They are able to do this because the use of simple lens spotlights still lingers on extensively whereas in America and Britain the more efficient Fresnels and Profiles have completely replaced them.

The condenser and objective optical systems of the projectors commonly available can be summarized as in Fig. 157. Masks and tinting filters can be inserted at positions *C*, *B*, and *A*. Position *B* is the gate occupied by the slide and in consequence anything inserted there, or just behind it at *C*, will function in much the same way. For example, a half filter of medium blue No. 32 will colour just that half of the picture. If the edge of this filter is not to be too sharply defined, although the slide design itself has to be, then position *C* will be appropriate. On the other hand, if the half filter is placed across the objective at *A*, then the whole picture will tend to be tinted with weak blue. This is because every part of the slide passes through every part of the objective lens on the way to the screen. Thus a white picture and a blue one are in effect superimposed. Use of masks in the various positions has much the same effect. Masks, unless used as gobos in Profile spotlights, are usually required to be out of focus and this can be helped by giving them irregular edges, the form on the left of Fig. 162 being known as vignetting.

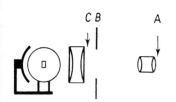

C B   A

FIG. 157 Positions for tinting in optical projector

In Britain, the commonest slide size for stage and TV projection is $3\frac{1}{4} \times 4$ in.,[1] and this is carried in something known as a turntable front since it allows rotation of the slide for angling purposes. A single slide can be carried in its own frame but where hand change is required the orthodox slide carrier, which slides to and fro, can be used. A motor-driven slide changer for six slides which can be remotely selected is also available. In this case provision is made to preset the focus of each slide separately, there being three knurled screws for the purpose, so that the objective lens does not have to be disturbed. Focus by slide angling in this way also has advantages when projecting from an oblique angle. German changers are made which can store a large number of slides in the 7-in. (18-cm) size when necessary.

Once the slide is determined, the size of the projected picture and its definition will depend on the focal length and quality of the objective lens. Some examples are given later, but readers are referred to suppliers' catalogues for detail. Care should be taken to specify landscape (horizontal) or portrait (vertical) format when photographs are being made.

Optical-effects projectors and associated equipment are mainly hired rather than purchased, at any rate in Britain, and the temptation to be perpetually using projected scenery or a cloud just because money has been laid out on these expensive devices is thereby curbed. This does mean one has to rely on hire stock and by far the commonest projector is the 1-kW size taking an A1 tubular lamp. However, a 2-kW model has recently been introduced to replace it and this is a much better unit and a reasonable compromise for most purposes including scene projection. Only in the larger theatres and more elaborate productions should it be necessary to consider the 4-kW or 5-kW scene projectors described on page 317.

Whatever the projector, it is important that it should be rigidly mounted. The slightest movement is amplified over the long throw. Unfortunately, the better the stage floor the more live it is; however, some modern stages have at least their wing areas mounted on concrete. Where stands are used they should be the tripod type. Suspension may be preferable provided it is well clear of flying scenery. Moving optical effects are not quite as sensitive as "stills" as the movement may disguise a slight rock, but although flames may dance clouds should not! Heat-absorbing glass filters are always inserted in the condenser system of any projector with pretensions to efficiency; but in the larger models this may be supplemented by a fan. Very occasionally a fan may develop

[1] The standard British "magic lantern" slide is $3\frac{1}{4}$ in. square; the common colour transparency is on 35-mm film in a 2-in. (5-cm) square frame.

a form of slight vibration which is transmitted to the picture and makes it look slightly out of focus. As out of focus is usually interpreted by the eye as "less bright," this could be serious in scene projection.

Slide Preparation

In my opinion, whenever possible the slide should be prepared photographically. At one time this meant black and white which then had to be tinted by hand. This led to the big 7-in. slide and thence it was but a step to paint the design direct on it. In Germany considerable proficiency has been acquired in this practice but this is a product of their large number of opera houses each staging their own repertories. In Britain, the designer can draw or paint what he likes on a sheet of paper or card roughly 24 in. wide and within forty-eight hours Ektachrome slides in full colours are available. Not only are these faithful reproductions but the necessary pre-distortion to correct for angle can be incorporated when taking the photographs. Fig. 158 of a scene by Jocelyn Herbert in the original production of the Wesker trilogy at the Royal Court Theatre in London is a good example of what can be done. There were two projectors, in this case only 2 kW each, and not only were these each sited at different angles to the screen but the screen itself hung at somewhat of an angle up and down stage instead of being parallel to the proscenium.

Slides can be made by specialist firms, such as Theatre Projects in London, to take account of distortions from the projection angles, but as a matter of interest a procedure is outlined here. This comes from Paul Weston, who has himself made colour slides for a number of different theatres and productions.

Angle-corrected Slides

For projected scenery using either front or back projection, it is seldom if ever possible to put the projector in the logical position for normal projection, that is, the lens in the centre of the picture both horizontally and vertically. Consequently, special slides have to be made to allow the projector to be placed where convenient.

The production of angle-corrected slides is not the simple matter some people believe of photographing an original at the same angle of view as that the projector will ultimately have. A little thought about the geometry will show that this cannot be so unless the ratio between the throw and the lens focal length are the same for projector and camera. This would mean an infinite number of focal lengths for the camera lens and is obviously not practicable.

The other problem, apart from getting the image the right

FIG. 158 Two scene projectors on flat screen and on multi-angled screens compared. The twin projections are (a) joined as Fig. 156 at centre of flat back-cloth, (b) crossed to cover a series of tall screens angled with mirrors between them on the opposite side of the stage (see page 307)

shape, is to get it the right size; because once the slide is made it is not possible to move the projector or the screen to make the picture larger or smaller. Thus it is imperative that the screen and projector positions are absolutely determined before any move is made to make slides.

Using a $3\frac{1}{4} \times 3\frac{1}{4}$ in. or a $4 \times 3\frac{1}{4}$ in. slide size, a 5×4 in. plate camera is very convenient. The method is as follows: first a mask is made which can be placed on the ground-glass screen while focusing and the camera moved so that the image just fills the mask. This is a tricky job as the final angle of the camera will be nothing like the angle the projector will be and takes some getting used to. After filling the mask to satisfaction, the process from then on is normal photography.

The production of the mask is the crux of the whole thing and while it is possible to produce it mathematically from given information, a more practical way is as follows: in a slide carrier, put the projector lens of the focal length suitable for the throw concerned and a piece of heavy frost Cinemoid. Mount the whole thing in the theatre *exactly* where the projector lens will be when attached to the projector, and then view the projection screen using the Cinemoid as the ground-glass screen in the camera. The projection screen will, of course, need some light on it from an external source such as a stage flood, or the working lights may perhaps be sufficient. Mark on the Cinemoid in pencil the four corners of the picture size required, remove it, join up the four points, and you have the exact shape and size of the image necessary. The cutting out of a mask is then a simple matter which does not need the agonies of higher maths and solid geometry.

Two projections are almost always used arranged to lap over down the centre line. There, either the design is sufficiently busy and irregular on a dark ground that it can interlock without showing or more usually the leading edge is dimmed out by spraying down on the slide. This can also be done by insertion of a suitable out-of-focus mask at position C (Fig. 157).

Provided glass is really clean it will take ink, and this led Allan Davy-Rae, an architect by profession, to use an interesting technique at the Mountview Little Theatre in North London. Using a series of trial slides, a grid was ultimately formed which when projected from a fixed angle came out as a regular squared pattern. This gave the distortion format and outline drawings were made in Indian ink direct on the glass to this. For colouring, Cinemoid filter shapes were cut out and stuck on the slides, sometimes lapping over each other. The result of the rigid discipline imposed by tinting in broad washes only was extremely pleasing and was eminently of the nature of projection. The scenes were varied and had a kind of stylized realism about them.

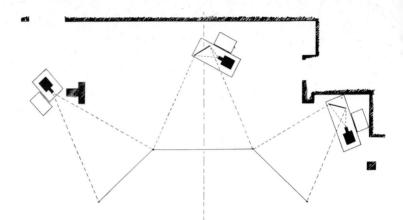

FIG. 159 *The Rise and Fall of the City of Mahogonny.* Back projection plan showing use of divertor mirrors to obtain beam spread and flat on angle for three screens on cramped stage at Sadler's Wells. The 4-kW projectors were on 4-ft rostrums at stage level

In the abstract field resort can sometimes be made to the nature of the glass itself—certain rolled and pattern glasses being particularly suitable. For example, a reeded glass when put in the projector can be focused to give a series of vertical columns. On putting a colour filter halfway across the lens (Fig. 157 at *A*) each column is tinted on one side. Further filters and masks can follow and a design built up.

The simplest method for home-made projected scenery and particularly for abstracts is the Linnebach projector described below. It also has the merit of being far and away the cheapest and least sensitive to problems of throw. These, however, can sometimes be eased for orthodox projectors by the use of divertor mirrors. There are two kinds: a small one carried on or near the objective lens and which allows the light to turn a corner in tight situations where it could be impossible to have the projector in a direct line with its beam; the other kind is a large mirror placed much farther down the beam to make it take a much longer travel. For this the plastic type of mirror is very convenient being lightweight, in effect front silvered and relatively low in cost. Fig. 159 shows the arrangement in plan of the three projectors used for the slides in the Weill and Brecht *Rise and Fall of the City of Mahogonny* at Sadlers Wells. The value of mirror diversion in this case is obvious.

Before considering moving effects, there is a use of stationary projection that must be mentioned. In some German theatres particularly, the slides of the projectors are painted to represent uneven shadows cast, for instance, by the boughs or leaves of a tree. This projection lights the acting area. Sometimes this is extended to the spotlighting by putting slotted or otherwise cut gobos in the gates of Profile spots. A patchy light known as Fleckenlicht results. Now I am all for dark patches, shadows, on the stage, but this kind of patchiness being small in scale cannot be dodged and, in consequence, confusion of the actors' features due to partial illumination, already probable in opera, is increased to certainty. If textured light there must be, I prefer the broken colour methods outlined on pages 95–96.

Moving Effects

It is a pity that projected effects other than scenery are always associated with excessive movement. Thus clouds hare across the sky and mist swirls around in a manner associated with its final expiry rather than prolonged blanketing. The sea rages right up to the horizon, whereas in reality the waves are only perceived as such in the foreground; anything farther out is far more likely to be due to the effects of light.

Now and then a moving effect can have an important part to play and, because what comes in a box labelled as "wave," "flame," or "cloud" needs considerable care and patience before the projected apparition justifies its name, we must go into some detail. The most obvious way of providing movement is to replace the slide by a large disc, only a small part of which passes behind the lens at a time. An obvious case is that of clouds which have to move across the sky passing out of view to be replaced by yet others. Cloud shapes are not very memorable and, in consequence, provided the disc is large enough it would need several revolutions before recognition is likely to occur. At one time effects were hand-painted on discs made up of large pieces of mica and the joins constituted an optical problem but nowadays, anyway in Britain, photographic processing on a toughened glass disc of 18-in. diameter is employed.

The driving mechanism used to be spring-driven clockwork but today electric clocks are a common method, except in those cases where remote speed regulation is required when a more orthodox electric motor has to be used. Clock motors are compact, lightweight, and above all quiet, but are, of course designed to keep exact time synchronized with the a.c. mains. This means that speed adjustment has to employ gearing. The procedure is to choose a fixed gear ratio, obviously much faster in the case of a flame than of a cloud, and then vary the speed beyond that by an adjustable gear. This latter appears as a disc (*D*) in Fig. 160 which is mounted on the same spindle (*E*) as carries the effect disc itself. The motor (*A*) drives a second spindle (*B*) at right angles to it and the two are connected to each other by a small rubber wheel (*C*). The wheel is fixed by a collet (*F*) which allows it to be loosened, whereupon the disc is pushed slightly down to allow the wheel to be repositioned. Near the centre of the disc one revolution of the driving wheel will equal one of the driven disc, whereas at the periphery three revs are required resulting in a reduction of the speed of three to one. If the driving wheel is carried over to the other side of the disc reversal of direction takes place.

It will be noticed that drive is applied to the centre of the effects disc and any backlash in the gearing would be amplified as jerking at the edge; a damping brake is therefore added to this spindle. In Germany effects discs are driven from the rim rather like the method used for gramophone turntables; backlash is minimized and the great reduction in speed inherent in driving from this position is another good point. Effects discs are also more readily exchanged and thus the one housing and drive can serve several effects. However, the assembly is not so neat as the British one and the quality of the discs themselves is way behind. Discs are likely to impart some of their circular motion to the projection though, as will be shown later, this can be compensated for to some extent. The Germans also make effects in which a flexible transparent material like an overlarge film loop is driven past the lens. There is a second version in which the film unwinds from one roller to another.

It so happens that actual movement of the slide is not the only way of imparting motion to an effect and, except for clouds, the two methods are combined. When a fixed glass with an untrue surface is interposed between disc and lens, distortion takes place which causes the projected image to twist and swirl. These break up glasses have to be picked very carefully for the particular type of work and an essential requirement is that the objective lens must focus exactly neither the glass nor the disc itself. In the one case there would be a series of fixed bright streaks and in the other a clear picture of some more than usually repellent abstract pattern rushing by.

Disc effects are supplied in an 18½-in. diameter aluminium protective case complete with break-up glass, where appropriate, and a turntable runner arrangement on the back to allow angling or complete inversion when mounted on an effects projector (Fig. 155). The front of the effect has runners for the objective lens and for mask and/or tinting filter. The spring retainer should always be clipped around the lens to guard against an accident should one decide to turn the thing upside down. It is also a safeguard against passing scenery lifting it out.

Another type of effect exists in which the movement comes from rocking break-up glasses gently up and down in front of a fixed slide. The principal effects obtained this way are wave and water ripple. They are easily recognizable by their tall rectangular cases. There are some moving effects which do not require an objective lens but they will be described as they arise. Unlike scene projection, moving effects do not require high-definition lenses—except perhaps in the case of

FIG. 160 Effects disc speed regulation by potter's wheel drive

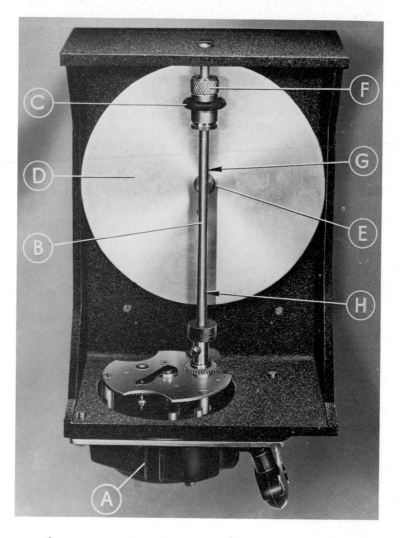

snow they are a positive drawback. The wide-angle objective lenses are known as sciop fronts and the commoner ones are: narrow-angle, giving 9-ft wide picture; wide-angle, giving 12-ft; and extra-wide-angle, giving an 18-ft picture. In each case a 4-in. wide slide and a 10-ft throw is assumed. Other lenses are always described by their focal length. For example, a 6-in., giving 5 ft at 10 ft, or much longer lengths may be required when working from the front of house or when a very small picture is required. A secondary support is advisable for the longer lens tubes.

Clouds

There are two basic forms of cloud. One consists of white clouds on a dark ground and is known as "fleecy cloud." The other is dark clouds on a light ground and is known as "storm cloud." A further effect referred to as a "thunder cloud" is now available. As both storm clouds have to provide their own sky light to show as dark against, so the only auxiliary light on the sky that can be used is a gentle washing out of the dark areas by some flooding on check, but there is little point in this when one has gone to the trouble to obtain a heavy storm. This, of course, must rely on the contrast of dark, really black areas of cloud against very occasional light (Fig. 161). Storm clouds can, however, benefit by some tinting on the lens itself with a No. 17 Steel or No. 45 Daylight. In moonlight scenes, the tints will have to marry with whatever is ultimately chosen to represent moonlight. Because storm clouds carry their own sky they will have to occupy as large an area of the backcloth or cyclorama as possible. Where some other light is needed to help out, it will have to be very patchy. A Linnebach projection is a useful aid. An alternative is to cut a mask something like those in Fig. 162, so that under no circumstances does any suggestion of a circular patch of light appear. Except in the thundercloud, two storm clouds lapping over each other are much better than one and the effect gains rather than loses from being projected somewhat from the side.

FIG. 161 Storm scene with projected clouds, *Rainbow Square*

FIG. 162   Effects masks

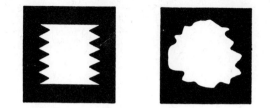

Fleecy clouds are intended to be projected on a surface already floodlit with some sort of blue—Nos. 40, 18, or even 32. Once again, more than one is advisable and personally I find the best combination is a fleecy and a storm cloud on top of each other as this gives the necessary depth and wispy lack of substance. A tint of No. 45 Daylight can be used to prevent their appearing too warm. Standard cloud speed is variable between one revolution in four-and-a-half minutes and one revolution in fourteen-and-a-half minutes, and the latter is to be preferred for fleecy clouds. Indeed, an extra slow speed gear range of thirty minutes to ninety minutes is available and its almost imperceptible motion is much more natural for fleecy clouds. It may be appropriate for storm clouds to run fast but they should not be left to do this for long for reasons dwelt on earlier. A convenient place to project clouds from is overhead. It is impossible to be specific as to how far down-stage. Too far away means too big pictures and too little light; too close leads to small patches. The best beginning is to know that one storm and one fleecy cloud together give good pictures when hanging 10 ft away and 12 ft above the stage to project on a cyclorama 20 ft wide × 18 ft high. The lamps are 1 kW and the stage with light drugget is lit to 25 foot-candles. This is how they are demonstrated and any increase in the size of cloth, worsening in its reflection factor or increase in light level on the acting area will have to be compensated for. The most ready method is to double the lamp wattage by making each 2 kW and after that one can use more projectors, each to concentrate on a particular part of the cyclorama. As was said earlier, it is not a good idea to add them all, one on top of the other, using wide-angle lenses on each. I have found that six 1 kW projectors, three fleecy and three storm, hanging on a bar roughly mid-stage makes a useful cloud machine for a large, not giant, curved cyclorama. This was some years ago before the present craze for very high lighting levels began. However, modern effects projectors are much more efficient and 2 kW lamps would now be substituted as well. The use of four 1 kW storm clouds at Sadlers Wells Opera is described later in this chapter.

Stationary clouds are, of course, a form of scene projection and some standard slides are available. On the other hand, for the small stage sometimes a simple outline cut-out will do and this can be hand-made, and one or more 500-watt Profile spots will put up quite a brave show provided great care is taken over the focus and the broken colour tinting on the front. The use of two spots, one with a wide-angle lens and the other with a standard lens superimposed, offers the way to quite a spectacular cloud. Painted mica slides are also available in this case. In the same way a Profile spot can be used to project the image of the moon but a diaphragm to reduce the lens aperture has to be put in the front runner as well to give the correct definition. By the way, there is a very good effect which allows clouds to pass over the moon on any cyclorama, be it solid or cloth. Two separate discs are used, one cloud only and the other moon with cloud. The two do not have to be synchronized; the fact that the moon's image has cloud passing over it leads automatically to the assumption that this is the same cloud as that moving over the rest of the sky (Fig. 143, page 253).

Lightning

Storms and thunder clouds imply lightning sooner or later. A lot of unnecessary fuss is made over this and in most cases a succession of two or three staccato flashes on a white batten circuit is all that is needed. One step better is to employ photoflood lamps instead of ordinary ones. These are used singly quite bare or grouped in a short length of batten according to how much lightning one wants. There is a device consisting of a flicker wheel and slide which can be focused to give forked lightning. A turntable front and pivoting in a stand allows the lightning to be placed differently each time it flashes. A lot of rehearsal is necessary to get this right and personally I suggest *one* quick flicker of fork to make an almost subliminal impression on the audience and let thunder supplemented by an occasional photoflood flash do the rest. Too often we are treated to a visual toy symphony simply because the device has been hired and cannot be wasted. Lightning has for me a visual stimulus equivalent to the clash of the cymbals and a little goes a long way. The last act of *Rigoletto* is murdered for me visually by the almost incessant use of lightning. There are, by the way, more complicated ways of producing lightning; these are made in Germany.

Flames, Smoke, and Firelight

Flame discs run at a speed adjustable between two and six revolutions a minute. The swirling motion is given by the break-up glass. Since brightness is all-important, the only hope is strictly to localize the area and make sure the reflection factor of the surface is good. A flame effect is supposed to include smoke and that is what the dark bits are intended by tradition to be. Discs are made which are completely smoke, no flame at all, and these should be adjusted to run much slower. Used sideways, particularly on gauzes, they become fog. Flame discs are also available without any colour at all, and although these are made primarily for television they have other applications. It is a great mistake to think that even the most realistic effect cannot be bent to some abstract purpose. For example, I have used the white flame running upside down and slightly sideways to suggest a rushing wind. Complete nonsense, really!

The most intense burning flame effect results from strips of silk over a blower and illuminated from below. The fact still remains, however, that the best fires take place off-stage in the imagination. What is then needed is the flickering glow reflected therefrom. This can be obtained by leaving the objective lens off the front of a flame disc but a less expensive method is to use a small-diameter motor-driven flame flicker disc which can be fitted in the front runners of a 6-in. Fresnel spot. Another way of producing flame, either direct or indirect, is by a high-speed drum which contains within it a 1-kW lamp. The great merit of this device is that it is successful even when placed very close to the object supposed to be on fire.

Real smoke can be produced by various pyrotechnic devices such as electrically fired smoke puffs or a powder which is heated over an electric element. Other devices give flashes and bangs. For these latter, maroons, which are particularly vicious, have to be fired in a tank for safety. A heavy low-lying smoke or mist is produced when steam is passed over dry ice and a special unit is made for the purpose of dispensing this inoffensive but impressive brew.

Snow and Rain

I remember soap flakes made wonderful snow floating down outside a window for *On Approval* long years ago, and for rain perforated pipes with real water have been used. The most convincing rain, both in appearance and sound, was rice shaken out of long boxes slung overhead for *Rainbow Square*. As is not unusual in theatre, the fake is better than the real thing. However, this kind of thing belongs to books on stage-craft. I must stick to light, or rather, in this case, dark. Rain as an optical effect is most difficult because the disc is ninety-five-per-cent black, the only opportunity for light to escape being through a series of thin scratches. The only hope is a very small patch tucked under a black storm cloud on the backcloth. Never, never try to put rain all over the acting area. Where this is required in some kind of light entertainment, a good impression is obtained from narrow-beam lamps with No. 18 Blue filters overhead pointing vertically downwards.

This, catching on shiny plastic macs and umbrellas, perfectly evoked a real downpour in one of Robert Nesbitt's Palladium shows.

Snow is one of the easier effects to use even all over the acting area, especially if a gauze is hung downstage. High-definition lenses provide an advantage in getting pin-sharp snowflakes against a black ground, but they are not vital. Wide-angle lenses must be avoided otherwise the flakes become tennis balls. The use of two effects at least, both projected over each other, is advisable. Speed is critical and a somewhat angled fall helps. I have seen snow pass my office window horizontally and going upwards in the heart of London. The woodland glade merits something more than an even fall all over. Some of the trees are going to do some interception and, in consequence, some gobo-type masking to the disc may give a more convincing effect.

Sea and Water

The most realistic of all the effects is the wave, though probably the least useful. It is said that it was devised for Arthur Bourchier's production of *Treasure Island* at the Strand Theatre in 1922, but I have my suspicions that the idea was around before that. It is also claimed that the slide used was taken from the stern of a ship in the Bay of Biscay. However true that may be, it can be used for most applications but must not run right up to the horizon as in most cases the scale then goes adrift.

In much the same way that storm and fleecy clouds combine well, so does the wave and the ripple, which in one form is much the same as the wave as far as action is concerned (Fig. 163). Keeping a horizon line clear can be difficult and a method is described later for *The Flying Dutchman*. Another method is to use an angled groundrow in front of the cyclorama or sky cloth and hang the effects projector vertically over it. As neither this effect nor its lamp takes kindly to this condition divertor mirrors have to be used on the front of the lens.

Running water is a disc effect which can be used vertically or horizontally and is a close relation of the flame disc. These two will never be out of work so long as there are *Magic Flutes* about.

Ripple effects can also be produced from "Tubular Ripple," which is a rotating drum and lamp unit somewhat on the lines of the flame drum. The whole drum with horizontal slots in it rotates between a long tubular filament lamp and the surface to be lit, whereas a flame drum rotates about the lamp. The result is the rise and fall of watery highlights in a most convincing manner. It is really a moving shadowgraph and is very convenient to use because it can be placed close to the cloth and is compact and shallow in shape (Fig. 164).

FIG. 163 Wave effect attachment

FIG. 164   Tubular ripple

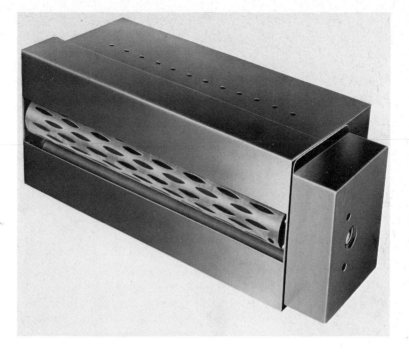

Ripples can be localized to give the romantic track of the moon or expanded to cover the whole stage. When this is done on a gauze the result is an under-water scene of which *Rheingold*, Act I, is the most enduring example. There are special underwater slides with seaweed and starfishes for use with wave-type ripple glasses though not, I hasten to add, for use in that particular opera! There are also discs with fishes and even one with a sinking ship of uncertain but antique appearance.

The making of optical discs and effects is a strange but little-known craft. As far as Britain is concerned, the whole output for the past half-century (and it is large) has been the responsibility of but two men, Frank Weston and his assistant and successor, Edward Biddle, both of Strand Electric. Almost anything has been and can be devised to order, including H-bomb explosions, fireworks, and astrocruisers, but the borderline between realism and farce is very narrow.

Correction and Focus

It is important when projecting from any angle to use the inevitable distortion to correct disc curvature rather than aggravate it. Assuming a cloud projector is pointing down-wards, the widest part of the picture will be at the bottom. This can make a considerable difference to the result depending on whether the effects disc rotates above or below the projector. Taking into account the fact that the picture is reversed through the lens, it will be found that the effect should be above when the projector hangs pointing downwards and below when pointing upwards. In this way the inner, more acutely curved part gets expanded into a larger, and therefore less obvious, curve. Sometimes the pin cushioning (elongated corners) defect of simple wide-angle lenses can be taken advantage of, as also can the curve of a cyclorama should there be one.

Flames, running water and other vertical running effects, when projected from the side behind the wings can lead to a similar result to that just discussed for clouds. Which side of the projector the disc runs can be critical. Unless curvature is deliberately wanted, and it might be for a water cascade, then the disc should point off stage.

Focus is very important and considerable experience is necessary to get the right effect. Except for projected scenery, it is wiser to assume that "out of focus" is the rule. An objective goes out of focus both when pulled too far out or when pushed too far in. The first distortion is more usual but it does not necessarily follow that it is always appropriate. In effects with a break-up glass there are two slides, one a short distance behind the other, to be concerned with. Positioning the lens can give the glass more or less chance to make its presence felt. Except in the case of scene projection and possibly snow, only low-definition lenses are needed or advisable.

"Flying Dutchman"

Dennis Arundell's production of this opera with sets by Timothy O'Brien and lighting by Charles Bristow is a useful example to show several types of optical effects used together in concert. The stage at Sadlers Wells is small and cramped by opera house standards. With an opening of 30 ft and a depth of 34 ft it sets problems and answers them in terms which readers of this book can be expected to comprehend. Mr. Bristow's own description below, reprinted from *Tabs*, perfectly exemplifies the admixture of artistry and ingenuity which has to be brought to the use of optical effects. It should be remembered that the layout did not stand for a run but had to be arranged to suit repertoire playing and revivals for some years after.

"The outstanding effect in the production is the arrival of the Dutchman's ghost ship, which appears on the distant horizon, and within approximately forty-five seconds, becomes moored alongside a stationary ship with its Dutch crew active on board. After several experiments, the best results were obtained by using four Pattern 52 lanterns (1000 W), each fitted with a low-geared optical flame effect (flames being untinted) with a specially designed slide carrier attached to the aperture. Four slides depicting the ship in silhouette, each one graduated in size, were then superimposed on to an unpainted backcloth, and by cross-fading each lantern from the smallest slide the desired motion was obtained.

"The object of using untinted flame discs is that, out of focus, they created a misty movement about the ship, thus enabling the cross-fade from one lantern to another (and consequent sudden increase in size) to be less noticeable. In conjunction with these, a fifth Pattern 52 fitted only with a flame disc (also untinted) was set to cover the entire backcloth horizontally so as to establish a mist from the onset.

"Following this sequence, the upstage area was then faded out to enable two ship cut-outs to be dropped into position. At this moment, two optical Chromotrope[1] effects were faded in to cover the downstage area, thereby causing a momentary visual distraction without interrupting the sequence of events. Immediately following this we returned to the general lighting exposing the ship.

"As the position of the lanterns employed is at rather an acute angle to the backcloth, the slides had to be 'angle-corrected' when printed.

"Having mastered the main problem, we were faced with yet one other. A backcloth featuring a painted sky and horizon was designed for Acts I and III. Had this been used, the definition of the ship projections would be lost. We therefore used an unprimed cloth lightly laid-in with grey, so that, by means of lighting, we could obtain an horizon and colour. Now, in the upstage area so much activity would be taking place moving boat trucks, and so on, that the use of ground rows or floods was quite out of the question. There remained but one alternative—backlighting—and our backcloth, being a translucent finely woven cotton duck, proved ideal. A disused straight border was hung upstage of the backcloth enabling the light from a six-way flood bar to be masked down to the sea area of backcloth. The arrangement was then reversed for the sky, this time using four sections of ground row and a 2-ft 6-in. scenic row (see Fig. 165). With the mixing of contrasting colours, ground row and floods being wired in three circuits, the backcloth began to take on a realistic appearance.

"Other scenes in the opera which involve the use of optical effects are the storm sequence, eerie atmospheres and the final rising of the sun.

"Act I commences with a raging sea, a violent storm, and flashing lightning. To accomplish this, the following effects

[1] This is a modern version of the old magic lantern slide which, by rotating one glass in the opposite direction to the other, produced perpetually expanding and contracting spirals and other changing patterns.

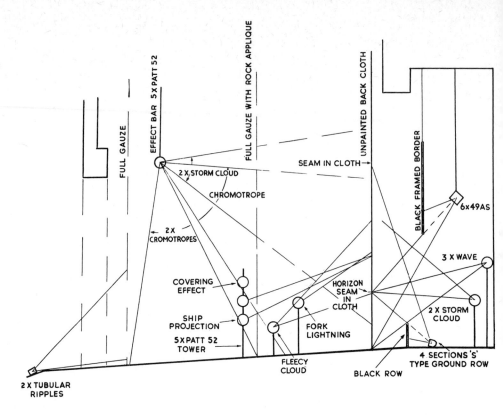

Labels within figure:

FULL GAUZE
EFFECT BAR 5 X PATT 52
FULL GAUZE WITH ROCK APPLIQUE
UNPAINTED BACK CLOTH
BLACK FRAMED BORDER
2 X STORM CLOUD
CHROMOTROPE
SEAM IN CLOTH →
6x49AS
2 X CROMOTROPES
3 X WAVE
COVERING EFFECT
HORIZON SEAM IN CLOTH
2 X STORM CLOUD
SHIP PROJECTION
5 X PATT 52 TOWER
FORK LIGHTNING
4 SECTIONS 'S' TYPE GROUND ROW
FLEECY CLOUD
BLACK ROW
2 X TUBULAR RIPPLES

FIG. 165 Section: showing set-up for *The Flying Dutchman* effects at Sadler's Wells

were used: four storm clouds, three wave effects, and one fork lightning. The three wave machines were mounted on high stands against the back wall of stage, being set to cover lower section of backcloth. Adjustable metal masks having a thin strip of No. 31 Frost glued to the blades cast a softening effect just below the horizon. The cloud effect was achieved by the use of two lanterns suspended from a bar hanging in the first bay, these (front) projecting storm clouds (their motors being set to a maximum speed) on to a mid-stage gauze, and penetrating through to the backcloth as well. In conjunction with these, two storm clouds (with motors set at a slower speed) were placed behind the backcloth. In this way we avoided a repetition of cloud formation, and by varying the intensity of either source it was possible to increase or abate the storm as often as required. Colour No. 56 was used to tint the cloud effects. For lightning, four short battens were used, each fitted with five photoflood lamps, these being distributed about the stage and controlled either in groups or independently to give distant or overhead lightning. In addition to those units, an optical fork lightning was projected on the backcloth. By using a selection of slides, and moving the direction slightly from left to right after each flash, a variety of pattern was obtained.

"Three less elaborate effects seem worth mentioning. A black proscenium gauze was used to give a haziness to the first scene and to emphasize this, two tubular ripples (Fig. 164) were laid in the footlights. By setting them tilted downwards at a slow speed to cover the lower part of the gauze an excellent ground mist was produced. During the last act, a few moments occur that require the Dutchman's ship to be surrounded by a ghostly atmosphere. A Chromotrope directed on to the mid-stage gauze from the centre of the effect bar gave the appearance of a strange, magical light radiating from the ship.

"From this point, during its last act, the opera slowly builds to its climax, until in a sudden blackout the Dutch ship vanishes, and from the darkness the sun slowly rises above the horizon after the violent storm. A gradual build of warm light behind the cloth, plus a single fleecy cloud effect (tinted No. 53) moving slowly across the sky, set a tranquil mood for the final moment of the opera."

Linnebach Projector

This is named after Adolf Linnebach, then technical director of the Munich Opera, who introduced it early in the century. It is really a shadowgraph and has appeared in every lighting textbook and on stage at irregular intervals ever since. A good photograph[1] is extant showing Molly McArthur's use of it to provide Henry Ainley with wings on the cyclorama of the very shallow stage at the Westminster Theatre, London, in 1931, for Bridie's *Tobias and the Angel*. The Linnebach principle was too well known and so obvious that few thought of it. It was James Hull Miller, well known for his imaginative theatres at Western Springs, Chicago, and elsewhere, who drew attention to its potentialities once again for projected backgrounds on his cycloramas. He uses the device suspended overhead centre, whereas most applications are usually from the floor at one side. This choice of position will probably settle itself because few stages are as well equipped with overhead access as those of Mr. Miller.

The Linnebach commends itself because it is inexpensive, the various bits and pieces including the slides can be home-made, and, lastly, it has a wide spread and therefore can be close to the cloth.

Optically, the Linnebach effect needs a compact source lamp in a housing with a blackened interior, no reflector or lens, but preferably some adjustable shutters on the front. These shutters must be capable of being angled as well as being pushed in and out as their purpose is to confine the beam to

---

[1] *Tabs*, Volume 22, Number 1, page 39.

FIG.166 Linnebach effect with
lantern and slide on the left

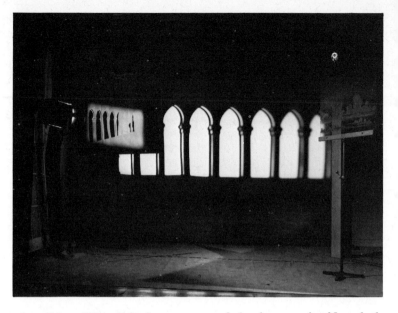

the slide. The slide is not part of the lantern itself and the
expression is something of a misnomer.

The Linnebach projector is a shadowgraph and silhouette
cut-outs could be placed anywhere between it and the surface
on which they are to appear. As everyone knows who has
played around as a child making animal and other fantasies
between a light source and a wall, the nearer to the screen and
the farther from the source, the clearer but smaller the picture.
The slide thus has to vary both in size and in distance from the
lantern, which explains why it is much better to keep it separate. Fortunately, for most effects, poor definition only is
required and the slide can be roughly 3 ft 6 in. × 2 ft 6 in.
and 1 ft or 2 ft away from the projector.

Fig. 166 shows a typical Linnebach effect, the arcade being
produced by such a lantern on the extreme left. As can be
seen, the slide is comparatively close to the projector. In this
case it is cut out of opaque material, black paper in fact, in
such a way as to allow for the increase in size as the image gets
farther away. As there is no objective lens no reversal takes
place. For slides which have to be painted, a piece of $\frac{1}{10}$-in.
thick Perspex or Oroglass, 3 × 2 ft or more, can be used carried
on a standard telescopic stand. Cinemoid in a frame, or even
glass, is also suitable there being no real heat to cope with.
The design can be painted on the slide using Photopak, a
photographic blanking-out brown-coloured material which
will appear black on the screen. Provided the slide is clean,
almost any painting material will take and if transparent
colour is used then the projected effect will be coloured
accordingly. For colour effects, pieces of Cinemoid can be

cut out and stuck on. Alternatively, if tinting not accurately located is required, as in sunset or dawn clouds, bits of broken Cinemoid can be added in an extra frame spaced just forward of the projector.

Designs can be carried out in cut-out pieces of Cinemoid mounted in turn on a sheet of clear Cinemoid, the whole being carried on a wooden frame. Little light is needed in most cases —a 500-watt T1 lamp or a 1000-watt T5 lamp. Which is used depends on the level of the main stage lighting and in keeping direct acting area light off the backcloth, but scatter and spill tend not to be critical because of the patterned projection. The contrast may be lessened by such spill but where it coincides with light patches, light is being added to light. Unwanted stray light and shadows are far more obvious when there is a plain, evenly lit background.

It is convenient to have the projector set up at stage level, except in those rare instances where there may be a side platform or perch to the stage. This means that projection will usually be at an acute angle from the side. Forms can be matched by keeping the slide more or less parallel to the screen, but the picture on the screen may be wedge-shaped and subject to distortion of shape. However, on a slide as large as this, the main features of the design can be laid in by trial and error on site. These can then be used for guidance as the detail is filled in elsewhere while the setting-up of the scenery or a rehearsal proceeds.

One reason for the undoubted fact that low intensity and stray patches of light get by whereas a proper optical projection might be ruined lies in the impressionist nature of the shadow projection. It cannot be anything else but a dreamlike evocation. This does not lead the designer to put a heavier burden of naturalism on it than it can bear. Clouds and ethereal evocations of distant landscape, mountains and forests are well within its range. So also are mirage-like towns shimmering through the heat haze. No one tries to transmit detail and, conversely, no one is disappointed at seeing detail gone wrong —out of focus.

Not that focus cannot be attempted: it is merely a matter of moving the slide somewhat nearer the screen. Of course, as this happens, it has to become very much larger and one is in reality building a large shadow frame and all kinds of other possibilities creep in—not only several frames but more than one light source, perhaps in several colours. This was the Penumbrascope of Malcolm Baker-Smith. The housing of these larger ventures can be troublesome, but one should keep in mind that it is not inconceivable that the structure should be on the stage itself, painted black, while an enlarged version of itself appears on the cyclorama beyond. This is what, in

FIG. 167 Strand Electric Theatre of 1939 with Light Console and shadow setting

fact, is happening in Fig. 167 above.

What the Linnebach projector effects above all is freedom from the tyranny of virginal blue cyclorama backgrounds liable to be violated by the first bit of stray light that comes along. Its use is open to all: it is only a matter of experiment and simple materials or slide building. Painting can go on and the result appear as one does it. This is an effect that fills a real need and is not a distraction. Indeed, a sky cloth is more likely to draw the eye in its floodlit purity. An effect like this adds something to, rather than steals something from, the stage picture and this is a good standard to judge the desirability of including any of the optical effects in this chapter.

Lamp Development and Projection

Projection is the one section of lighting equipment where technical development has been able to show some progress at all equivalent to what has gone on in dimmers and lighting control. New improved light sources, notably the tungsten halogen and CSI (described in Chapter 5), when used in optical systems specifically designed for them, have made their impact.

However, the result has not been to use them to provide a less expensive and more convenient form of changeable scenery but because of the designer's demands they become a *different* form of changeable scenery. Just as it is likely that memory control systems will increase the number of lighting changes, so too better scene projectors and more skill in their use lead to more complex effects. The simple can be as far away as ever and fashion and the search for some new thing, rather than the budget, will decide whether scene projection is used. As I write there is something of a lull—it is almost as if after the orgy of projection the top designers had got tired of it.

The work of Pat Robertson, particularly at the Nottingham Playhouse, probably represents the ultimate in the economical deployment of equipment. There he has had only two Strand Patt. 752, 4 kW projectors—used from positions somewhat as Fig. 156. His effects are obtained from the multiplicity of surfaces he projects upon and he is a master at making the necessary distorted slides. It is a great mistake to think of projection as always on to a simple screen as in that diagram. He has used screens in different planes and in at least one ingenious solution has managed to get the light to turn round a corner. Tall detached vertical screens faced across the stage at their projector on the opposite side. Thus those on stage left carried the image from the projector on the right and vice versa. Joining the screens together were equally tall mirrors. Each was placed at right angles to its neighbouring screen and carried its image—albeit reversed—round the corner. (Fig. 158b) Small built sets were placed in the foreground inhabited by the actors. Both this production and another by Pat Robertson on the open thrust stage at Chichester Festival theatre have been detailed in *Tabs*.

In the case of Timothy O'Brien's set for the production of *Knot Garden*, one slide had to cover the whole proscenium opening and stage beyond of the Covent Garden Opera House. Originally a special adaptation of a film projector with a Xenon source was used and a pair of these in a special temporary room annexed the space normally occupied by the centre 24 seats of the Grand tier. To get the necessary flat-on throw for the beam, the projectors had, so to speak, the best position to "see" the effect they were producing. A *pair* of projectors was necessary to crossfade slides instead of just changing them. Light was a problem since the screen consisted of a series of ropes hanging in rows behind each other. This idea originated as far as I know with Svoboda and gives a wonderful depth and life especially when, as here, tree and foliage slides are used. The Pani BP4 HMI projector would certainly now provide the intensities of light this kind of work requires and a special projector would not be needed.

One slide covering a whole stage is rather an extreme test and the use of two or more projectors as described earlier in the chapter is more usual.

In the amateur theatre, using three Patt. 252 projectors of only 2 kW and 4 × 3¾ in. slides, Bob Anderson has been able to show what could be done on the open stage of the Questors. In that case three 8 ft square back-projection screens were built into a simple architectural formation. The slides, taken on location at Osterley House and elsewhere, provided the walls lined with bookcases, the windows with a view beyond, the picture gallery—in all six different scenes for *School for Scandal*. Eighteen slides, three for each scene, were required. An interesting feature was that all detail including some of the furniture was on the slides, only the necessary practical pieces being set in front. As regards the lighting of the actors it was reported that "faces and costumes were loudly visible."

The better and the more compact the source and its optics the more one has to resort to artificial cooling to supplement the heat-absorbing glasses. This applies both to the slide and the lamp. Although the wattage may only be 150, small 35 mm transparency projectors have a blower as an integral part. The Kodak Carousel with its drum for remote change of eighty slides has often been used in theatre. The standard version has a 150 or 250 watt lamp but an adaptation for a 1200 watt 120 volt lamp is obtainable. Although a 15 mm f2·8 lens producing a 10 ft wide picture at a 4 ft throw has been around for some time now, most shows have used multiple projection— several pictures side by side.

The ultimate in this kind of thing would seem to be the use of thirty-two Carousels for back-projection at the Piccadilly theatre in the musical *I and Albert*. In fact sixteen were used at a time, the second set being to allow a crossfade or dissolve from one scene to another. The largest of the ten screens used became the backcloth. This had nine framed apertures in it to allow the light beams to go through and arrive on the other screens hanging downstage of it. Some of the screens were flown out at various times and the whole lot, including the backcloth, at one part of the show. The projections then relied on smoke to make them visible. Even when they were all in, the screens did not always all carry pictures at the same time. The lighting and projection was by Robert Ornbo in conjunction with Theatre Projects Lighting. A firm which does a lot of multiple projection with Carousels is Electrosonic Ltd. of Greenwich. Much of this is automatic and linked to sound and dimming systems for exhibitions and other displays.

In the case of the production just described it was necessary to build a structure on to the rear wall of the stage to carry all the equipment and there had to be a special sound-absorbent wall downstage of it, because of the considerable noise from all the projectors. It has to be remarked that in spite of all this fiendish ingenuity the show *I and Albert* did not run whereas Housman's *Victoria Regina* on the same subject has been popping up here and there ever since the first London production of 1935. Its needs are few and I have seen it both with the original Rex Whistler painted sets and in the round with but a few modest pieces of furniture.

Now that real light intensity is at last becoming available for scene projection, one is tempted to wonder whether the effect of pictures in depth cannot be got by single all-over simple screens or a single screen. In this I echo, a few years later, the opening two pages of this chapter. Depth is in fact shadow and shadow is contrast in intensity. What has made this difficult has been to get enough punch for the highlights. It is tempting to go on from here and speculate whether a few such scene projectors could one day provide the ingredients of the pattern of light and shade within which the actors move—in other words act as the stage lighting itself. Operating on this theory, the lighting from the front of house might be represented by a projector on the left and another on the right. These would be duplicated for crossfades and on-stage the same kind of thing repeats and we might end up with a dozen sources instead of two hundred. The scenery itself would of course be projected, so in order to avoid obstructions a giant all-embracing cyclorama is needed and we are back to the Bel Geddes project of 1922.

Such a background is a fixed distance from the actor and although it is easy by optical illusion to make it appear even further away, the reverse is difficult, perhaps impossible. Maybe the multi-screen techniques already described give a hint of how it might be done but how the slides are to be made is another problem. Where slides are not hand-painted, and few are nowadays, there has to be something to photograph. One thing is certain: it is going to be a matter of much drawing and planning on the board. The lighting designer will have to be trained to draw and paint—perhaps he will be the scene designer!

All five productions mentioned in the last section above have been described in detail with diagrams and photographs in *Tabs*: the references are: (1) Vol. 26, No. 2, (2) Vol. 31, No. 3, (3) Vol. 28, No. 3, (4) Vol. 29, No. 1, (5) Vol. 31, No. 2.

13 Equipment
in Common Use

THIS chapter provides a guide to equipment in common use in 1976. These references are dealt with in some detail, but naturally are more likely to be comprehensive in respect of Britain. This is all the more understandable when it is realized that I make it a rule that I must have seen the equipment for myself. The retailing of information at second-hand is a practice that does not commend itself to me.

Owing in part to the misleading nature of the names that tradition or trade has attached to equipment, it is not possible to adopt alphabetical order if this summary is to be readable, or indeed to make sense. Items are grouped, therefore, in classes or families, and when seeking by name without much clue as to what it represents the Index or Glossary may be more helpful in the first place.

Lanterns, Lighting Fittings, Instruments, or Luminaires

All the above terms can mean the same thing. "Lighting Fittings" I dislike although it is used in a British Standards Specification and elsewhere to cover the type of thing we are talking about. The term "fitting" is better reserved for chandeliers, pendants, wall brackets, and table lamps, practical or otherwise, with which the set is decorated. The term "instrument" is in common usage in American stage lighting but would leave readers on my own side of the Atlantic completely at sea. "Luminaire" is the illuminating engineers' term, but they are a small fraternity and it is not identified precisely enough with a single source anyway. All in all, the best word for a source of light enclosed in a housing is the good old English "Lantern." This is the "lanthorn" of Shakespeare and the "magic lantern" of Victorian and Edwardian days which translates beautifully into French as *Lanterne*. In German it is still recognizable as *Laterne* and mercifully this is the *Laterna* I can recognize in the pages of *Acta Scaenographica* from Prague. This is more than can be said for the place in which we propose to use them, for "theatre" becomes *Divadlo!* Lanterns divide into three main classes: the "spotlights," the

FIG. 168   1000-watt focus lantern

effects or optical "projectors," and the "floodlights."

Thanks to the versatility of modern Profile and Fresnel spotlights it is possible to form a large layout by repeating basically a few components only. However, stage lighting equipment is usually made not to wear out in spite of the hard life it leads. Both in the stocks of firms which hire and on our own stages and in their stores many types now supplanted will continue to linger. There follow brief descriptions of all those main models which have been commonly at large in Britain from the 1920s onward and which are likely to be still in service. To these have been added some of the better-known ones encountered in, for example, Germany and America in so far as they represent schools of thought or of design differing from British practice. Also included are some of those, like the Leko, which perplex because of their trade name; posterity may be grateful to inventors who perpetuate their names thus but it is a little hard on strangers. Pattern numbers are, however, just as perplexing and appear to be applied with even less logic and in this I am not free of guilt.

Spotlights

These are provided with a relatively crude, though often efficient, optical system which gives a beam whose spread can be varied over wide limits.

Focus Lamp or Focus Lantern

These two terms have been used to describe the simplest form of spotlight—a fixed plano-convex lens and a lamp, often with a spherical reflector, which can be moved to and fro behind it. It was also known as a "half-watt spotlight," or to add further to the confusion, simply as a 1000-watt or 500-watt spot. It has been replaced by the Fresnel spot (see below) except in the German orbit (see Lens Spot below). The common lens diameter was 6 in. for 1000 watts but a few 8 in. 2000 watt were made. The smallest in common use was the "float spot" with a 3-in. diameter lens. Compared to the Fresnel spot, the focus lamp is inefficient and prone to give a streaky light when spotted down; the beam edges are however clearer and there is less tendency to scatter of light outside the beam at any rate while the lens remains clean. Beam angle 13–42 degrees approximately.

Lens Spot (Linsenscheinwerfer)

This is a focus lamp (see above) which lingers on in German theatre, particularly opera houses, where in 1 kW, 2 kW, and 3 kW usually with an 8-in. diameter lens it is the traditional multi-purpose unit. An adaptor is always available which goes in the front and carries an extra lens to make a suitable condenser for optical projection. A runner on this can take a slide carrier or any of the moving effects and these in their turn can carry the appropriate objective lens. Of course a gobo slide, masking shutters or an iris diaphragm can equally well be used and in consequence a "lens spot" can also deputize for a Profile spot (q.v.) albeit with comparatively inefficient light output.

Condenser Spotlight
American term for Focus Lamp (see above).

Fresnel Spot
Fixed Fresnel (step) lens with moving lamp and reflector. The commonest unit in use in theatre today. The short focus possible with this type of lens gives twice the light, wattage for wattage, compared to corresponding Focus Lamp (see above). Beam has soft edges plus a tendency to scatter outside which can be corrected somewhat by fitting a lens which has blackened risers (said to be colouvred) or, of course, by using barndoors. Common theatre wattages range up to 2 kW and have lenses of $4\frac{1}{2}$, 6, 8, or 10 in. diameter (3, 6, 8, and 12 in. in America) but larger ones, such as 5 kW with lenses of 16 in. diameter, are made by film and television studio specialists such as Berkey or Ianiro. Beam angle 15–50 degrees approximately.

Profile Spot
This is the correct term for a spotlight in which the light is collected by a reflector system and redirected through a gate, the outline of which can be altered by shutters or iris or cut-out slides (gobos). The gate itself is then focused by an objective lens to give a hard-edged shaped beam. An essential feature is that the principal aim is efficient collection of light, the nature of the field and definition of focus being secondary and need for the latter is in the main confined to the Profile. Maximum beam angles are set by the focal length of the lens: for example, 22 degrees standard, with 37 degrees wide angle on the one hand and 11 degrees narrow on the other.

Bifocal Spot
Trade name for Profile spot (q.v.) with two sets of gate shutters: one in the focal position for hard profiling and the other with serrated edges and out of focus for soft. Hard and soft profiling can be mixed in the same beam and front lens diffusers become unnecessary.

Ellipsoidal Spot
A general American expression for Profile spot (q.v.) originating with geometric shape of the reflector commonly used.

Ellipsenspiegel-Linsenscheinwerfer
The German for Profile or ellipsoidal spot.

Klieglite
Trade name used by Kliegl for Profile spots of their manufacture. Kliegl were the first to launch these in a really big way in the early 1930s and it is Kliegleye that went into the language to describe the effects of glare in studios. Levy and Kook claim prior invention, but presumably Lekeye was something film stars did not care to announce they suffered from.

Lekolite or Leko
Trade name compounded from the names, Levy and Kook, and used by Century Lighting for Profile spots (q.v.) of their manufacture.

Mirror Spot
The name I gave to the early Profile spots I designed for Strand Electric. Deep ellipsoidal reflectors were out of the question owing to the unsuitable lamps in Britain in the 1930s, therefore a large mirror reflector stood behind the lamp. This had to be removed for access to the lamp when the rear door was used. A removable lid to the top of the spot was included to avoid this when possible. A further complication was the absence of suitable prefocus holders in Europe until well after the 1939–45 War. Post-war some Profiles (Patt 83) were made in skeleton form to put in circle front housings and reduce the access problem. This was later modified and put in a coffin-shaped housing which though ugly was reasonably precise in manufacture and easy to adjust. (See Fig. 169.) The production of the 1000-watt cap-up burning T4 lamp in 1963 put an end to this.

Silhouette 1000 and 2000
Profile spotlights manufactured by C.C.T. Theatre Lighting Ltd. They are for tungsten halogen lamps of 1 kW and 2 kW and have, in addition to the usual four shutters, a second "zoom" lens which gives angles between 10° and 22° with the 15° lens tube and 16° to 30° with the 25°, 20° to 36° with the 40° and 35° to 45° with the 40°. The combination of the two lenses can also be used to give a hard or soft profile to the beam (see also Fig. 111).

Twenty-three
The first mass-produced die-cast stage lighting spot. This, the Patt 23 baby Profile, introduced in 1951 by Strand Electric, so caught the imagination that it almost became synonymous with a spotlight and it was ordered whether profiling was

required or not. It is still not uncommon to see it used without diaphragms and, worse still, upside down!

Dynabeam
Kliegl's long-range version of Profile spot using tungsten lamps of 2 kW or more and, in consequence, large in size. Used fixed or for following, all the principal manufacturers now have models of something of the sort doing an equivalent job.

Halospot and Highspot
Trade name for follow spots by Rank Strand Electric using profile optical system, iris and horizontal barndoor in conjunction with 600-watt and 1000-watt CSI lamps respectively. Auxiliary control unit necessary and dimming is only possible by shutter (Fig. 47).

Stelmar
Trade name compounded from Steele and Martin who invented the optical system in 1929. The Stelmar was an early Profile spot but with concentric reflectors between the tungsten lamp and gate. It was mainly used as 1000-watt for following though there were a few 500-watt models made. About the time the Stelmar was losing out to the Mirror Spot in the tungsten field, the system was taken over by Frank Brockliss for use as a high power arc follow-spot, some of which are still in service (Fig. 12, page 43).

Sunspot

Trade name for Strand Electric's mirror arc follow-spot. Usually used as a.c. from an inductor and therefore very modest in its power input. Some d.c. models are also about, also some with automatic feed arcs. Essentially this is an enlarged power narrow-angle Profile spot. Iris, vertical and horizontal barn-doors are arranged for rapid operation and the first named can be locked to mirror focus to make sure automatically of maximum possible intensity when opening and closing the aperture. A colour magazine of five colours is fitted to the front.

Trouper and Trouperette

Follow-spots using carbon arc and tungsten respectively, made by the Strong Company in America. Much copied, they have a characteristic streamlined external appearance. This type of casing can tend to impede the full logical development of the optics and some derived models by others, although very neat and handy to work, have bought their appearance at the expense of reduced optical efficiency.

Zenspot

A version of the Sunspot above, arranged to use an AEI Xenon three-electrode lamp and reflector instead of carbon arc. Auxiliary control unit necessary and dimming is only by shutter. (See Fig. 46, page 82.)

Optical Effects

Cloud Machine (Wolkenapparat)

This originated with Schwabe. The device used a 3-kW lamp round which the housing slowly turned by electric motor. Light, which passed through separate photographic slides of clouds, was diverted by 45-degree mirrors through a series of ten lenses each pointing vertically upwards. This served to keep the diameter of the machine down but also allowed divertor mirrors to be fitted over each lens to bring the light out horizontally once more. The mirrors were pivoted and joined together by small gears and shafting so that their tilt could be altered by remote control. The large model of the machine had two tiers each of ten lenses and each tier independently controlled as to mirror tilt so that clouds could be made to pass over each other. (Fig. 170.)

Effects Projector

This has a condenser system specifically designed for optical projection and runners to take eight-and-one-eighth inch square

FIG. 170 3-kW single lamp German double-tier cloud machine with 20 lenses and slides

standard effects turntable backplates. Before the 1939–45 War models were commonly of 1 kW and had two components to the condenser. A third lens was then added, also a heat absorbing glass to protect the slide. There are a lot of these still about in Britain, and while satisfactory for clouds they are unsuitable for pin-sharp focusing as, for example, in snow effects especially if they have been knocking around a theatre or hire store for some time. The latest Strand Electric effects projector takes either a 1-kW or 2-kW lamp. The condenser has three components and a heat absorbing glass. Treated with respect as a precision instrument, it can be used to project scenery slides with reasonable success. (Fig. 155.)

Linnebach Projector

This is not really a projector but a shadowgraph. In one form it is a sheet metal lamp housing with sloping sides to ensure a very large front which carries a slide of perhaps as much as 40 × 30 in. across its full width. In the other form, the lamp housing is quite separate from the slide and this is described

316   *The Art of Stage Lighting*

on pages 303–6. The large slide overhead projector with its divertor mirror common in lecture theatres can be used to much the same effect.

Scene Projector

The boundary between a scene and an effects projector is poorly defined since each can do the job of the other. Generally, what is implied by the term "scene projector" is a large machine of 4 kW or 5 kW complete with its own special stand to give a rigid mounting. Some degree of blowing to assist slide and/or lamp cooling is also not uncommon.

The traditional 5-kW German scene projector of, for example, Reiche and Vogel, is always for 7-in. slides and employs two rods which overhang the front and carry the various lenses and attachments. A remote changer for 7-in. slides is available. A 10-kW model is also made.

Strand Electric used to make two models for a 4 kW 110-volt lamp, the Patt 152 for a $3\frac{1}{4} \times 4$ in. slide and Patt 752 for a 7-in. (18 cm) slide. Since 1973 as Rank Strand Electric they have decided to market projectors made by Ludwig Pani of Vienna. There is a 5 kW tungsten halogen model BP5 but particularly interesting is the Pani BP4 HMI. (See Fig. 48.) This is designed for a 4 kW HMI lamp, the German equivalent of our CSI lamp. CCT make a 1kW model for 5-inch slides and optical effects. Both represent a real breakthrough in intensity for scene projection. Another projector that is in use for this purpose is the Kodak Carousel. Pictures are built up with a number of these lined up side by side. Often large numbers are used and what is more with a specially boosted light source of 1200 watts in spite of the problem of fan noise.

Floodlights

These are either separate lanterns or magazine equipment of several sources collected together in one housing. The various types can represent a wide range of beam spread but all share the common disadvantage that the range of individual adjustment to this spread is either small or non-existent.

Acting Area Flood

In British practice this means a vertical floodlight, introduced in the mid-thirties, with a fixed beam of roughly 26 degrees and sharp cut-off. Used massed together on bars first by Robert Nesbitt for his spectacular shows in the late 1930s, it became the common solution for high intensity lighting particularly during the 1939–45 War and immediately after. Massed use of Patt 23 Baby Profile Spots and finally the availability of Fresnels, both of which had adjustable beam coverage, killed

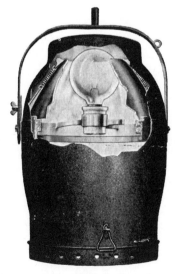

FIG. 171   1-kW Acting Area flood—phantom view

it. In a way, both the Nedervolt and the higher wattages of Sealed-beam Lamps (q.v.), when used massed together, produce a similar type of lighting to this use of Acting Areas.

In Germany in the 1920s, probably earlier, an Acting Area flood (*Spielflächenleuchte*) had been designed to be used as a vertical coverage in areas encompassed by the cyclorama. But the lanterns themselves were less efficient than their British successors and in any case only a few were used to each installation. The essential difference between the two usages may be summed up by saying that in Germany the Acting Area lantern was an auxiliary unit only whereas in Britain it was often the main source of overhead light.

Batten

This in its stage-lighting connotation is taken in Britain to mean magazine compartment equipment wired to alternate as two, three, or four colours. Used unqualified a wide-angle softlight would be expected, but other versions with narrower distribution from concentrating reflectors or PAR lamps are also used (Fig. 133, page 232).

Beamlight

A much better term used in America for the Pageant type of parallel-beam lantern (q.v.). Rank Strand Electric reintroduced a version with a 1000-watt tungsten halogen lamp in 1970.

Borderlight

American expression for "batten," not very happy as it suggests the lighting of the borders, but better than the term "X-ray" which was completely misleading. I am told that "striplight" is now the way to describe this equipment over there, but unfortunately in Britain this would imply a fluorescent tube or small-wattage lamp with a line filament or even the festoons of coloured lamps used to decorate seaside resorts.

Cyclorama Lighting

Television studios have become great users of colour mixing on cycloramas. Special 4-colour tungsten halogen units and corresponding ground rows have been developed by studio lighting firms notably Berkey and Ianiro. Where a large theatre cyclorama is concerned the claims of such equipment should be considered.

Flood

A sheet metal housing for 150, 500 and 1000 watt containing separate reflector mounted inside (cf. Olivette, opposite). During the thirties, with the silvered glass sunray type of reflector, quite a variety of floods were developed which had

to cover up the gap in Britain occasioned by lack of commercial production of cheap Fresnel lenses. Each flood had wide-angle and medium-angle alternatives; nowadays the wide-angle, but in anodized aluminium instead of glass, is standard.

Horizon Lamp (Horizontleuchte)

This vertical cylindrical lantern originated with the Schwabe Company. Nearly half is reflector and half is aperture into which special glasses can be fitted. The 1000-watt lamp is tubular with a line filament. The wide, even spread of 170 degrees which results was designed specifically for seven-colour lighting of the large cylindrical cyclorama or Hasait cloth. This task has mainly been taken over by banks of hot-cathode fluorescent tubes, three to a fitting used vertically.

Nedervolt-Spiegelscheinwerfer

German low-voltage transformer spot which became very popular there in the immediate post-war temporary theatres. Reiche and Vogel and others make models using either built-in transformers or separate ones permanently coupled by a short loop of thick cable. The low voltage gives a very efficient compact source; but there is no denying that the extra weight of a transformer for a 1000-watt or 500-watt 24-volt lamp is an awful encumbrance which is tolerable only on the German type stage with its bridges and towers. Essentially a narrow-angle spot, little adjustment of beam spread is possible, though diffuser glasses can be used to help out but at the risk of some scatter. Various sizes down to 100 watt 12 volt are made and some have a lens optical system, but this is less common than a reflector system.

Olivette

American term, seemingly on the decline, for wide-angle flood. Reflector spinning acts as its own housing. This survives in television as a softlight known as a "scoop."

Pageant Lantern

Trade name for 1000-watt parallel-beam reflector spot originally with spill rings and latterly blanking mask to cut out direct light from lamp. Although when spotted down the Fresnel spot does not do exactly the same job, its far greater versatility has caused it to replace the Pageant which ceased to be listed in 1960 by Strand Electric. Strictly speaking, its real substitute is the much more efficient Nedervolt spot.

Panorama Lamp

See Horizon Flood. For some reason the Strand Electric

version of the German lamp was known by this name.

Spielflächenleuchte

According to Basil Dean, known as *Spielflächenbeleuchtungskörper* when he first met it. The original Acting Area lantern (q.v.).

Lighting Control

Considerable replacement of the older control systems is always going on. This springs in part from the availability of better systems (often at a remarkably reasonable price considering the effect of inflation) and the understandable reluctance of Rank Strand Electric to service earlier systems, particularly of the mechanical or electro-mechanical type. Nevertheless some of them survive, largely due to an under-cover cannibalization service between the electricians of one theatre and another in parts which become available as equipment is dismantled for replacement.

Modern control systems of the simpler types are omitted from this summary. There are now, thanks to the thyristor and today's electronics, so many of these about. It is only in points of detail that there is any difference between the work of reputable firms. Once one leaves basic presetting and elementary grouping there is much of interest. Since these are discussed in Chapter 8 they receive brief treatment here and yesterday's controls inevitably receive more attention than their influence on the future warrants. Overseas systems I have seen and which represent a distinctive solution to the control problem have also been included. However one-offs—no matter how intriguing or exciting their nature—have been excluded. The test of any switchboard must be, did anyone want another and could they afford it?

Manual and Electro-mechanical Dimmer Systems

Resistance dimmers are strictly speaking fixed load but windings giving two-to-one load variation with displaced curve are usual. Transformer dimmers are of the auto-wound type and are load independent.

Bordoni Dimmer Regulator

Standard for many years in Germany and in other European countries. Arranged to operate multi-channel transformers and prior to that resistance by remote control using tracker wire over considerable distances. Dimmer levers are at $1\frac{3}{4}$-in. centres and provide locking to move up or down, usually by turning an arrow-pointed lever head. Sliding covers pull down to limit top or bottom travel of each dimmer lever thereby providing some degree of presetting. Grand Master cross-gearing is usual and is sometimes duplicated by motor drive with Ward Leonard variable speed control to each shaft. Switchboard and fuses quite separate and often not even adjacent. A French example is shown in Fig. 14 but so many were made by various European firms that they are bound to be encountered for many years yet all over the place.

Chromon or Chromoselector
The four colours, Red, Yellow, Green and Blue, each fed from dimmers are linked to a single pointer which by its positioning integrates the intensities to produce any additive colour mixture of the above. Devised by M. Leblanc, of Clemançon.

Delicolor
Proprietary name given to three primary colour mixing equipment using dimmers operated from a single dial with a series of colour names against a pointer for selection. Supplied at one time by W. J. Furse to the design of Rollo Gillespie Williams.

Direct-operated or Manual Switchboards
Minimum control is by slider dimmers with only very occasional mastering provided by larger dimmers. Alternatively, radial dimmers back of board mounted to allow mechanical interlocking of their levers to a master at the end of the shaft on which they are carried. Handles are commonly at $4\frac{1}{2}$-in. centres and some allow for slip at the end of travel and are known as self-release, but the majority of "bracket handles" do not. When fitted with cross gearing between shafts are known as Grand Master Boards (Fig. 16) but dimmers on individual shafts are condemned to travel in the same direction and do not have any means of limiting their travel. Switching usually of the two-way and off type giving "On Master Blackout," "Off" and "Independent." On the larger installations, master blackouts are by remote contactors. American forms of this control use slot interlocking but in other respects are just as poor if not worse because of the amount of mechanical friction to overcome. The only reason for direct-operated control is relatively low price which may excuse very small installations but not the large ones such as the ninety-six dimmers at the Phoenix Theatre in London, installed as late as 1949—now replaced.

Jeu d'Orgue Classique
Entirely peculiar to France, made by Clemançon, and notable for flat edge-to-edge mounting of dial-type levers with con-

tinuous wire connection to dimmers instead of usual single-tracker wire and counterweight. Interlocking otherwise to same effect as the Bordoni Regulator above. Unique provision to select dimmers for short circuiting using tram-type multi-way controllers to bring lights suddenly full on (Fig. 15).

Junior 8

Until 1951 the amateur theatre had to be content with cut down versions of professional controls. These being special tended to defeat the aim of keeping down the cost. To remedy this we at Strand Electric made in quantity our HA series with either twelve circuits and six dimmers or six and three—later changed to eight and four as the combination effect was more useful. The original frames were of angle iron, later sheet metal and the dimmers were plugged in with wander leads. The sockets had shorting switches and were fed by 2-way switches from blackout or independent. The idea caught on and there must be hundreds of this type of control still about.

In 1962 I had a new slider dimmer made and four were integrally wired to be available to adjacent sockets. This the Junior 8 (Fig. 174) still in 1976 occupies the bottom of the cost table but it is becoming a question of how long manufacturers will *want* to make this kind of thing.

Electro-Mechanical Dimmer Bank

The extensive use of these prior to 1964 by Strand Electric had no parallel anywhere else. Based on the Mansell clutch, in

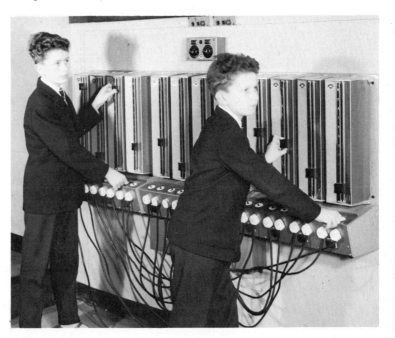

FIG. 174 Three Junior-8 units combined as one control of 12 dimmers 24 circuits

which pairs of 15–17 volt electro-magnets grip either side of an iron wheel and are linked to a dimmer crank above and below the pivot to obtain reversal; the original centres were 7 in., but refinement in 1954 reduced them to 5 in. The dimmer wheels were mounted on horizontal shafts and driven, sometimes as many as 120, as a single bank by one variable-speed motor (Fig. 175). The dimmers were resistances or special double-sided 5 kW transformers. From 1955 a polarized relay servo was used (Fig. 177). When the dimmer lever potentiometer is moved, DC current in the centre line causes the sensitive relay to switch in the appropriate clutch and drive the dimmer and its slave potentiometer until they balance. Current ceases to flow and the relay cuts out. Time taken is determined by the motor speed—usually variable between 3 sec and 45 sec. Contactor switches in series with the dimmer, and in the case of the Light Console (q.v.) in parallel as well, were used for instantaneous changes.

Light Console

Each channel selected by stopkey to be "played" on a master keyboard (Fig. 176). When off the dimmer stays where last driven. Each master consists of twelve keys, three of each colour—white, red, blue, and green. The stopkeys are coloured similarly and splitting a production layout with some care over the colours and masters is advisable. Dimmers can, however, be moved against their colour master by using "Reverse" and "General Move." Master keys are double-touch giving in fours from the left: Blackout/Dim, Raise/Dim, Full-on/Raise. Dimmers have both *series* and *short-circuiting*

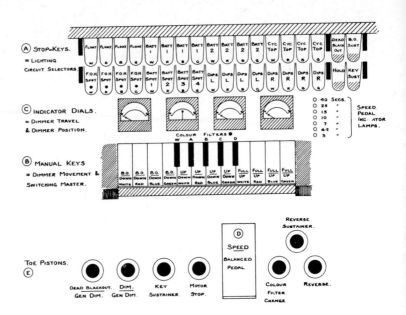

FIG. 176 Basic controls for Light Console; diagram reproduced from 1950 instruction book

contactors. Speed of dimmer movement is by balanced (swell) pedal usually one per keyboard. Each keyboard has a left master and a right master with a centre set of keys to operate both at once. Where there is more than one keyboard they also couple together. There are usually between thirty-two and forty channels per master of four colours. Stopkeys are subject to organ-type memory combination action from pistons in the keyslip. Second touch on a stopkey reads the position of the dimmer on a dial, one per colour, which at other times reads a dummy dimmer ("setter") to measure amount of movement imparted. The groups of five black notes give colour filters, *A, B, C, D* and white on any channels whose lanterns are so fitted and whose stopkeys are selected.

The description above is of the post-war models and therefore applies only in general principle, not in detail, to that in S'Carlos Opera in Lisbon. Some fourteen were installed, of which the best known are the Palladium (replaced by a C/AE control for 240 thyristor channels, December, 1966) and Drury Lane; 152 and 216 channels respectively (Fig. 18).

Polarized Relay Servo (System PR)

Originally an attempt to reproduce with electro-mechanical servo (Fig. 177) the facilities of the "Electronic" preset (q.v.). There is a 136-channel example in the New Theatre in London and a fifty-two channel one in the Belgrade in Coventry, both with twin preset panels, row masters and combined dimmer and contactor grouping three-position switches to each channel. The cross-fader becomes a motor drive with speed regulator.

Being electro-mechanical, inertia gives a two preset ahead

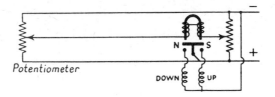

FIG. 177 Schematic: polarised relay servo for use with magnetic clutches

Potentiometer

DOWN   UP

effect. This is further exploited in later models housed in vertical control cabinets where dimmer grouping and contactor switching is given separate three-position amber tablet switches so that three groups can be formed for movement within the presets.

System CD

A combination of the polarized relay servo and the Light Console (see Fig. 178) designed to exploit fully the "inertia" possibilities of electro-mechanical servo.

One or two sets of dimmer levers as presets is usual and, in addition, each channel has a stopkey as a selector. Combinations of these may be captured and moved whenever required by memory action, fourteen or twenty memories being usual. Normally only the dimmers of the channels selected will move no matter what the position of the levers on the preset, the speed of movement being governed by a balanced foot pedal. A full-on and a dim push can be used to raise or lower them without need to reset their preset levers. "Remainder Dim" takes out all channels not selected and when used with a preset provides a very easy cross-fade. Individual dimmer positions can be read on a dial by second touching each channel stopkey.

The system has been the common control for the larger theatres in Britain, for example, Playhouse, Nottingham; Apollo, Shaftesbury, Lyric, and in many television studios. Beyond 120 channels use is made of wing units and up to

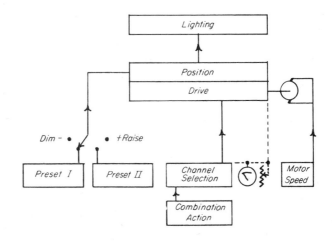

FIG. 178 System CD; to obtain lighting change both servo positioning and selection for mechanical drive must take place. The selectors for the latter (stopkeys) are operated both manually and as combinations by instant memory action

Lighting

Position

Drive

Dim −   + Raise

Preset I   Preset II   Channel Selection   Motor Speed

Combination Action

Equipment in Common Use   325

240 channels have been so accommodated, the principle of operation remaining the same. The CD in the Adelphi Theatre is unique in possessing a full-on control since it represents a modernization of the previous Light Console banks and the contactors already existed. The Piccadilly Theatre has the only three-preset example, one being on the console itself, the others on a wing added later.

Note: Theatre cues are mainly dimming ones, whereas in television they are switching. Therefore it was theatre practice in System CD to keep the channel contactors closed and only trip them out when a blackout is required. On the other hand, in television models contactors are normally open and selected to close only when required. For this reason the equivalent to the "Blackout" push becomes the "Go" control.

System C

This is a variant of CD with a further extension of facilities which has been employed only for television, and there principally by the BBC for Grade 1 studios. It uses a luminous stophead selector adjacent to each pair of preset levers in the earlier versions and in the later a touch contact illuminated scale integral with the dimmer levers. The main advantage is the location of selection and dimmer control together but considerably more cost is involved in the relay circuitry than in stopkey control.

All-electric Dimmer Systems

There have been to date seven main forms of these dimmers: Saturable Reactor, Thyratron-controlled Reactor, Transistor-controlled Reactor, Magnetic Amplifier, Two-valve Thyratron, Three-valve Thyratron, and Thyristor. The main distinction is that in the first four the load-carrying unit is an iron-cored reactor whose impedance is varied, whereas the other three function by chopping the a.c. wave to allow a varying part to be transmitted directly through them. In its simplest and least expensive form the reactor was not suitable for presetting.

Where the type of dimmer is not specifically mentioned it can be assumed to be the thyristor.

Saturable Reactor Dimmers

Limited load variation of two to one requiring tap changing at dimmer to achieve best performance. Dimmer sizes commonly 1 kW and 2 kW but also 500 watt, 3 kW and 5 kW. Weight considerable. Control by saturation of iron core with d.c. winding fed through metal rectifier from a.c. potentiometer network. Contactor to each channel to disconnect load line essential.

Simple Reactor Control

Single dimmer lever per channel with, in Strand Electric (System SR) examples, twenty-one steps covered by reactor time lag. Grouping switches to select on master X or master Y. In smaller models combined with contactor feed to give "off" at mid position. When separate contactor switches are fitted, centre position of dimmer switch (coloured amber) becomes independent live allowing cross-fade between two groups with a third remaining stationary. Channel contactor switches then connect to Blackout A or B or off. Very many examples of up to fifty-four channels were built, including one in Criterion Theatre, replaced by system MMS, and another in The Mermaid in London, where there is now a Q-Master.

Double-reactor Preset

Pre-transistor attempt by Strand Electric (System SR Preset) to provide true preset with cross-fade using small reactor in control line to main reactor. Defects of saturable reactor as a dimmer emphasized thereby and in consequence more than usually poor load variation and retapping essential. Very few made, supplanted by system LC (below) whose desk controls were virtually the same.

Preset Reactor Control System LC

Transistor amplifiers with feedback in control line to give presetting and improve variable load performance within the same curve. Four to one possible in good examples but pronounced time-lag at quarter load.

Two presets standard with amber tablet switches to form groups X, Y, and Z on rotary masters three per preset. Switches to couple together to any one preset master. Second set of switches connects channel contactor to either master blackout, A or B or off. Maximum number of possible channels was ninety-six but forty-eight or seventy-two was usual. There were very many examples of this system in floor-standing and desk forms a number of which are likely to survive some time yet.

Magnetic Amplifier Control

No examples in Britain but there are many in Europe and America. Load variation possible is wide. Examples of controls, see under Century, Graham Brothers (ASEA) and Siemens.

Thyratron-controlled Reactor

Several examples in the United States, including Radio City Music Hall (see page 51). Only theatre example in Britain, the Odeon, Leicester Square (1938) by BTH, which was replaced

FIG. 179   2-preset 3-group transistor/reactor control, system LC

in 1962 by, of all things, a second-hand Grand Master direct operated board. The stage was only very occasionally used and maintenance of the by then obsolete indirect thyratron equipment was probably a nuisance.

Two-valve Thyratron

No stage-lighting examples in Britain, but some fluorescent dimming installations by Thorn and GEC. Used for some years by Century in America. First important German use by AEG for Hamburg Opera in 1952. Load independent. Examples of controls see under Century and AEG below. (See also "Hysterset" under "C-Core.")

Three-valve Thyratron

Known in Britain as "The Electronic" and was made by Strand Electric in Europe and Kliegl (under licence) in America. Load independent. Used with complete twin desk preset connected by fast and slow motion integrating cross-fader. Master and independent fader to each preset desk. Row master to every twelve dimmers and switch to each channel to connect "on" or "off" or "independent." Maximum 144 channels usually 2 kW but some 5 kW. See also page 53 and Fig. 85.

AEG Regulator

A control panel with group master and cross-faders feeds twin panels similar to the Strand electronic desk principle above. In addition, each channel lever is fitted with cam-operated movement mechanically to shift the levers when the particular preset panel is no longer electrically connected, the lighting being held on the other. The cams are integral in each channel lever and about six preset levels could be stored, but this has been greatly increased in recent models. Examples: with thyratron valves in Hamburg and Munster now replaced.

C-Core

A kind of halfway house to the direct thyristor dimmer. By Century originally using a reactor and a single thyristor in shunt across it. The term was afterwards used to cover normal twin thyristor dimmers. A rather similar arrangement was marketed by Ward Leonard under the name "Hysterset" using a single thyratron at about the time George Izenour first introduced the twin valve direct thyratron. C-core dimmers were used with standard Century control consoles.

C-Card

Century's term for their platten system (q.v.).

Century CI Control

Centre desk with a set of large levers specially shaped for use as a rehearsal system and for "playing" with the fingers. Switch under each to transfer channel to preset. Pushes to select any preset either side of the cross-fader, originally only odd numbers on one side and only evens on the other. Presets mounted as five or ten edge-operated wheels in vertical lines per channel to form a wing unit (Fig. 90).

At one time the remote control most frequently met with in the United States with a host of examples. Maximum practicable number of channels from the handling point of view would appear to me to be one hundred.

DDM

This system based on a mini-computer and using rockers for channel control was the last to be devised and made under my immediate direction. It was installed at Stratford-upon-Avon in the Winter of 1971. If the Light Console is the alpha then this is the omega of that side of my Strand Electric career. Subsequently Rank Strand engineers slightly altered the ergonomic basis of the master panel and in the revised form a good number have been installed of which the largest is that for La Scala Milan with 320 channels.

Graham Bros. (ASEA) Regulator

This was a straightforward preset. Usually of four presets in larger installations arranged in a curved shape for ease of reading and reach. An example of 120 channels is in the theatre at Gelsenkirchen in Germany. Graham Bros. of Sweden were the first to use punched card on a large scale. It has been used in combination with a variant of their normal preset regulator so that levels are punched off a preset once it has been set up, but as there is no mechanical action (unlike Siemens) the dimmer itself, not its control lever, is operated by the card when read. To modify part of a change, the dimmer or dimmers must be switched over individually to a lever or levers in one of the presets and a new card then punched to include this if required. Examples: The Royal Dramatic Theatre in Stockholm (180 channels) and new Opera House in Warsaw (300 channels).

IDM

Introduced by Strand Electric in 1967 and superseded four years later by Rank Strand's system MSR with improved electronics. Complete set of luminous mimic micro-switch levers with A and B manual masters. Mechanical numerical selectors (IDM) or keyboard type (MSR) for Record and Playback. C and D faders and crossfader for playback. For IDM/R see under WHZ.

Infinite Preset

Term used in United States for control systems using means other than repeat dimmer levers for presets. Thus applied to punch card and to other record cards or plattens.

Kliegl Three-preset

This system, installed to control sixty thyristor dimmers in the Tyrone Guthrie Theatre in Minneapolis, is of interest as it uses three horizontal rows of levers representing the three presets and, in addition, a set of eight pushes to each channel to set up eight groups to restrict a change to part of a preset.

Luminous Preset (LP and Lightset)

Three presets in horizontal rows. Touch contact dimmer scales light in red and white to form and display group X and Y separately or together or off. Cross-fades within presets with third group stationary are therefore possible. Further, while different groups can be set on each preset, they can be instantly matched for cross-fades at the touch of the appropriate push when required. Examples are The Theatre Royal, York, and Coventry Theatre, each 100 channels.

FIG. 180 3-preset control with luminous lever formation of groups

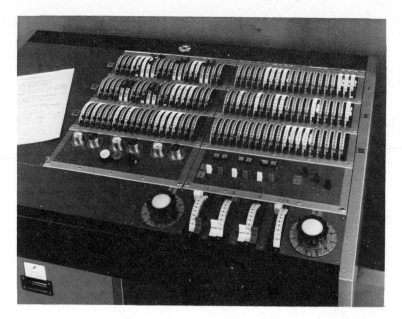

A later Rank Strand version of this system known as Lightset had Copy between the red and white groups within a preset instead of between presets.

Memocard

The Danish Grosman punched card system with automatic punch but manual readers (usually three or four) marketed and in part manufactured by Rank Strand. Pair of levers per channel (see page 153). Good example for 150 dimmers installed in King's Theatre, Edinburgh in 1972, and several others but system has been overtaken by for example MMS (q.v.). The Grosman firm now have a cassette and other magnetic memory systems.

Memolight

Memory systems made by ADB (Adrian de Backer) and marketed in Britain by CCT Theatre Lighting Ltd. Their model ST150 is for 150 channels and employs a cassette with 600 memories to each side. Selection of channels is by individual push buttons and there is a crossfader with three group faders. There are 24 manual levers duplicated to give a preset. A maximum of four channels can be plugged to each by jumper leads; when so connected they are independent of the memory system and its supply.

MMS

A Rank Strand system in which electronically complete modules can be plugged together to provide facilities of different degrees of sophistication for installations of varying sizes. The principal modules are:

Push button per channel
Channel control wheel and dial
    OR
Channel mimic
Channel selector keyboard, wheel and dial
    WITH
Manual playback with A and B faders and master fader
    OR
Rate playback with full facilities.

Along with these go modules for varying capacities of memory, cassettes and other items. "Compact", a portable model, is also made.

MSR

See under *IDM*.

MEMO-Q

This was the version of the IDM memory system made in the United States for Century Strand and Strand Century in Canada. The keyboard call-up represented an improvement

Multi-group Preset (C/AE MGP)

Two or three preset solid state switching version of what was known in its relay form as C/AE. Each preset has a set of touch-contact dimmer scales lit in red and white, corresponding to a red (active) master and a white (park) master. Memory action can record the red combination in use as on or off for recall (hence **MG** = multi-group). Transfer from the red master to the white or vice versa can take place at any time these are approximately lined up. The white master is mainly intended to hold a channel in use but not active, said to be "parked." Cross-fades can take place within a preset by using both masters. This is the nearest all-electric equivalent to System CD.

Platten System

A form of what the Americans call "Infinite Preset" (q.v.) in which miniature dimmer levers are mounted on trays (plattens) and are inserted in substitute for the normal preset.

Punch

Century's name for their punch-card dimmer control. Example in the Vivian Beaumont Theatre at the Lincoln Center has 180 channels with four standard IBM cards per cue. Now replaced by Q-File.

FIG. 181   240-channel 2-preset
40-memory group system C/AE
at London Palladium

Q-File

Thorn instant memory systems with numerical call-up for
dimmer channels with servo-operated master fader. Two complete rate playbacks giving AB fade and CD fade. Full facilities
including manual faders for Preset and Stage, mimic diagrams
for both the memories and the channels. This control, introduced for television in 1966, was the original numerical dimmer
system and the latest stage version is known as the Q-File
2000. (See Fig. 92.)

Q-Level

Kliegl markets Q-Master (q.v.) in North America under this name.

Q-Master

Thorn memory system with dimmer levers to each channel. Two masters A and B for manual playback and a third C for manual and rate crossfade. Memories can be added or subtracted. Channel mimic available. (See Fig. 94.)

Series PM

A Thorn system in which ten groups can be formed by pin-matrix as part of a two or three preset control. This makes in the latter case a total of 13 or 14 master faders (if the optional Grand master is specified). Claimed as suitable for 20 to 140 channels (see Fig. 89).

Siemens Regulator

Although originally designed for use with all-electric magnetic amplifier dimmers, the control panel is equipped with electro-mechanical clutch servo and motor drive (dimmer levers at one inch centres) to simulate all the facilities of the Bordoni Regulator (q.v.). Locking to travel up or down is by three position tablets which can also all be centred to neutral row by row on using a cancel trip. Presetting was developed later and consists of sets of potentiometers which can be connected to main desk servo and drive the levers there to correspond to the preset levels. Preset levers are mounted in groups of fours side by side but picking out is facilitated by bringing the appropriate preset levers forward mechanically from behind a comb shield where they can otherwise be seen but not operated.

A further step has been to provide in addition punch-card equipment to record on a large card of $11\frac{3}{4} \times 8\frac{3}{8}$ in. for 200 channels and to set the dimmer levels to which the main desk levers are driven. Later still ferrite stores giving dimmer memory were added, the control regulator remaining basically the same. It was only in 1974 that a change from this regulator was announced. There must be hundreds of them about, either straight or with card or ferrite memory. (See Sitralux.)

Sitralux

The trade term used by Siemens for their lighting control in recent years. Rather confusingly it has been extended to cover a totally different ergonomic approach using encoder wheels while merely adding "B" for the full theatre control and "M" for a more general-purpose application. (See page 165.)

FIG. 182 Siemens servo dimmer levers in foreground with 8-preset beyond the central master panel. Nationaltheater, Mannheim

Threeset

A Rank Strand system with 3-presets and 3-way group switches to each channel in each preset to allow control from nine masters. Claimed as suitable for 40 to 120 channels. (See Fig. 87.)

WHZ

This Strand Electric system managed to stagger through its demonstration in February 1966 to become "the world's first stage lighting control to record dimmer positions instantly by magnetic means, access for playback or modification being immediate also." The first such system to work *reliably* was, however, Q-File four months later. WHZ (then known as IDM/R) was installed with different electronics by Sperry but only two installations were completed. The spirit of what WHZ should have done lives in the rockers of DDM.

Glossary

ABTT. Association of British Theatre Technicians.

Acting Area. The part of the stage on which the actors move or speak. Also short for Acting Area Flood (*AA*), a lantern which provides vertical lighting of this area, not to be confused with Acting Area Lighting which should apply to *any* lighting specifically for this area.

Actor's Left or Right. Also known as Stage Left, Stage Right, it assumes that the actor is facing the audience. His Right is the audience's Left. Lanterns and spotlights on a batten are numbered from his left.

All-electric. A lighting-control system in which no mechanical linkages of any kind are involved.

Apron Stage. See "Forestage."

Arc. From "arc lamp" (US *Arc Light*), a high-power light source burning carbons. The term is usually coupled with Front-of-House (FOH) to refer to the spotlight projectors at the back of the auditorium used for picking out and following Music Hall artists and others.

Amphitheatre. Strictly the oval building with seats surrounding the arena of Roman times but later applied to the upper part or gallery of a theatre, as is still the case at the Royal Opera House, Covent Garden.

Arena Theatre. Our equivalent for this American term is "Theatre-in-the-Round," i.e. complete encirclement of the acting area by the audience. Arena in Latin means sand, hence the stage of an amphitheatre (q.v.).

Auditorium. The area of a theatre which certainly houses the audience but in some forms the actors as well. It is curious that people set off to the theatre which is a place for seeing, but once they get inside they give this notion up and sit in a place which by definition is dedicated to hearing.

Automation. A distinction must be made between Automation and Power Assistance. A stage lift and revolve which have to have their stopping points determined for them by the operator pushing the stop button at the appropriate time are merely power assisted. The essential qualification for automation is "feedback" which does not necessarily mean a lot of electronics or a computer. Feedback is the circuit which enables the equipment to compare its instruction with its present state and make all necessary adjustments to bring the two in line, thereby removing the drudgery from the human operator's work.

Backcloth (US *Backdrop*). See "Cloth."

Backing. A cloth or flat (q.v.) placed behind windows, doors, and other openings in the scenery.

Barrel (US *Pipe*). Usually a $1\frac{1}{2}$-in. gas-pipe (2-in. OD) hanging horizontally for carrying scenery or lanterns, abbreviated to "bar," or vertically as a support to which lanterns can be clamped as "boom."

Barndoor. Four separately hinged doors on pivoted frame for use on front of spotlights, particularly Fresnels.

Batten. Metal or wooden "bar" from which scenery or lanterns can hang. Loosely applied to a barrel and lighting equipment, especially compartment type (see Fig. 133, page 232).

BDL. The British Drama League, now British Theatre Association (BTA).

Blackout. No light. Used as a verb to indicate the switching out of lights, properly a group of lights. Dead blackout (*DBO*) is most important and must be attainable by a simple switch override.

Board. An all-embracing term used to cover the main control point for the stage lighting. More appropriate to the old direct-operated (US *Manual*) control where switches, dimmers, and fuses were housed together. See also Console and Control Desk.

Boomerang (Boom). Vertical barrel carrying spotlights at the sides of the stage behind the wings, fixed to the floor and made off at the top.

Border. A strip of canvas or curtain used to prevent the regions above the stage beyond the scenery being seen.

Box Set. Also known as a *Chamber Set*, still the staple form of interior setting today—a room with the proscenium opening as the "fourth wall."

Brail. To draw a lighting batten or piece of hanging scenery up or down stage out of its normal vertical hanging position.

Bridge (US Elevator or Stage Elevator). A large rectangular section of the stage floor formed as a lift to travel some distance above or below the normal stage level. May be power- or manually-driven and lessens the need for large rostrums. A *Lighting Bridge* is a narrow gallery about 20 in. (50 cm) deep suspended over stage or forestage. Lanterns fixed to the bridge are accessible during rehearsal or performance.

BSI. The British Standards Institution, which publishes BS specifications.

Busbar (US Bus). A metal conductor to which many electrical circuits sharing a common supply may be connected, derived from "omnibus."

Cathode. An electrode in a discharge lamp or radio valve designed to emit electrons. An Anode is an electrode designed to receive the electrons. As the direction of the current in a discharge lamp reverses with the alternating current, both electrodes are designed to emit electrons and are therefore known as cathodes, e.g. hot-cathode lamp.

Chamber Set. See "Box Set."

Channel. Much the best term for a controllable stage-lighting circuit complete with dimmer. It is also used in respect of sound to cover much the same thing. One channel, whether light or sound, can be used or regulated quite independently of another.

Check. An intermediate position on the travel of a dimmer, or, as a verb, to alter lighting intensity on dimmers. The reverse is to "bring in" or "fade in," but "dim in" and "dim out" are not unknown and surely descriptive enough to justify the contradiction.

CIE. (Commission Internationale de L'Eclairage). A medium of international exchange on lighting matters. Committee E3192 deals with Cinema, Theatre, and Television production lighting.

Cinemoid. The trade mark "Cinemoid" denotes a particular brand of self-extinguishing (to BS 3944) cellulose acetate sheeting made in England by Courtaulds and used as stage colour filters.

Circle (US Balcony). The tiers over the stalls, the first (bottom) being the "Grand" or, more often still, the "Dress," then the "Upper," followed by the "Gallery," sometimes called the "Amphitheatre."

Circuit. Any complete path from source of electrical supply and back, but more specifically in stage work a lamp or lamps, plug socket or sockets which are connected to a switch on the stageboard or a jack on a patch panel (q.v.). A dimmer circuit should be referred to as a "channel."

Cloth (US Drop). A large area of painted canvas to hang with a wood batten top and bottom. Up stage there is a Backcloth, down stage a Front cloth, and between them are Drop cloths, or Cut cloths of arches or trees.

Console. The key desk from which an organ is played, now extended to cover any compact desk for remote control of lighting or sound.

Contactor. A switch carrying a large current to a lamp or lamps which is operated by an electromagnet requiring a small current (see "Relay").

Control Desk. Used interchangeably with Console (q.v.).

Counterweight System. The usual method of flying scenery in which the apparatus can be loaded so that hanging scenery is exactly balanced. May be arranged to operate from stage level or from a fly gallery above. But in either case when the bar is down for scenery or lighting to be attached the counterweight cradle is up and, in consequence, a "loading gallery" becomes necessary to enable the balance weights to be put on or off.

CSA. Canadian Standards Association.

Cue. This is the signal given by the Stage Manager (or taken directly from the action on the stage) to carry out a plotted change of lighting. The change may be slow or fast. A cue is of course not restricted to lighting.

Cut. Applied to immediate switching, usually from one lighting or sound effect to another.

Cyclorama. Properly applied to a plain cylindrical background or sky dome or cloth completely bounding the stage behind the proscenium, but now applied to almost any plain cloth or background up-stage on which an extra flood of light is directed. "Cyc" is a common abbreviation.

Dim (verb). See "Check."

Dimmer. This term, when unqualified, means a power-regulating device in the circuit feeding the lamp.

Dip (US *Floor Pocket*). Socket outlets usually beneath traps but at any rate at stage-floor level unless qualified as, for example, "Fly Dips."

Direct-operated (US *Manual*). A form of control in which dimmers are mechanically connected to operating levers in close proximity.

Dis-board. A unit consisting of fuses and busbars from which the electrical supply is distributed to the various circuits. Sometimes switches are included instead of or in addition to switches local to the lighting or apparatus controlled.

Disc Stage. A revolving stage sufficiently shallow to be laid on top of a normal stage. The orthodox type of revolve with under-stage mechanism is nowadays required only when power-operated bridges and lifts form part of the unit.

Drapes. Curtains or any fabrics hanging in folds.

Earth (US *Ground*). Electric supply systems usually have one side connected to earth so that only the "live" wire presents a shock hazard. All metal casings associated with the equipment have to be "earthed" ("grounded") for reasons that are explained in Chapter 7.

Effect. Applied to apparatus for a specific optical result, such as a wave or cloud effect, or to a particular stage picture as painted with light— a dawn effect, fine-day effect.

Electrode. See "Cathode."

Electromagnet. A device which forms a magnet only as long as current flows through its coil.

End Stage. An open stage across one end of the auditorium and not separated from it by a proscenium.

ETU. Electrical Trades Union, now Electrical Electronic, Telecommunication, Plumbing Union.

Fader. The equivalent device to a dimmer but in a sound channel, but very useful term to apply to master controls in light control also. Thus, master "fader" but individual "dimmer" levers.

Filter. Colour medium, also an electrical device to smooth out irregularities in an electrical supply.

Fit-up. A temporary arrangement easily assembled to provide a proscenium and scenery rigging on an existing open platform or the complete stage, floor included.

Flat. A rectangular piece of scenery constructed of canvas stretched on a wooden frame consisting of two stiles (the uprights) and horizontal rails between. There are various elaborations to take door and window units or hinged together as the self-explanatory "book flats." A series of flats battened together to fly as one unit is known as a French flat: perhaps because it commonly includes a french window?

Flex (US *Stranded Cable*). Not any loose cable but a cable whose conductor is made up of fine strands to withstand twisting without breaking. Must be of the finest quality with heavy insulation for stage work, normal domestic twisted flex being unsuitable.

Float. A traditional name for footlights.

Flood (verb) *and Floodlight.* This term is obviously the reverse of to "spot" but it is important to realize that most spotlights can both be spotted and flooded and that even in the case of a wide-angle floodlight the result may not resemble a softlight (q.v.) as although the beam may radiate widely it may still have its origin in a source small in area and therefore capable of creating pronounced shadows.

Flys. I do not like the spelling "flies" which suggests insects of some sort. To me "Flys" is a contraction of *"Fly* tower and galleries" which is the upper part of the stage where scenery can be suspended out of sight (flown). Also refers more particularly to the gallery at the side of the stage where the ropes and controls for this scenery are placed.

Focus (verb). Quite apart from the technical meaning of the word "focus" it is often used very loosely in the theatre. "Focus that spot over here" may involve putting the lamp even farther out of focus. Hence "hard" and "soft" focus.

FOH. "Front of house," that part of the theatre used by the public, i.e. in front of the curtain, but also taken in another context means lighting positioned in the auditorium and directed at the stage.

Forestage. There seems to be a tendency to use "apron" and "forestage" interchangeably but I think it is more convenient if apron is applied to the area between footlights and house tabs when it is of sufficient size to allow one to compère a show or sing the prologue to *Pagliacci* without risk of getting knocked over by the house tabs. A forestage on the other hand should be an acting area in its own right capable of carrying a large part of the action even when the house tabs are lowered. (See also "Space Stage" and "Thrust Stage.")

Frost. A gelatine or Cinemoid diffuser. For Profile spots the right degree of diffusion is difficult to get in Cinemoid and a rolled textured glass, such as cathedral, has to be used, and the term frost is then a complete misnomer which might lead to etched or sandblasted glass being used.

Gauze (US *Scrim*). There are several forms depending upon whether it is required to paint on them, but all have the property of becoming invisible when objects upstage of them are lit and not the gauze itself.

GE and GEC. Some confusion arises because these initials stand for two very large but entirely separate companies of the same name. Both figure in the present book and when they occur General Electric is used for the American company and GEC for the British one.

Gelatines. Sometimes "gellies" or "gels" in the US. Dyed gelatine was for a long time the only way of obtaining a wide range of colour filters; in consequence, the term is often taken to cover modern plastic materials such as Cinemoid (q.v.).

Grand Master. This term has become synonymous for any large collection of mechanical shafting, levers, switches, and dimmers of the pre-remote-control era. It really applies to one precise form. (See "Direct-operated Switchboard," page 321.)

GLC. Greater London Council. Theatre licensing for this area now falls to them in place of the now defunct London County Council.

Grid (Stage). The framework above the stage from which scenery and lighting can be suspended provided it conforms to a close gridiron formation on which it is possible to walk and position extra pulleys, etc. Should be at least two-and-a-half times the height of the working proscenium from the stage floor.

Grid (Valve). The gate in a thermionic valve which regulates the flow of electrons.

Ground Row. A piece of scenery, possibly painted "profile," to mask the bottom of a cloth or cyclorama, but also applies to lengths of shallow lighting equipment designed for use behind the ground rows.

Heater. The filament of a thermionic valve which causes electrons to be emitted.

Hemp Line. Originally scenery was hung from hemp lines made off to the fly-rail. Although replaced for most purposes by counter-weighted lines (q.v.) some hemp lines should be retained; for items which are detached when set on the stage they may be more convenient.

IEE. Institution of Electrical Engineers. Chartered Electrical Engineers are FIEE (Fellow) and MIEE (Member), but there are other membership grades.

IES. Illuminating Engineering Society, hence F Illum ES (Fellow) and M Illum ES (Member) for qualified illuminating engineers, but there are other membership grades.

Independents. Originally stage circuits conformed to colour groupings and shafts on the switchboard were so identified. When spotlights became common they obviously did not comply, therefore separate shafts known as "independents" (of colour) were fitted. Another later use was "blackout" or "independent," a two-way switch being used for the purpose. Today the term can apply only to a few live socket outlets on the stage independent of the main control and used for testing, but see also "Non-dim" below.

Intake. The room in which the electricity supply authority's mains enter the customer's premises. Here are housed the meters and main switchgear for stage lighting, other lighting, power, and so on. A large theatre with a fire curtain may have one in the front of house and another for the stage, only the stage lighting in the FOH crossing the great divide.

Ladder. A suspended frame to carry spotlights in the wings but well clear of the floor to avoid obstruction to entrances.

Lantern. Otherwise known as "Instrument" (US) or "Luminaire" (IES). See Chapter 13, page 310.

Lantern (Stage). The haystack-shaped glass skylight which must be fitted in the roof of any stage fitted with a safety curtain. Its object is to allow escape of smoke and the high pressure caused by the expansion of air in a fire.

Legs. Vertical curtains or unframed scenery hanging to mask the sides of the stage.

Length. A series of lamps originally on a length of wood batten now of the usual compartment type of equipment mainly to hang vertically just behind the leading edges of scenery or to light backings. Not often encountered today.

Lighting Bridge. See "Bridge."

Lime. An expression for the powerful following spots in the FOH (q.v.). The source of light, now an electric arc, used to be a gas jet impinged on a lozenge of lime.

Live or *Line*. The feed to an electric circuit (see Chapter 7, page 113).

Monopole. A telescopic suspension unit originally introduced by Mole Richardson Ltd., commonly used in television to carry and position spotlights and other lanterns from an overall grid in television studios. May have some application to stage lighting, particularly of open stages.

Moon Box. A shallow square box with a large circular aperture, the white interior of which is illuminated by lamps concealed in the corners. This device is hung behind a cut-out moon in a backcloth.

Movable. Not equivalent to "portable" (q.v.).

NATKE. National Association of Theatrical and Kinematograph Employees.

Neutral. The return side of an alternating-current circuit (see Chapter 7, pages 113 and 132).

NODA. The National Operatic and Dramatic Association.

Non-dim. It is an American custom to specify a number of circuits which are what we would call "switched only" in order to economize in the number of dimmers used. This has no logic today when thyristor dimmers have made dimming relatively inexpensive, but like a lot of traditions it is hard to get rid of and in consequence it is not unknown for thyristors to be controlled as switches and not permitted to dim in order to fulfil the specification. All stage lighting control channels must have dimmers (but see also "Independents").

Objective. The final lens or combination of lenses in one jacket used to focus a lantern slide (or equivalent) sharply.

Open Stage. A stage within the same room as the audience and not separated from it by proscenium or tabs.

Optical Effect. A device which when attached to a projector and fitted with an objective produces movement such as clouds or flames without resort to the elaboration of cinema film. Can be legitimately extended to cover devices self-contained with lamp, like the ripple box, which do not require a projector.

Paint Frame. In Britain scene painters work vertically, the cloths being raised or lowered past them on this frame. In other countries the cloth is spread out on the floor and the painter stands on it as he paints.

Panorama. At one time a painted cloth which could be unwound from one side of the stage and rewound on the other to give a changing view. The traditional staging of *The Ring* included such a device for Siegfried's journeyings and in vertical form for the descent to Nibelheim.

Patch (verb—originally American, now adopted over here). To share out a lesser number of dimmers among a greater number of circuits. (For Patching methods, see Chapter 7.)

Perches. Originally shelf-like platforms on the stage side of the proscenium wall. The term is often applied to spotlights in that position whether there are perch platforms or not. In such cases they may be known in US as "Torm-(entor) spots."

Picture-frame Stage. Not synonymous for "Proscenium" (q.v.).

Pilots (stage). Reduced lighting for use in scene changes and to find one's way about behind scenes. They are insufficient for rehearsals or any other prolonged work and should not therefore be confused with WORKING LIGHTS which can and should be bright and cheerful.

Plan. A drawing showing a horizontal cut taken through, for example, a building. Unless otherwise stated (first-floor plan, roof plan, etc.) it is the one a few feet above the actual ground or stage floor so that all the windows and door openings in the walls show on it.

Portable. This means being capable of being carried by one or two men through any normal door. Larger objects may be "movable" but they are not "portable."

Preset. A preset must have a minimum of two controls to each channel so that an alternative choice is possible. Such controls must be duplicates both as to size and facility. A control with three such controls is then a three-preset. (See "Rehearsal System.")

Profile. Rigid but flat scenery, the edges of which are cut out in the shape of trees, and so on. It is constructed of thin plywood faced with scrim, but substitutes such as hardboard are not unknown. (See also "Profile Spot," in Chapter 13, page 312.)

Proscenium Theatre. A theatre with an opening dividing auditorium and stage. This opening has its origin in the use of a curtain and later a fire curtain, but this does not mean that it need be defined; in consequence, "Picture-frame Stage" is not an interchangeable expression for proscenium. A production or theatre can be designed to stress the frame and fourth-wall idea or not, as desired.

Pros(cenium) Border (US *Teaser*). The position of this border just upstage of the tabs determines the working height of the stage.

Rake. The slope applied to a stage or auditorium floor. This latter is the proper place for it though the maximum permitted of one in ten is usually not enough and stepping has to be resorted to. Rakes, sometimes very steep, are often applied to stages for particular scenic purposes but the permanent stage floor itself should be flat as this facilitates mounting of any scenic and mechanical device.

Rectifier. A device for converting alternating current to direct current.

Relay. Strictly an electro-magnetic switch which requires a minute current to work it. It is used to supply the larger current for the coil of a contactor switch or magnetic clutch and thereby avoid a long run of heavy wire between remote-control point and the latter.

Rehearsal System. An extra set of dimmer levers often larger than the presets on certain American controls carried on the main console, the latter being relegated to an auxiliary wing.

Rostrum. A movable platform to provide a raised area of the stage. The larger ones are constructed of a strong folding frame with a separate top so that they are easy to strike and store.

Run. Electric installation term for the wires and their housing between one position and another. The wires may be run in tube or conduit, trunking (US *Gutters*), or with integral armouring or occasionally open-on trays (US *Raceways*).

SBTD. Society of British Theatre Designers.

Sciopticon (*Sciop*). Originally an American term for optical effects projector; it is often used now in Britain as well.

Secondary Lighting. Emergency lighting from an independent supply, usually a battery.

Section. A view of a building or stage showing a vertical cut through it. Lines are sometimes drawn on the Plan (q.v.) view marked *A–A*, *B–B*, and particular sections drawn for each position. If, however, the section is located on the centre line of the plan or some other obvious position such as the proscenium, it is not necessary to specify beyond the word section.

Servo. An electro-mechanical positioning system with feedback in which the degree of movement at a remote point is determined by the amount of movement of the control lever.

Setting Line. The line on the stage side of the proscenium to which the setting may be brought and from which its dimensions are taken.

Sight Lines. Imaginary lines from the eyes of each member of the audience to the stage. These lines are straight and cannot pass through or round *any* obstruction. One aim of good theatre design is to ensure that the proportion of the stage common to all these lines is as large as possible.

Sightline. Journal of the ABTT (q.v.).

Softlight. A source large enough in area to give shadowless lighting or at any rate hardly perceptible shadows.

Solenoid. A form of electro-magnet in which the core is not fixed and used to attract a moving part, but is free to be drawn up inside the coil when current passes through it. For the same current in the coil an electro-magnet will exert a greater attraction, but a solenoid can pull through a greater distance.

Solid State Switching. Using electronic devices, particularly controlled rectifiers (thyristors), to perform operations which would have required contacts on moving relays.

Space Stage. A stage which has an indefinite proscenium and is so wide as to give a sense of embracing the audience. Opposite to "Thrust" (q.v.).

Stalls. This seating area is described as the "orchestra" in the United States.

Tabs. Derived from "tableaux curtains," which part in the centre and draw up in loops either side of the proscenium, but now applied to any set of stage curtains. Curtains forming part of the furnishing of a setting are drapes, but this is not always adhered to. "House tabs" is the name given to the curtain which cuts off the stage and forms part of the auditorium decorative scheme. Where, as is usually the case, this curtain is used to terminate the act it may be known as the "act drop," but the term really belongs to a painted curtain formerly used for this purpose, the house tabs merely opening and closing the show.

TAC. Theatres' Advisory Council.

Tails. The heat-resisting wiring of lanterns and other apparatus is often extended for one to three feet outside. These ends are known as tails and are used to connect up. They must not be replaced by running the ordinary wiring into the lantern, as the cable used for normal purposes does not have a heat-resisting covering.

Theatre-in-the-round (US *Arena*). Open stage with audience all round or 360-degree encirclement.

Throw. The distance along the centre line of a beam from a projector to screen; size of picture is also required in order to obtain correct lens. The problem of projection from an angle is dealt with in Chapter 12.

Thrust Stage. A stage with the audience on three sides, as at Stratford in Ontario.

Tier. A theatre with one floor is a single-tier house; with a dress circle, upper circle, and gallery all on separate balconies it is a four-tier house.

Tormentors. Masking flats angled between the edge of the proscenium and upstage of the tabs, thereby determining the working width of the stage. Sometimes these and the proscenium borders are combined as a "false proscenium" special to a production.

Tower. A mobile structure capable of carrying both lighting and men to operate it. Common in the German theatre either side of the proscenium in our perch position and always operated in conjunction with a bridge overhead. The stage is thus provided with an adjustable frame with lighting equipment all round its edges.

Transverse Stage. The audience sit on two sides facing each other across the stage.

Tripe. General term for flexible cables.

Truck. Low trolley for movement of built scenery (see also "Wagon").

Tumble. To roll cloth up on a tumbler rather than fly it in and out in one piece because of lack of height. An alternative is to "trip" by raising both top and bottom of the cloth when flying, thereby causing it to occupy half the height.

Tungsten Lamp. Any lamp with a filament.

USITT. United States Institute for Theatre Technology.

Wagon. It seems desirable to make a clear distinction between this and "truck." A wagon stage has a permanent power-driven installation of rolling stages with or without lifts by means of which several alternative stage floors are available for the building of scenery. This is typical of German practice. In Britain and the United States trucks, which are very shallow and may or may not travel on tracks, carry the larger pieces of built scenery—perhaps, as in Higgins' study, the whole set. Motor drive is more often than not unnecessary.

Wings. The off-stage areas each side beyond the working proscenium; also certain kinds of scenery masking them. It is important that there should be plenty of wing space but its provision needs careful planning as the fly tower may become too wide (and therefore too expensive) or double-purchase counterweights, which are much disliked, become necessary. One simple solution is to provide much more wing space on the side which does not house them as this would not need to be covered by the grid.

Appendix 1

All references to colour by number in this book belong to the standard Cinemoid range

STANDARD CINEMOID STAGE FILTERS

Colour Order

LAVENDER–GOLD–PINK

Pale Violet	42	Pale Salmon	53	Dark Pink	11
Lavender	71	Pale Rose	54	Salmon Pink	78
Pale Lavender	36	Light Salmon	9	Bright Rose	48
Gold Tint	51	Light Rose	7	Deep Rose	12
Pale Gold	52	Pink	57	Smoky Pink	27
Pale Golden Rose	75	Middle Rose	10	Magenta	13

YELLOW–AMBER–RED

Pale Yellow	50	Chrome Yellow	46	Deep Golden	
Straw Tint	73	Deep Amber	33	Amber	35
Straw	3	Golden Amber	34	Pale Red	66
Yellow	1	Deep Salmon*	8	Medium Red	64
Canary	49	Apricot	47	Primary Red	6
Light Amber	2	Orange	5	Red Frost	74
Medium Amber	4	Deep Orange*	5A	Ruby	14

BLUE–PURPLE–VIOLET

Turquoise	62	Pale Blue	40	Blue Frost	72
Cyan		Giselle Blue	68	Sky Blue	63
(Blue-green)	16	Pale Navy Blue	43	Dark Blue	19
Peacock Blue	15	Light Blue	18	Deep Blue	20
Ariel Blue	69	Bright Blue	41	Purple	25
Steel Tint	67	Slate Blue	61	Mauve	26
Steel Blue	17	Medium Blue	32	Pale Violet	42
Daylight	45				

GREEN–NEUTRAL–FROST

Green Tint	77	Primary Green	39	Pale Chocolate	56
Pale Green	38	Blue-green	16	Pale Grey	60
Pea Green	21	Turquoise	62	Light Frost	31
Moss Green	22	Peacock Blue	15	Heavy Frost	29
Light Green	23	Chocolate Tint	55	Clear	30
Dark Green	24				

STANDARD CINEMOID STAGE FILTERS

Numerical Order

1. Yellow
2. Light Amber
3. Straw
4. Medium Amber
5. Orange
5A Deep Orange
6. Red (Primary)
7. Light Rose
8. Deep Salmon*
9. Light Salmon
10. Middle Rose
11. Dark Pink
12. Deep Rose
13. Magenta
14. Ruby
15. Peacock Blue
16. Blue-green
17. Steel Blue
18. Light Blue
19. Dark Blue
20. Deep Blue (Primary)
21. Pea Green
22. Moss Green
23. Light Green
24. Dark Green
25. Purple
26. Mauve
27. Smoky Pink
29. Heavy Frost
30. Clear
31. Light Frost
32. Medium Blue
33. Deep Amber
34. Golden Amber
35. Deep Golden Amber

36. Pale Lavender
38. Pale Green
39. Primary Green
40. Pale Blue
41. Bright Blue
42. Pale Violet
43. Pale Navy Blue
45. Daylight
46. Chrome Yellow
47. Apricot
48. Bright Rose
49. Canary
50. Pale Yellow
51. Gold Tint
52. Pale Gold
53. Pale Salmon
54. Pale Rose
55. Chocolate Tint
56. Pale Chocolate
57. Pink
60. Pale Grey
61. Slate Blue
62. Turquoise
63. Sky Blue
64. Medium Red
66. Pale Red
67. Steel Tint
68. Giselle Blue
69. Ariel Blue
71. Lavender
73. Straw Tint
74. Red Frost
75. Pale Golden Rose
77. Green Tint
78. Salmon Pink

* Discontinued.

Appendix 2

The international symbols referred to on page 214 are illustrated opposite. In the left-hand column is the printed version for half-inch scale plans but, as the middle columns show, these can be rapidly sketched and yet still be recognizable. Where small-scale reproduction is concerned as in architects' $\frac{1}{8}$-inch scale plans, a filled-in figure as in the right-hand column may be used. These last can be freehand versions as in the sketches and diagrams in this book, or of course be miniature versions of the left-hand column filled in appropriately.

Direction of the beam is readily indicated by arrows, the symbol itself not necessarily being aligned along this axis. Difficulty is however encountered when the unit is to point vertically downwards and in these somewhat rare cases it is now proposed that the symbol have a circle drawn round it.

A. **FLOODLIGHT** One-half peak divergence exceeding 100° and cut-off not less than 180°.			
B. **SPECIAL FLOODLIGHT** Specified one-half peak divergence (less than 100°) and specified cut-off angle.			
C. **REFLECTOR SPOTLIGHT** Simple reflector system capable of adjustment of divergence by relative movement of lamp and mirror.			
D. **SEALED-BEAM SPOTLIGHT** Beam divergence depends entirely on the shaped and metallized bulb of the lamp and in consequence can be altered only by a change of lamp.			
E. **LENS SPOTLIGHT** Simple lens with or without reflector and capable of adjustment of divergence by relative movement of lamp and lens.			
F. **FRESNEL SPOTLIGHT** As *E* above but with a short-focus stepped lens to provide greater light and a soft edge to the beam.			
G. **PROFILE SPOTLIGHT** Hard-edged beam which can be varied in outline by diaphragms, shutters or silhouette cut-out masks.			
H. **EFFECTS PROJECTOR** Specifically designed to give even field illumination of slides and well-defined projection using objective lenses. Slide can be stationary or moving-effects type.			
I. **SOFTLIGHT** Size sufficient to produce diffused lighting with indefinite shadow boundaries.			
J. **BIFOCAL SPOTLIGHT** Profile spotlight as *G.* above but with double shutters to provide, when required, a beam outline part of which is hard and part soft.			

Appendix 3

COLOUR MUSIC

In all the not inconsiderable time I have enjoyed playing around with the fitting of colour (coloured light) to music, the only link which works for me is emotional. Certain music arouses a desire to do certain things visually. At first tentatively, here and there. Then with further study eventually given the right music, and only some is at all suitable, a composition is built up. Thereafter, rehearsal is merely to ensure the dexterity to play it; there is no longer any question whatever of improvisation. Not only do I not by then feel the need for change but it would in any case be fatal because one might be caught on the wrong foot in respect of the state of the switchboard.

We are, in fact, talking of an art in which the novelty lies in using light to provide the change, the story line so to speak. It uses the fact that the audience does not know what the settings consist of to tease their imagination. With really low levels one can first open up a vista here and there, model first this shape, then that. These then are variations in light or there is the gradual development method until at last all becomes clear. Whether one ends on that or is taken back to the original entry—a *reprise*—depends on the music. Repetition of musical motifs can have their equivalent in light.

I am one of those who had the urge to experiment but because of the war there was obviously an enormous gap. Once I picked it up again I have had, much to my regret, virtually no time to spend on it and, in consequence, it has been a matter mainly of revival of pre-war work, at any rate as far as the sets are concerned.

On joining Strand Electric in 1932 it was natural to import my model-theatre technique for demonstrating lighting in their then new theatre. The completion of my Light Console, invented with more than half an eye on colour music, gave an added fillip to this kind of demonstration. After all, our problem was to demonstrate lighting as and when customers dropped in and we obviously could not have a play complete with actors standing by for the purpose. Even at the full-scale demonstrations, the relatively small size of the stage, together with the extra cost involved, gave encouragement to the idea of making do without. For this, colour music was to hand and even a demonstration of three-colour lighting on the cyclorama went down better with music to give it form.

In 1958 it became possible to consider a full-scale recital of Colour Music once more. Odd pieces had been slipped in here and there in the demonstrations before this but now the original Light Console, which had been pensioned off from the Palladium when the new one went in, was available and there was a more or less suitable clutch-operated dimmer bank

There has always been a hint that the technique imposed by the control itself had been helping by providing the limitations within which one could compose. The limitations of piano, violin, or whatever, are a stimulant to the composer though he often works to extend the player. In the case of lighting, it might be said that there are much the same forces at work. Personally, I think that in the limitations of a lighting control there can be a danger. I am sometimes so busy amazing myself at the feats of dexterity and memory I perform that it could be that this becomes the show itself and therefore capable of appreciation only by myself, the player.

In truth, Colour Music should be concerned at all times to provide an effect with an artistic message. There should be no case of mere transition to get from one picture to another. The journey itself has to have a message. This is asking a lot of the human memory when one considers that little can be written down. To look at the controls, at a score or plot, and at the stage, all at the same time, is impossible. The memory has therefore to be used for all this, and this means rehearsal and still more rehearsal—not only to attain the necessary virtuosity at the controls but to remember all the visual effects which are supposed to be the end product.

How are these effects determined? Speaking for myself, and in no wise wishing to pontificate, the process is as follows. The particular piece of music has already been seen in the mind's eye in terms of visual effects, most of which are impossible to achieve. Compromise steps in here and it is a matter of which part of this vision can take material shape. Later some bits of the vision which do take shape turn out to be a failure anyway. However, it is true to say that some route has been mapped out before finger is set to dimmer. It is this that enables the lighting to be arranged at all. Some picture landmarks are created and then it is a matter of making a way from one to the other as the music suggests. Some pictures which have been created may never be needed at all, and yet others may arise from under the fingers. After several repeats, a shape begins to emerge.

This suggests that orchestration very much affects the colouring, and I must confess this is so and is one reason for my preference for full orchestra. There are other direct correspondences to be found. A crescendo in sound equals a crescendo in light, but there are no rules: it is still a matter of emotion. Where lighting entries do happen to marry to instrumental ones, it is very important to anticipate not follow them. For a horn to be followed by a flood of golden amber is to turn it into a joke. What must happen is that the audience become aware that at the time of hearing the horn passage there has been a change somewhere to correspond.

The tailpiece to the chapter on this subject in the 1968 edition of this book and to a similar one in my book of 1950 was "The Future." I find more interest now in looking back at what I did and what wasn't done in doing it. Artist friends have been puzzled that it did not become a way of life for me. Was it only my very serious illness that stopped London having its Colour Music equivalent of Prague's *Laterna Magika*? Recently we managed to hold an audience at Wyndham's for six minutes with nothing better than the improbable *Godspell* wire cage and its lighting rig to play our crude *Manfred* finale on. What might have been done with a blown-up version of the Strand Electric theatre rig and sets? Who knows. One thing is certain, it is harder now for a newcomer to attempt this art form because anything can be done. Where can the discipline—the framework within which to create—come from?

With the Stockhausens at work and the Moog synthesizers to play with, that which calls to be accompanied can be lost further and further in a Laocoön of tapes. Where is there a place for someone bumbling on trying to bend his stage lighting installation to give colour to the passions of say Tchaikovsky? Then again, if one can plug in for direct modulation of the difficult bits and finally put the whole lot together as a videotape or film to be performed exactly again and again, then the only challenge is where will the audience come from? It is not difficult to imagine a visual accompaniment to Mike Oldfield's "Tubular Bells" assembled with all the painstaking care and electronic wizardry bestowed on the original sound track and relying just as much on a mechanical reproducer for each replaying.

All this is not for me; I still haven't tired in 1976 of my settings of 1939! Given half a chance, out they come with guess what music and each time I play upon virtually the original lighting rig—and upon the original audience as well, it would almost appear, or one very like it.

Index

Drapes, 108–9
  black, 9, 34, 224, 240, 257, 266, 270
  'silver-grey', 240, 250, 252
Dressing rooms, 109
Drop cloth, 219, 265
Drottningholm Theatre, 39
Drury Lane, Theatre Royal, 3, 7, 24, 324
  console, 8
  lighting, 81, 100, 262, 263, 265, 269
Dublin, Abbey Theatre, 19–20
Dusseldorf, Opera House, 276, 279
Dynamic Technology Ltd., 159, 164, 171

Ealing, The Questors Theatre, 13, 14, 15, 32, 308
Earls Court
  Empress Hall, 272
  Exhibition Hall, 52
Edinburgh
  Assembly Hall, 5, 15
  Kings Theatre, 27, 331
Edwardian theatre, 2, 39, 250
Effects, moving, 291–6
  projector(s), 66–7, 285–7
  see also effect by name (e.g. Cloud, Wave)
Electrician, 55, 113, 139, 184, 185, 186, 196, 320
Electricity
  circuit, 112, 114–16
  competent supervision, 113
  danger of shock, 113
  earthing, 113–14, 132
  fear of its disciplines, 184
  flow (actual v conventional), 121
  frequency, 121
  fuses, 112–13, 134
  generation, 120–2
  installation, 113, 132–4, 135–6
    need for flexibility, 136
  insulation, 112, 113–14, 115
  mains, 112, 121, 132–3
  motors, 122
  neutral, 113, 122, 132
  power, 115
  regulations, 113
  RMS value, 121, 127
  technology, advances in, 142, 158, 173, 273, 306
  three-phase, 132–3
Electronic, The, 53–4, 148, 150, 328
Electrosonic Ltd., 308
Elliott, Michael, 18, 32
Ellipsoidal spots, 43, 61, 68–9, 312–3
Emmet, Alfred, 32, 34
End stage, 19, 209–14
English, John, 14, 16, 201
European practice, 121, 123, 148, 153, 161, 317, 321
  see also Czech, French, German and Swedish
Evening, 241
Exit signs, 192

Expressionism, 234
Exterior scenes, lighting of, 231, 250, 252–4
Eye
  adaptation by, 204, 234
  interpretation by, 204–9, 215, 250, 273, 287

Facial illumination, 109, 207, 209–10, 212
Farnham, Redgrave Theatre, 8, 32
Farrah, Abd'Elkader, 240
Fill light, 209
Filters, 88, 89–91
  changing of, 200
  Cinemoid, 89–90, 104, 344–5
  colour, 80
  dichroic, 91, 92
  efficiency of, 99, 105, 107
  electrical, see Choke
  fading, 90, 96, 191
  flammability, 89
  gelatine, 38, 89, 90
  glass, 90–1
  identification and specification, 104–7, 195
  lamp lacquer, 38
  remote control of, 180, 202–3, 314
  Roscolene and Roscolor, 90
  transmission curves, 105–7
  Wratten, 101
Finish in lighting, 273–4
Fire
  curtain, 17, 19, 23, 25, 34–5
  effects, see Flame
  risk, 46, 120
Firelight, 246, 259, 296–7
Fisher, Jules, 28
Fitting(s)
  property lighting, 241–4
  switching of, 248–9
  table lamp, 242–3
  wall bracket, 241–2
Fitzgerald, Percy, 45
Flame, 94, 296–7
Flashes and bangs, 297
Fleckenlicht, 290
Floodlights, 61, 71, 254, 257, 317–20
  baby, 236, 241
  wing, 261, 267
  see also Battens
Fluorescent
  colours, 89, 110–11
  effects, 110–11, 270–2
  lamps, 80, 84–6, 108
  lighting, 12, 29, 86, 234
Flying Dutchman, The, 300–3
Flys and flying, 22–3, 29, 41, 136, 269
Focus lamps (lanterns), 40
Fog, see Mist

Pitlochry, Festival Theatre, 19
Plan(s), 185–8
Plastics, 89–90
Plaza Cinema, London, 41
Plotting, 157, 191–5
Plugging systems, *see* Patching
Plugs and sockets, 113, 135–6, 138–9
Polaroid camera, 202
Power cut, 9
Power of Persuasion, 188
Prague, 45, 283–4, 310
   National Theatre, 219
Preset control, 146–7
  colour preset, 321
  group(ing),
    fixed, 147–8
    switch, 147–8
  infinite, 330
  mechanical inertia, 130
  multi, 151–2
  multi-group, 54, 56, 325–6, 332–3
  park, 170
  platten, 332
  punched card, 153, 161, 331–2, 334
  shift, 165
Producer (Director), 3, 9, 16, 17, 34, 158, 183–4, 205,
    215, 223, 249, 257, 275
Projection
  as stage lighting, 9, 309
  effects, 284–5
  lamps, 74–6, 84
  lenses, 64–5
  projector, 66–7, 285–7, 306–7, 315–17
  scene, 22, 280–4
  screen(s), 280–1, 307–9
  slides, 285–91
    carousel, 308, 317
Prompt corner, 197
Properties, stage, 243
  see also Fittings
Proscenium, 17, 19, 22, 23–5, 35, 205, 221, 223
  lighting opportunities, 212, 214
  lighting position, 24, 136, 236
Psychological lighting, 234, 260–1

Q-File control, *see* Thorn
Quartz lamps, *see* Lamps, Tungsten Halogen
Queens Theatre, 26

Radio City Music Hall, 51–2, 125
Rainbow Square, 189–91, 294
Rain effects, 297–8
Ramon, George, 190
Rank Strand
  DDM, 155–6, 163, 170, 175, 176, 329, 335
  equipment, 149, 158, 174, 175, 314, 317, 320, 329,
    330–1

Lightboard, 180
  MMS, 158, 164, 167, 169–70, 331–2
Reactance, 124
Reactor, saturable, *see* Dimmer(s)
Realism, *see* Naturalism
"Real world", 16
Regent's Park, Open Air Theatre, 6
Regulations, 28, 113–14
Rehearsal(s)
  control desk, 165, 178, 181
  dress, 183, 191–2, 195–6
  lighting for, 192
  station, 196
  time critical, 182
Reid, Francis, 150, 168, 181
Reiche and Vogel, 40, 317, 319
Reinhardt, Max, 219
Repertoire, 35, 153, 175, 189, 197–201, 202, 284
Revolving stage, 35
Rheingold, 299
Ridge, Harold, 41
Rigging and setting, 189–90, 197–8, 203
Rigoletto, 95, 296
Ring, The, 6, 85, 162, 284
Ripple, (water), 292, 298–9, 303
Rise and Fall of the City of Mahogonny, 290
Robertson, Patrick, 307
Romans, The, 6
Royal
  Ballet, 267
  Court Theatre, 245, 287
  Exchange, 5
  Festival Hall, 7, 25, 26, 86, 180
  Opera House, *see* Covent Garden
  Shakespeare Company, 3, 33, 39, 40, 224, 240,
    251, 266

Sadler's Wells Opera, 201, 290, 300–3
St Martin's Theatre, 40
Samoiloff, Adrian, 38, 102, 103, 105
Saville Theatre, 275
Savoy Theatre, 37, 45
Scale
  architectural, 221
  in lighting, 234–5
  models, 185
Scales
  dimmer lever, 144, 151–2
  spotlight, 200, 201
Scarborough, Library Theatre, 31
Scene(ry), 2–4, 13–14, 23, 219–22, 240, 251, 270, 280
  effect of light on, 108, 278
  flame resistant, 19
  jumbo mobile, as a, 6
  lighting of, 210, 237–9, 246, 254, 265, 283
  model, 185
  plan, 185